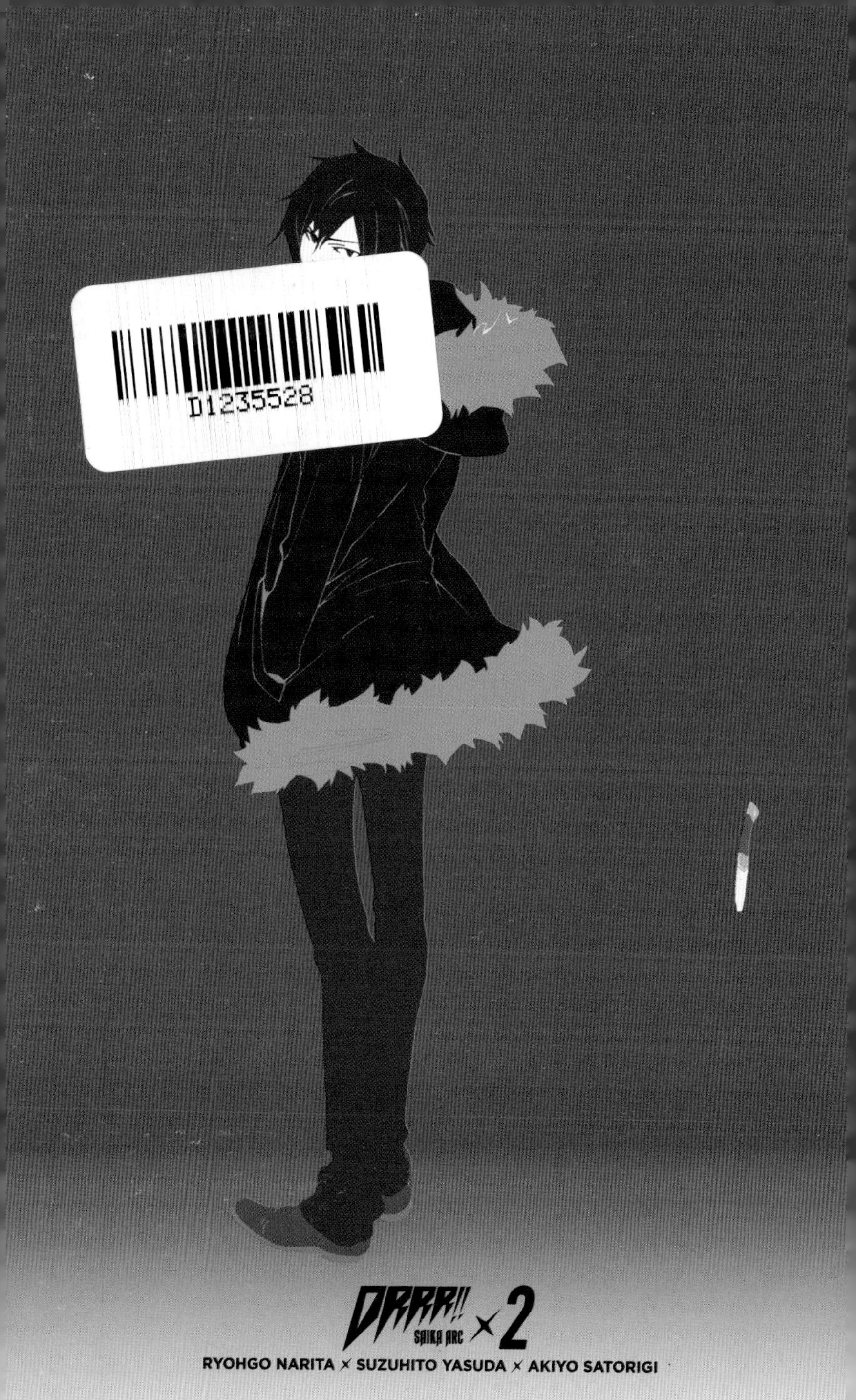

DRRR!! SAIKA ARC ×2

RYOHGO NARITA × SUZUHITO YASUDA × AKIYO SATORIGI

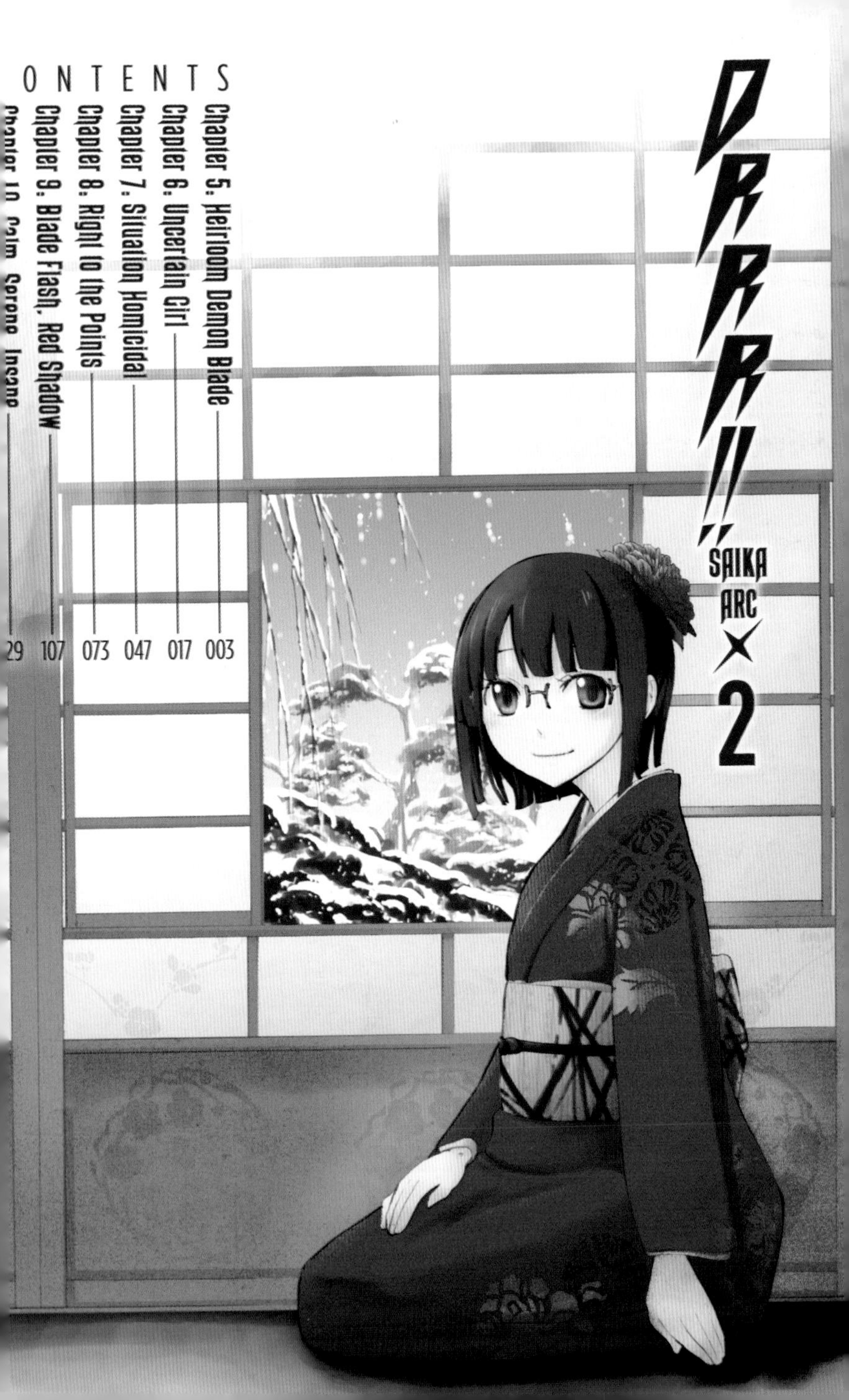
DRRR!!
SAIKA ARC
×2

ONTENTS

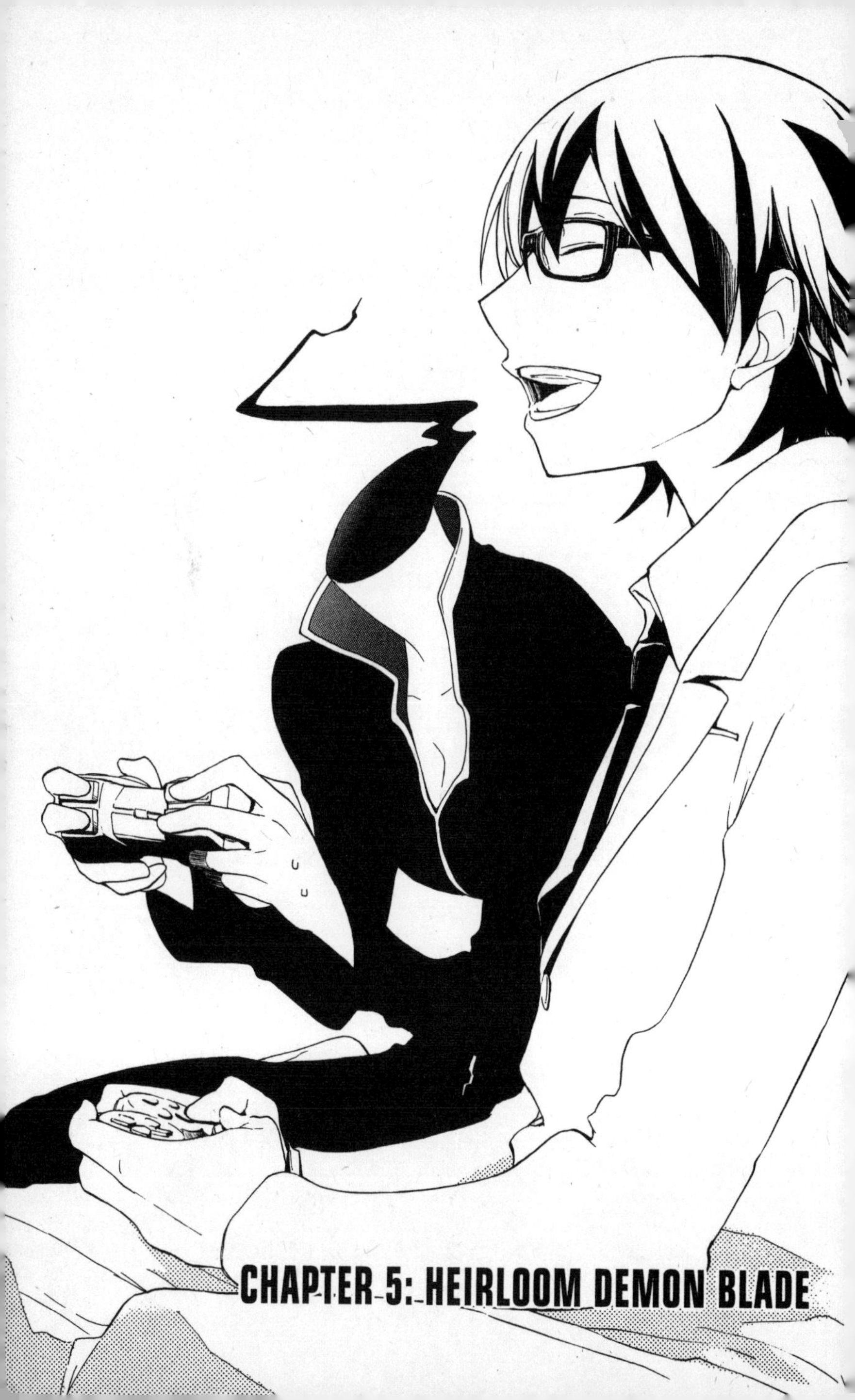
CHAPTER 5: HEIRLOOM DEMON BLADE

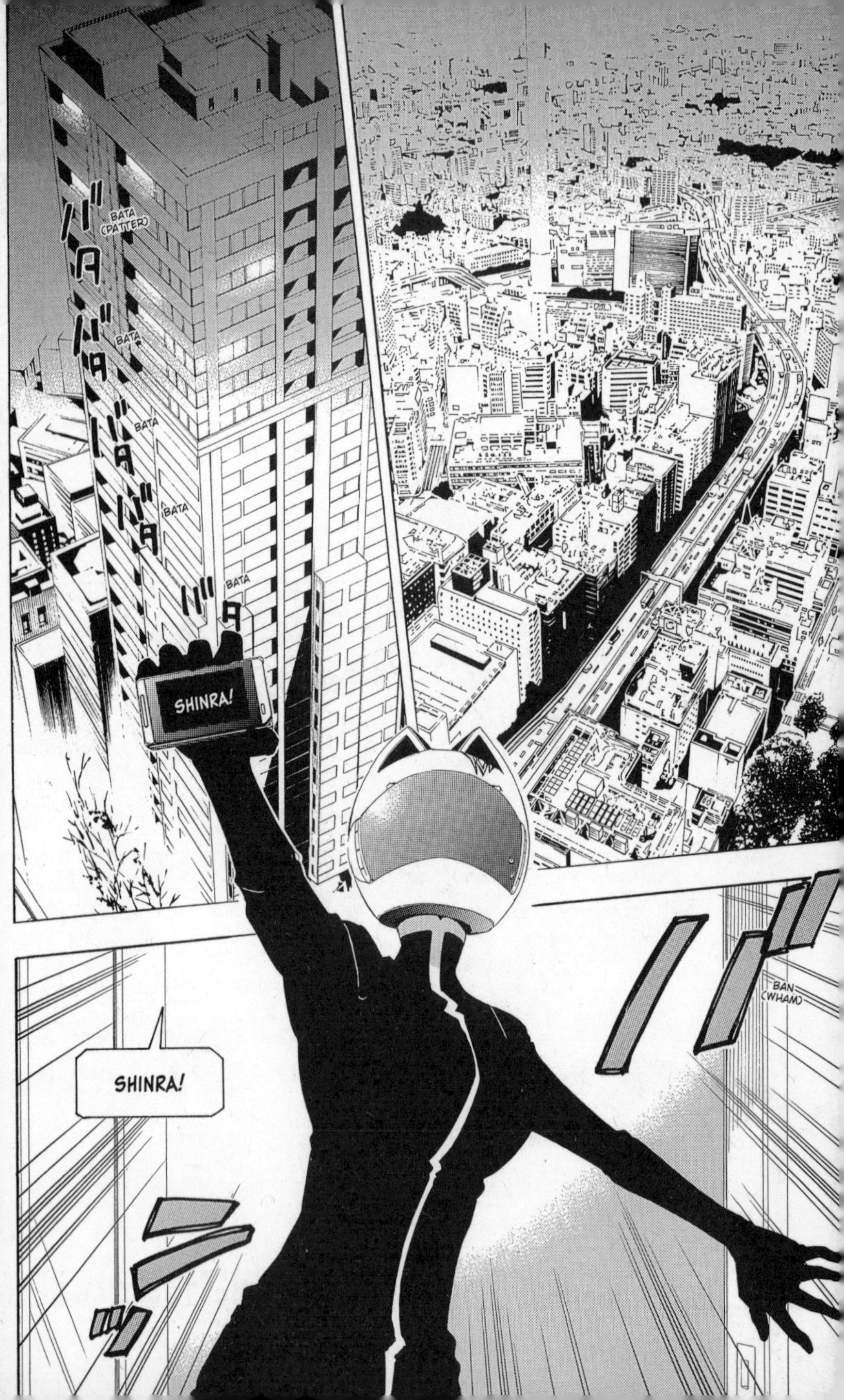
BATA (PATTER)
BATA
BATA
BATA
BATA
SHINRA!
BAN (WHAM)
SHINRA!

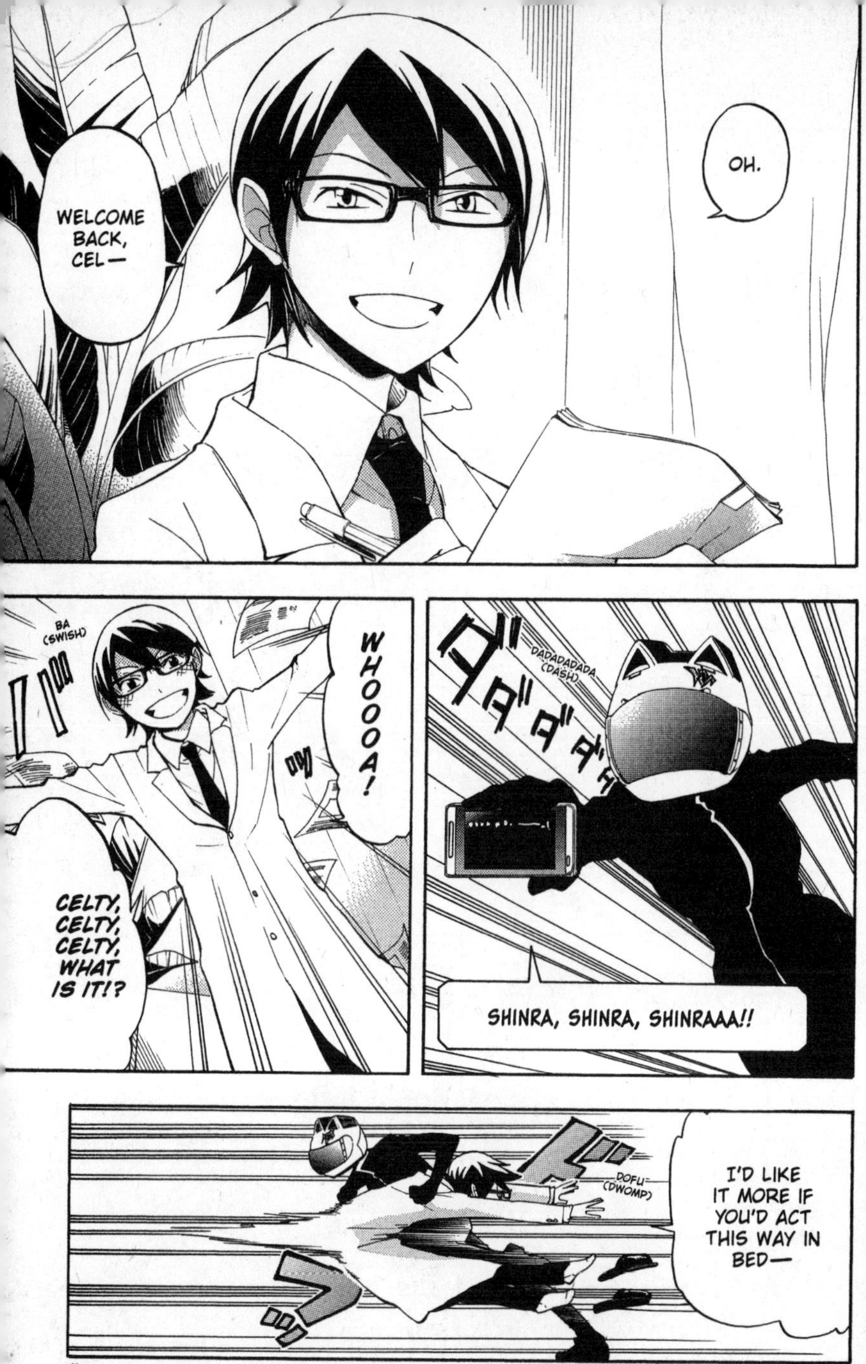

OH.
WELCOME BACK, CEL—
DADADADADA (DASH)
SHINRA, SHINRA, SHINRAAA!!
WHOOOOA!
BA (SWISH)
CELTY, CELTY, CELTY, WHAT IS IT!?
I'D LIKE IT MORE IF YOU'D ACT THIS WAY IN BED—
DOFU (DWOMP)

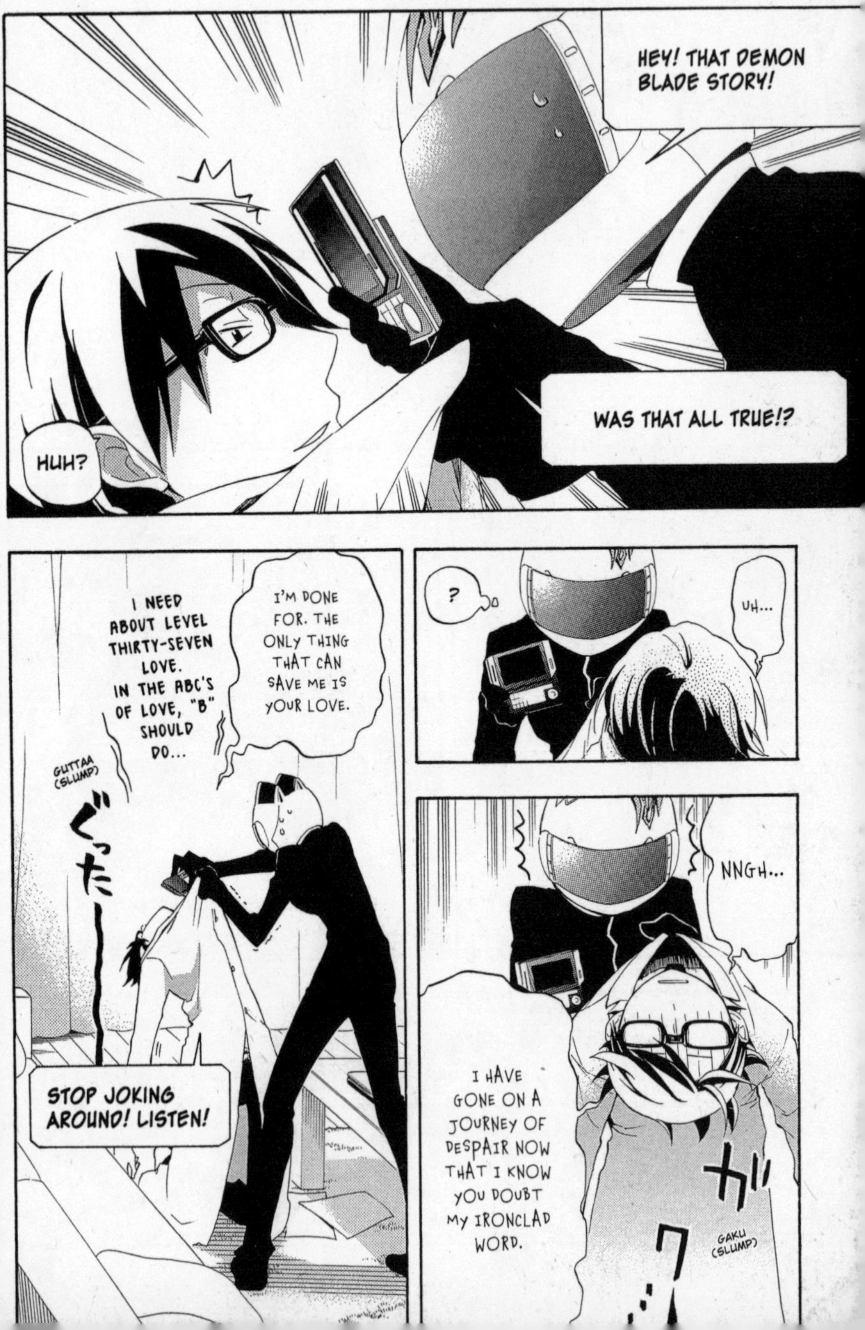
HEY! THAT DEMON BLADE STORY!
WAS THAT ALL TRUE!?
HUH?
UH...
?
NNGH...
I HAVE GONE ON A JOURNEY OF DESPAIR NOW THAT I KNOW YOU DOUBT MY IRONCLAD WORD.
ガクッ
GAKU (SLUMP)
I'M DONE FOR. THE ONLY THING THAT CAN SAVE ME IS YOUR LOVE.
I NEED ABOUT LEVEL THIRTY-SEVEN LOVE. IN THE ABC'S OF LOVE, "B" SHOULD DO...
GUTTAA (SLUMP)
ぐったー
STOP JOKING AROUND! LISTEN!

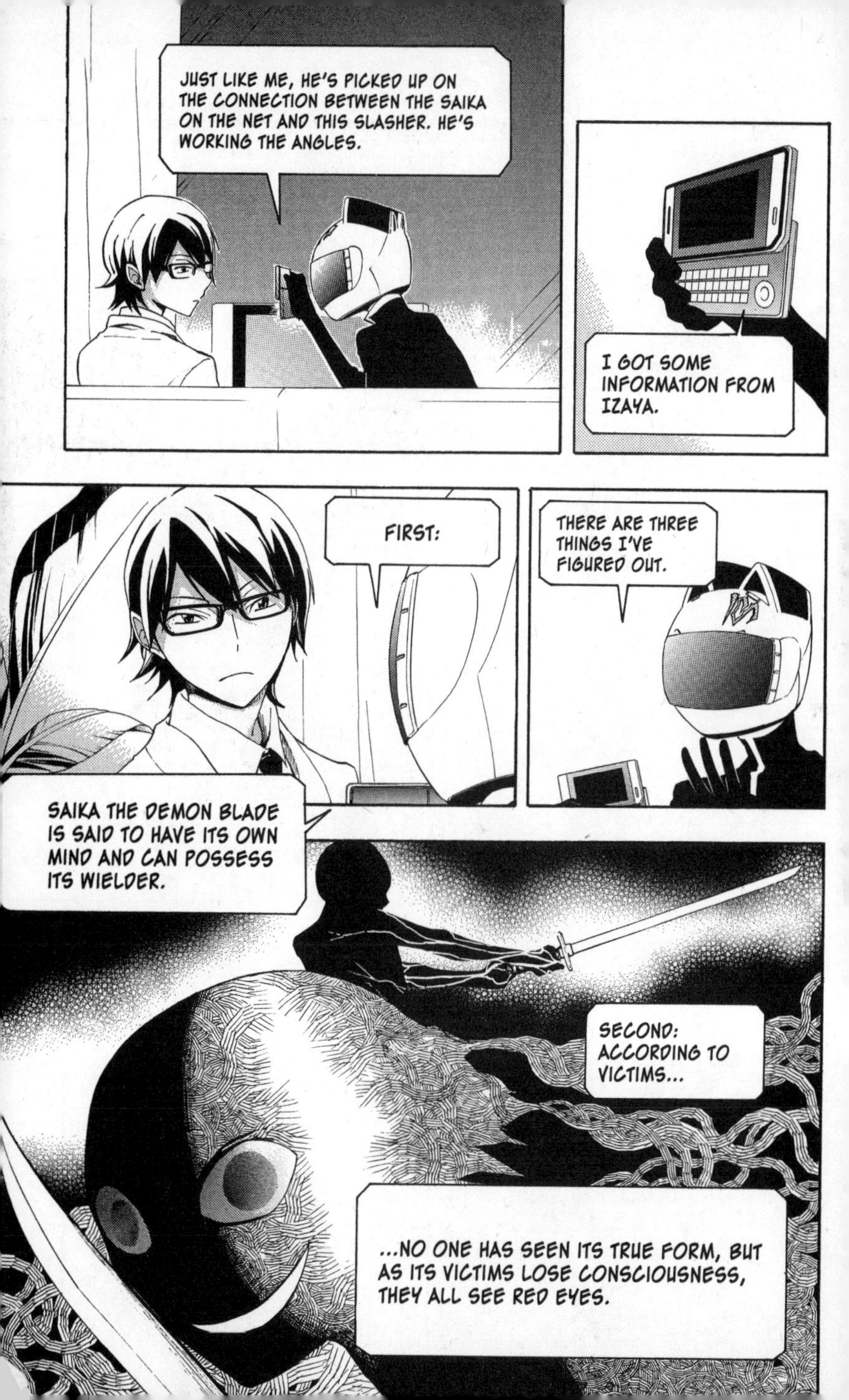
I GOT SOME INFORMATION FROM IZAYA.
JUST LIKE ME, HE'S PICKED UP ON THE CONNECTION BETWEEN THE SAIKA ON THE NET AND THIS SLASHER. HE'S WORKING THE ANGLES.
THERE ARE THREE THINGS I'VE FIGURED OUT.
FIRST:
SAIKA THE DEMON BLADE IS SAID TO HAVE ITS OWN MIND AND CAN POSSESS ITS WIELDER.
SECOND: ACCORDING TO VICTIMS...
...NO ONE HAS SEEN ITS TRUE FORM, BUT AS ITS VICTIMS LOSE CONSCIOUSNESS, THEY ALL SEE RED EYES.

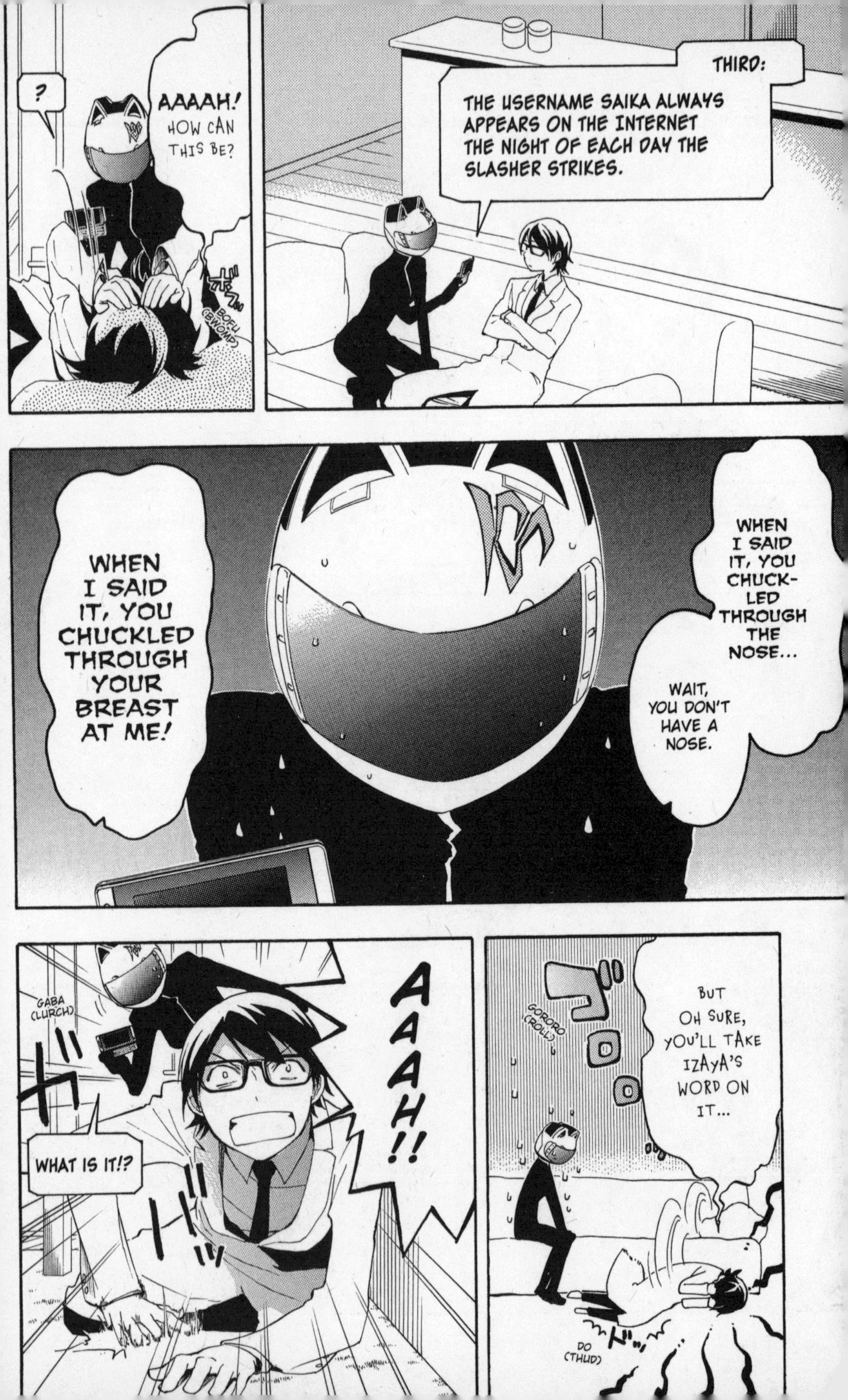
THIRD:
THE USERNAME SAIKA ALWAYS APPEARS ON THE INTERNET THE NIGHT OF EACH DAY THE SLASHER STRIKES.
AAAAH! HOW CAN THIS BE?
?
BOFU (BWOMP)
WHEN I SAID IT, YOU CHUCK-LED THROUGH THE NOSE...
WAIT, YOU DON'T HAVE A NOSE.
WHEN I SAID IT, YOU CHUCKLED THROUGH YOUR BREAST AT ME!
GORORO (ROLL)
BUT OH SURE, YOU'LL TAKE IZAYA'S WORD ON IT...
DO (THUD)
AAAAH!!
GABA (LURCH)
WHAT IS IT!?

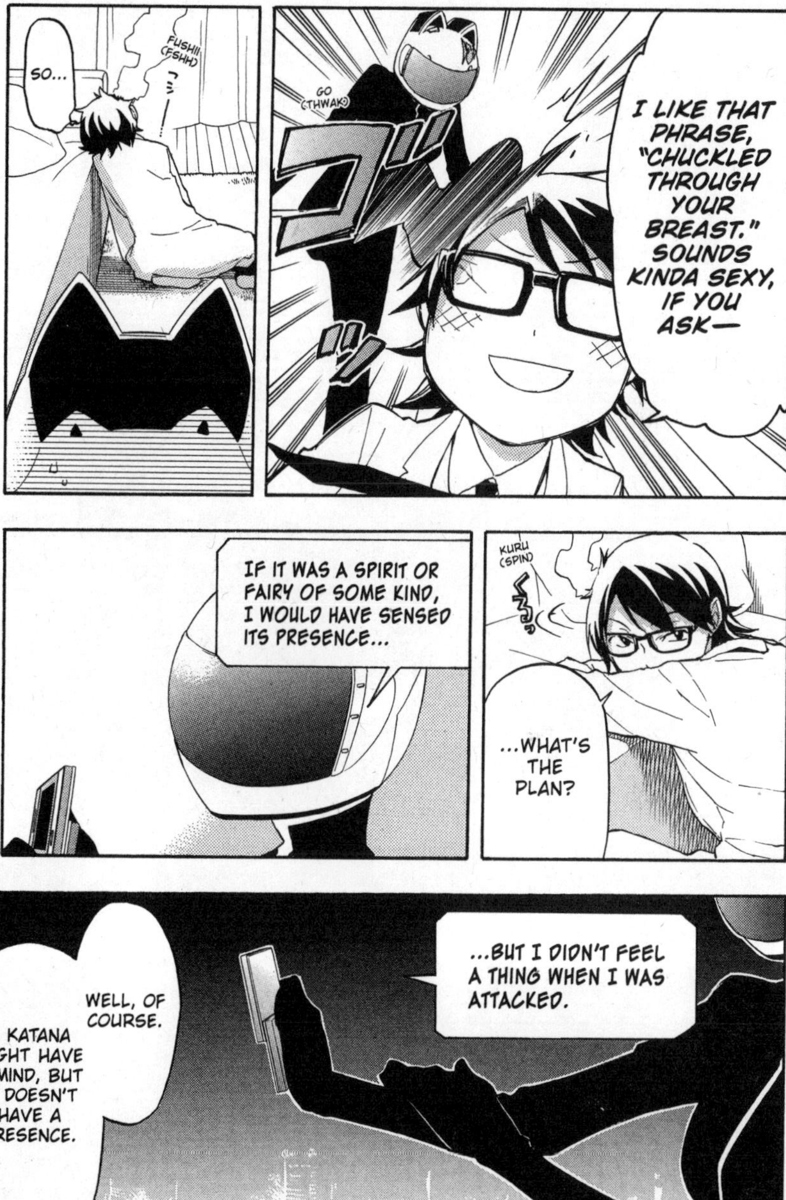
I LIKE THAT PHRASE, "CHUCKLED THROUGH YOUR BREAST." SOUNDS KINDA SEXY, IF YOU ASK—
GO (THWAK)
FUSHII (FSHH)
SO...
KURU (SPIN)
...WHAT'S THE PLAN?
IF IT WAS A SPIRIT OR FAIRY OF SOME KIND, I WOULD HAVE SENSED ITS PRESENCE...
...BUT I DIDN'T FEEL A THING WHEN I WAS ATTACKED.
WELL, OF COURSE.
A KATANA MIGHT HAVE A MIND, BUT IT DOESN'T HAVE A PRESENCE.

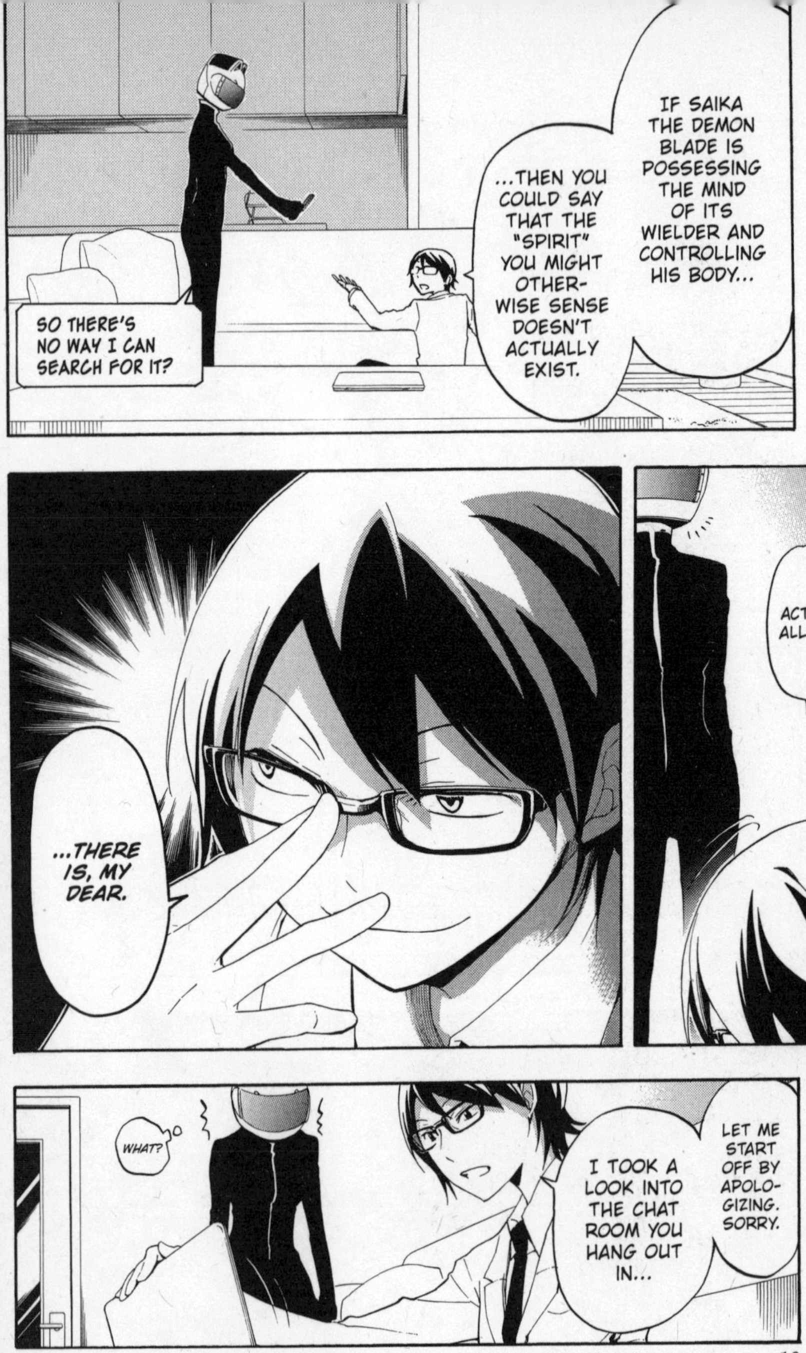
IF SAIKA THE DEMON BLADE IS POSSESSING THE MIND OF ITS WIELDER AND CONTROLLING HIS BODY...
...THEN YOU COULD SAY THAT THE "SPIRIT" YOU MIGHT OTHER-WISE SENSE DOESN'T ACTUALLY EXIST.
SO THERE'S NO WAY I CAN SEARCH FOR IT?
ACTU-ALLY...
...THERE IS, MY DEAR.
LET ME START OFF BY APOLO-GIZING. SORRY.
I TOOK A LOOK INTO THE CHAT ROOM YOU HANG OUT IN...
WHAT?

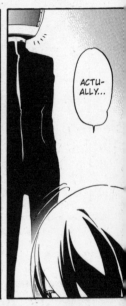

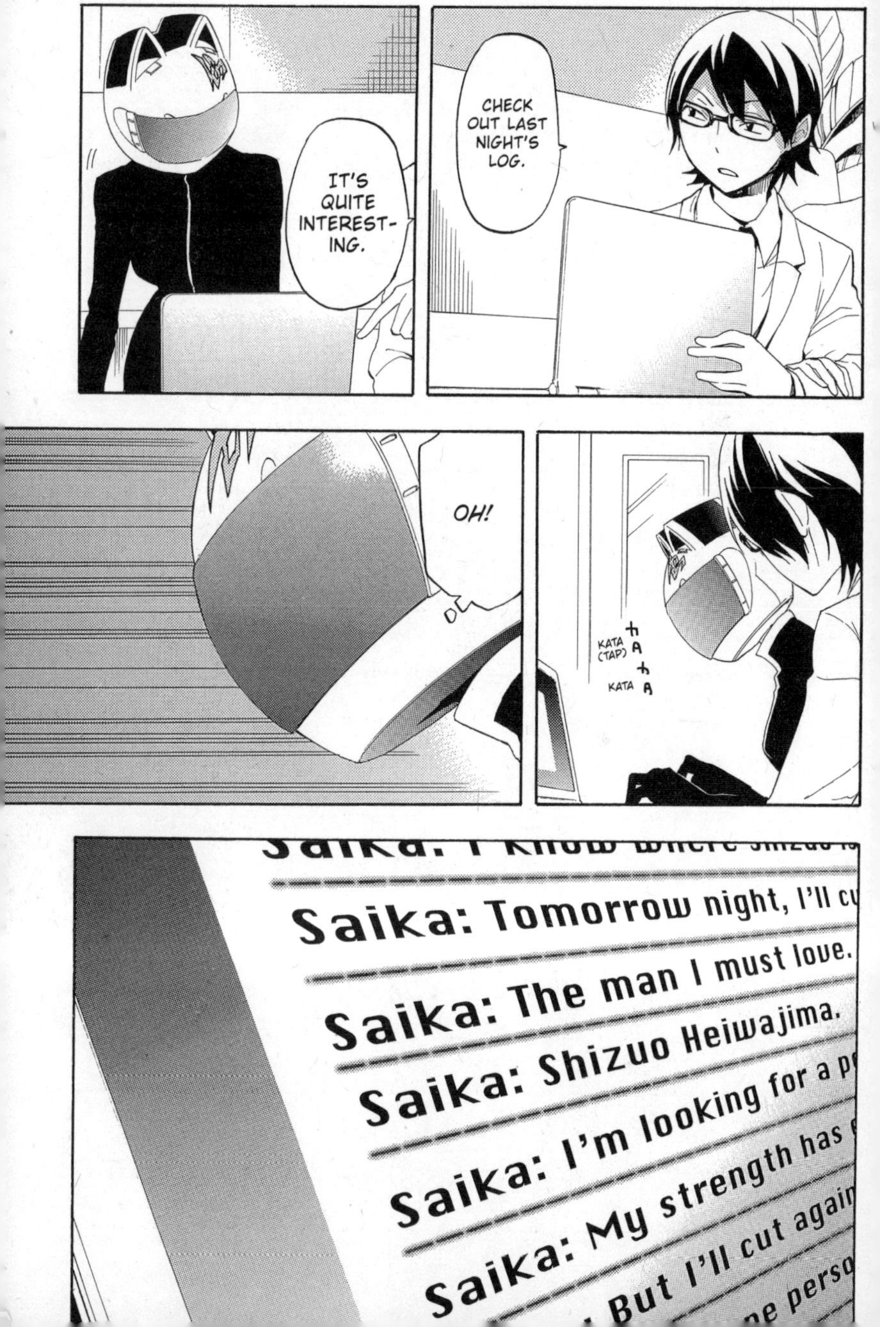
CHECK OUT LAST NIGHT'S LOG.
IT'S QUITE INTERESTING.
KATA (TAP) KATA
OH!
Saika: Tomorrow night, I'll
Saika: The man I must love.
Saika: Shizuo Heiwajima.
Saika: I'm looking for a
Saika: My strength has
Saika: But I'll cut again

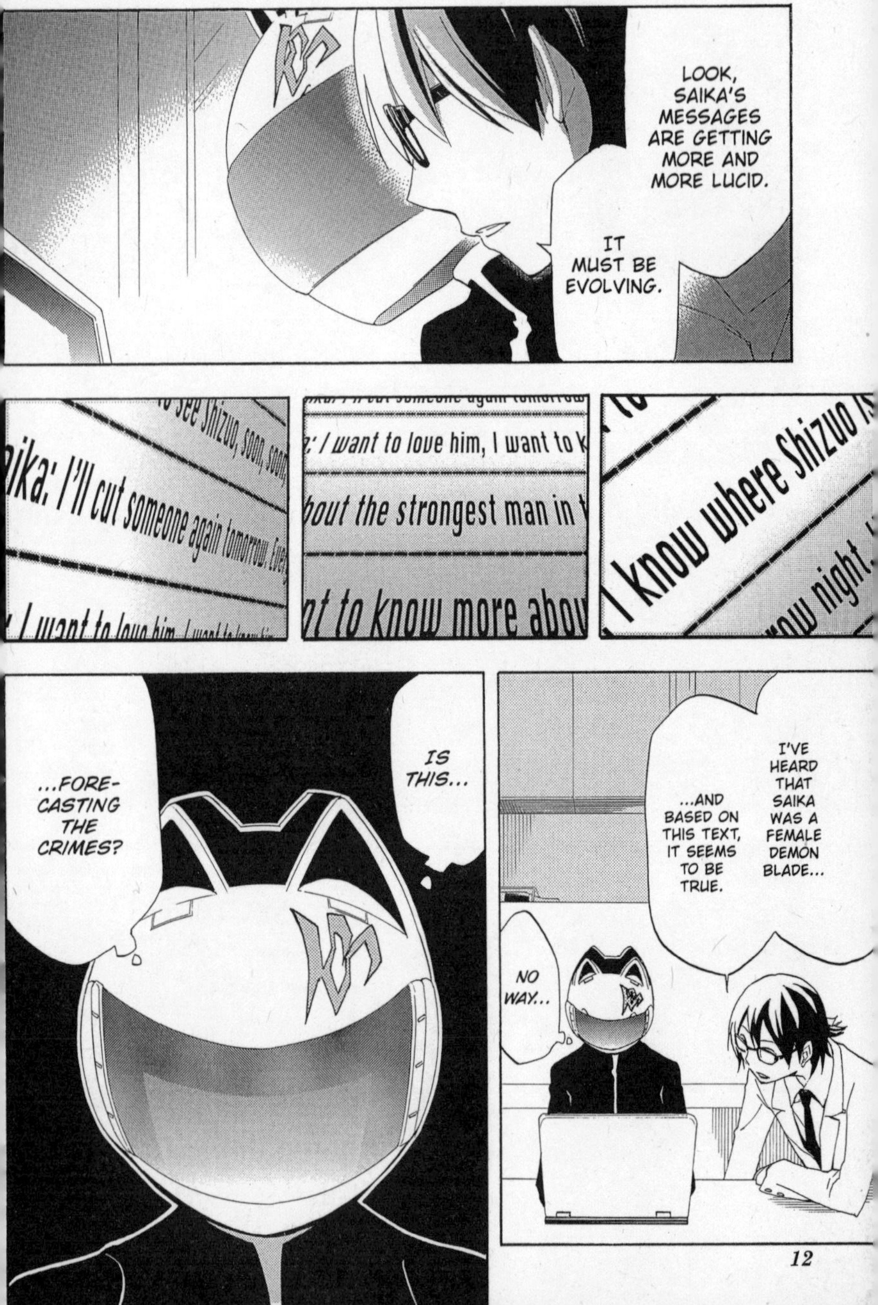

LOOK, SAIKA'S MESSAGES ARE GETTING MORE AND MORE LUCID.
IT MUST BE EVOLVING.
I know where Shizuo is
row night.
: I want to love him, I want to k
bout the strongest man in t
nt to know more abov
to see Shizuo, soon, soon
aika: I'll cut someone again tomorrow.
I'VE HEARD THAT SAIKA WAS A FEMALE DEMON BLADE...
...AND BASED ON THIS TEXT, IT SEEMS TO BE TRUE.
NO WAY...
IS THIS...
...FORE-CASTING THE CRIMES?

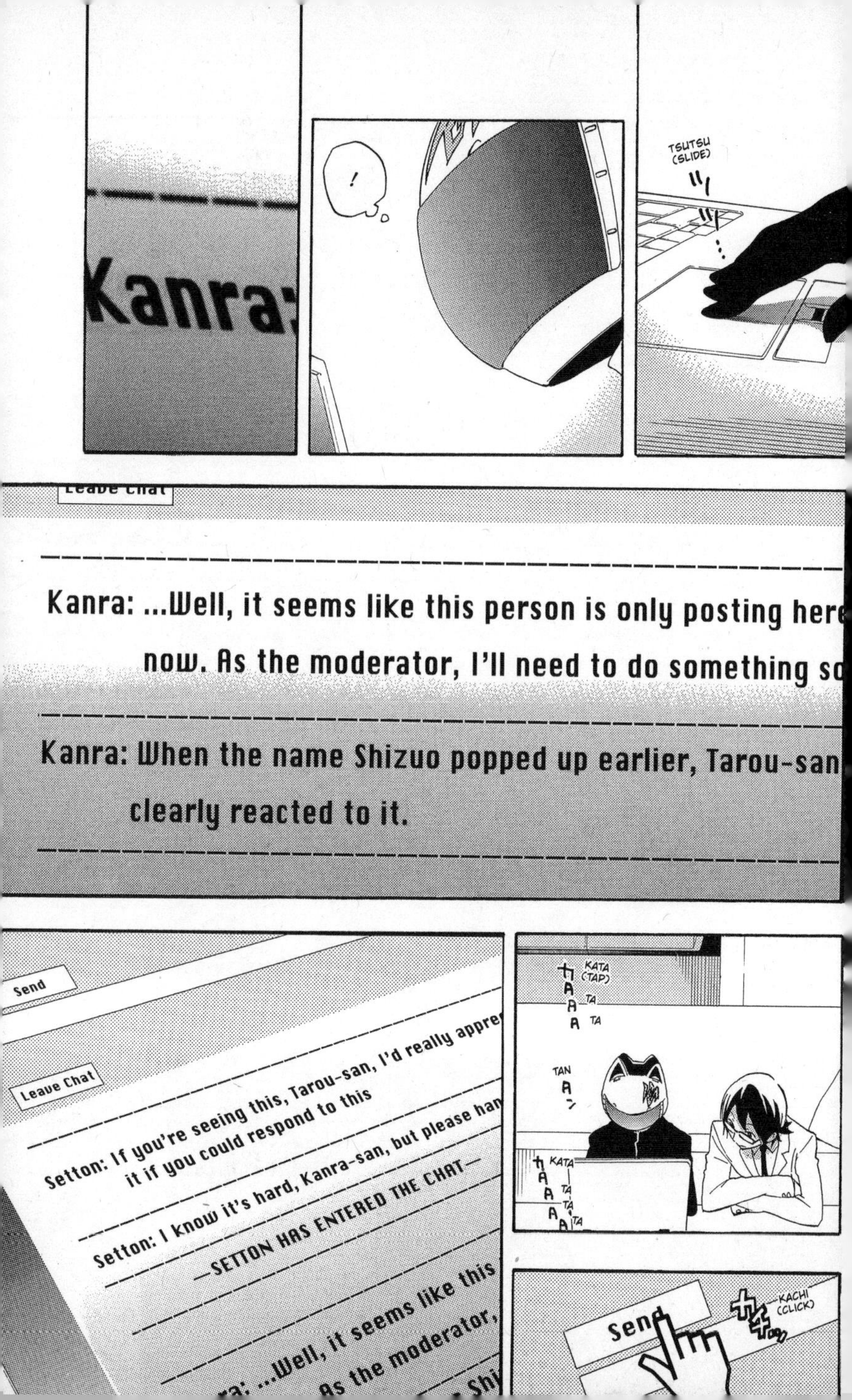

TSUTSU (SLIDE)
!
Kanra:
Leave Chat
Kanra: ...Well, it seems like this person is only posting here
now. As the moderator, I'll need to do something so
Kanra: When the name Shizuo popped up earlier, Tarou-san
clearly reacted to it.
KATA (TAP) TA TA
TAN
KATA TA TA TA
Send
KACHI (CLICK)
Send
Leave Chat
Setton: If you're seeing this, Tarou-san, I'd really appre
it if you could respond to this
Setton: I know it's hard, Kanra-san, but please han
—SETTON HAS ENTERED THE CHAT—
...Well, it seems like this
As the moderator,

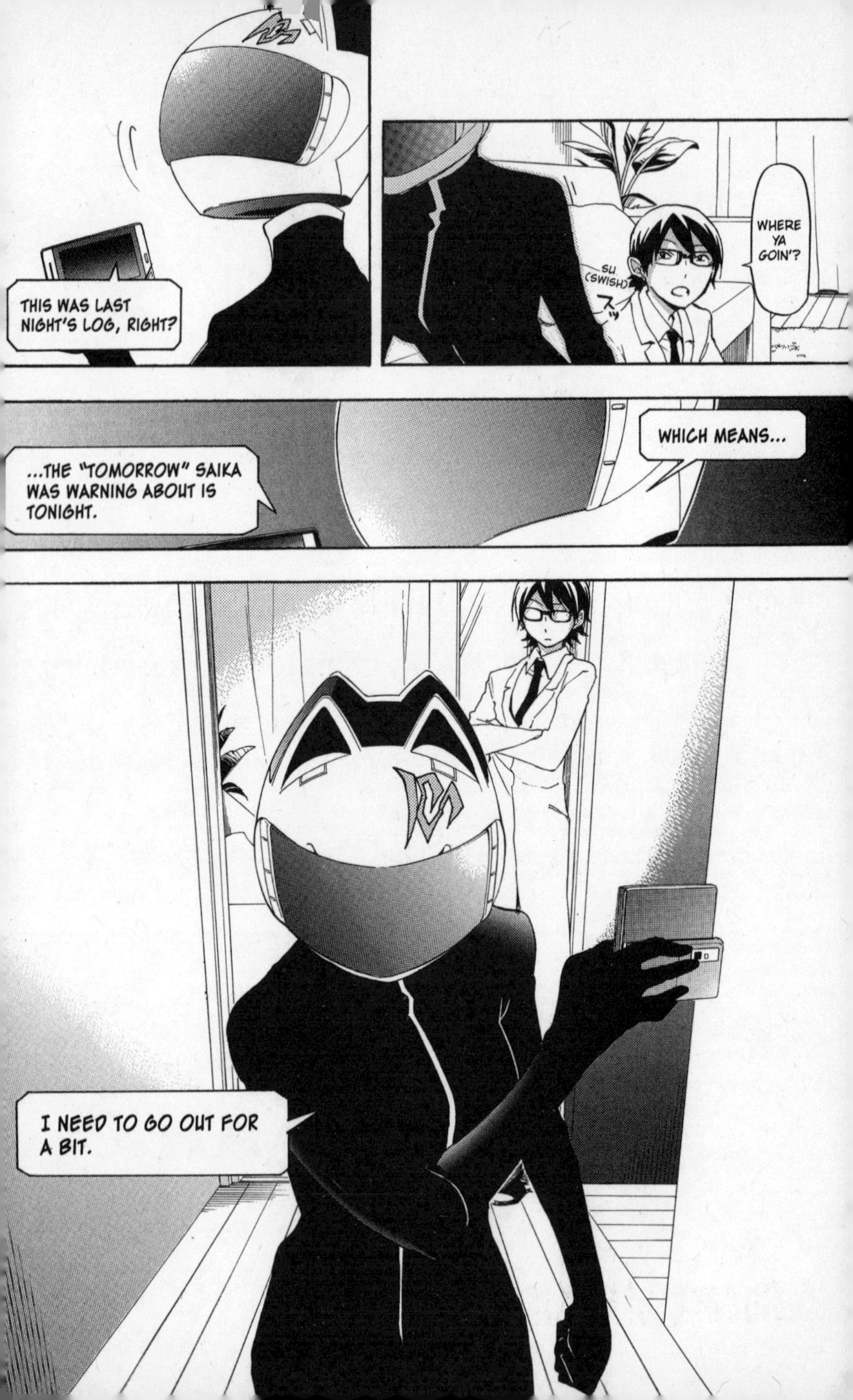
WHERE YA GOIN'?
SU (SWISH)
ズッ
THIS WAS LAST NIGHT'S LOG, RIGHT?
WHICH MEANS...
..."THE "TOMORROW" SAIKA WAS WARNING ABOUT IS TONIGHT.
I NEED TO GO OUT FOR A BIT.

Durarara!! Saika Arc

DRRR!!

CHAPTER 6: UNCERTAIN GIRL

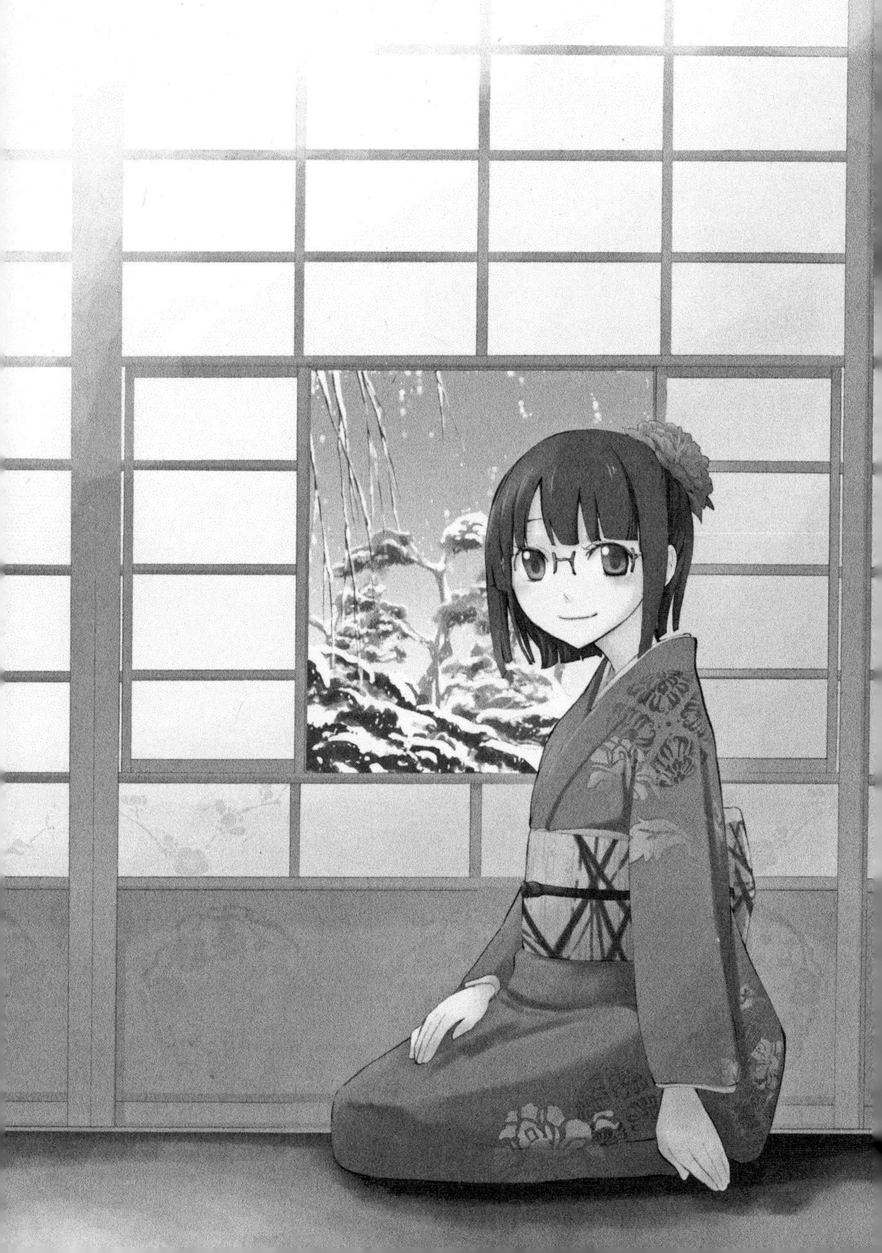

DRRR!!

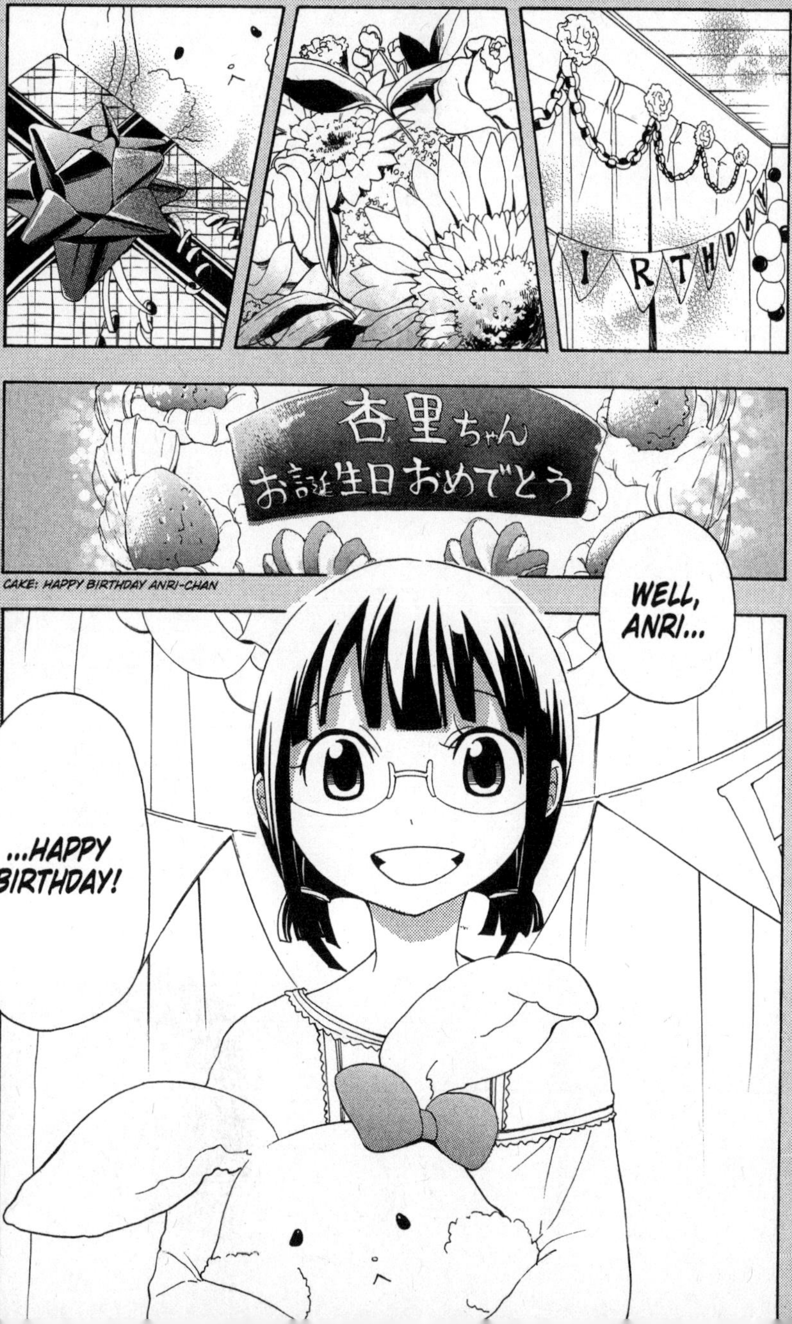
杏里ちゃん
お誕生日おめでとう
CAKE: HAPPY BIRTHDAY ANRI-CHAN
WELL, ANRI...
...HAPPY BIRTHDAY!

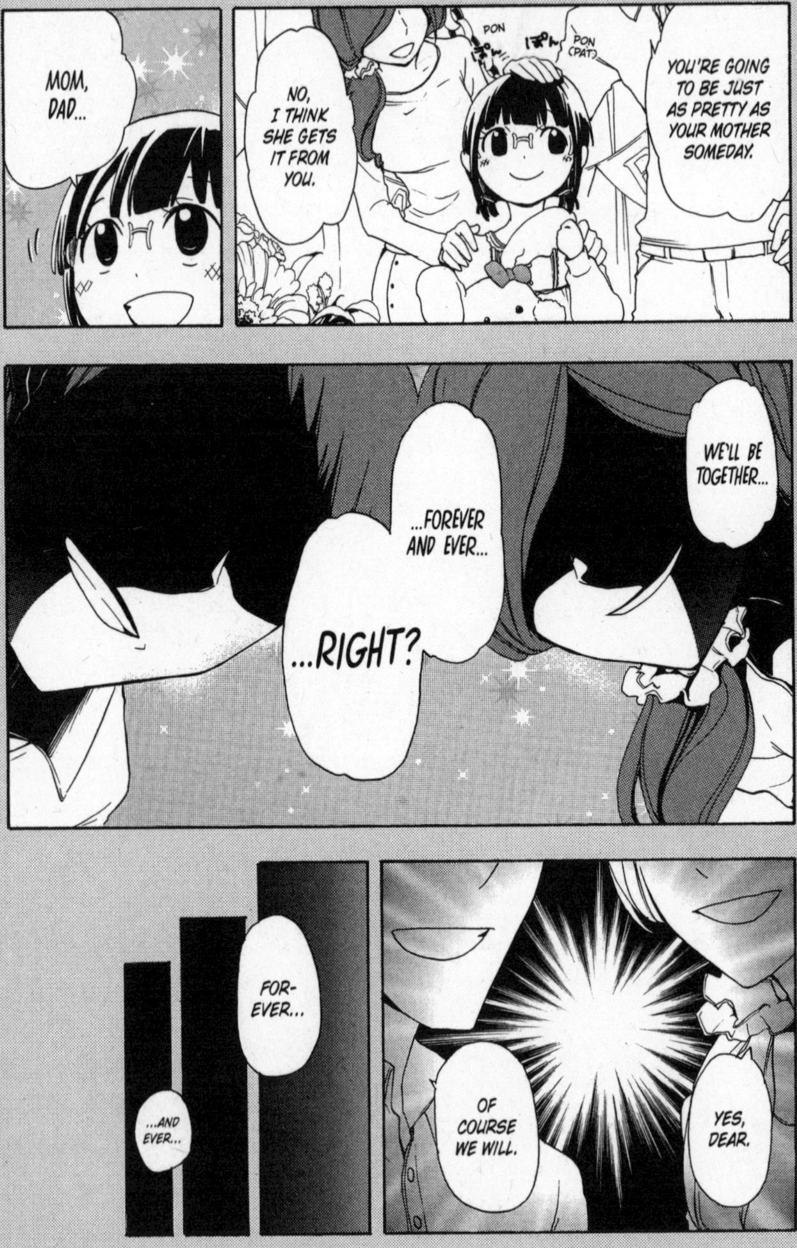
YOU'RE GOING TO BE JUST AS PRETTY AS YOUR MOTHER SOMEDAY.
PON (PAT)
ぽん
PON
ぽん
NO, I THINK SHE GETS IT FROM YOU.
MOM, DAD...
WE'LL BE TOGETHER...
...FOREVER AND EVER...
...RIGHT?
YES, DEAR.
OF COURSE WE WILL.
FOR-EVER...
...AND EVER...

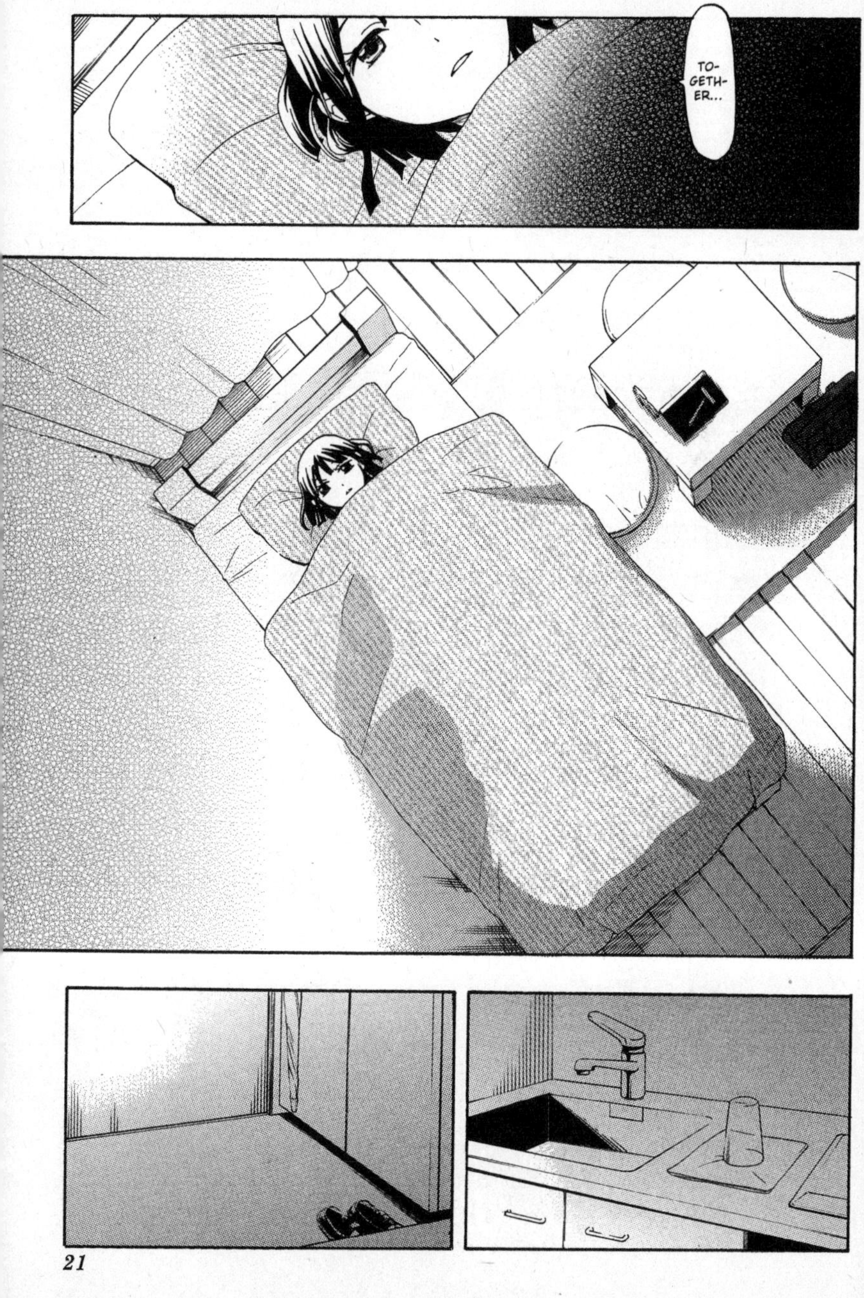
TO-GETH-ER...

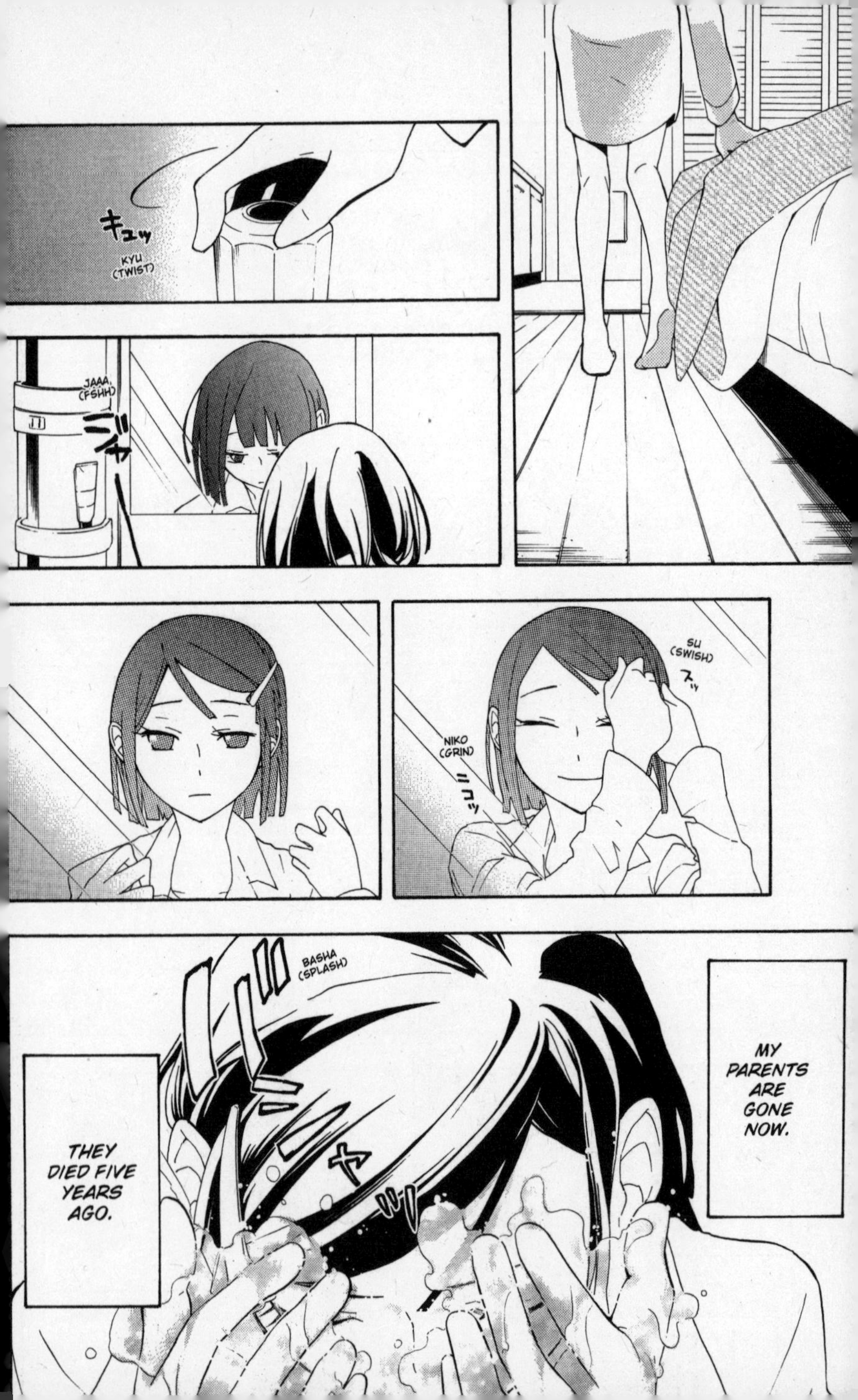
キュッ
KYU (TWIST)
JAAA, (FSHH)
ジャ
SU (SWISH)
スッ
NIKO (GRIN)
ニコッ
MY PARENTS ARE GONE NOW.
BASHA (SPLASH)
バシャッ
THEY DIED FIVE YEARS AGO.

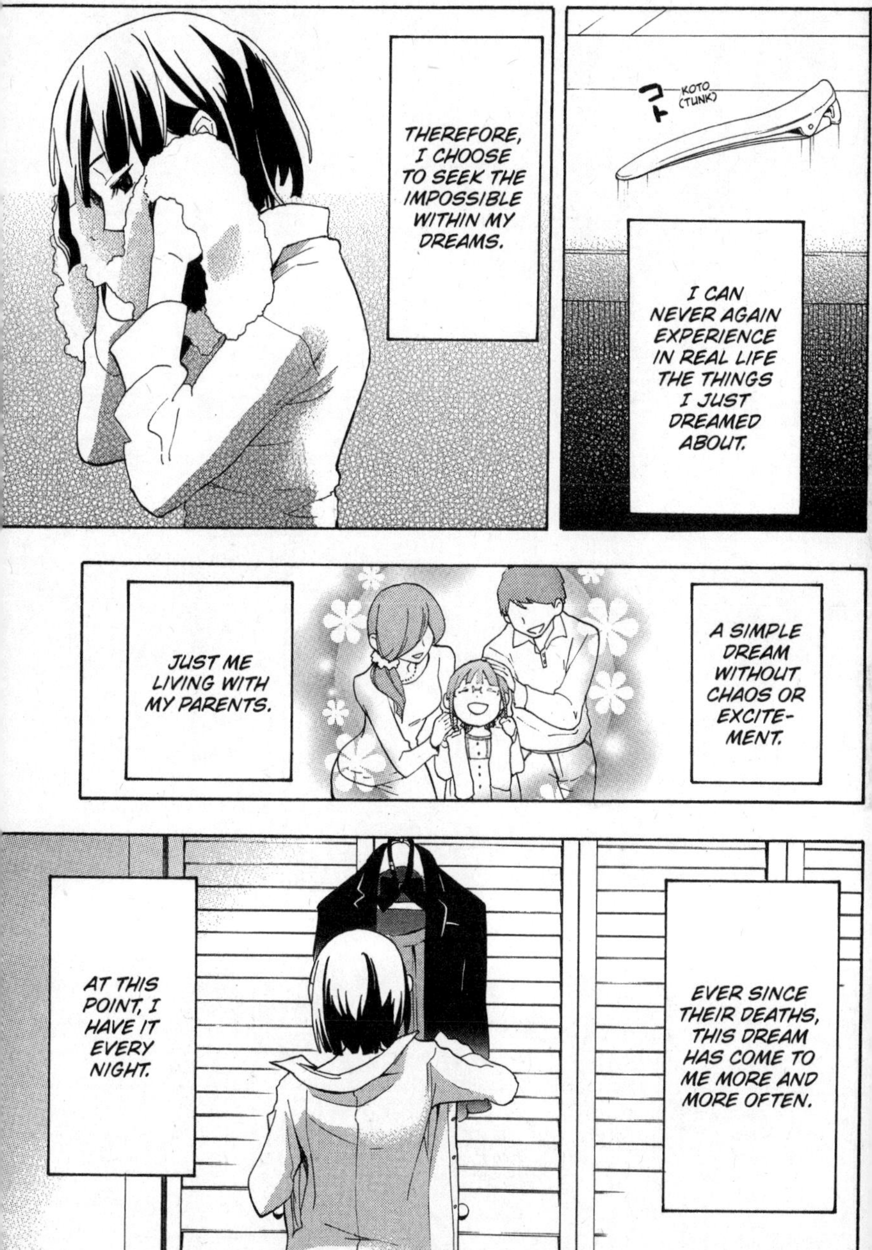
コト
KOTO (TUNK)
I CAN NEVER AGAIN EXPERIENCE IN REAL LIFE THE THINGS I JUST DREAMED ABOUT.
THEREFORE, I CHOOSE TO SEEK THE IMPOSSIBLE WITHIN MY DREAMS.
A SIMPLE DREAM WITHOUT CHAOS OR EXCITE-MENT.
JUST ME LIVING WITH MY PARENTS.
EVER SINCE THEIR DEATHS, THIS DREAM HAS COME TO ME MORE AND MORE OFTEN.
AT THIS POINT, I HAVE IT EVERY NIGHT.

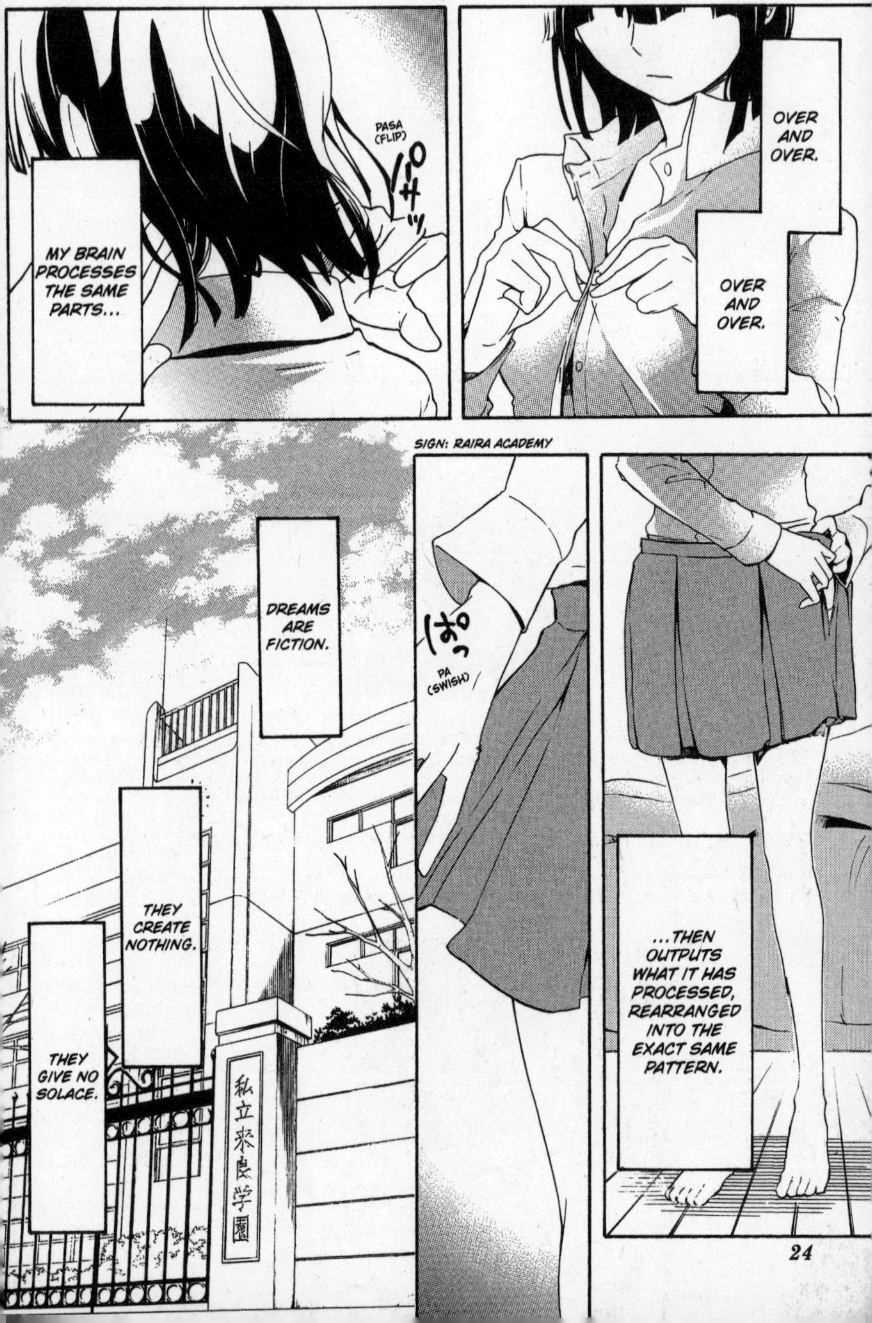
OVER AND OVER.
OVER AND OVER.
PASA (FLIP)
パサッ
MY BRAIN PROCESSES THE SAME PARTS...
...THEN OUTPUTS WHAT IT HAS PROCESSED, REARRANGED INTO THE EXACT SAME PATTERN.
ぱっ
PA (SWISH)
SIGN: RAIRA ACADEMY
DREAMS ARE FICTION.
THEY CREATE NOTHING.
THEY GIVE NO SOLACE.
私立来良学園

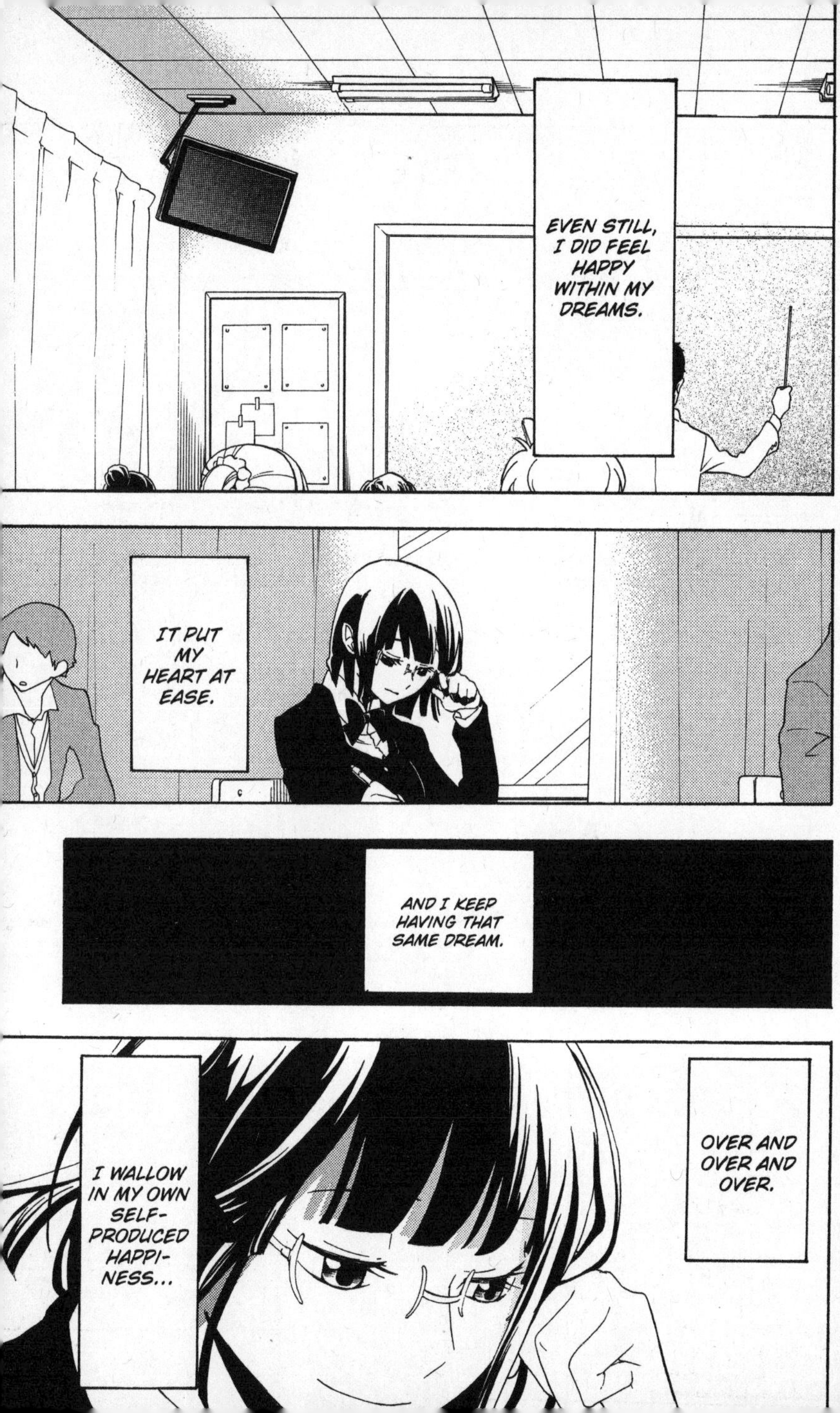
EVEN STILL, I DID FEEL HAPPY WITHIN MY DREAMS.
IT PUT MY HEART AT EASE.
AND I KEEP HAVING THAT SAME DREAM.
OVER AND OVER AND OVER.
I WALLOW IN MY OWN SELF-PRODUCED HAPPINESS...

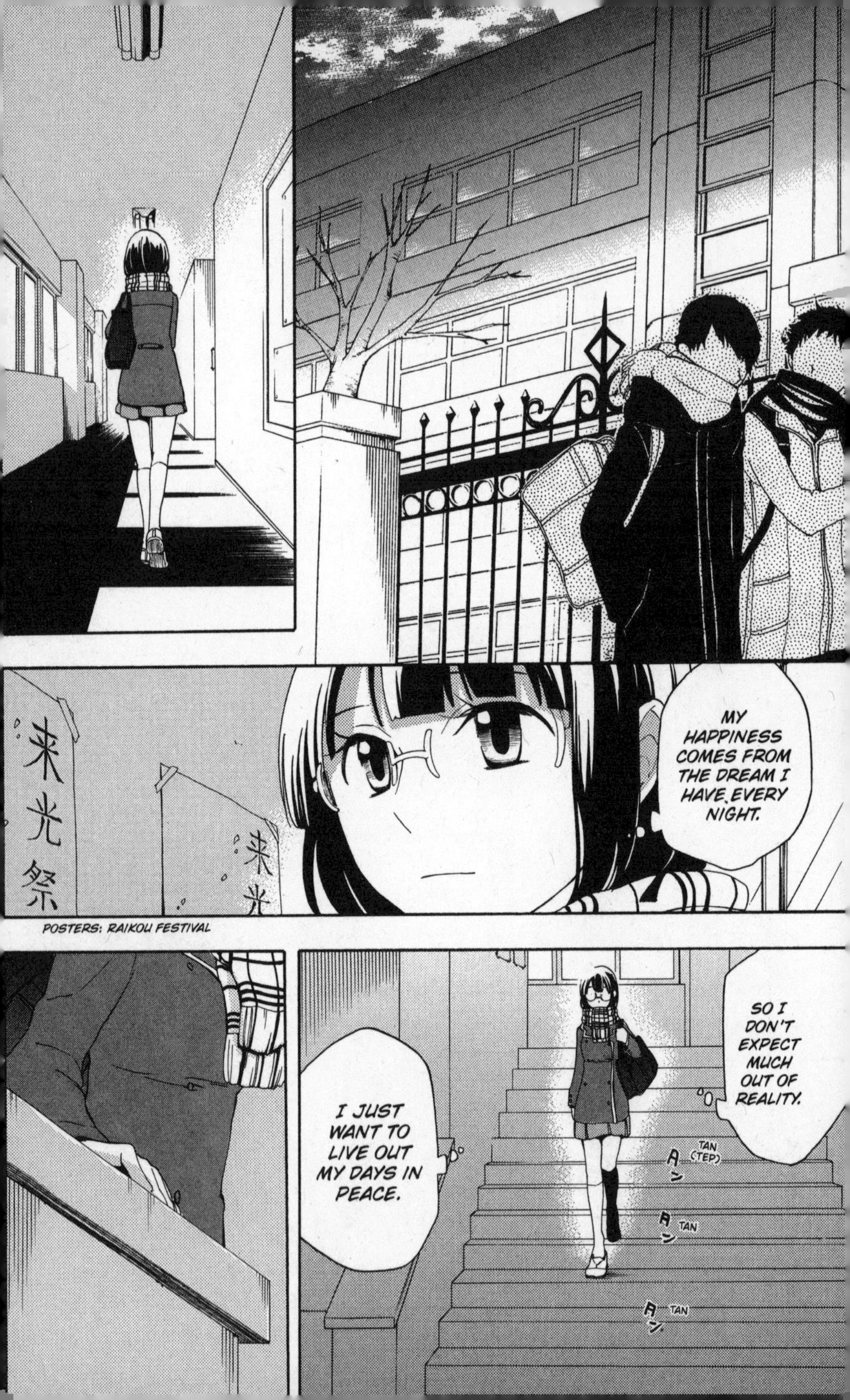
MY HAPPINESS COMES FROM THE DREAM I HAVE EVERY NIGHT.
来光祭
来光
POSTERS: RAIKOU FESTIVAL
SO I DON'T EXPECT MUCH OUT OF REALITY.
I JUST WANT TO LIVE OUT MY DAYS IN PEACE.
タン TAN (TEP)
タン TAN
タン TAN

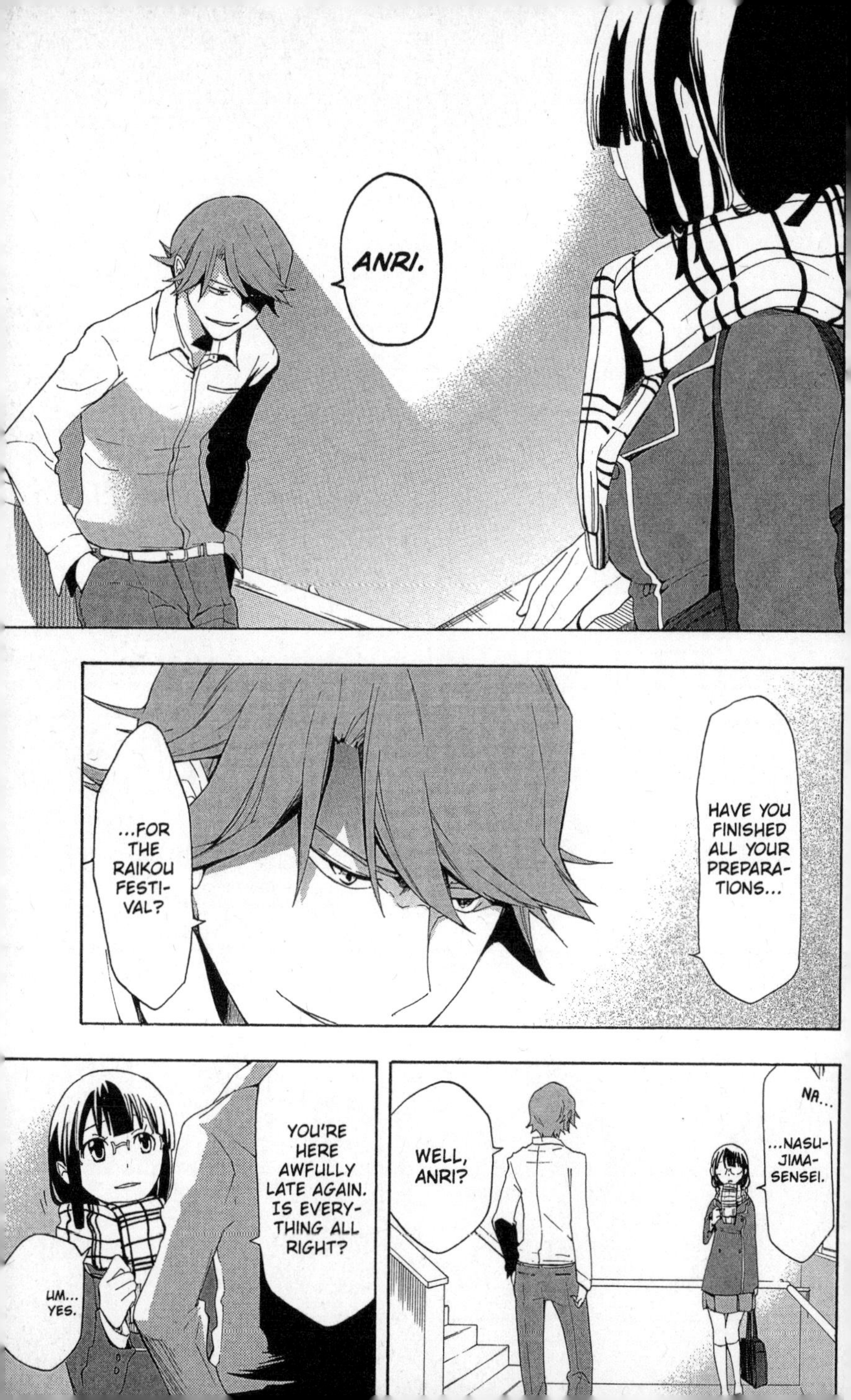
ANRI.
HAVE YOU FINISHED ALL YOUR PREPARATIONS...
...FOR THE RAIKOU FESTIVAL?
NA...
...NASUJIMA-SENSEI.
WELL, ANRI?
YOU'RE HERE AWFULLY LATE AGAIN. IS EVERYTHING ALL RIGHT?
UM... YES.

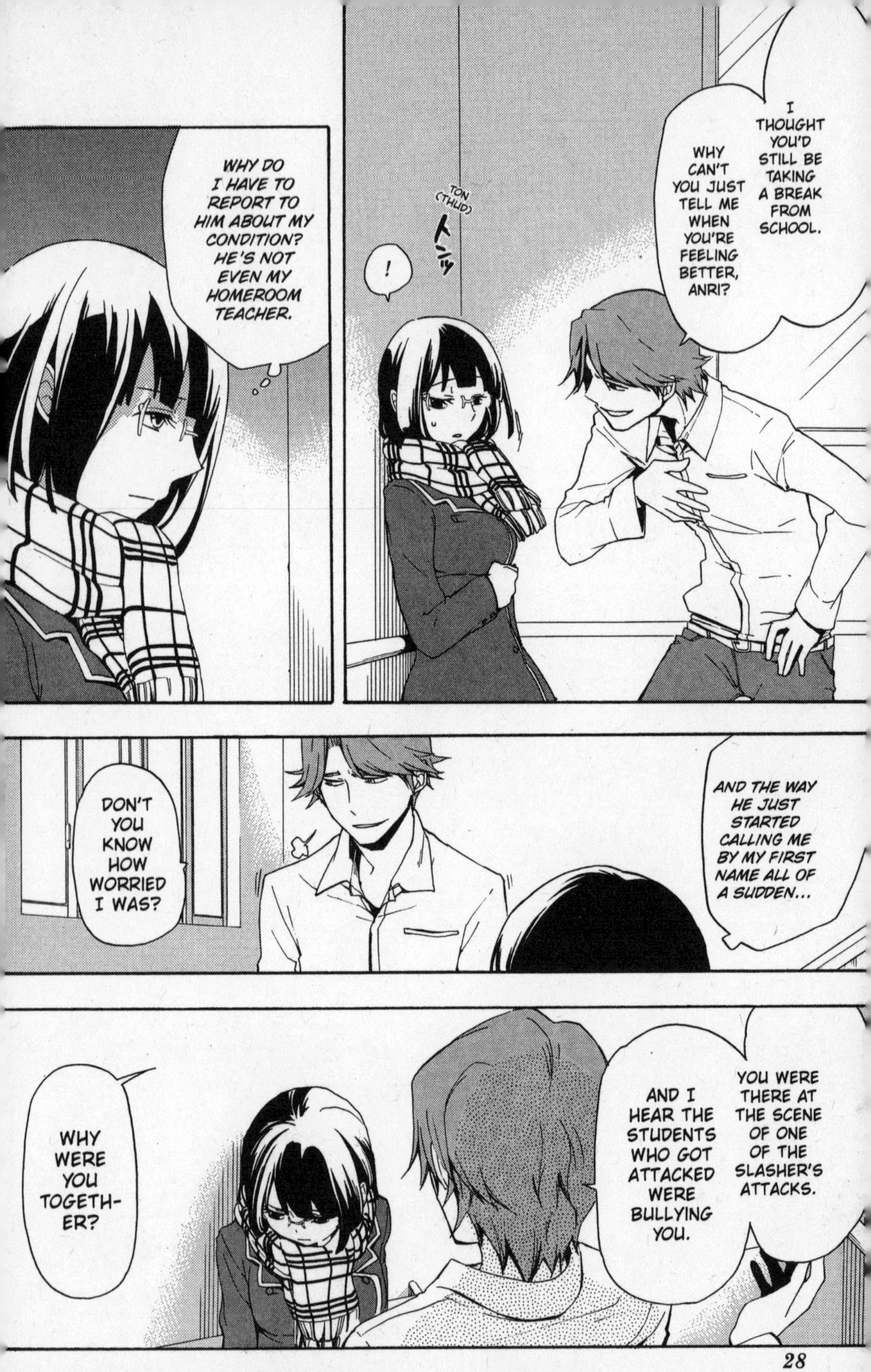
I THOUGHT YOU'D STILL BE TAKING A BREAK FROM SCHOOL.
WHY CAN'T YOU JUST TELL ME WHEN YOU'RE FEELING BETTER, ANRI?
TON (THUD)
トッ
!
WHY DO I HAVE TO REPORT TO HIM ABOUT MY CONDITION? HE'S NOT EVEN MY HOMEROOM TEACHER.
AND THE WAY HE JUST STARTED CALLING ME BY MY FIRST NAME ALL OF A SUDDEN...
DON'T YOU KNOW HOW WORRIED I WAS?
YOU WERE THERE AT THE SCENE OF ONE OF THE SLASHER'S ATTACKS.
AND I HEAR THE STUDENTS WHO GOT ATTACKED WERE BULLYING YOU.
WHY WERE YOU TOGETHER?

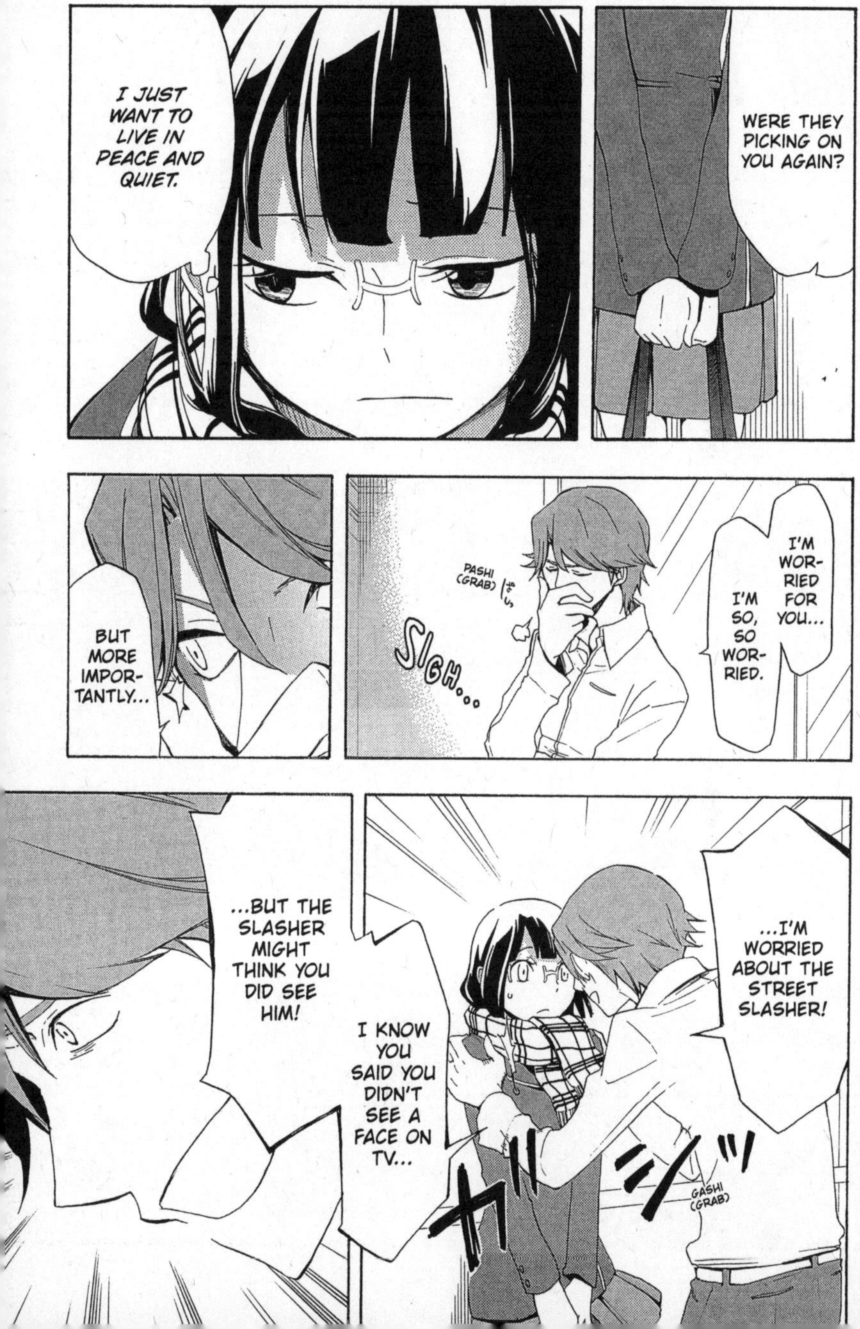
WERE THEY PICKING ON YOU AGAIN?
I JUST WANT TO LIVE IN PEACE AND QUIET.
I'M WORRIED FOR YOU...
I'M SO, SO WORRIED.
PASHI (GRAB)
SIGH...
BUT MORE IMPORTANTLY...
...I'M WORRIED ABOUT THE STREET SLASHER!
I KNOW YOU SAID YOU DIDN'T SEE A FACE ON TV...
GASHI (GRAB)
...BUT THE SLASHER MIGHT THINK YOU DID SEE HIM!

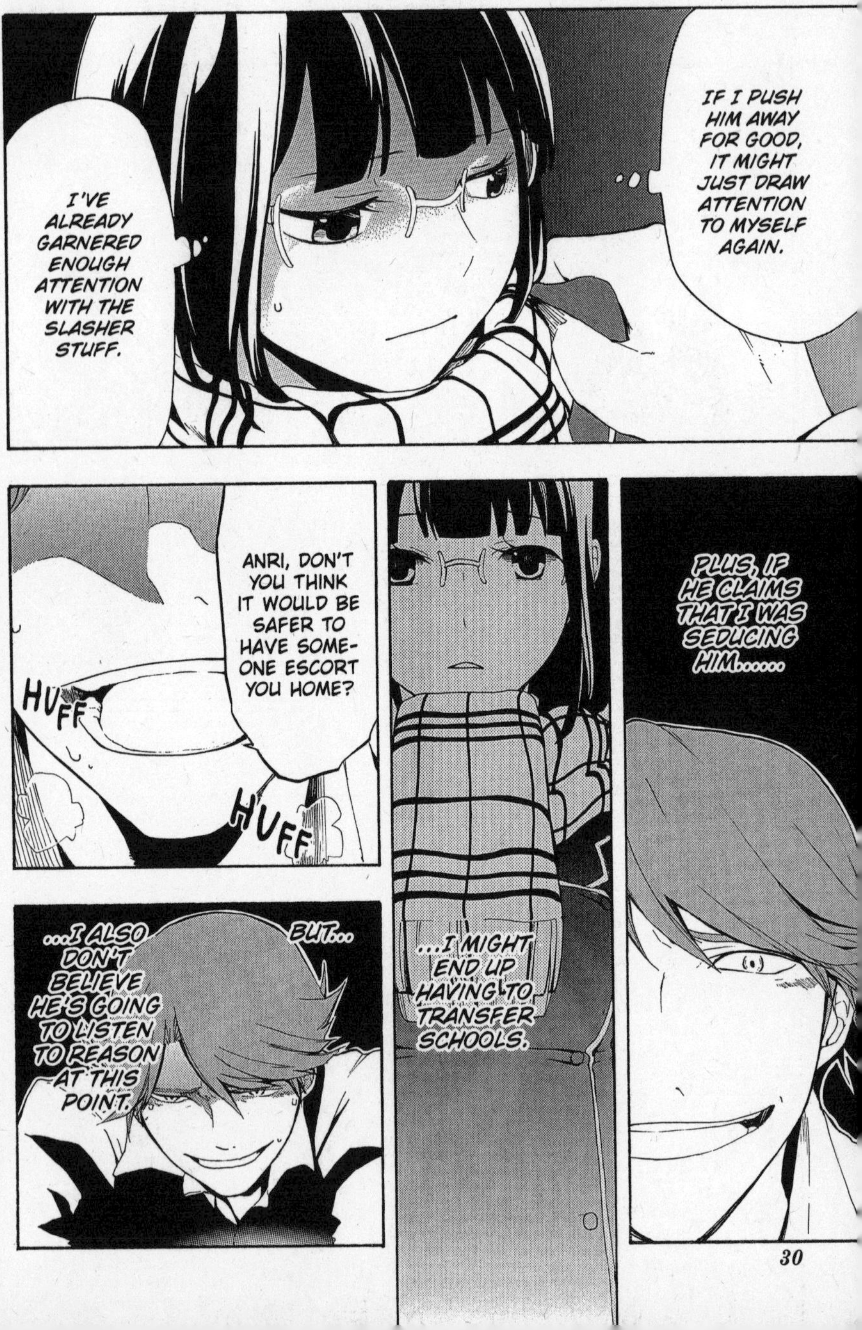
IF I PUSH HIM AWAY FOR GOOD, IT MIGHT JUST DRAW ATTENTION TO MYSELF AGAIN.
I'VE ALREADY GARNERED ENOUGH ATTENTION WITH THE SLASHER STUFF.
PLUS, IF HE CLAIMS THAT I WAS SEDUCING HIM......
...I MIGHT END UP HAVING TO TRANSFER SCHOOLS.
ANRI, DON'T YOU THINK IT WOULD BE SAFER TO HAVE SOME-ONE ESCORT YOU HOME?
HUFF
HUFF
BUT...
...I ALSO DON'T BELIEVE HE'S GOING TO LISTEN TO REASON AT THIS POINT.

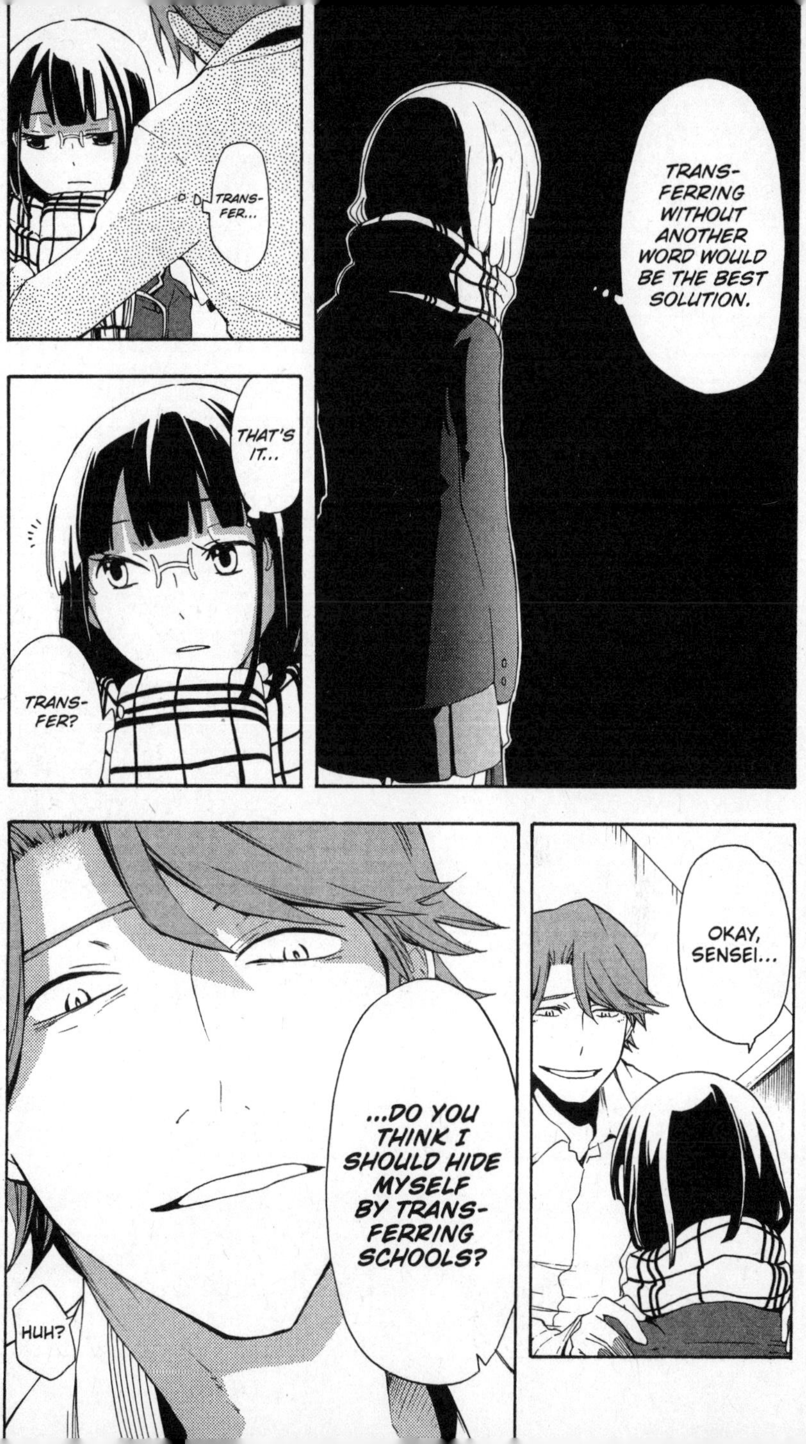
TRANS-FERRING WITHOUT ANOTHER WORD WOULD BE THE BEST SOLUTION.
TRANS-FER...
THAT'S IT...
TRANS-FER?
OKAY, SENSEI...
...DO YOU THINK I SHOULD HIDE MYSELF BY TRANS-FERRING SCHOOLS?
HUH?

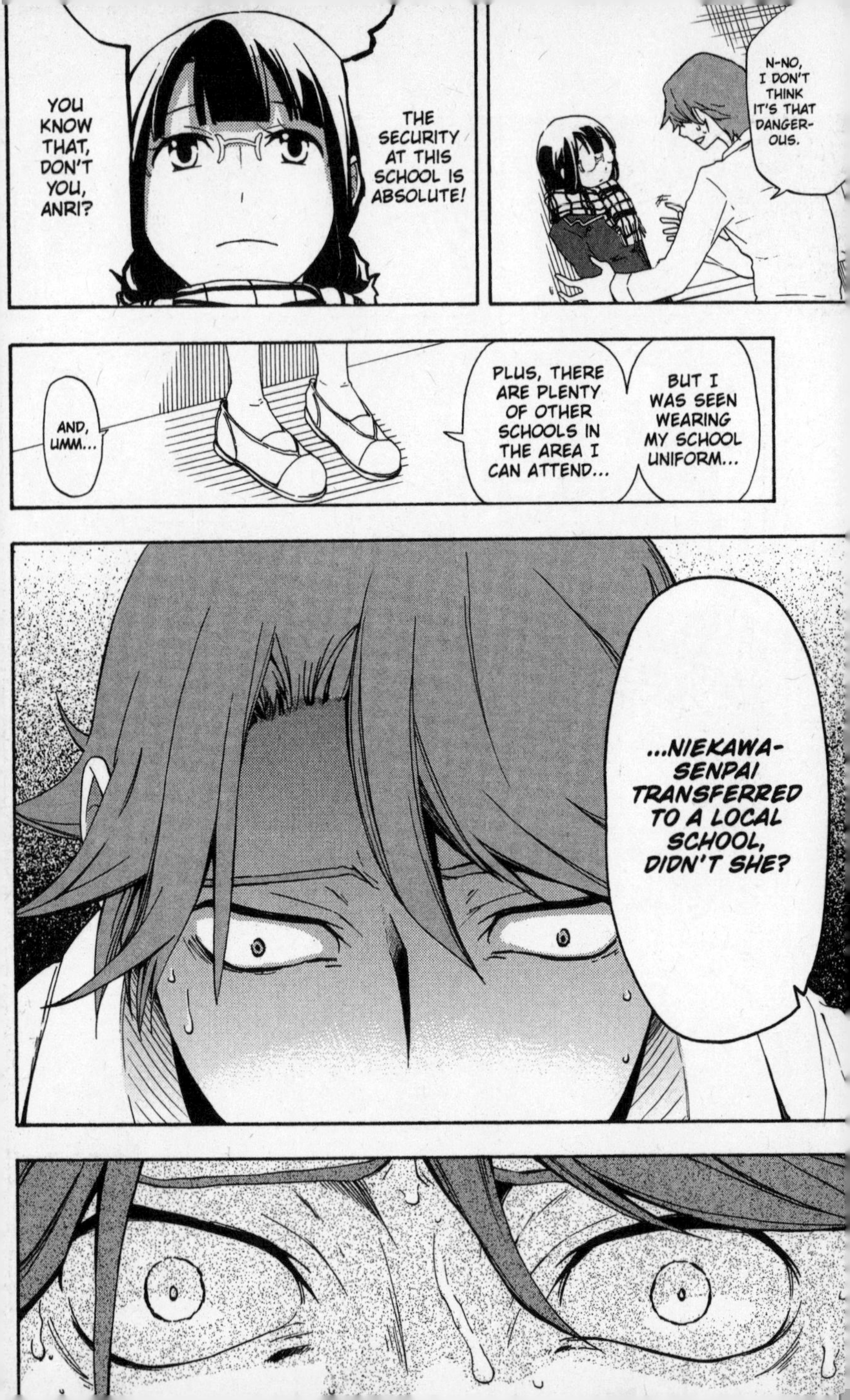
N-NO, I DON'T THINK IT'S THAT DANGER-OUS.
THE SECURITY AT THIS SCHOOL IS ABSOLUTE!
YOU KNOW THAT, DON'T YOU, ANRI?
BUT I WAS SEEN WEARING MY SCHOOL UNIFORM...
PLUS, THERE ARE PLENTY OF OTHER SCHOOLS IN THE AREA I CAN ATTEND...
AND, UMM...
...NIEKAWA-SENPAI TRANSFERRED TO A LOCAL SCHOOL, DIDN'T SHE?

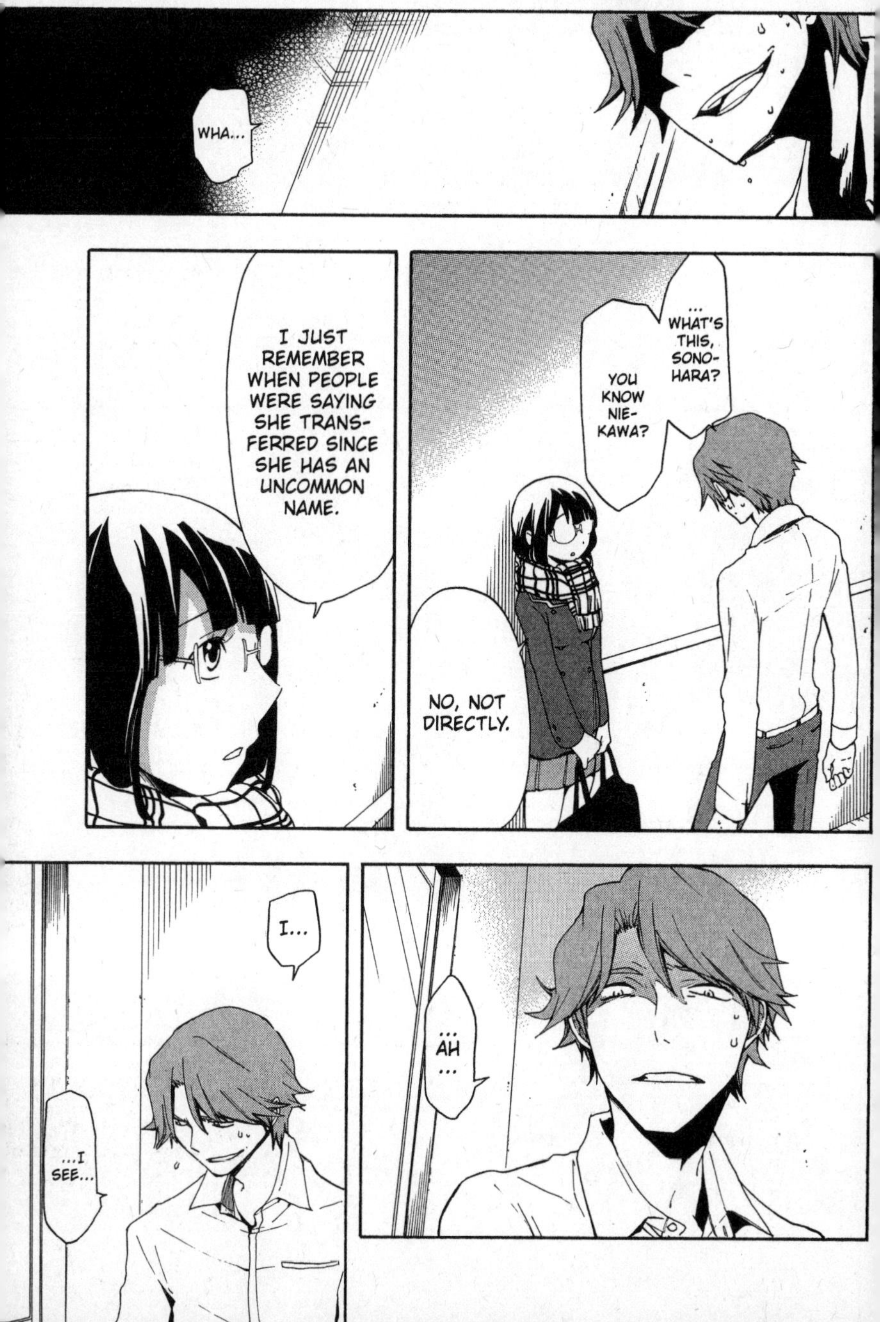
WHA...
...WHAT'S THIS, SONO-HARA?
YOU KNOW NIE-KAWA?
NO, NOT DIRECTLY.
I JUST REMEMBER WHEN PEOPLE WERE SAYING SHE TRANS-FERRED SINCE SHE HAS AN UNCOMMON NAME.
...AH...
I...
...I SEE...

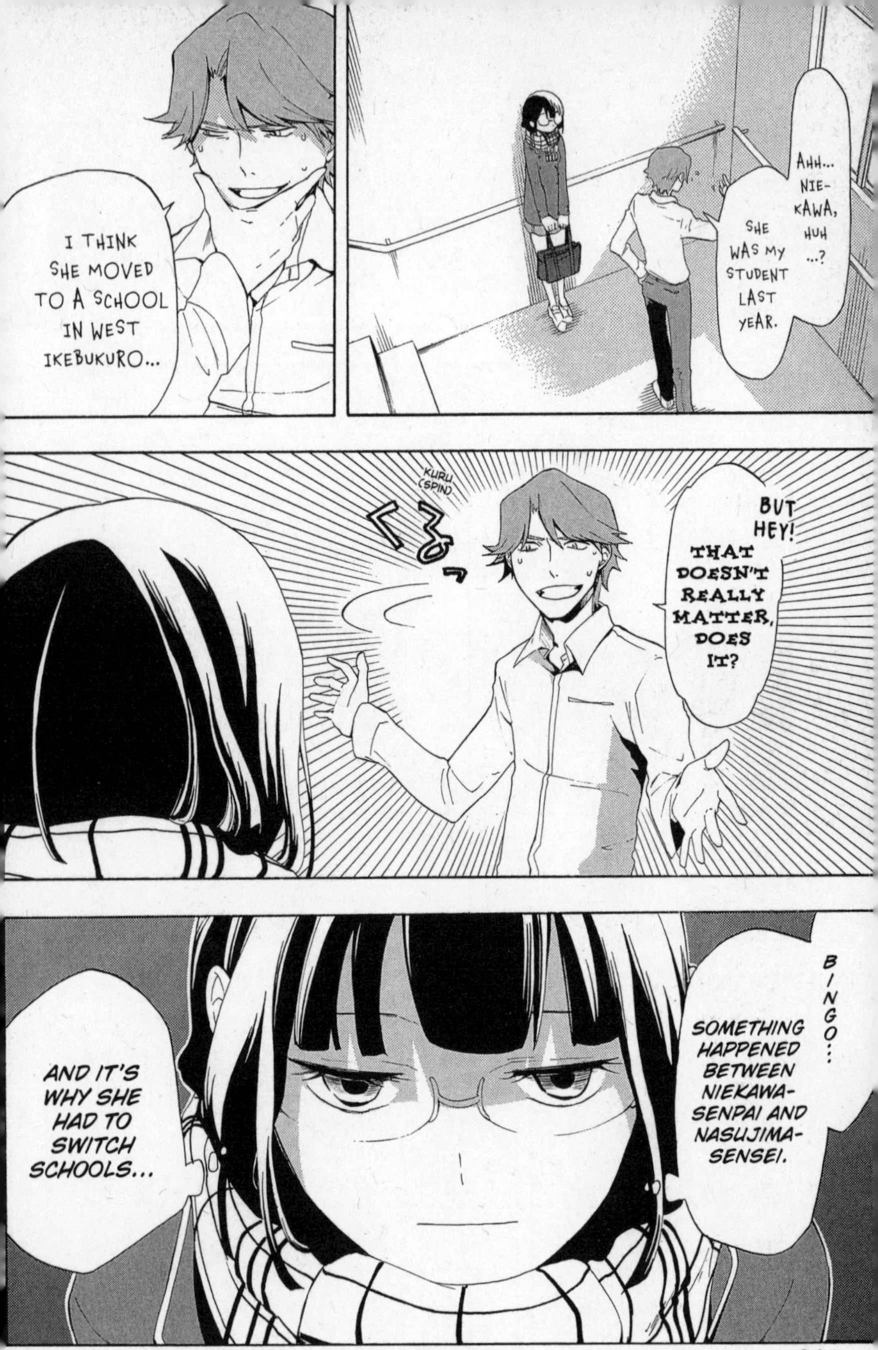

AHH... NIEKAWA, HUH ...?
SHE WAS MY STUDENT LAST YEAR.
I THINK SHE MOVED TO A SCHOOL IN WEST IKEBUKURO...
くる
KURU (SPIN)
BUT HEY!
THAT DOESN'T REALLY MATTER, DOES IT?
BINGO...
SOMETHING HAPPENED BETWEEN NIEKAWA-SENPAI AND NASUJIMA-SENSEI.
AND IT'S WHY SHE HAD TO SWITCH SCHOOLS...

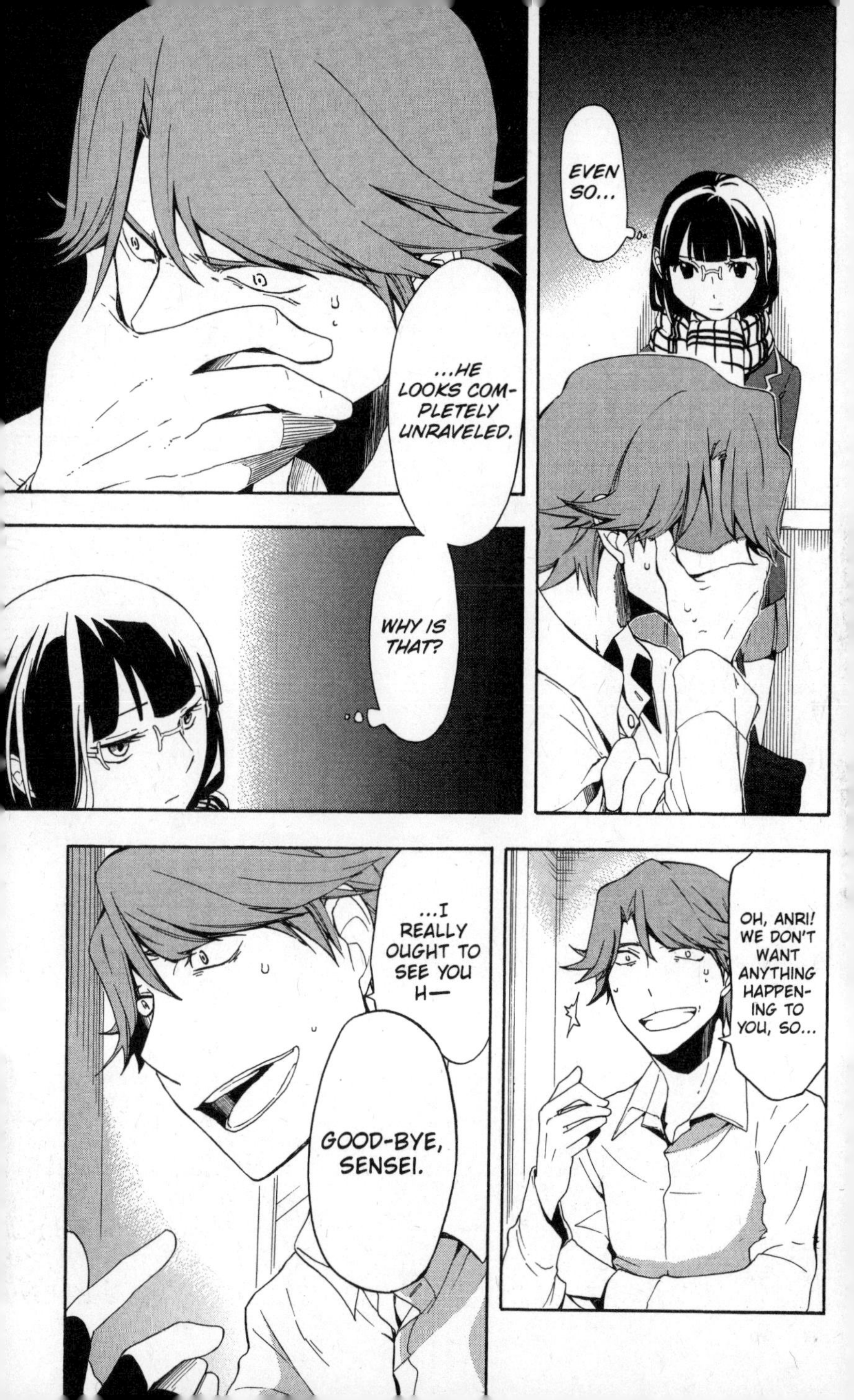
EVEN SO...
...HE LOOKS COMPLETELY UNRAVELED.
WHY IS THAT?
OH, ANRI! WE DON'T WANT ANYTHING HAPPENING TO YOU, SO...
...I REALLY OUGHT TO SEE YOU H—
GOOD-BYE, SENSEI.

I NEED TO GET GOING.

PEKORI (BOW)

... AH ...

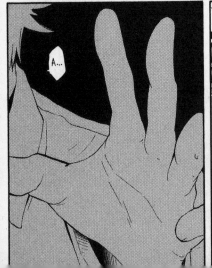

A...

BA (FWP)

SUTA (STRIDE)

SUTA

SUTA

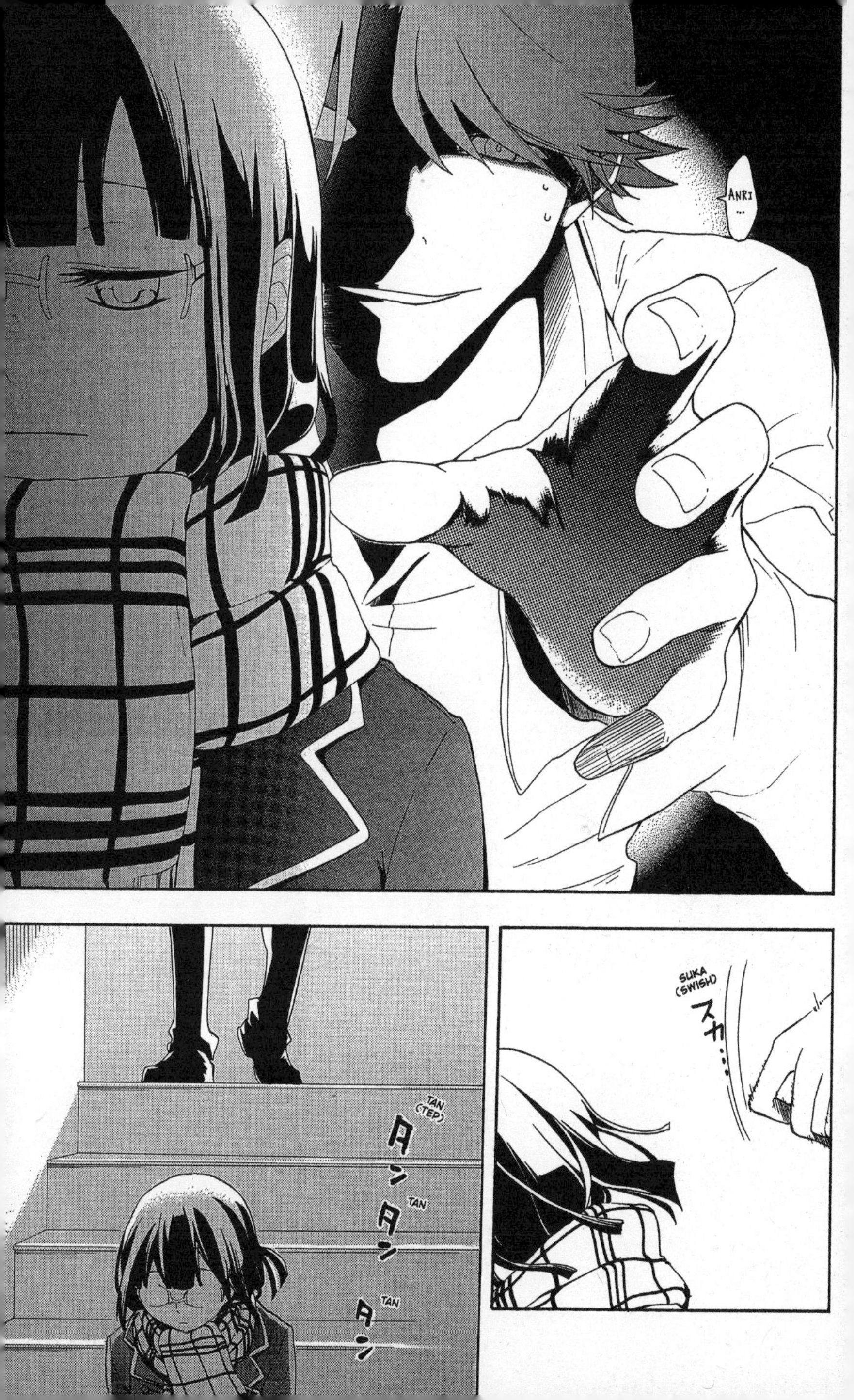
ANRI ...
SUKA (SWISH)
スカ…
TAN (TEP)
タン
TAN
タン
TAN
タン

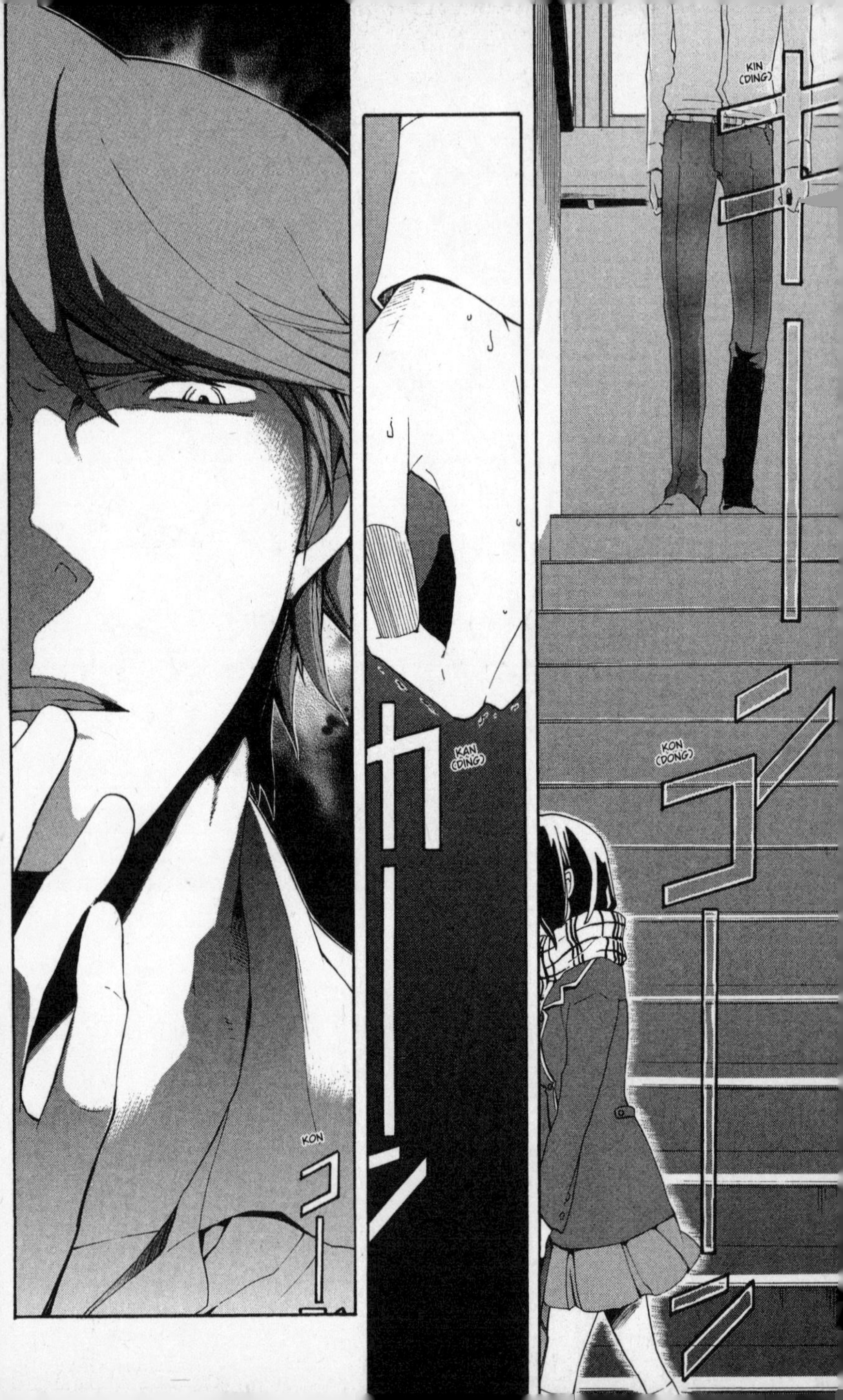
KIN
(DING)
KON
(DONG)
KAN
(DING)
KON

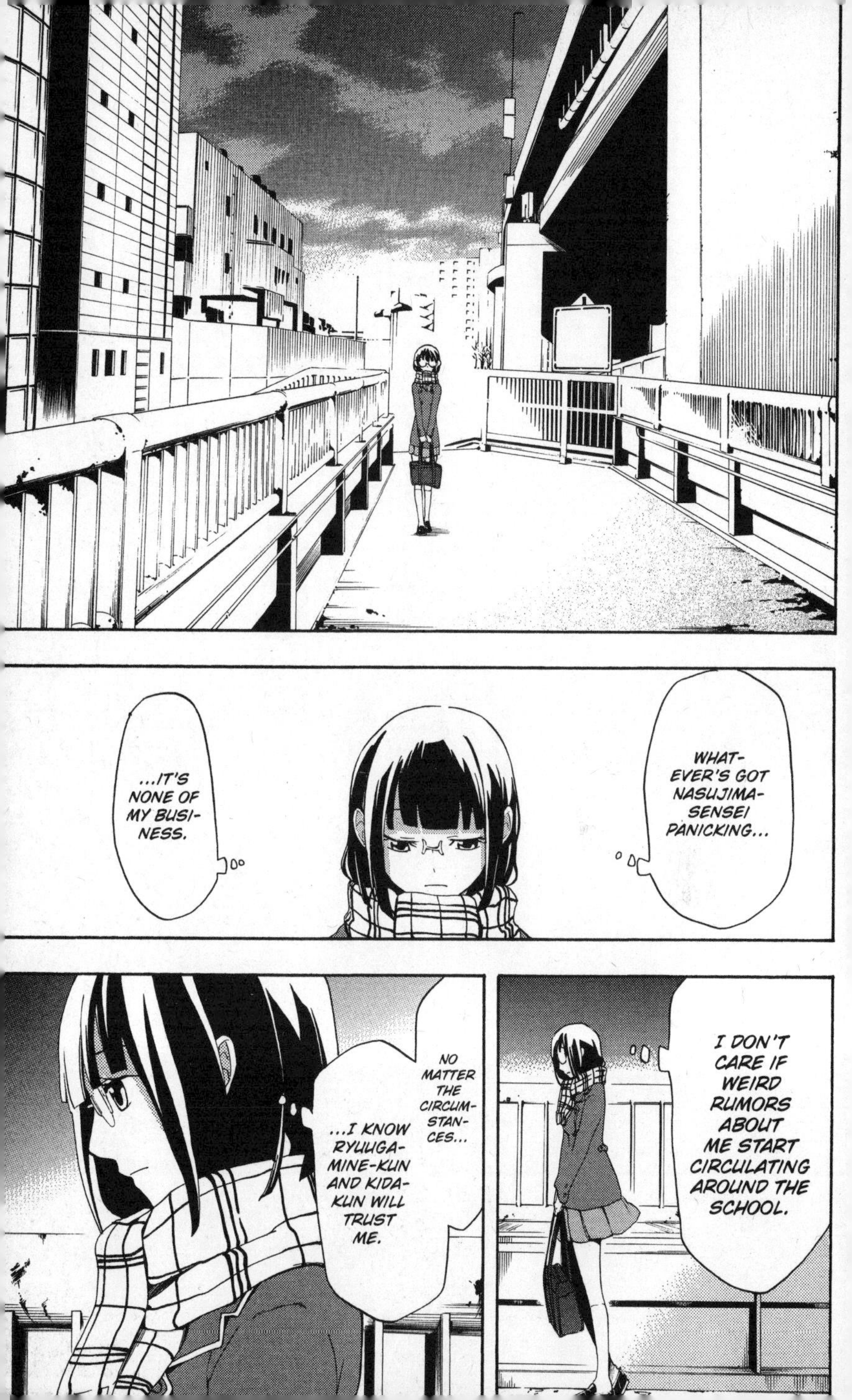

WHAT-EVER'S GOT NASUJIMA-SENSEI PANICKING...
...IT'S NONE OF MY BUSI-NESS.
I DON'T CARE IF WEIRD RUMORS ABOUT ME START CIRCULATING AROUND THE SCHOOL.
NO MATTER THE CIRCUM-STAN-CES...
...I KNOW RYUUGA-MINE-KUN AND KIDA-KUN WILL TRUST ME.

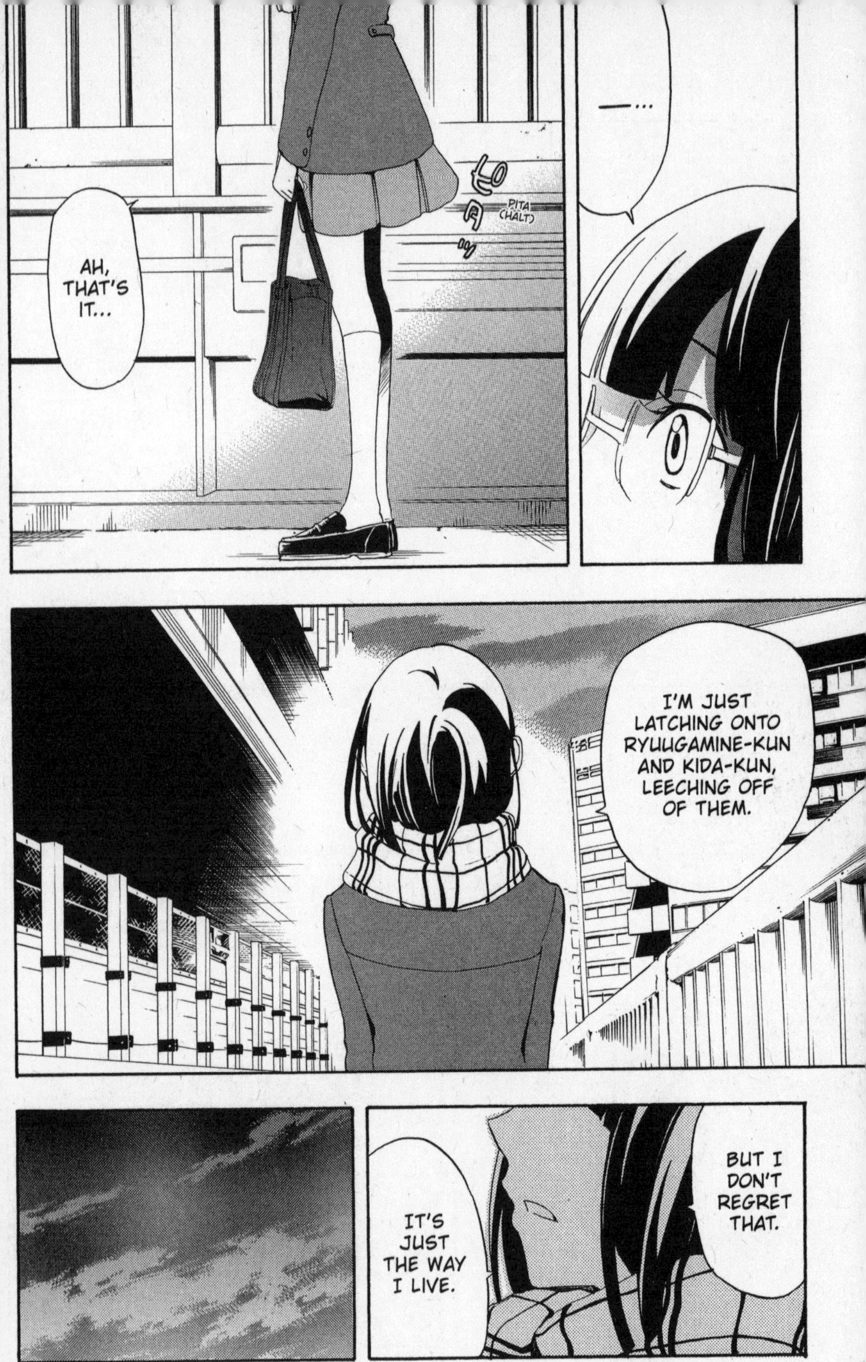
—...
AH, THAT'S IT...
PITA (HALT)
I'M JUST LATCHING ONTO RYUUGAMINE-KUN AND KIDA-KUN, LEECHING OFF OF THEM.
BUT I DON'T REGRET THAT.
IT'S JUST THE WAY I LIVE.

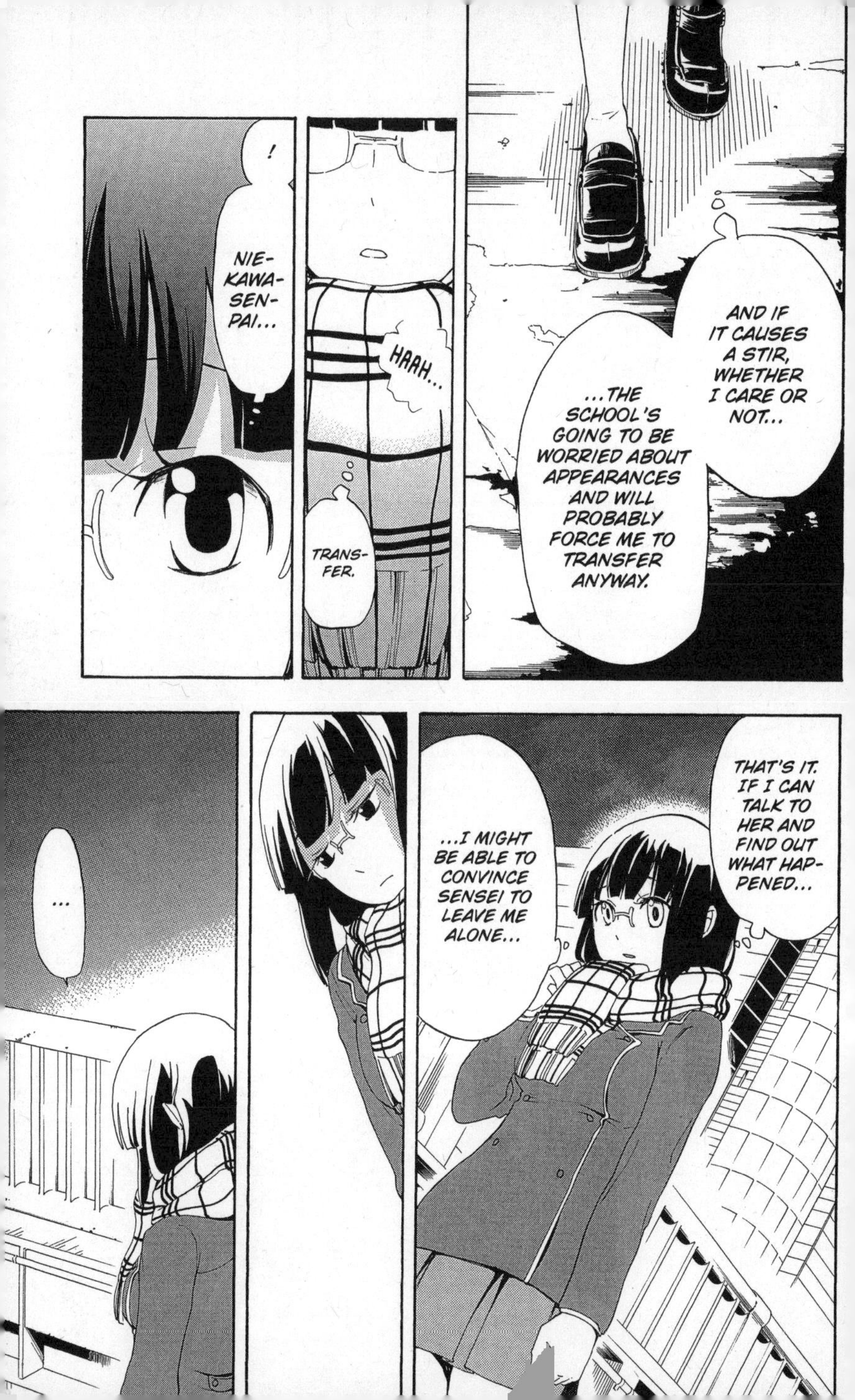
AND IF IT CAUSES A STIR, WHETHER I CARE OR NOT...
...THE SCHOOL'S GOING TO BE WORRIED ABOUT APPEARANCES AND WILL PROBABLY FORCE ME TO TRANSFER ANYWAY.
HAAH...
TRANSFER.
!
NIEKAWA-SENPAI...
THAT'S IT. IF I CAN TALK TO HER AND FIND OUT WHAT HAPPENED...
...I MIGHT BE ABLE TO CONVINCE SENSEI TO LEAVE ME ALONE...
...

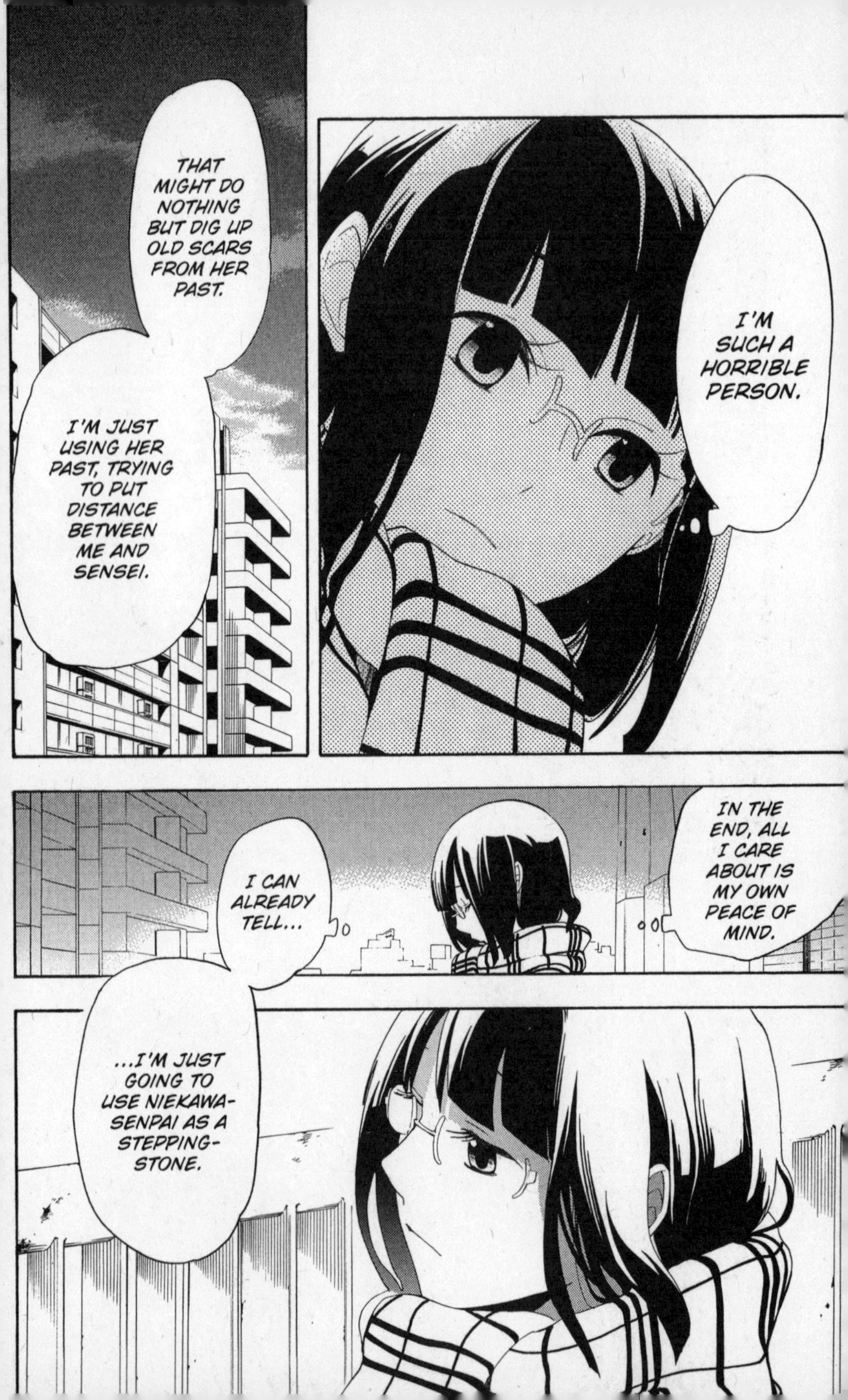
I'M SUCH A HORRIBLE PERSON.
THAT MIGHT DO NOTHING BUT DIG UP OLD SCARS FROM HER PAST.
I'M JUST USING HER PAST, TRYING TO PUT DISTANCE BETWEEN ME AND SENSEI.
IN THE END, ALL I CARE ABOUT IS MY OWN PEACE OF MIND.
I CAN ALREADY TELL...
...I'M JUST GOING TO USE NIEKAWA-SENPAI AS A STEPPING-STONE.

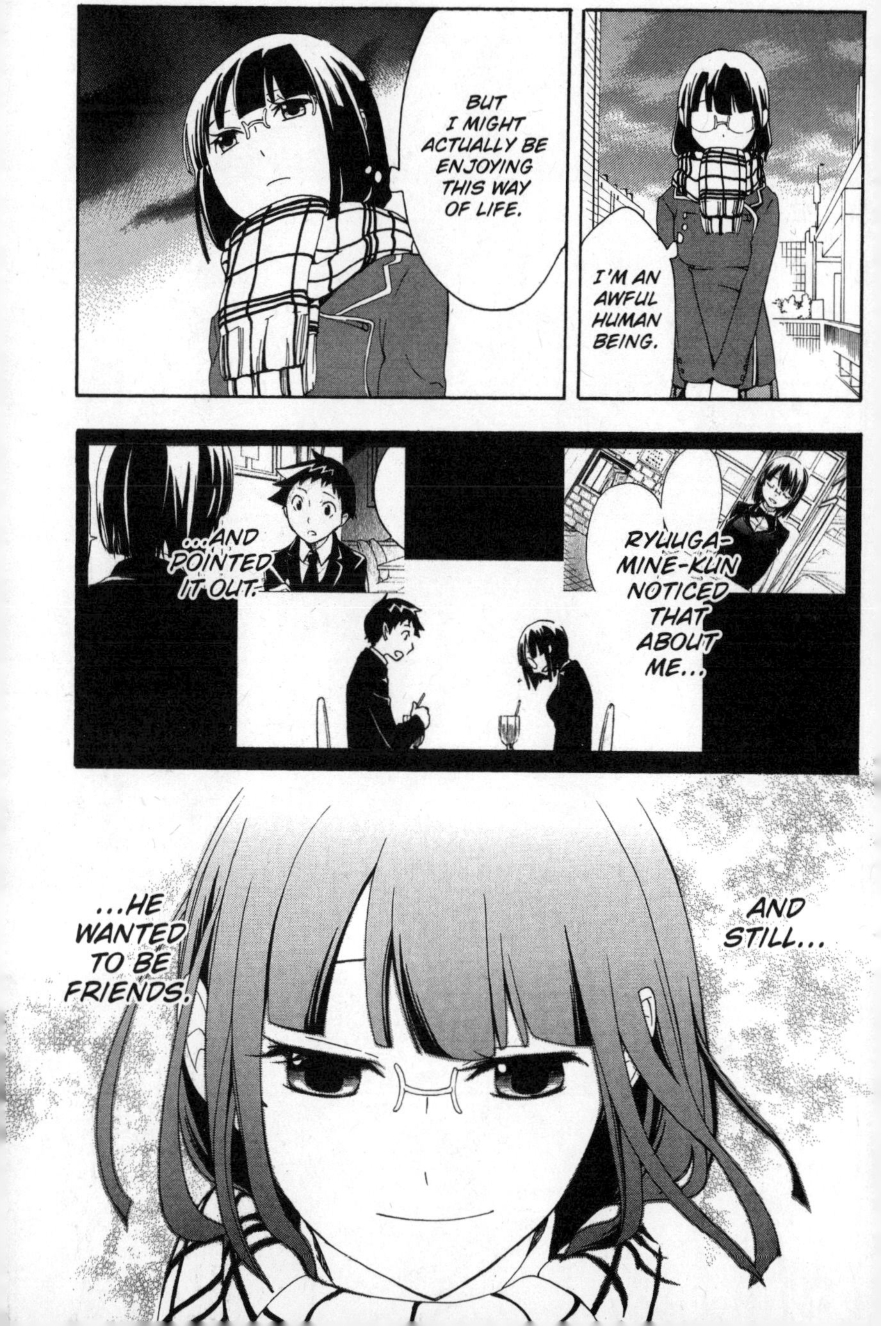
I'M AN AWFUL HUMAN BEING.
BUT I MIGHT ACTUALLY BE ENJOYING THIS WAY OF LIFE.
RYUUGA-MINE-KUN NOTICED THAT ABOUT ME...
...AND POINTED IT OUT.
AND STILL...
...HE WANTED TO BE FRIENDS.

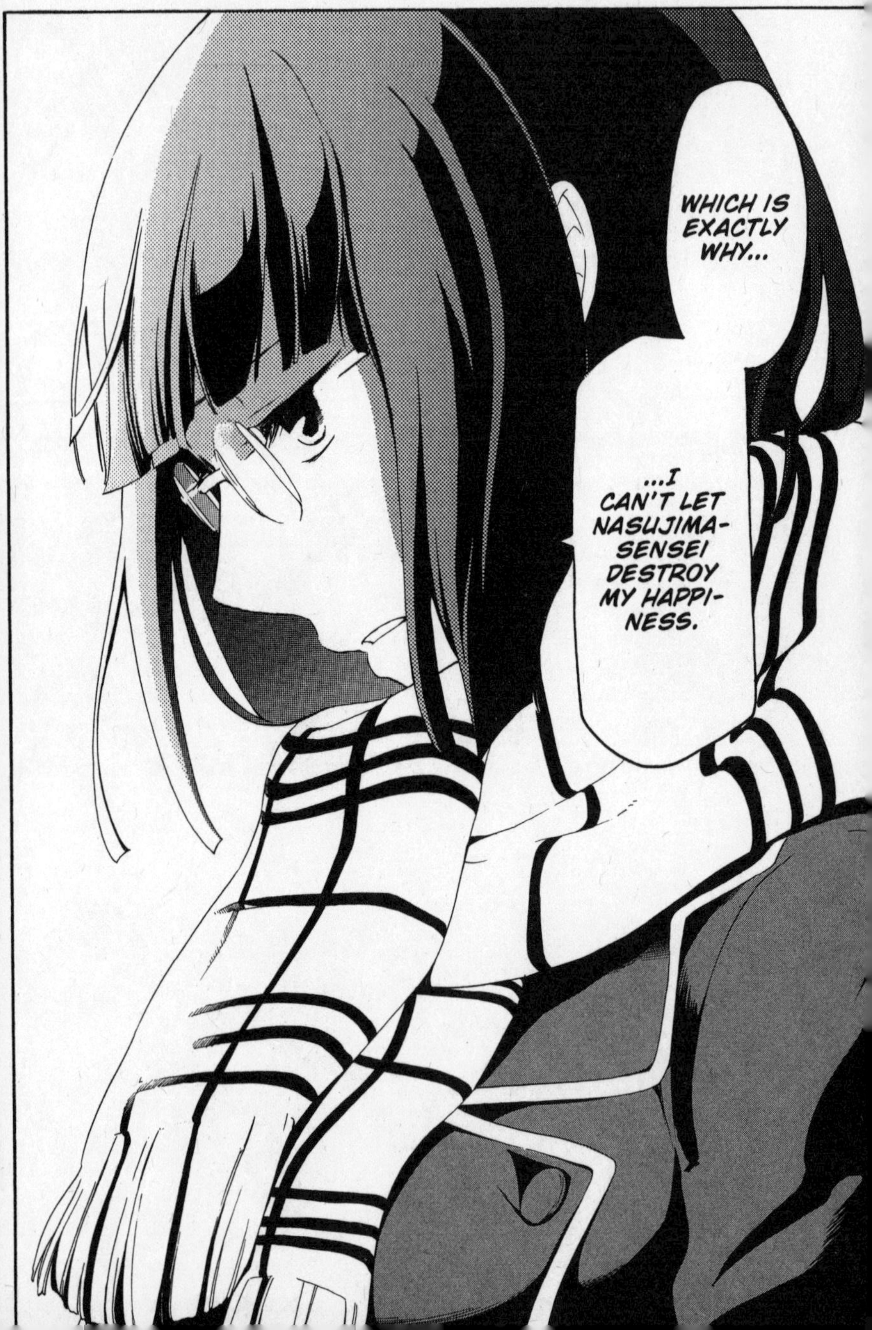
WHICH IS EXACTLY WHY...
...I CAN'T LET NASUJIMA-SENSEI DESTROY MY HAPPI-NESS.

Durarara!! Saika Arc

DRRR!!

CHAPTER 7: SITUATION HOMICIDAL

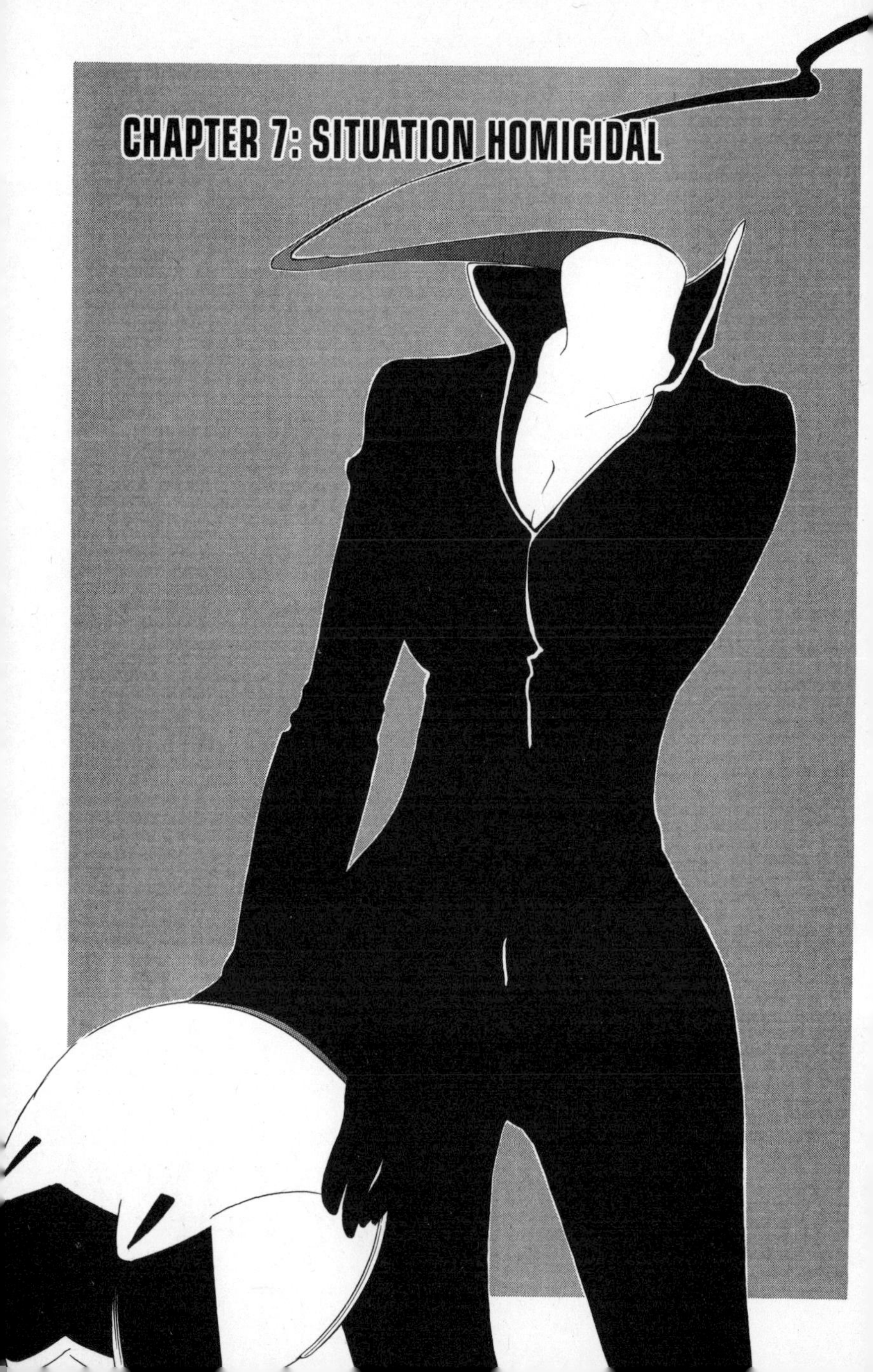

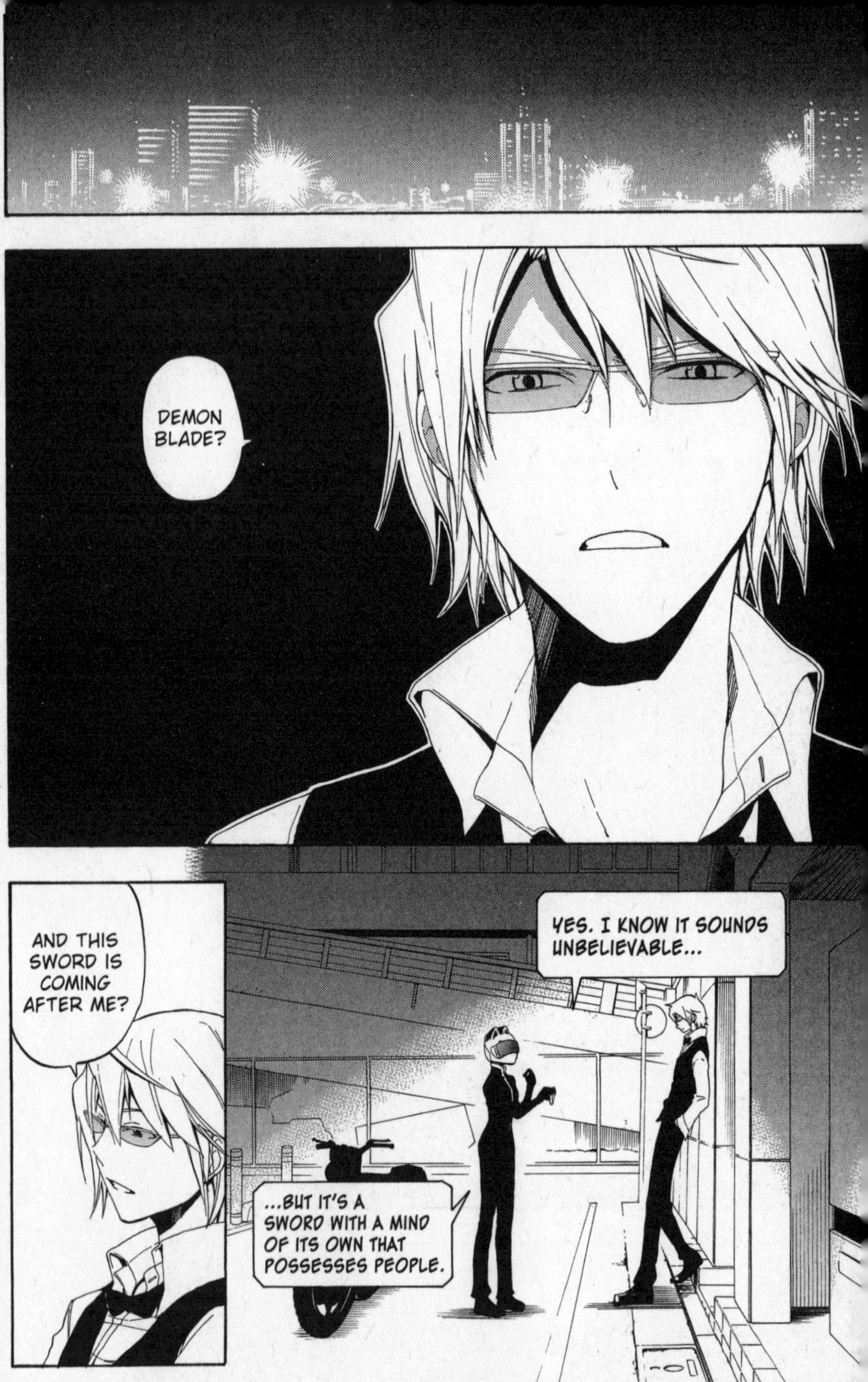
DEMON BLADE?
YES. I KNOW IT SOUNDS UNBELIEVABLE...
...BUT IT'S A SWORD WITH A MIND OF ITS OWN THAT POSSESSES PEOPLE.
AND THIS SWORD IS COMING AFTER ME?

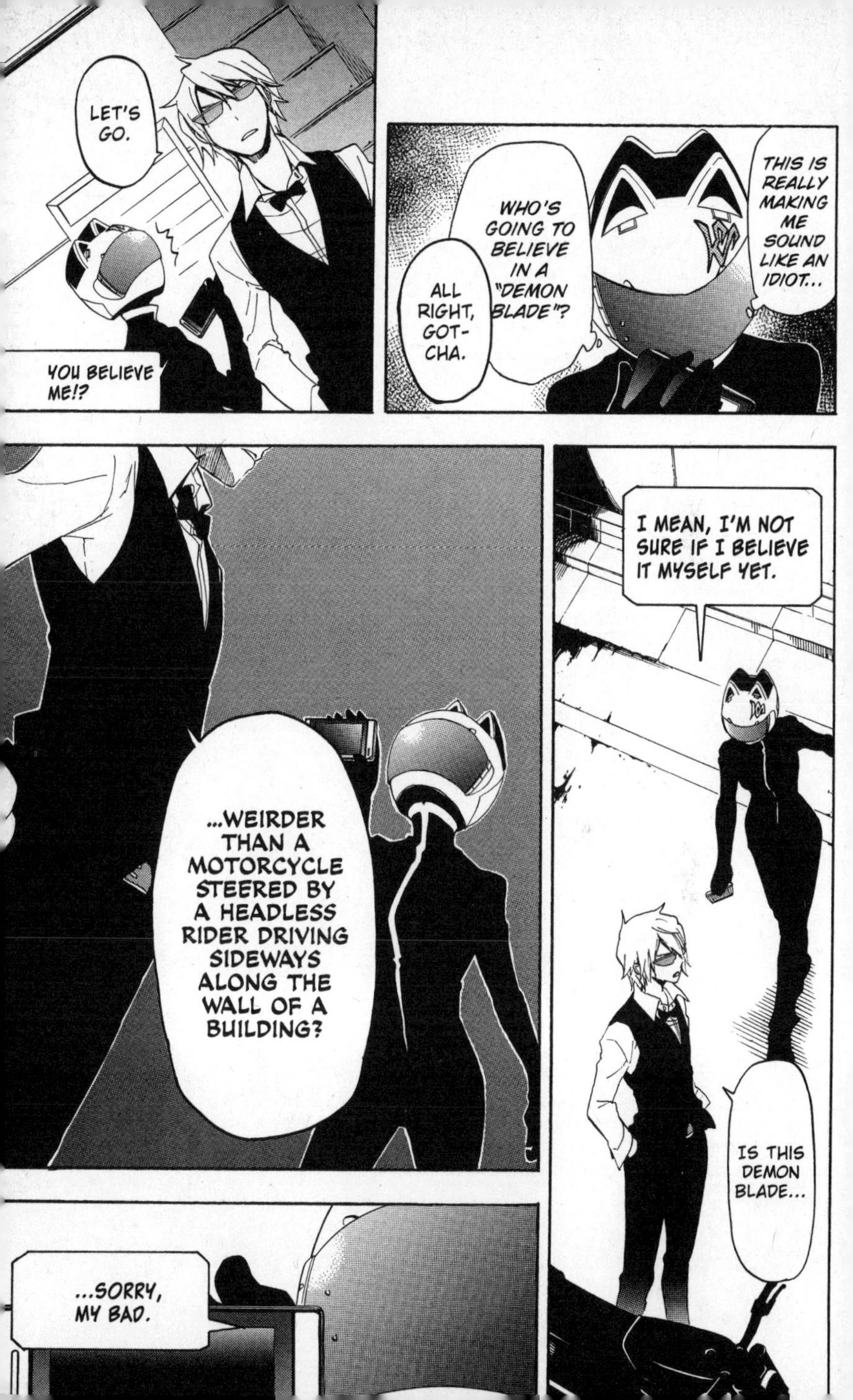
THIS IS REALLY MAKING ME SOUND LIKE AN IDIOT...
WHO'S GOING TO BELIEVE IN A "DEMON BLADE"?
ALL RIGHT, GOT-CHA.
LET'S GO.
YOU BELIEVE ME!?
I MEAN, I'M NOT SURE IF I BELIEVE IT MYSELF YET.
IS THIS DEMON BLADE...
...WEIRDER THAN A MOTORCYCLE STEERED BY A HEADLESS RIDER DRIVING SIDEWAYS ALONG THE WALL OF A BUILDING?
...SORRY, MY BAD.

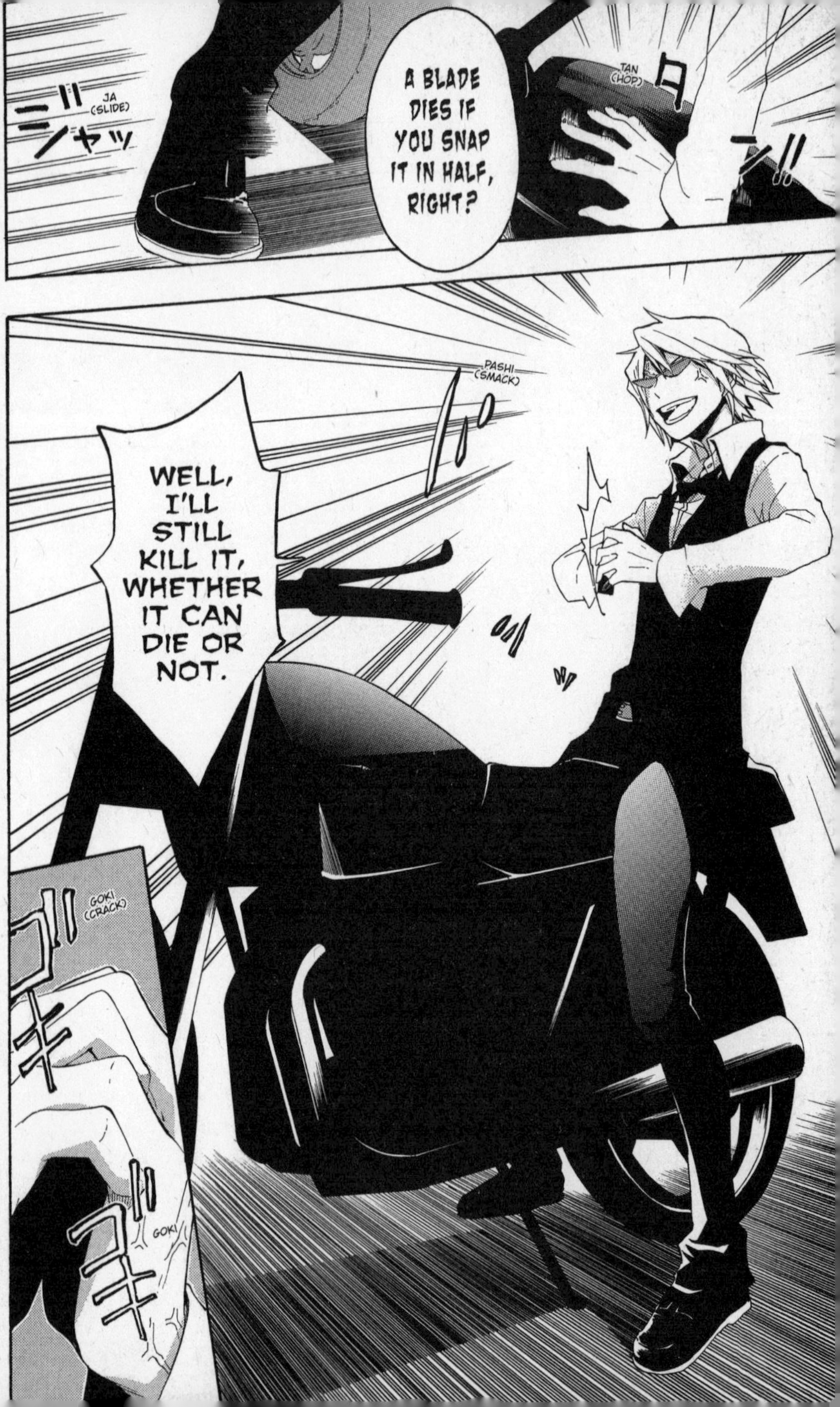
TAN (HOP)
A BLADE DIES IF YOU SNAP IT IN HALF, RIGHT?
JA (SLIDE)
PASHI (SMACK)
WELL, I'LL STILL KILL IT, WHETHER IT CAN DIE OR NOT.
GOKI (CRACK)
GOKI

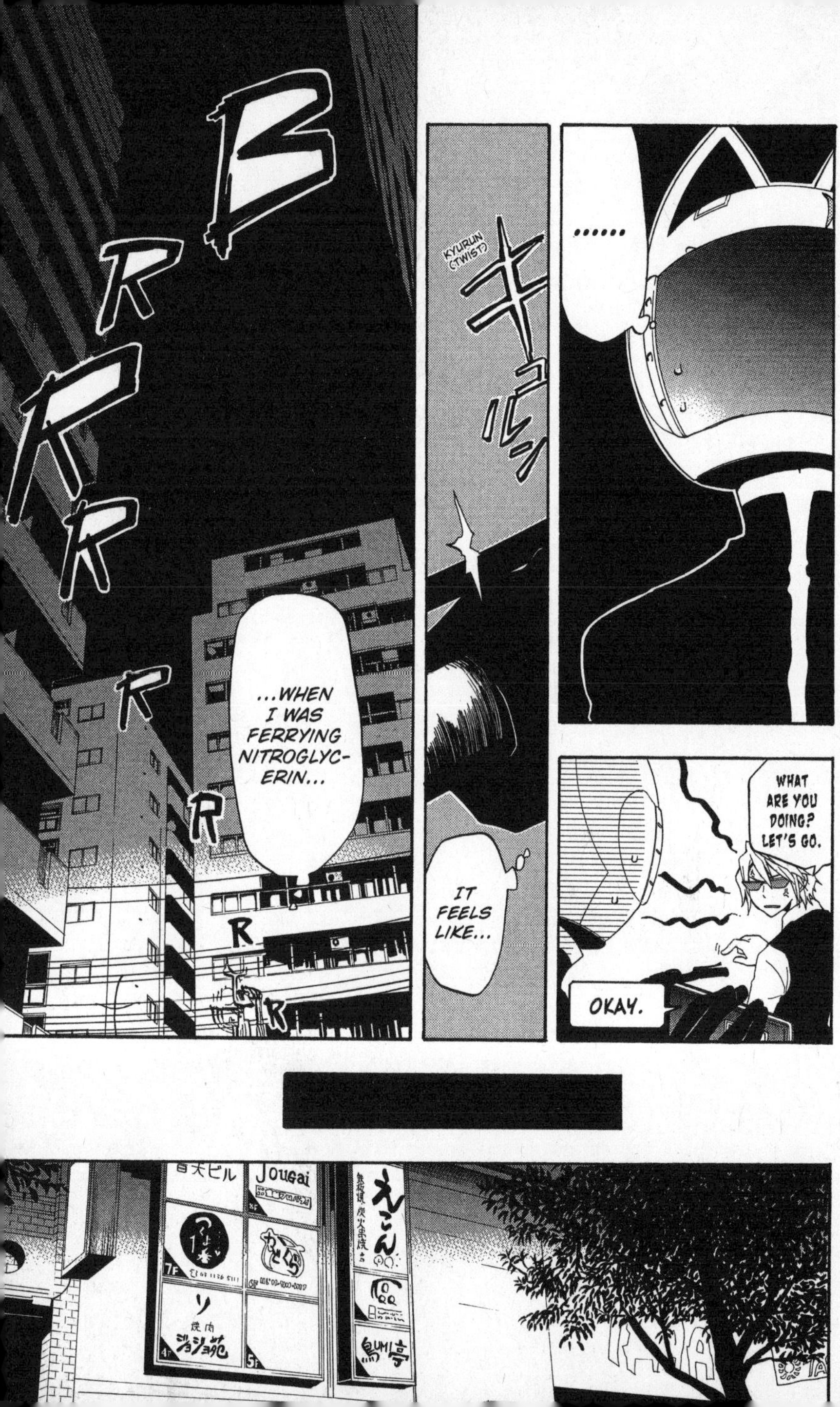
......
WHAT ARE YOU DOING? LET'S GO.
OKAY.
KYURUN (TWIST)
キュルン
IT FEELS LIKE...
BRRRRRRRR
...WHEN I WAS FERRYING NITROGLYCERIN...
Jougai

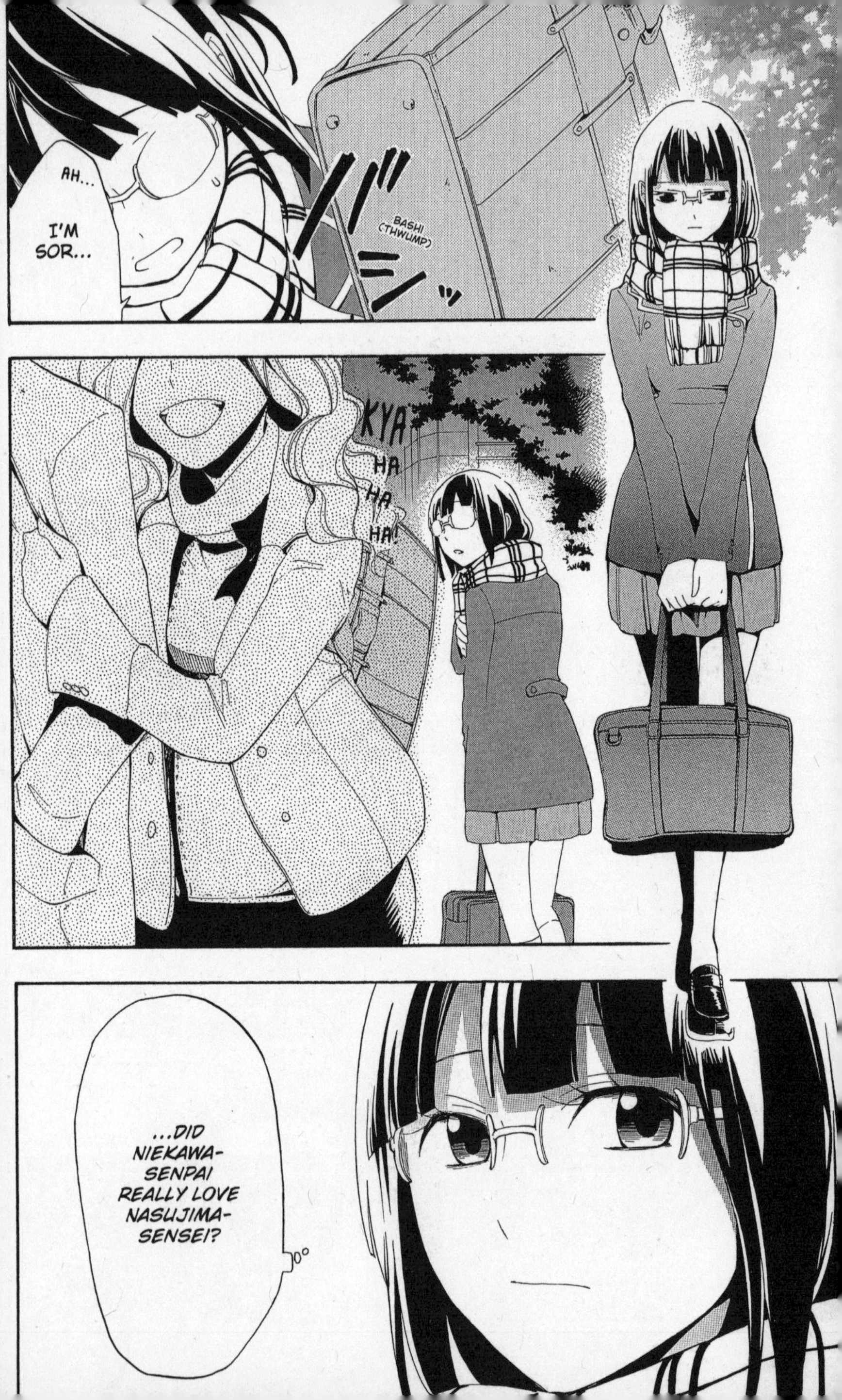

AH...
I'M SOR...
BASHI (THWUMP)
KYA HA HA HA!
...DID NIEKAWA-SENPAI REALLY LOVE NASUJIMA-SENSEI?

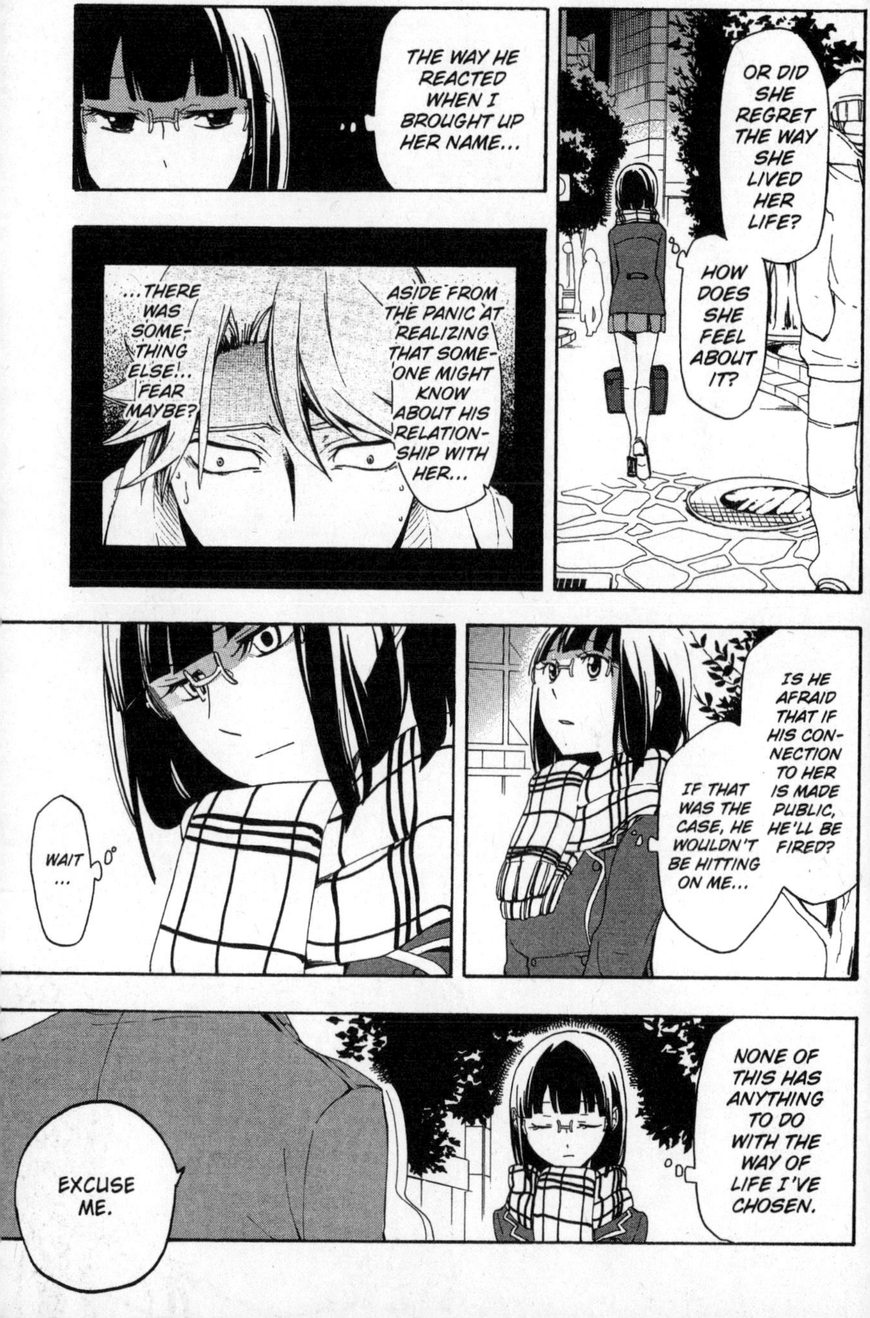
OR DID SHE REGRET THE WAY SHE LIVED HER LIFE?
HOW DOES SHE FEEL ABOUT IT?
...
THE WAY HE REACTED WHEN I BROUGHT UP HER NAME...
ASIDE FROM THE PANIC AT REALIZING THAT SOME-ONE MIGHT KNOW ABOUT HIS RELATION-SHIP WITH HER...
...THERE WAS SOME-THING ELSE!... FEAR MAYBE?
IS HE AFRAID THAT IF HIS CON-NECTION TO HER IS MADE PUBLIC, HE'LL BE FIRED?
IF THAT WAS THE CASE, HE WOULDN'T BE HITTING ON ME...
WAIT...
NONE OF THIS HAS ANYTHING TO DO WITH THE WAY OF LIFE I'VE CHOSEN.
EXCUSE ME.

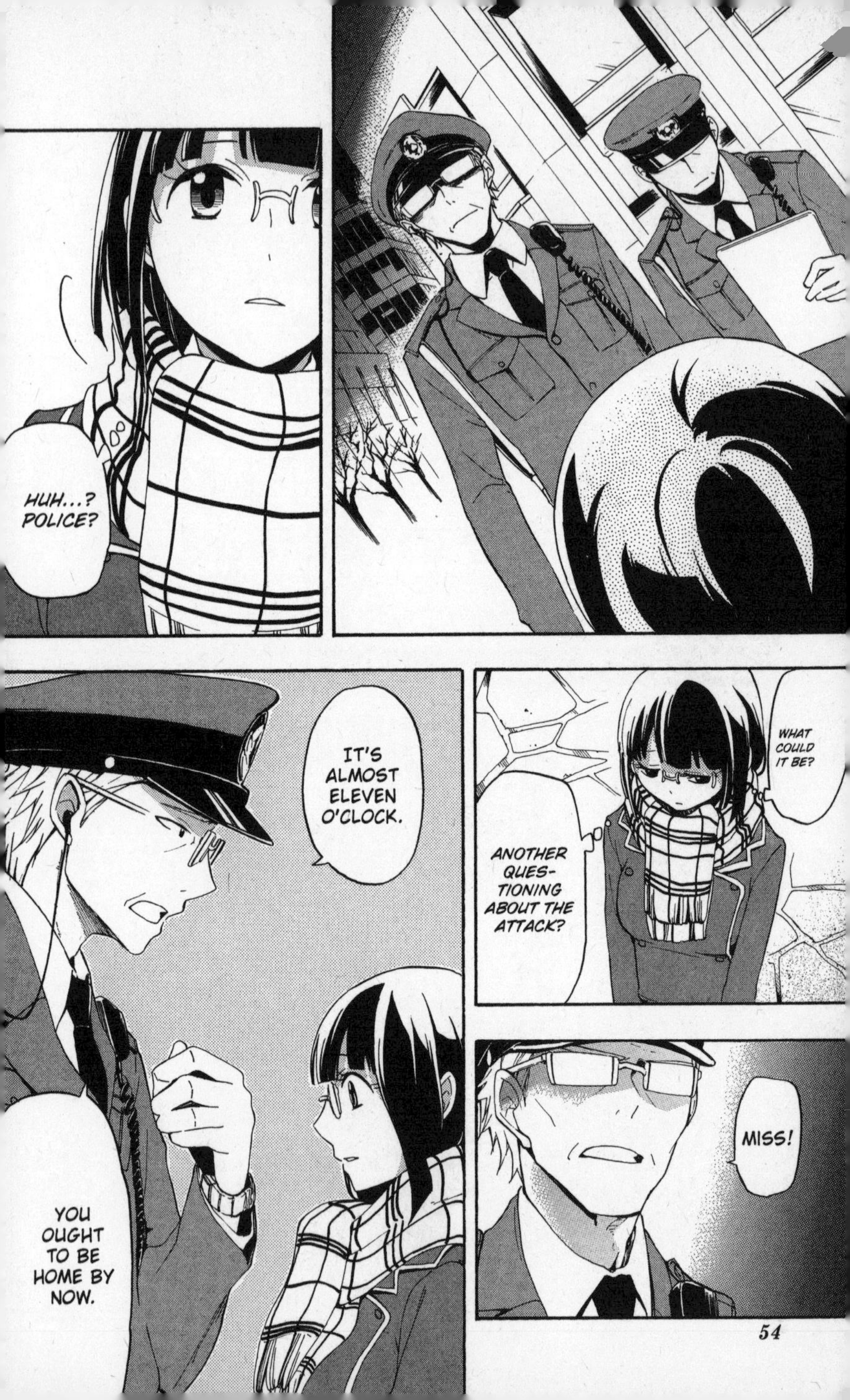
HUH...? POLICE?
WHAT COULD IT BE?
ANOTHER QUES-TIONING ABOUT THE ATTACK?
MISS!
IT'S ALMOST ELEVEN O'CLOCK.
YOU OUGHT TO BE HOME BY NOW.

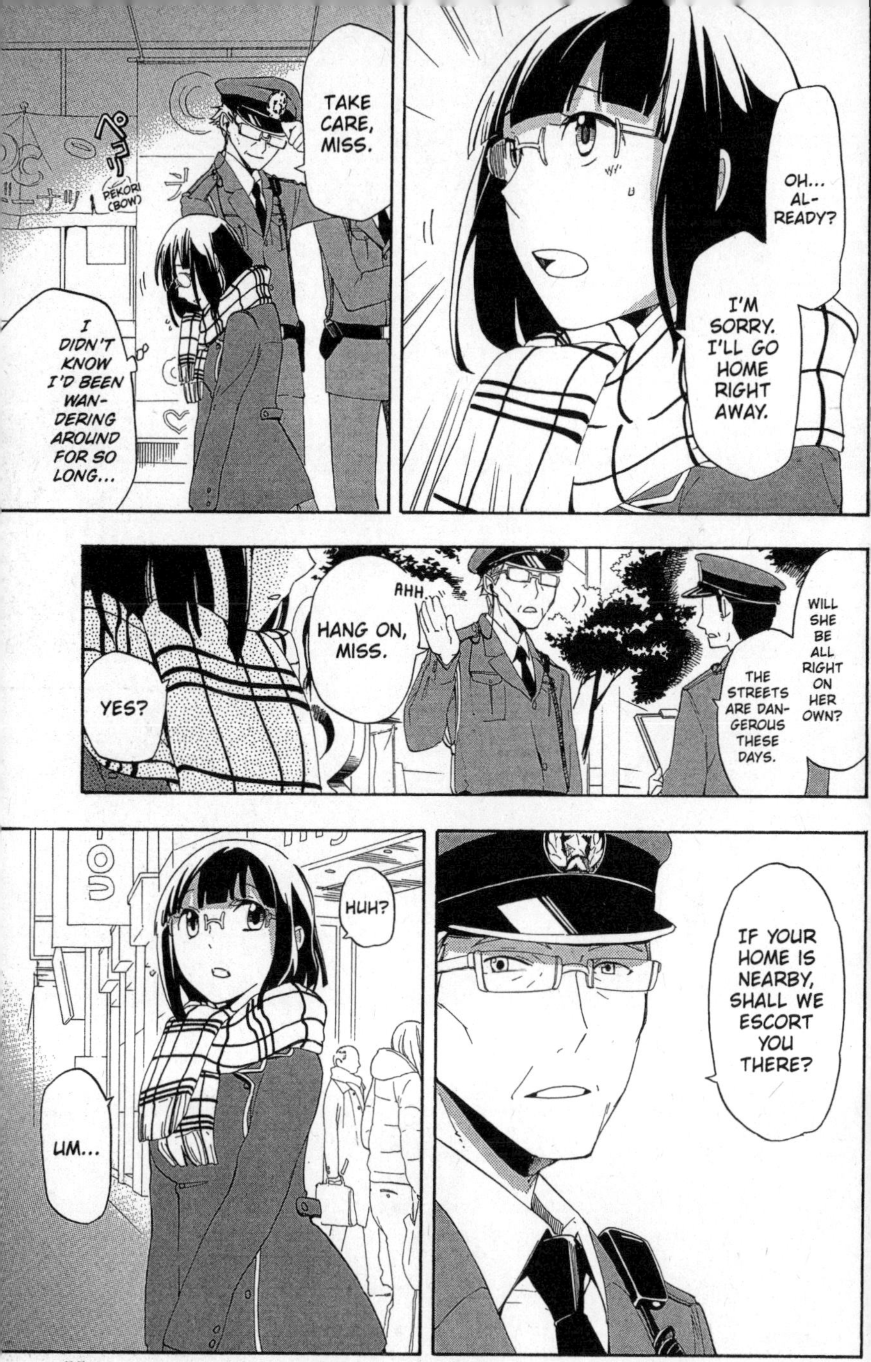
OH... AL-READY?
I'M SORRY. I'LL GO HOME RIGHT AWAY.
TAKE CARE, MISS.
ペコリ
PEKORI (BOW)
I DIDN'T KNOW I'D BEEN WAN-DERING AROUND FOR SO LONG...
WILL SHE BE ALL RIGHT ON HER OWN?
THE STREETS ARE DAN-GEROUS THESE DAYS.
AHH.
HANG ON, MISS.
YES?
IF YOUR HOME IS NEARBY, SHALL WE ESCORT YOU THERE?
HUH?
UM...

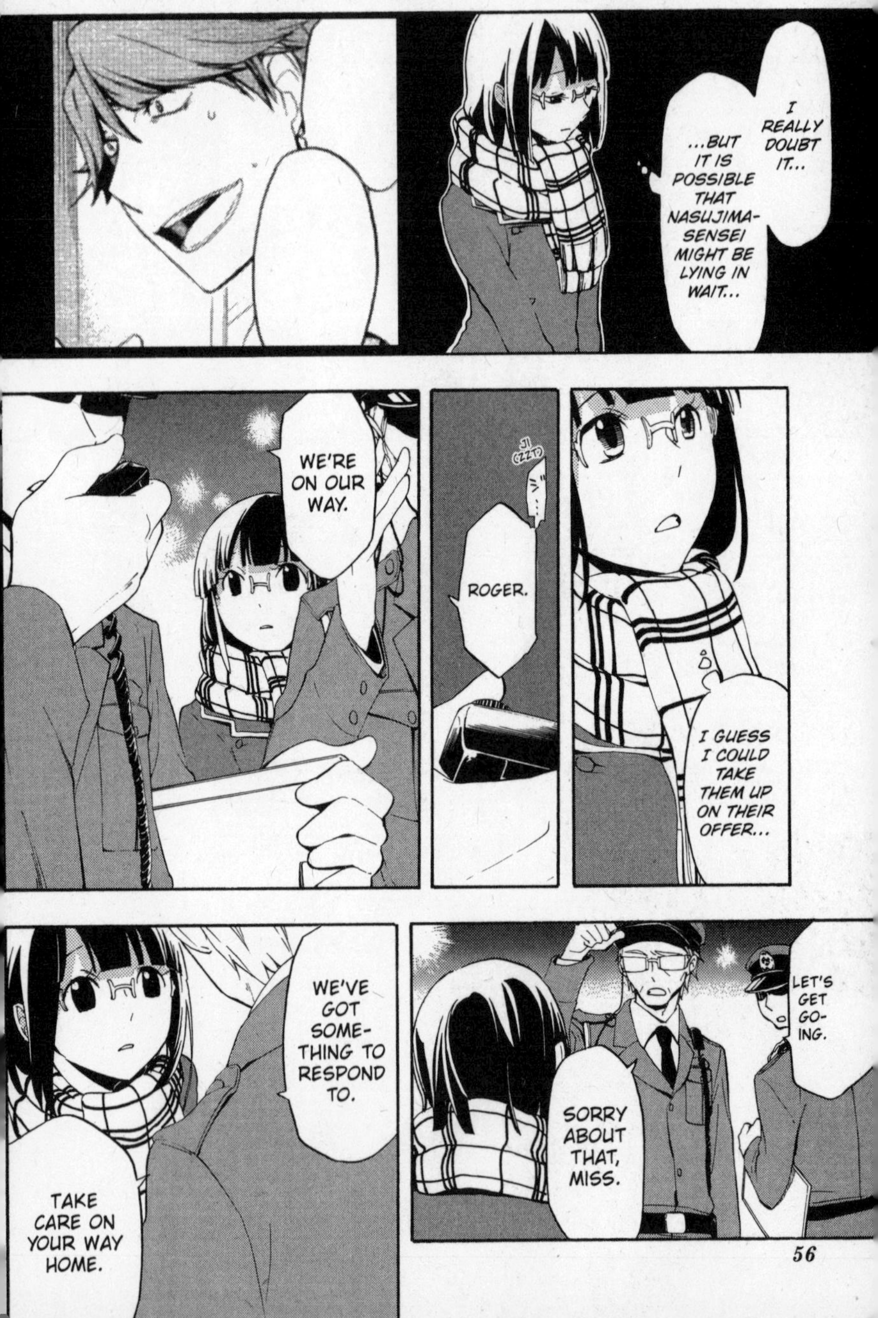
I REALLY DOUBT IT...
...BUT IT IS POSSIBLE THAT NASUJIMA-SENSEI MIGHT BE LYING IN WAIT...
I GUESS I COULD TAKE THEM UP ON THEIR OFFER...
JI (ZZZT)
ROGER.
WE'RE ON OUR WAY.
LET'S GET GO-ING.
SORRY ABOUT THAT, MISS.
WE'VE GOT SOMETHING TO RESPOND TO.
TAKE CARE ON YOUR WAY HOME.

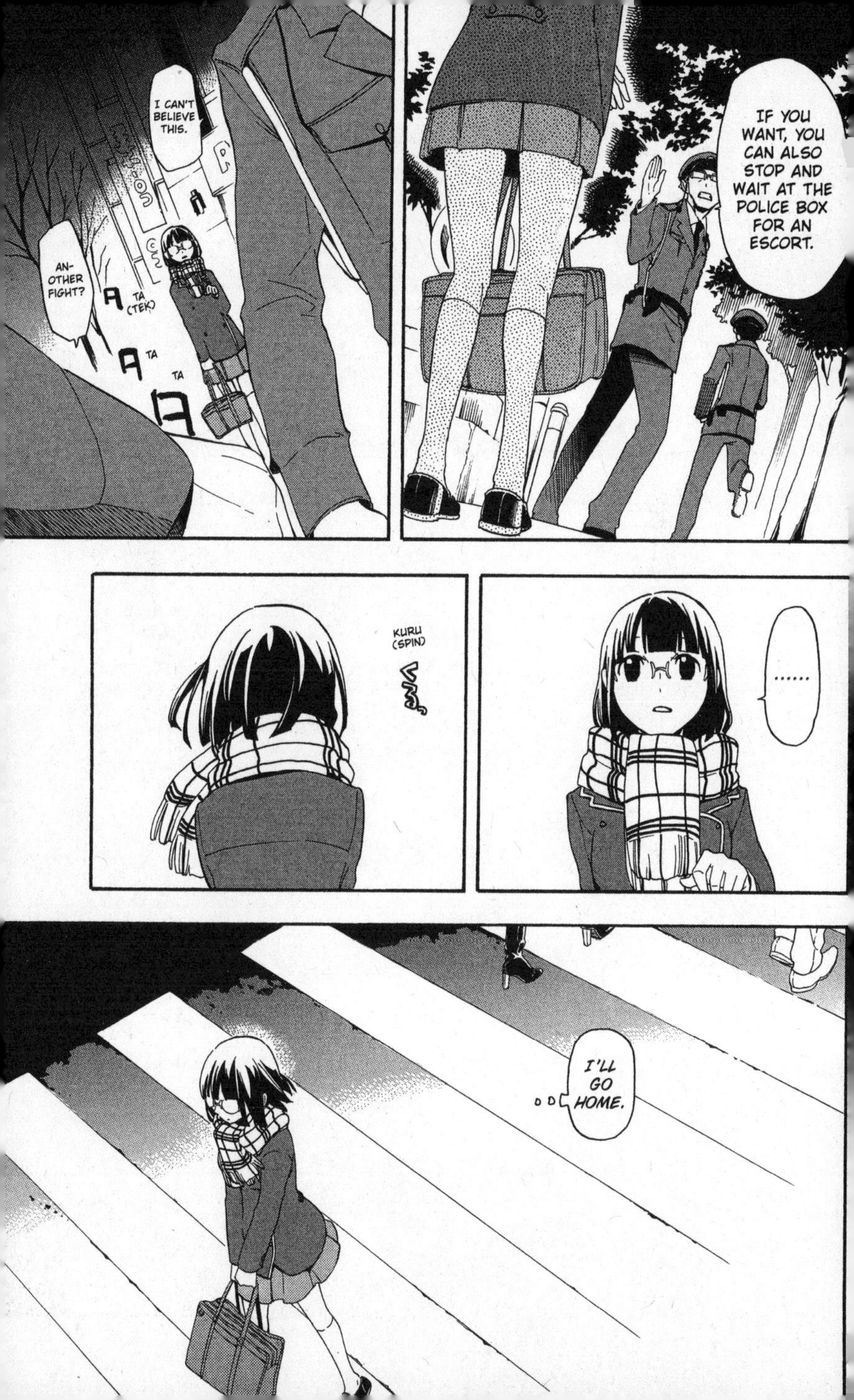
IF YOU WANT, YOU CAN ALSO STOP AND WAIT AT THE POLICE BOX FOR AN ESCORT.
I CAN'T BELIEVE THIS.
AN-OTHER FIGHT?
TA (TEK)
TA
TA
......
KURU (SPIN)
I'LL GO HOME.

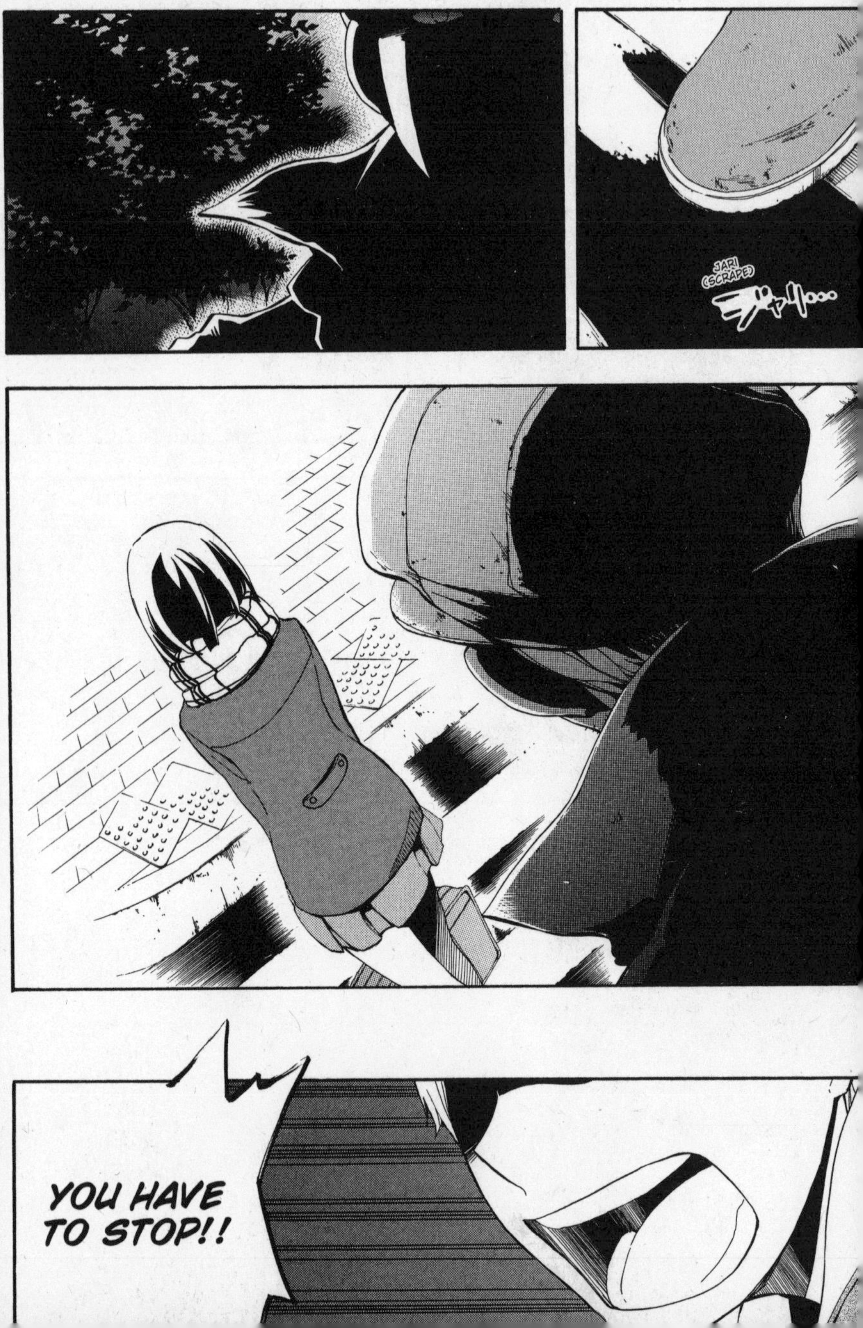
JARI (SCRAPE)
ジャリ…
YOU HAVE TO STOP!!

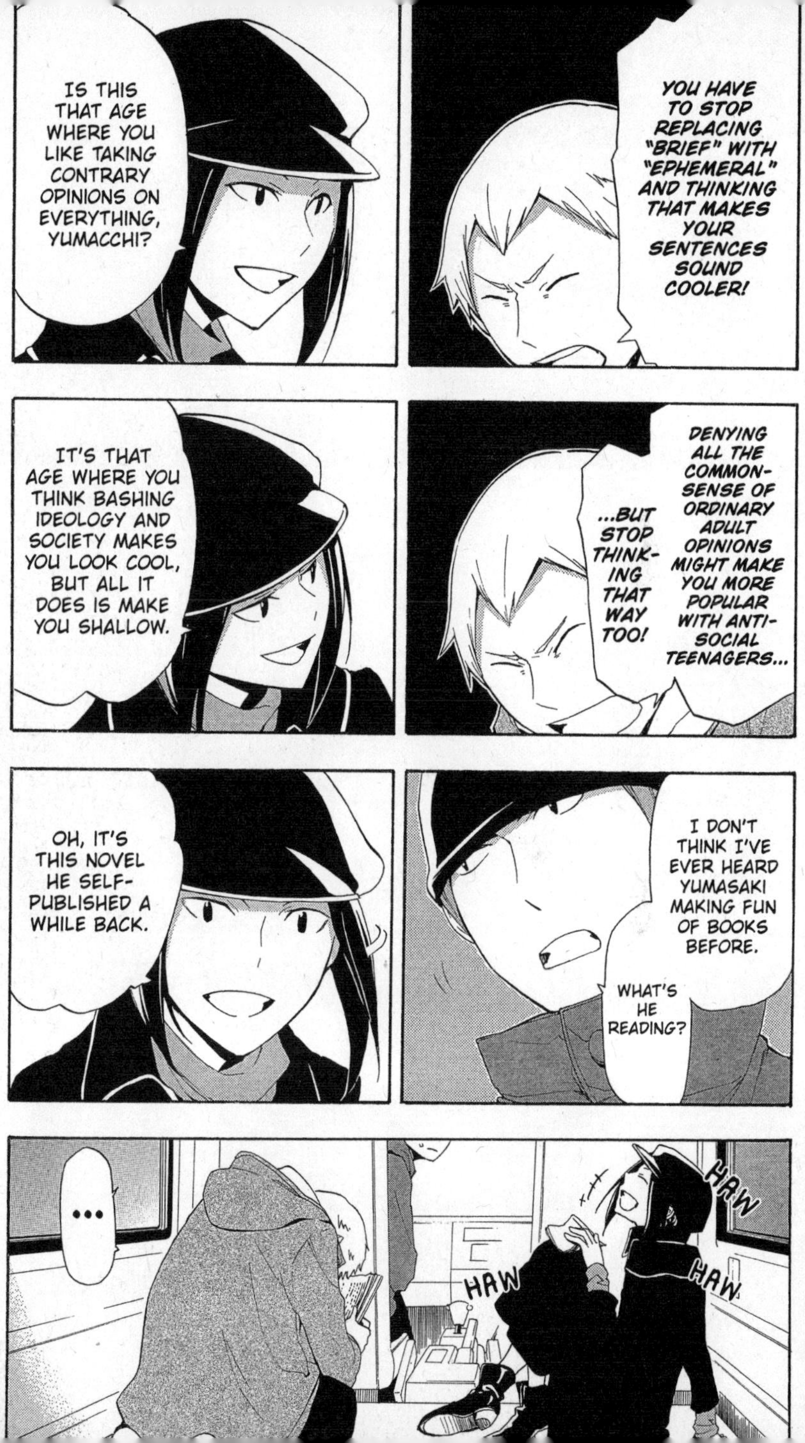
YOU HAVE TO STOP REPLACING "BRIEF" WITH "EPHEMERAL" AND THINKING THAT MAKES YOUR SENTENCES SOUND COOLER!
IS THIS THAT AGE WHERE YOU LIKE TAKING CONTRARY OPINIONS ON EVERYTHING, YUMACCHI?
DENYING ALL THE COMMON-SENSE OF ORDINARY ADULT OPINIONS MIGHT MAKE YOU MORE POPULAR WITH ANTI-SOCIAL TEENAGERS...
...BUT STOP THINK-ING THAT WAY TOO!
IT'S THAT AGE WHERE YOU THINK BASHING IDEOLOGY AND SOCIETY MAKES YOU LOOK COOL, BUT ALL IT DOES IS MAKE YOU SHALLOW.
I DON'T THINK I'VE EVER HEARD YUMASAKI MAKING FUN OF BOOKS BEFORE.
WHAT'S HE READING?
OH, IT'S THIS NOVEL HE SELF-PUBLISHED A WHILE BACK.
HAW
HAW
HAW
...

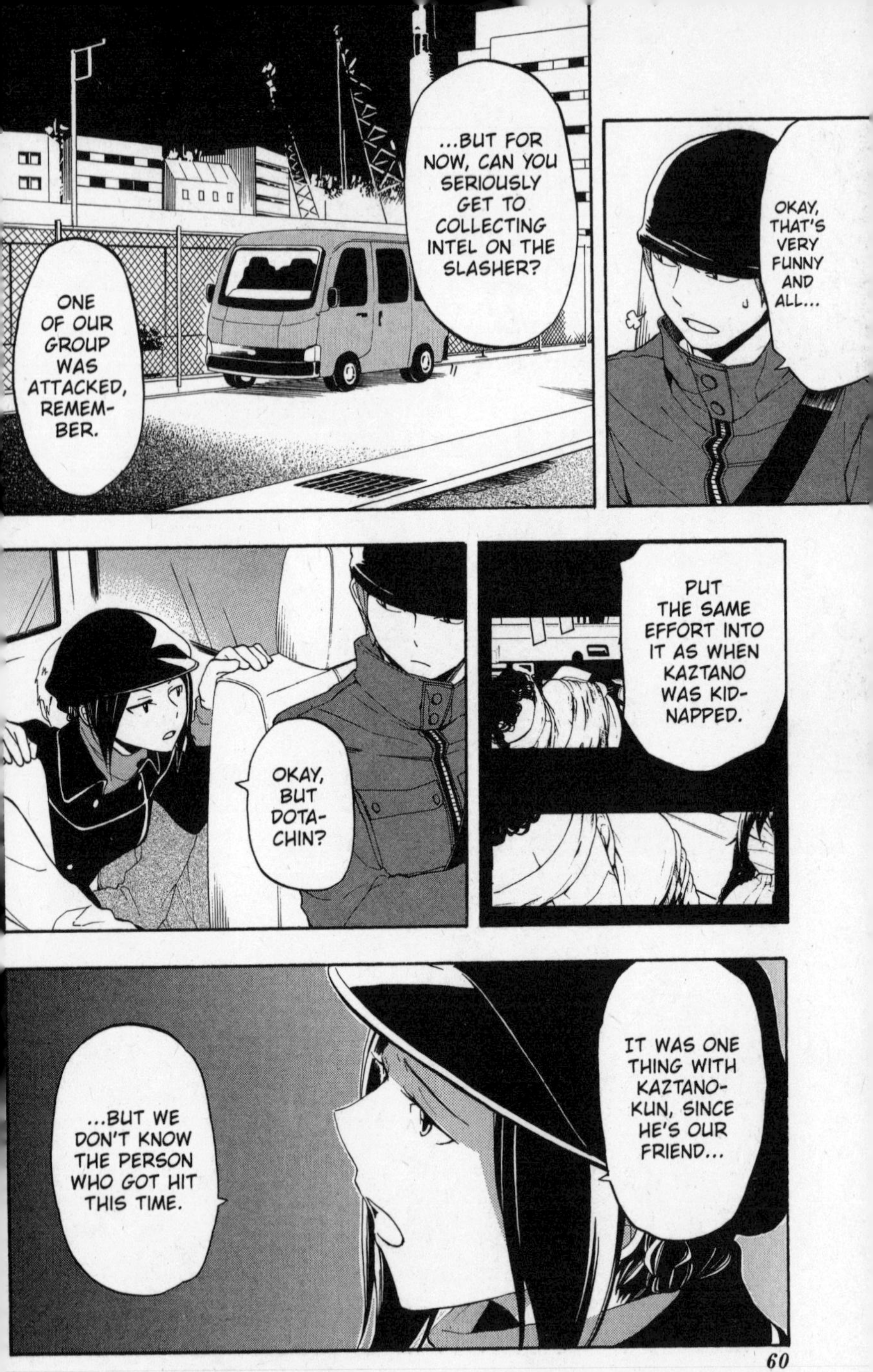
OKAY, THAT'S VERY FUNNY AND ALL...
...BUT FOR NOW, CAN YOU SERIOUSLY GET TO COLLECTING INTEL ON THE SLASHER?
ONE OF OUR GROUP WAS ATTACKED, REMEMBER.
PUT THE SAME EFFORT INTO IT AS WHEN KAZTANO WAS KID-NAPPED.
OKAY, BUT DOTA-CHIN?
IT WAS ONE THING WITH KAZTANO-KUN, SINCE HE'S OUR FRIEND...
...BUT WE DON'T KNOW THE PERSON WHO GOT HIT THIS TIME.

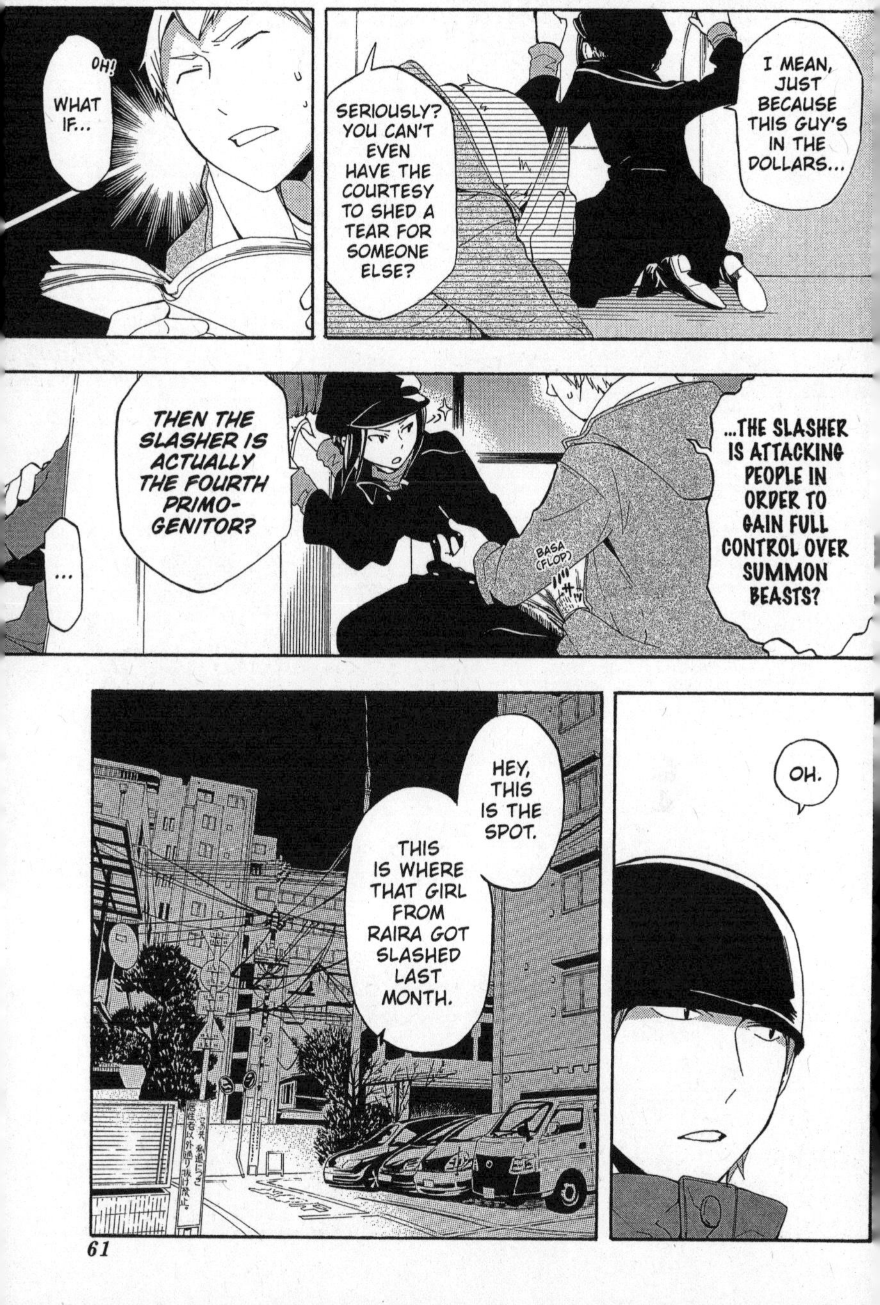
I MEAN, JUST BECAUSE THIS GUY'S IN THE DOLLARS...
SERIOUSLY? YOU CAN'T EVEN HAVE THE COURTESY TO SHED A TEAR FOR SOMEONE ELSE?
OH!
WHAT IF...
...THE SLASHER IS ATTACKING PEOPLE IN ORDER TO GAIN FULL CONTROL OVER SUMMON BEASTS?
BASA (FLOP)
THEN THE SLASHER IS ACTUALLY THE FOURTH PRIMO-GENITOR?
...
OH.
HEY, THIS IS THE SPOT.
THIS IS WHERE THAT GIRL FROM RAIRA GOT SLASHED LAST MONTH.

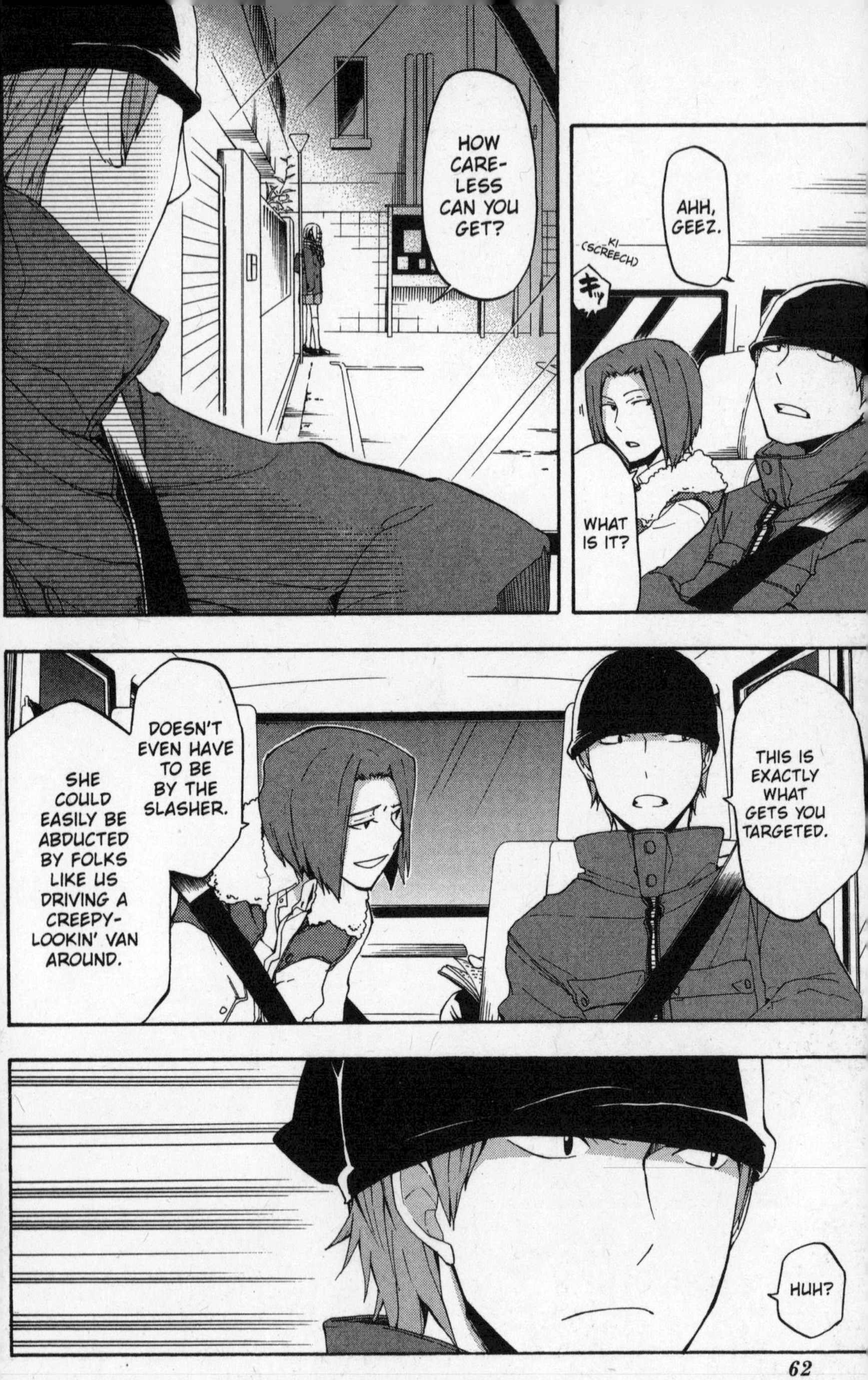
AHH, GEEZ.
KI (SCREECH)
WHAT IS IT?
HOW CARELESS CAN YOU GET?
THIS IS EXACTLY WHAT GETS YOU TARGETED.
DOESN'T EVEN HAVE TO BE BY THE SLASHER.
SHE COULD EASILY BE ABDUCTED BY FOLKS LIKE US DRIVING A CREEPY-LOOKIN' VAN AROUND.
HUH?

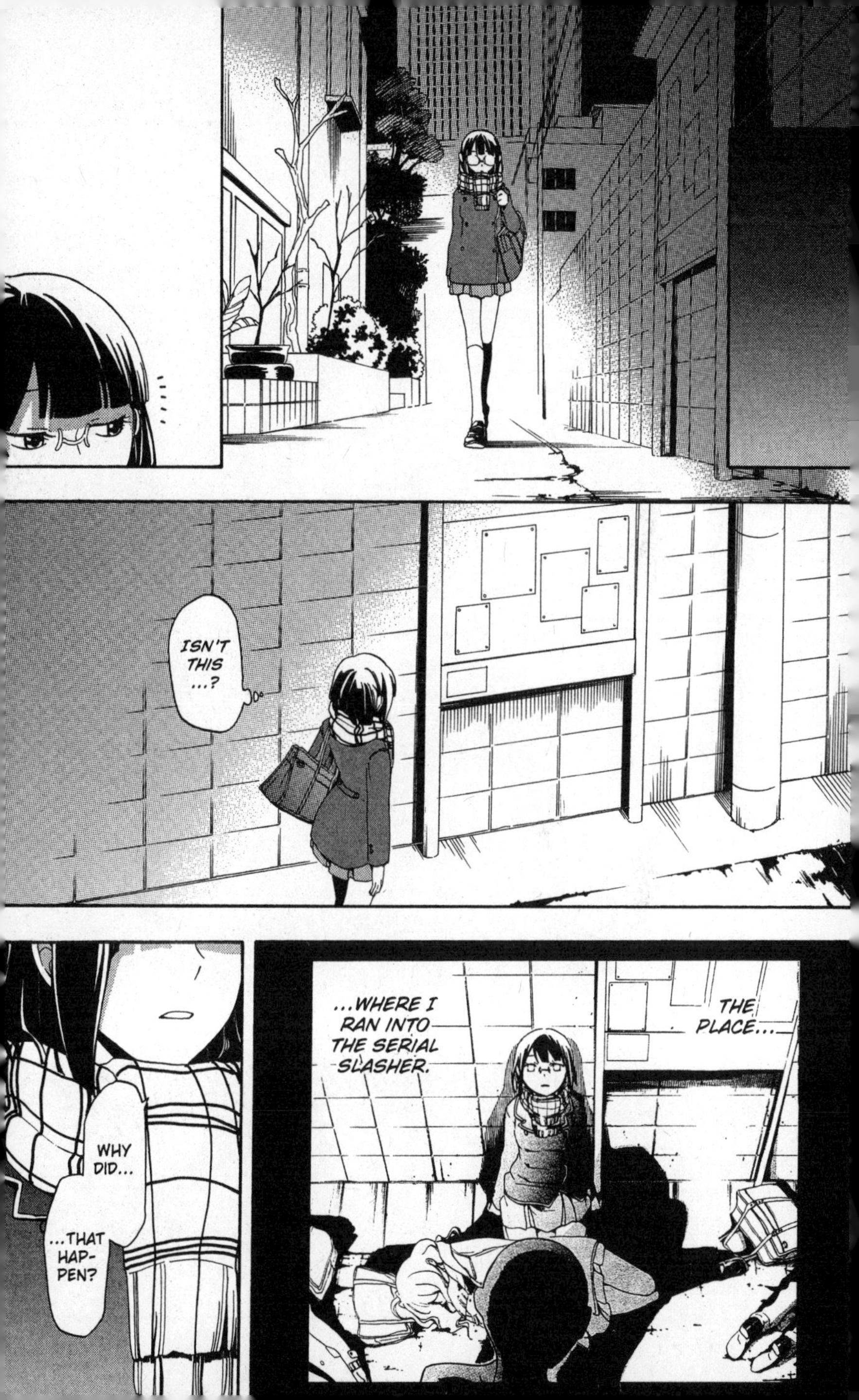
ISN'T THIS ...?
THE PLACE...
...WHERE I RAN INTO THE SERIAL SLASHER.
WHY DID...
...THAT HAP-PEN?

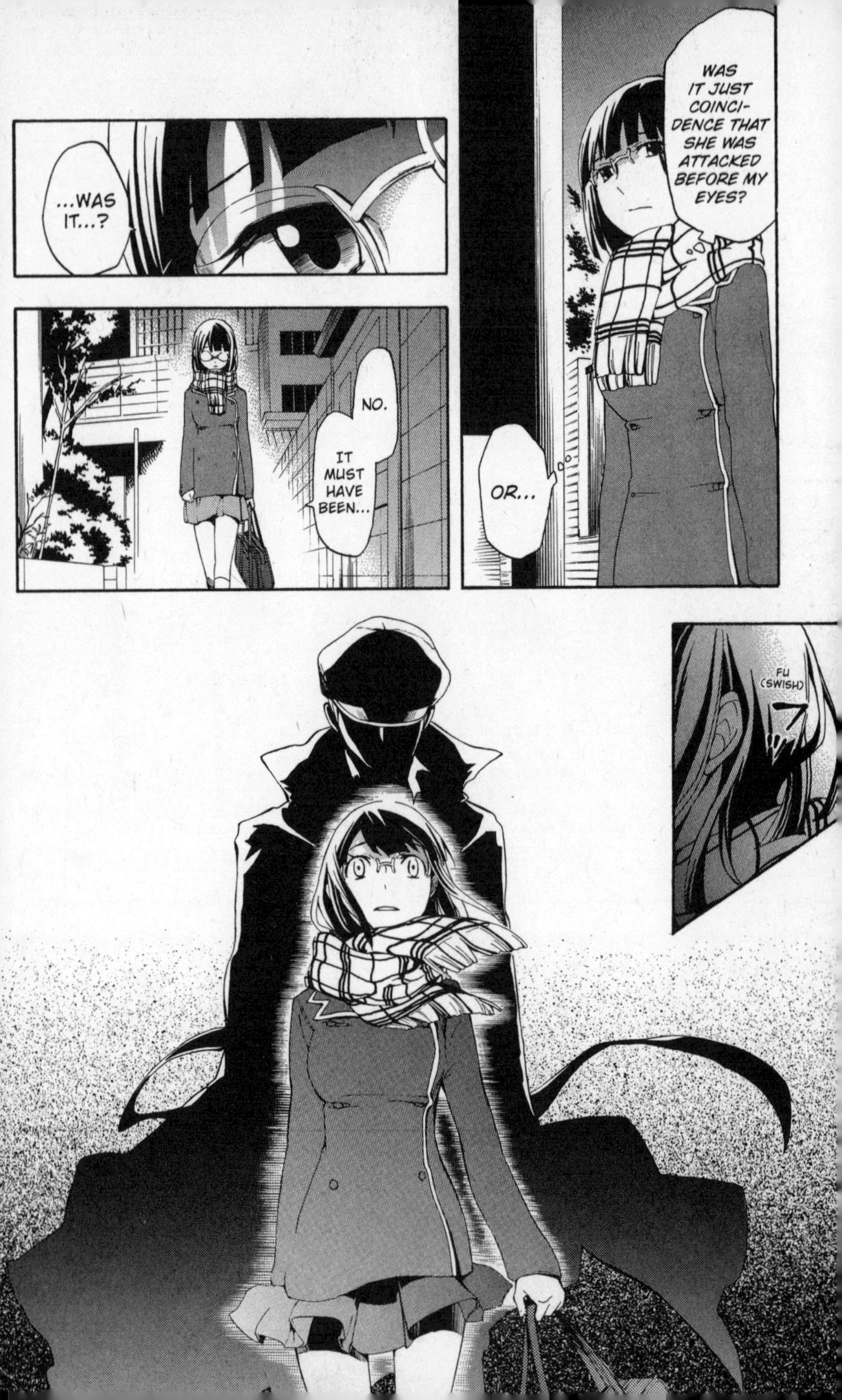
WAS IT JUST COINCIDENCE THAT SHE WAS ATTACKED BEFORE MY EYES?
OR...
...WAS IT...?
NO.
IT MUST HAVE BEEN...
FU (SWISH)

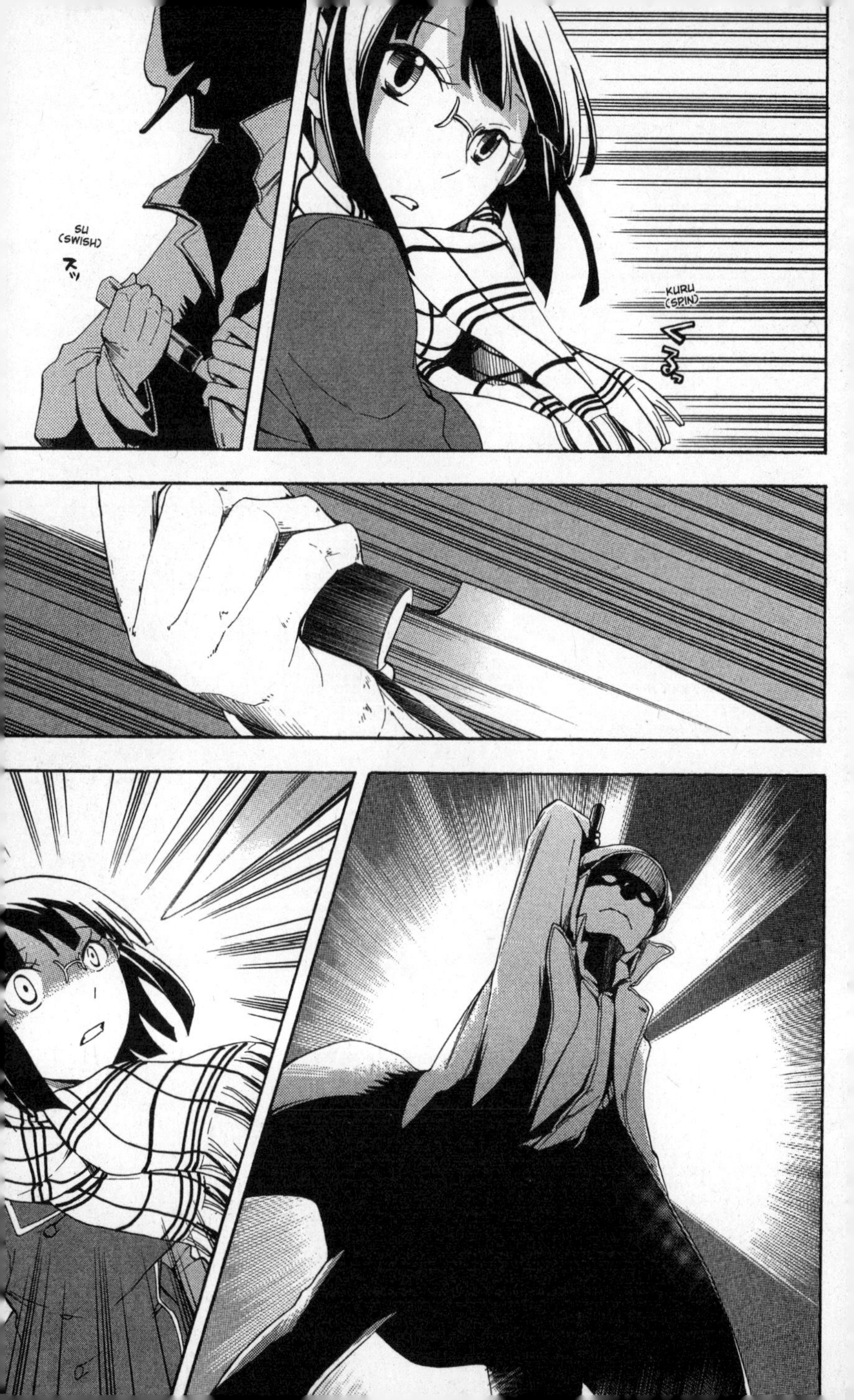
KURU
(SPIN)
くる
SU
(SWISH)
スッ

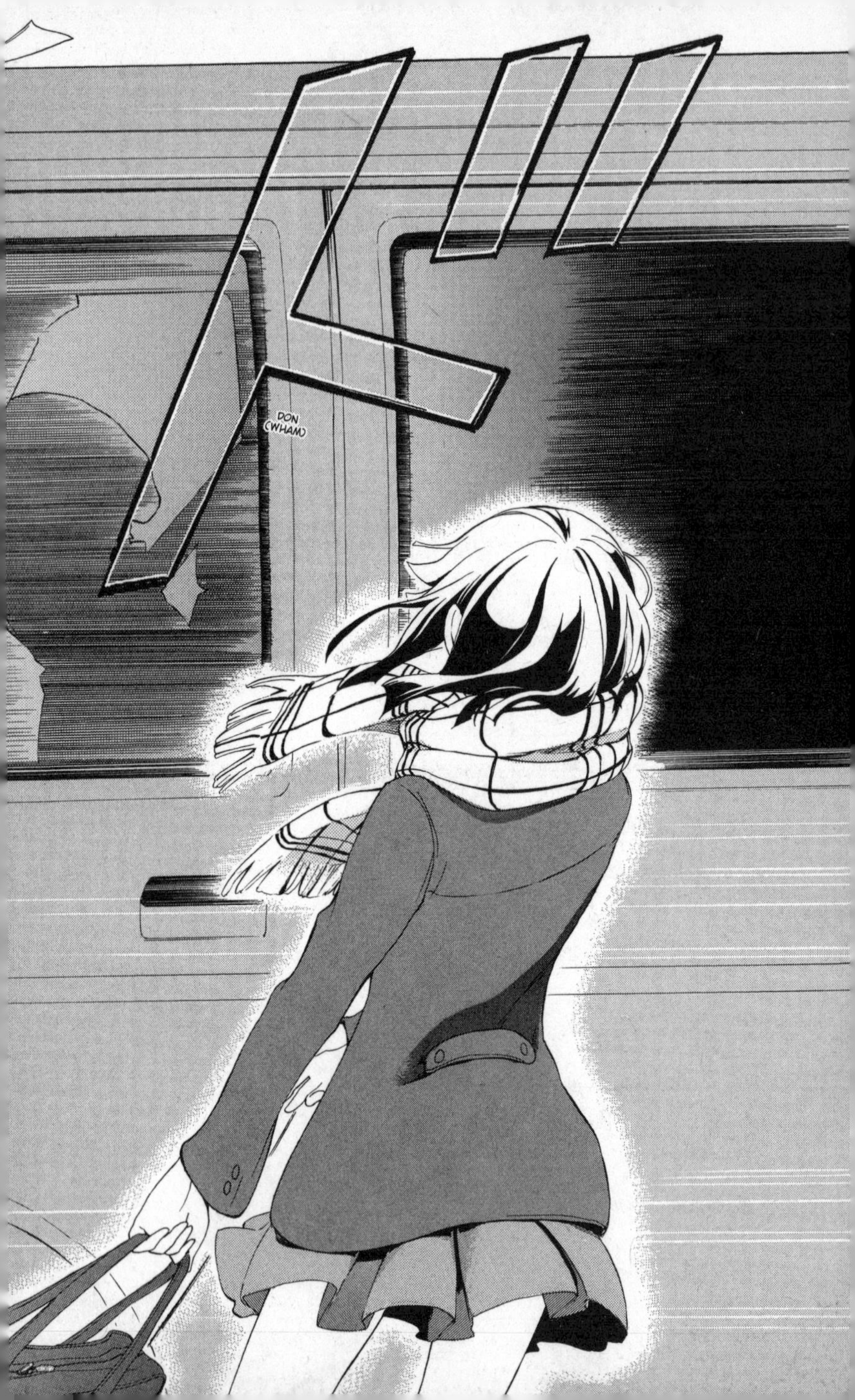
DON
(WHAM)

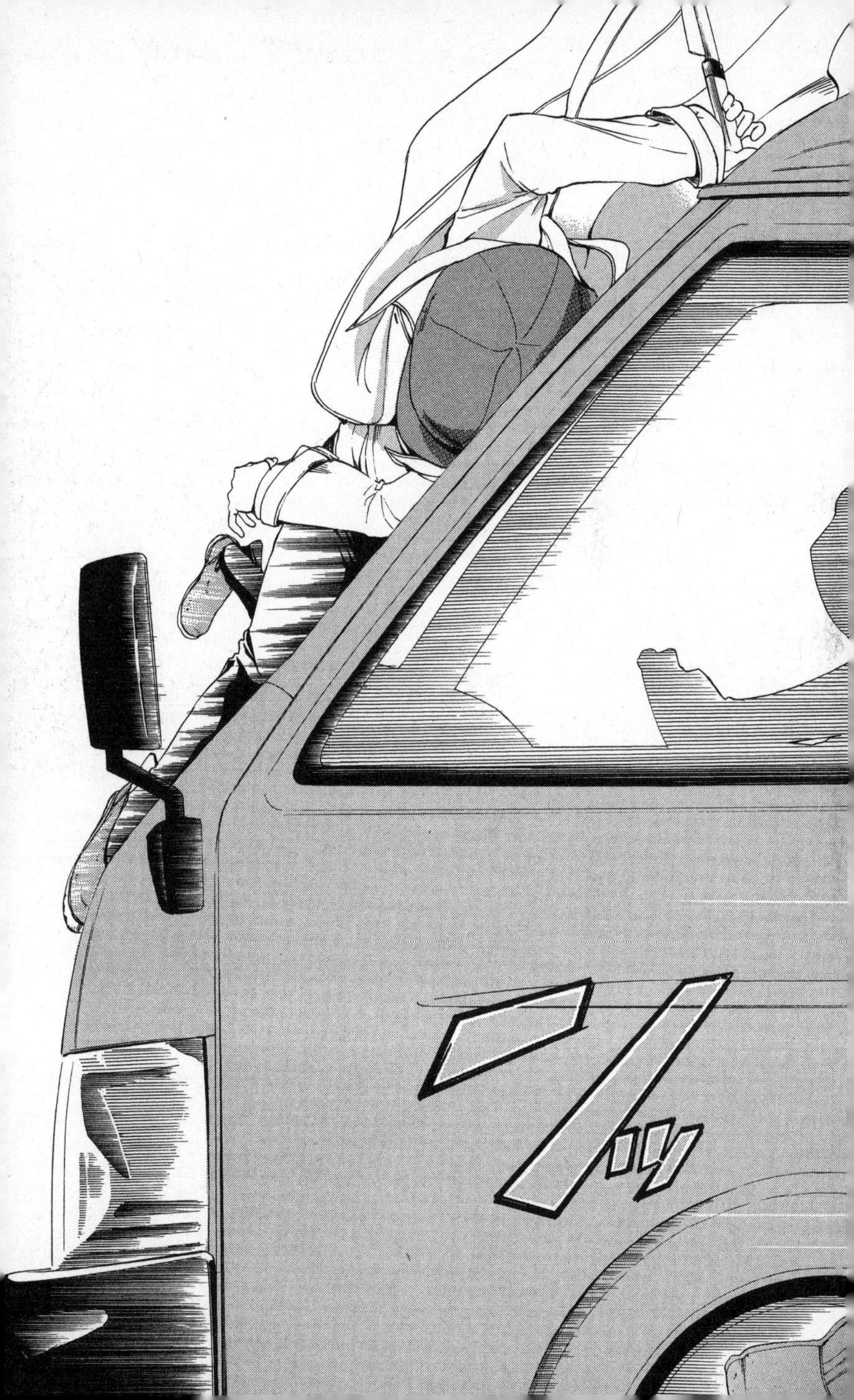

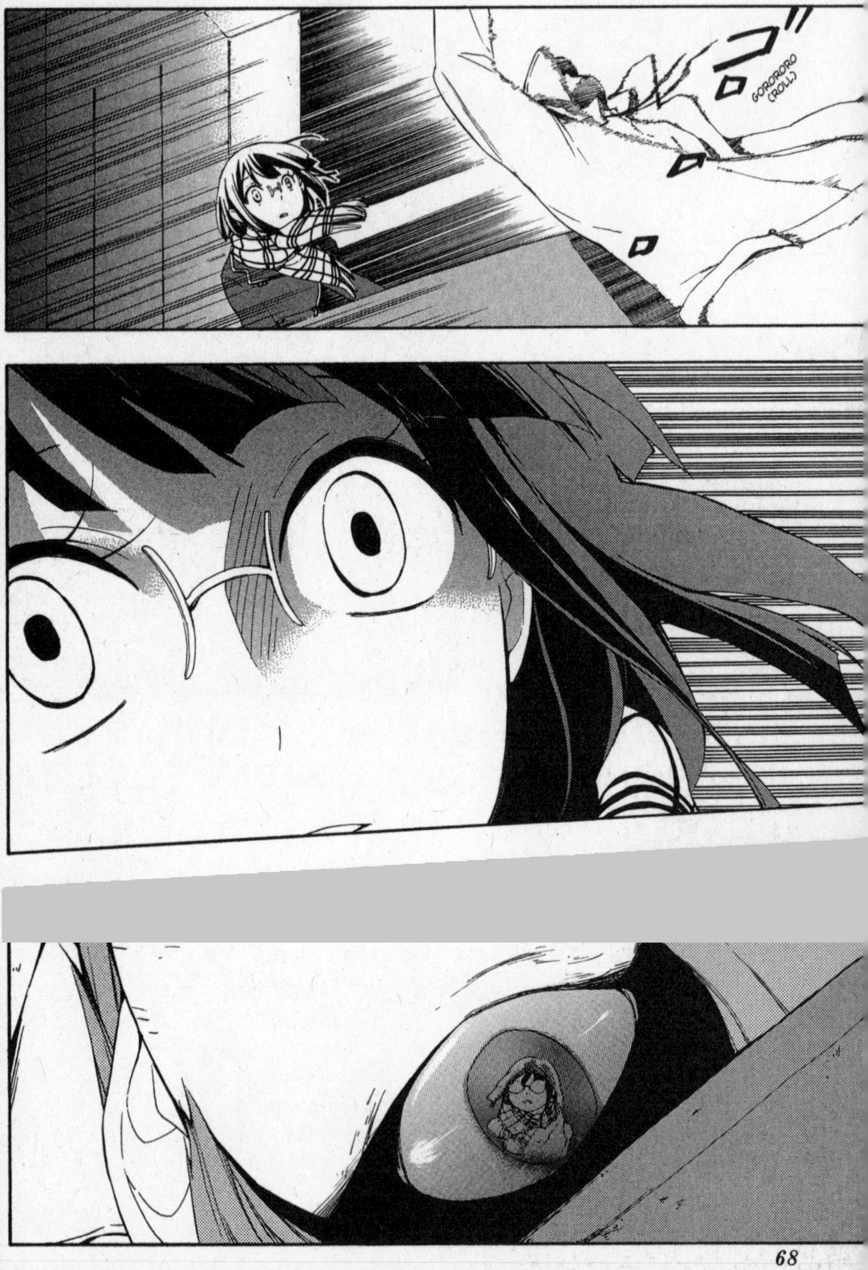
GORORORO
(ROLL)

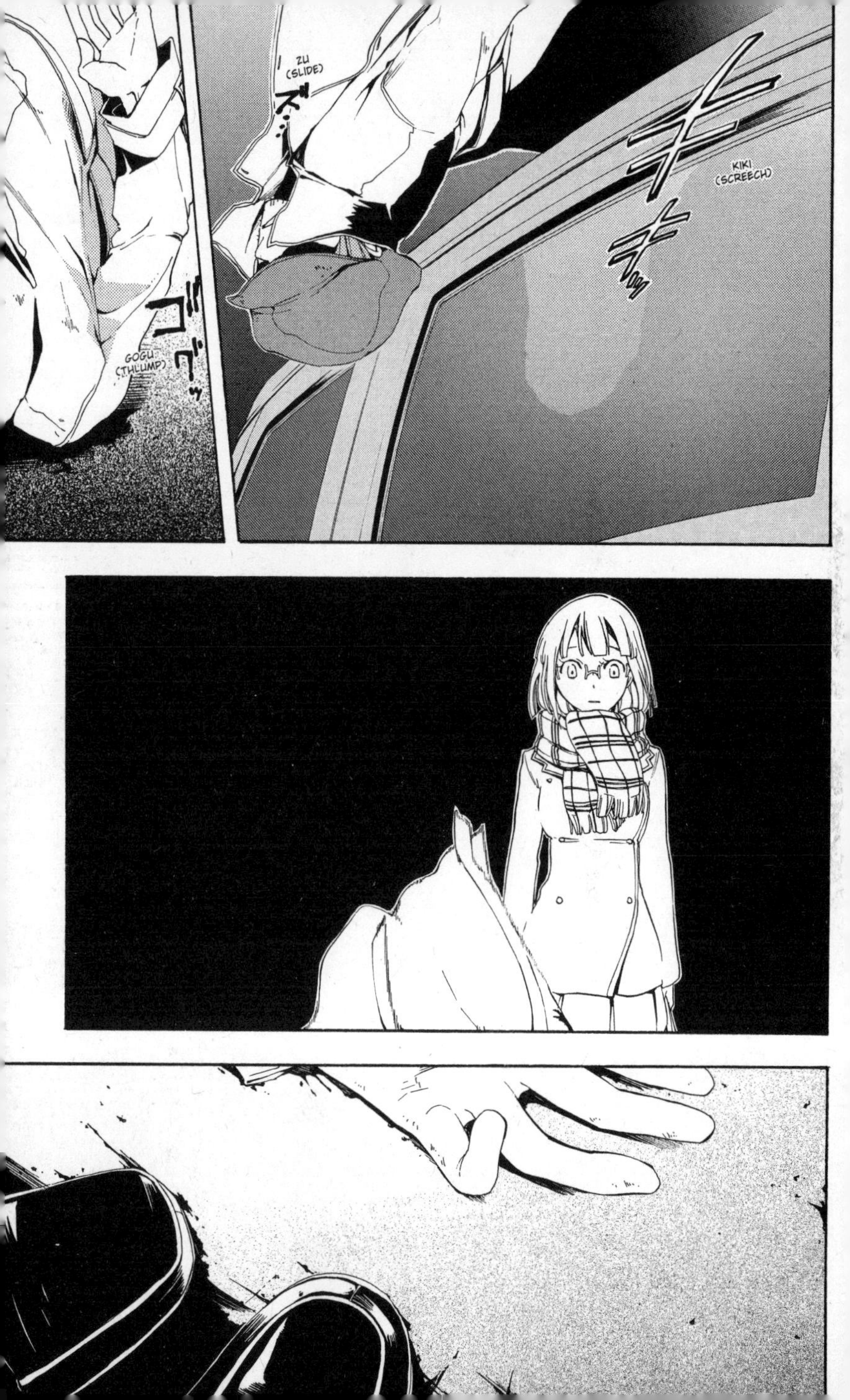
KIKI (SCREECH)
ZU (SLIDE)
GOGU (THUMP)

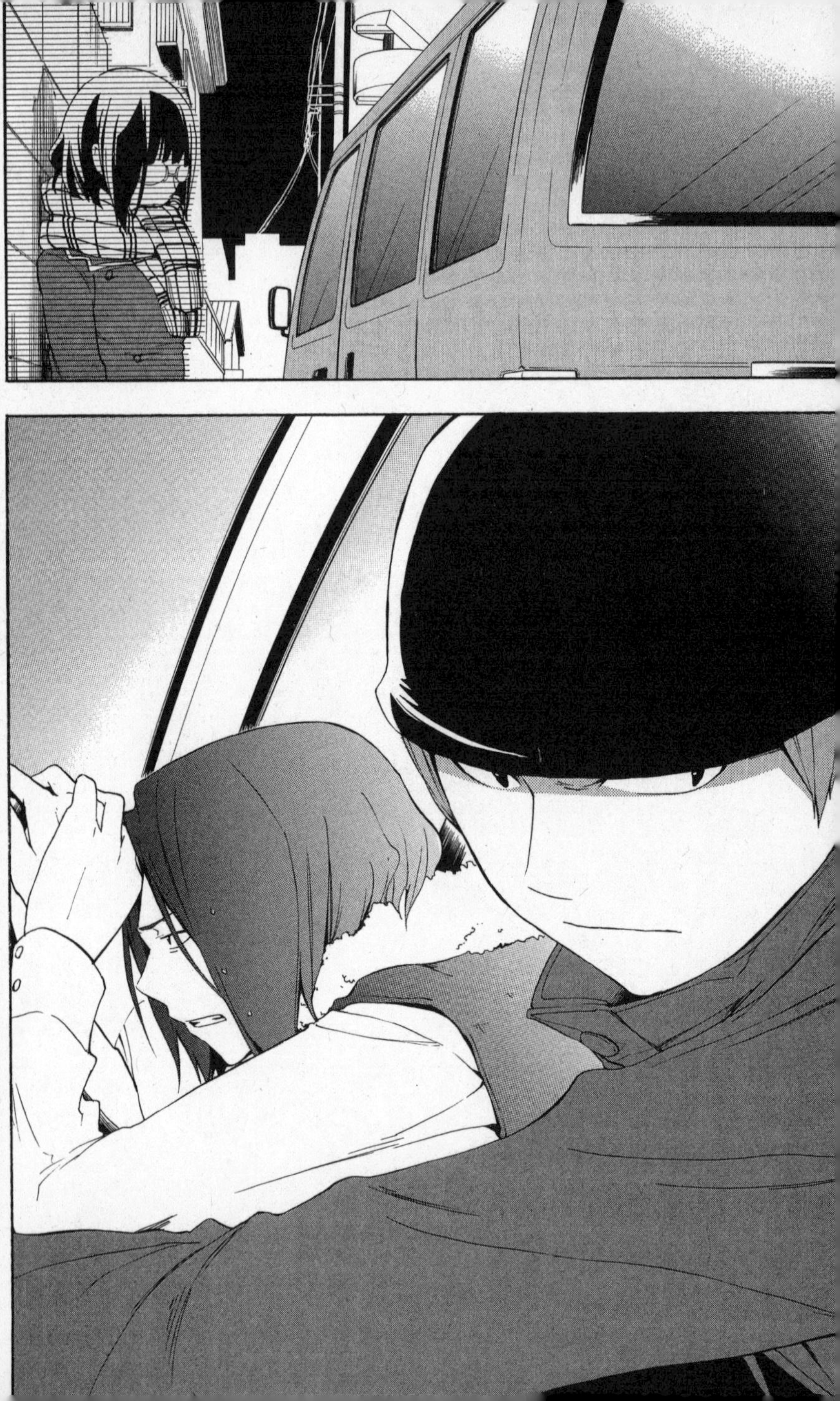

Durarara!! Saika Arc

DRRR!!

CHAPTER 8: RIGHT TO THE POINTS

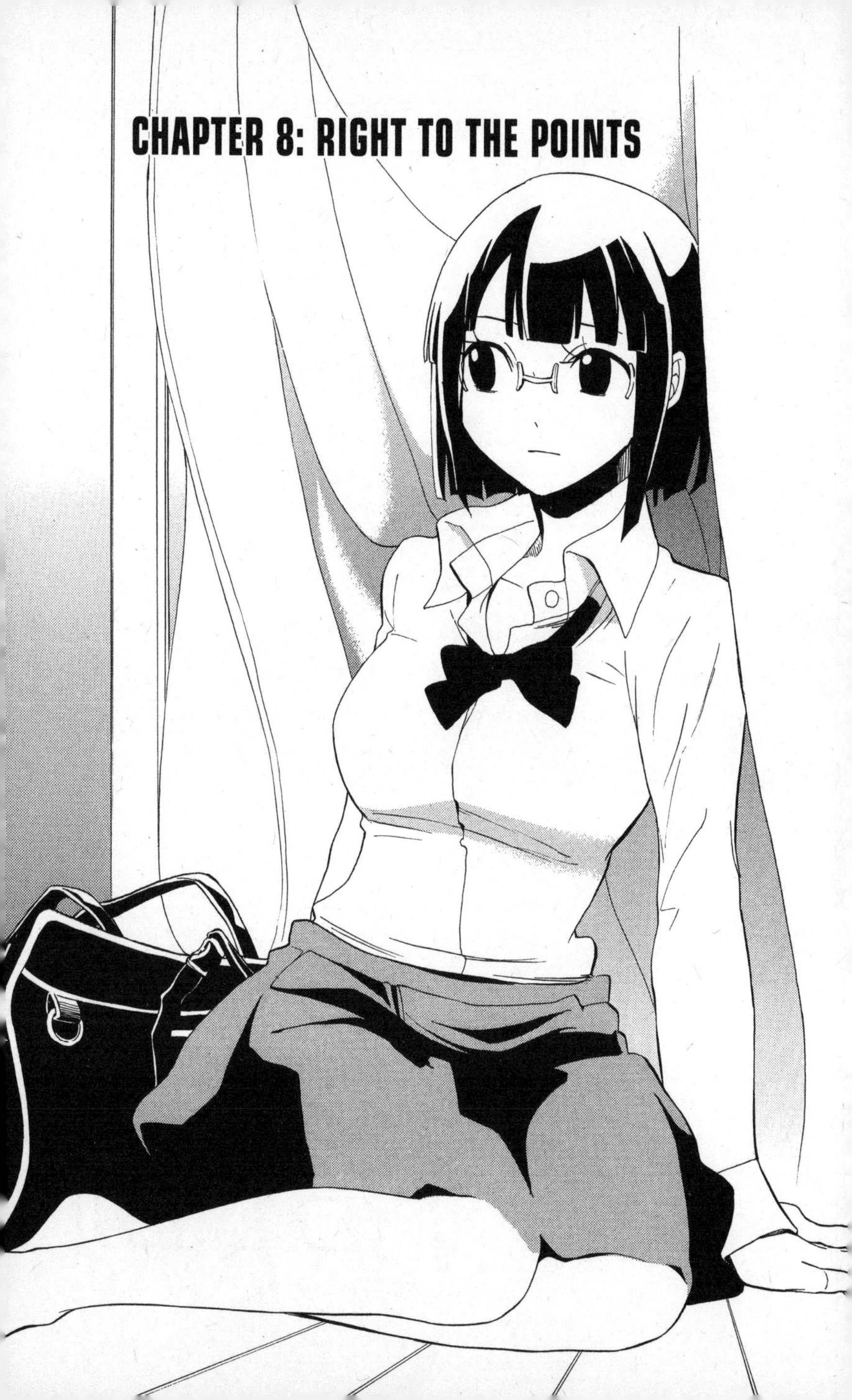

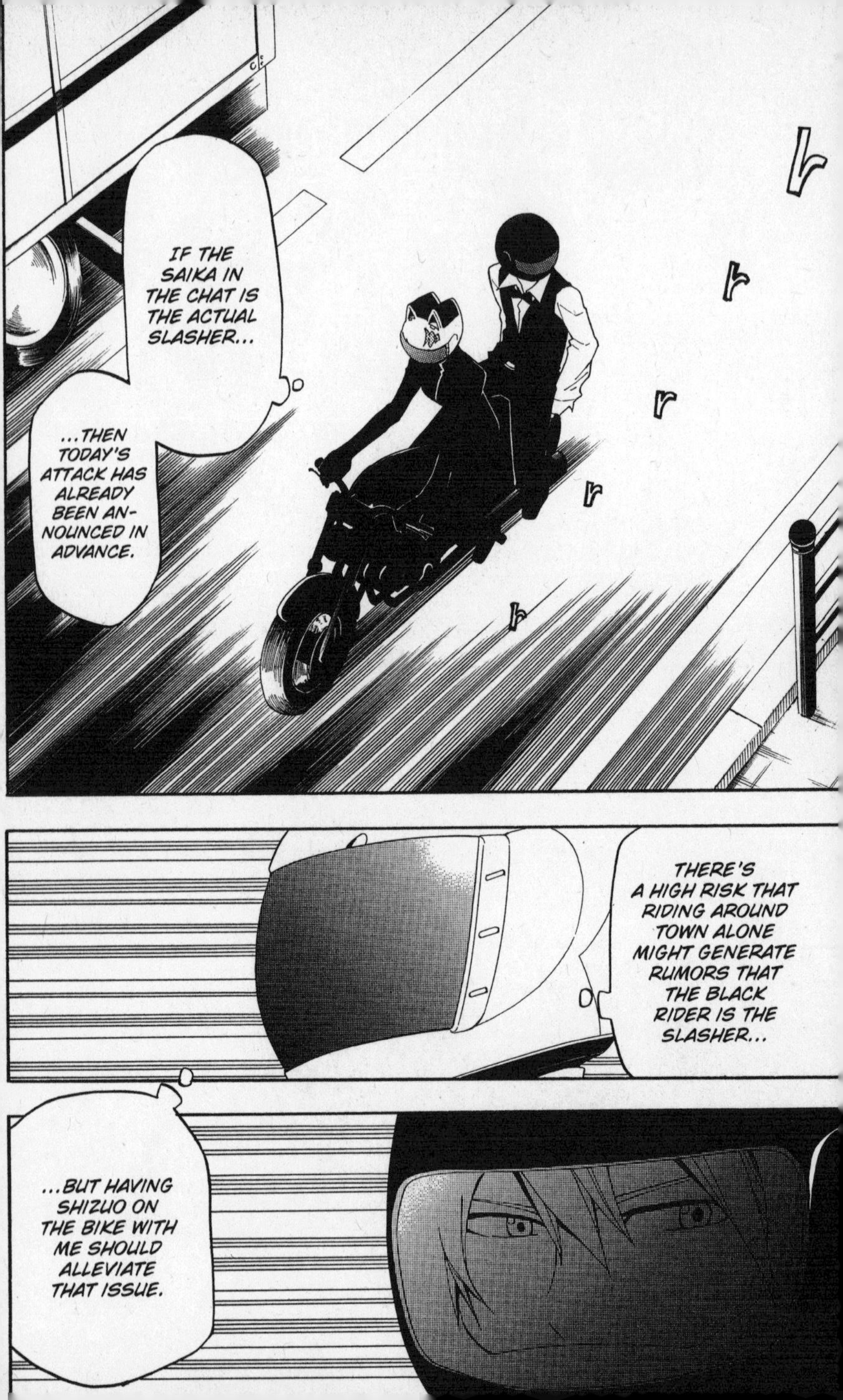

rrrrr
IF THE SAIKA IN THE CHAT IS THE ACTUAL SLASHER...
...THEN TODAY'S ATTACK HAS ALREADY BEEN AN-NOUNCED IN ADVANCE.
THERE'S A HIGH RISK THAT RIDING AROUND TOWN ALONE MIGHT GENERATE RUMORS THAT THE BLACK RIDER IS THE SLASHER...
...BUT HAVING SHIZUO ON THE BIKE WITH ME SHOULD ALLEVIATE THAT ISSUE.

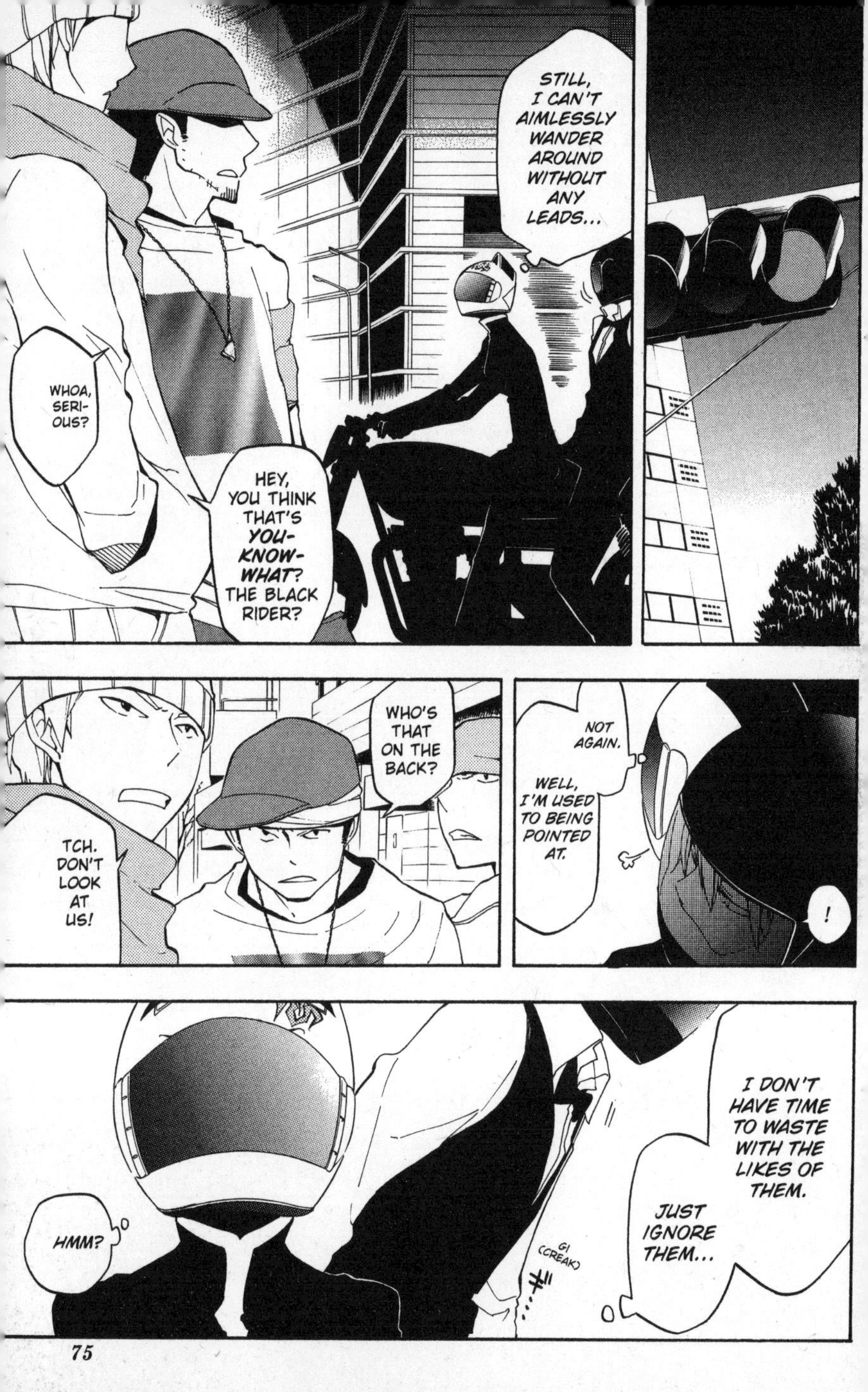
STILL, I CAN'T AIMLESSLY WANDER AROUND WITHOUT ANY LEADS...
HEY, YOU THINK THAT'S *YOU-KNOW-WHAT*? THE BLACK RIDER?
WHOA, SERI-OUS?
NOT AGAIN.
WELL, I'M USED TO BEING POINTED AT.
!
WHO'S THAT ON THE BACK?
TCH. DON'T LOOK AT US!
I DON'T HAVE TIME TO WASTE WITH THE LIKES OF THEM.
JUST IGNORE THEM...
GI (CREAK)
HMM?

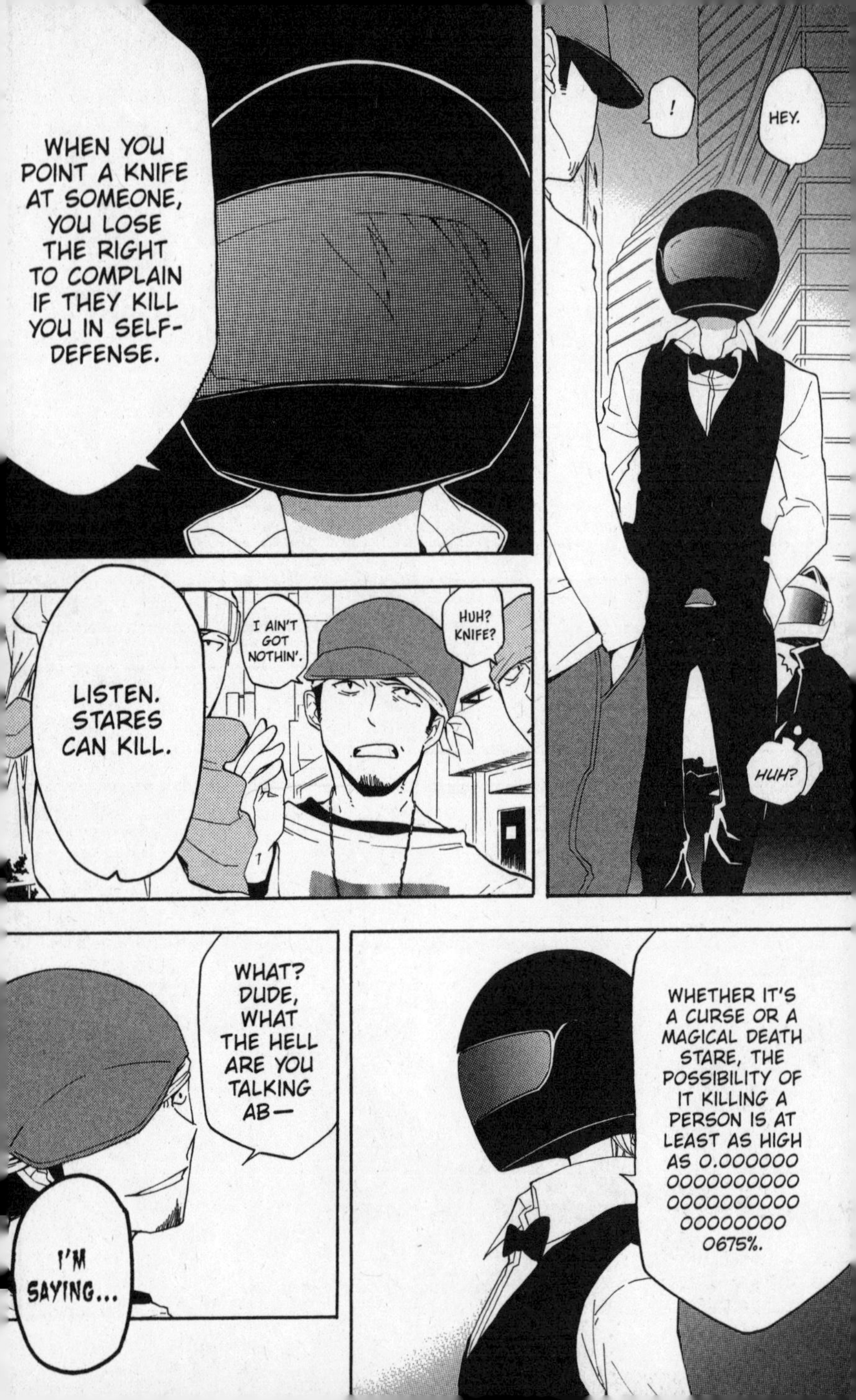
HEY.
!
HUH?
WHEN YOU POINT A KNIFE AT SOMEONE, YOU LOSE THE RIGHT TO COMPLAIN IF THEY KILL YOU IN SELF-DEFENSE.
HUH? KNIFE?
I AIN'T GOT NOTHIN'.
LISTEN. STARES CAN KILL.
WHETHER IT'S A CURSE OR A MAGICAL DEATH STARE, THE POSSIBILITY OF IT KILLING A PERSON IS AT LEAST AS HIGH AS 0.000000000000000000000000000000000675%.
WHAT? DUDE, WHAT THE HELL ARE YOU TALKING AB—
I'M SAYING...

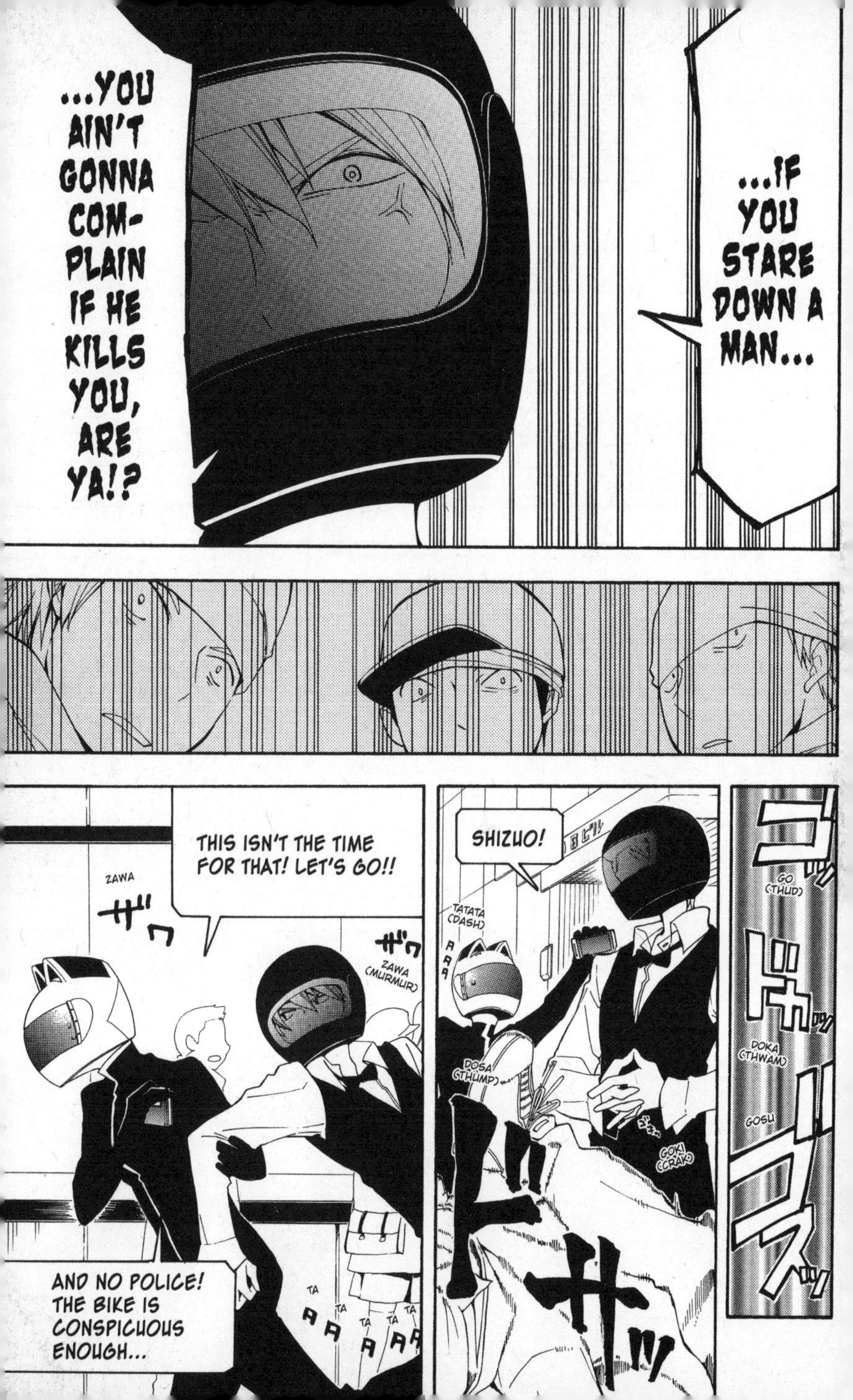
...IF YOU STARE DOWN A MAN...
...YOU AIN'T GONNA COMPLAIN IF HE KILLS YOU, ARE YA!?
GO (THUD)
DOKA (THWAM)
GOSU
SHIZUO!
TATATA (DASH)
DOSA (THUMP)
GOKI (CRAK)
THIS ISN'T THE TIME FOR THAT! LET'S GO!!
ZAWA
ZAWA (MURMUR)
AND NO POLICE! THE BIKE IS CONSPICUOUS ENOUGH...
TA TA TA TA

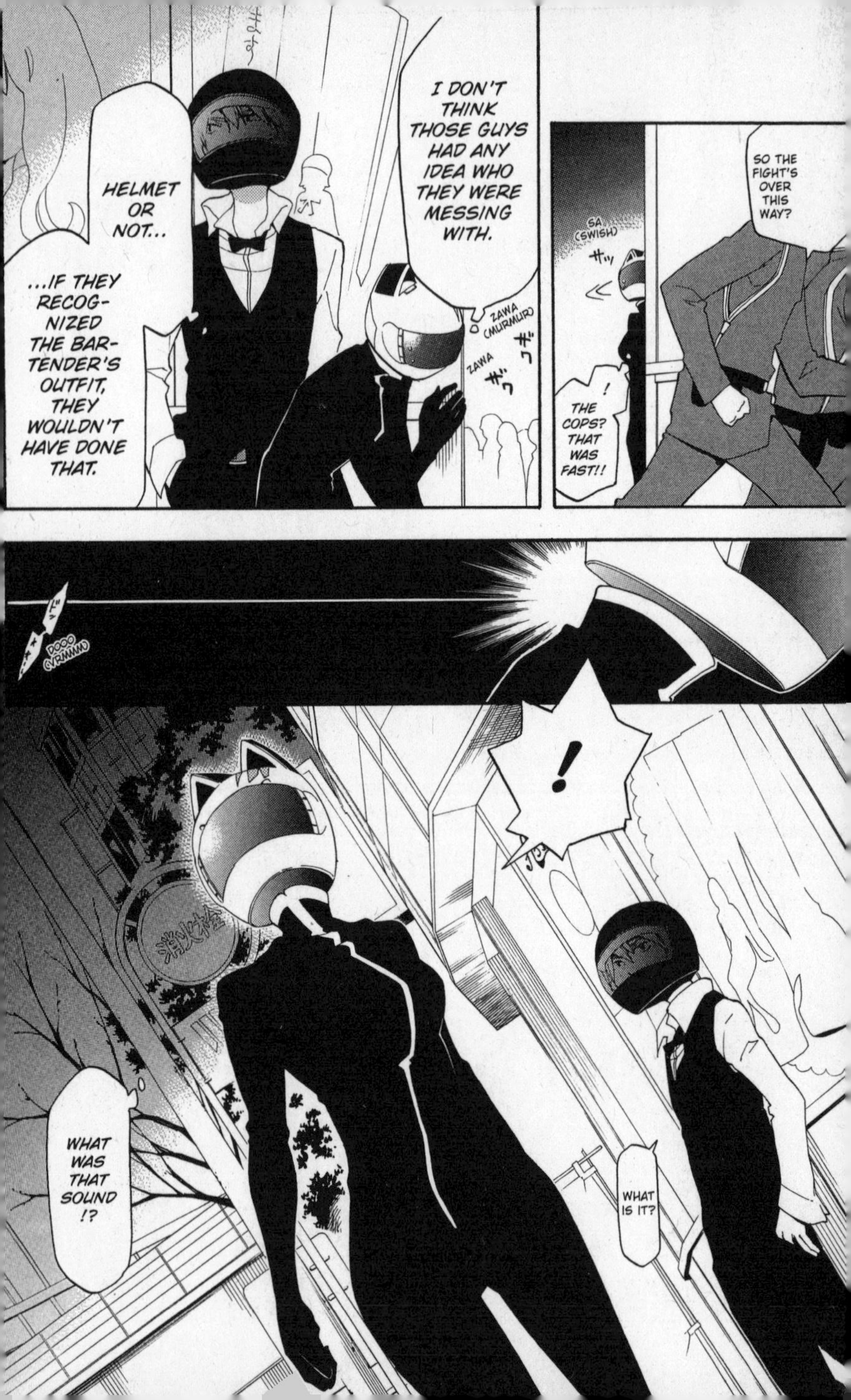
SO THE FIGHT'S OVER THIS WAY?
SA (SWISH)
THE COPS? THAT WAS FAST!!
I DON'T THINK THOSE GUYS HAD ANY IDEA WHO THEY WERE MESSING WITH.
ZAWA (MURMUR)
ZAWA
HELMET OR NOT...
...IF THEY RECOG-NIZED THE BAR-TENDER'S OUTFIT, THEY WOULDN'T HAVE DONE THAT.
DOOO (VRMMM)
!
WHAT IS IT?
WHAT WAS THAT SOUND !?

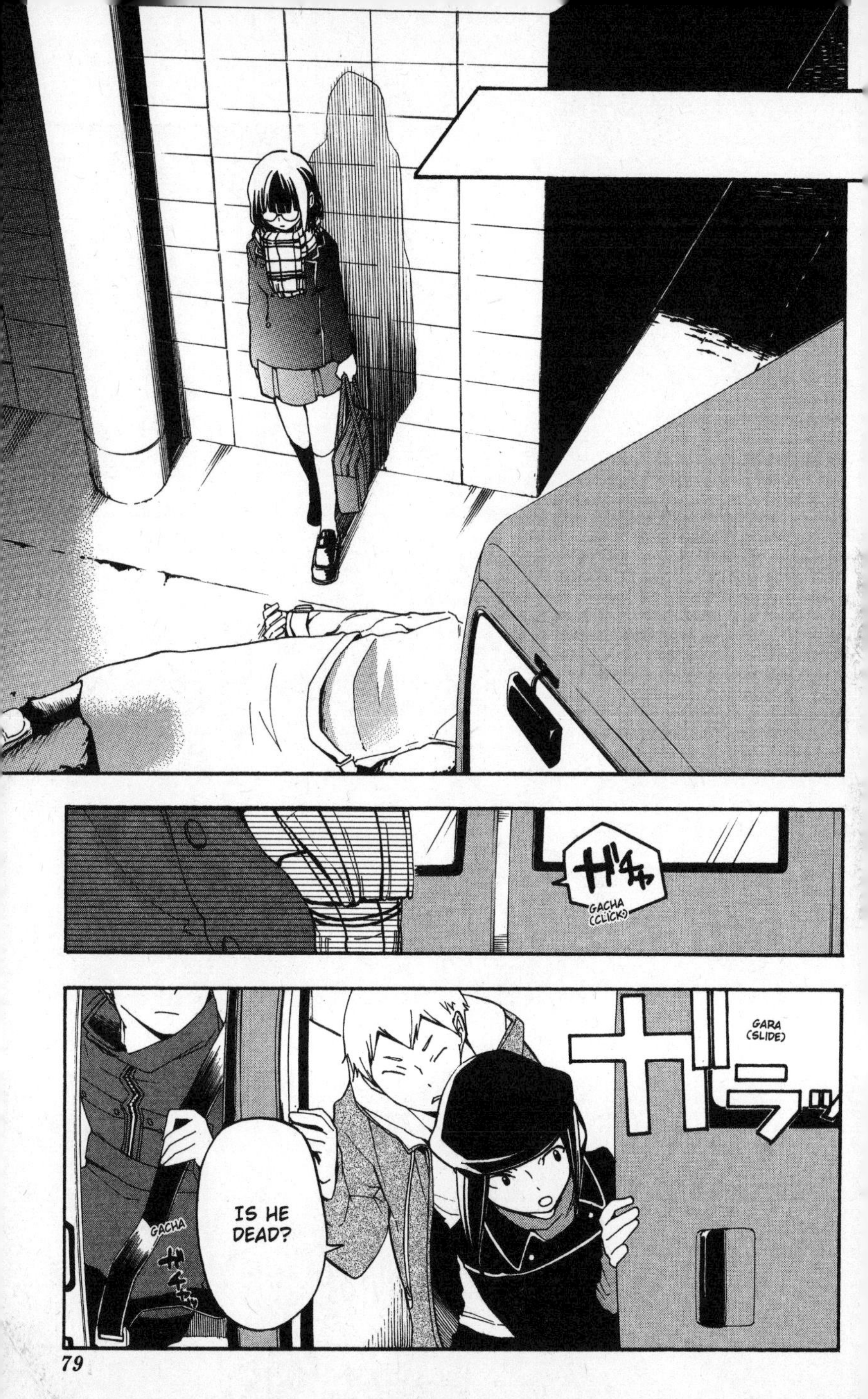
GACHA (CLICK)
GARA (SLIDE)
ガラッ
IS HE DEAD?
GACHA

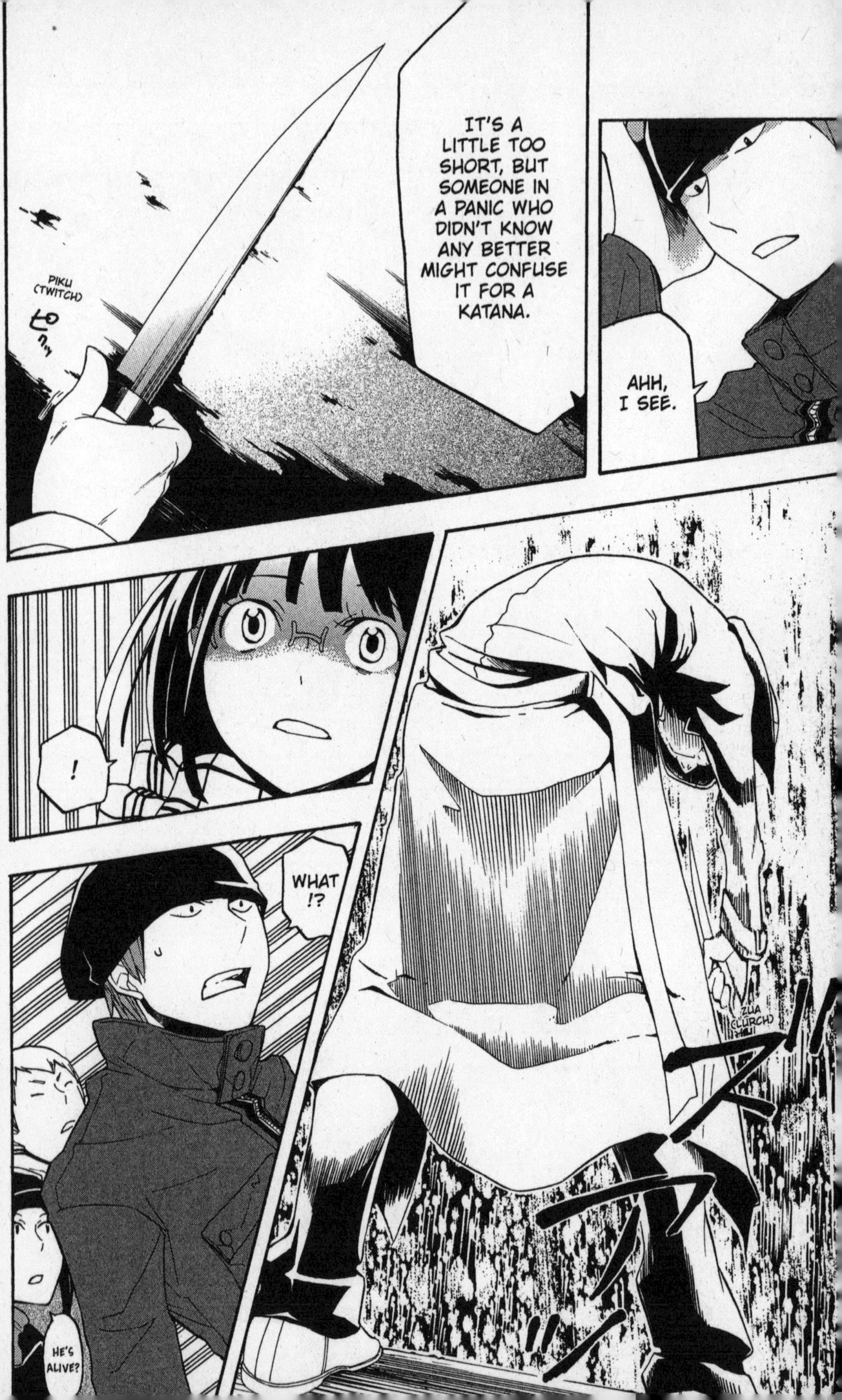

IT'S A LITTLE TOO SHORT, BUT SOMEONE IN A PANIC WHO DIDN'T KNOW ANY BETTER MIGHT CONFUSE IT FOR A KATANA.
AHH, I SEE.
PIKU (TWITCH)
ZUA (LURCH)
!
WHAT !?
HE'S ALIVE?

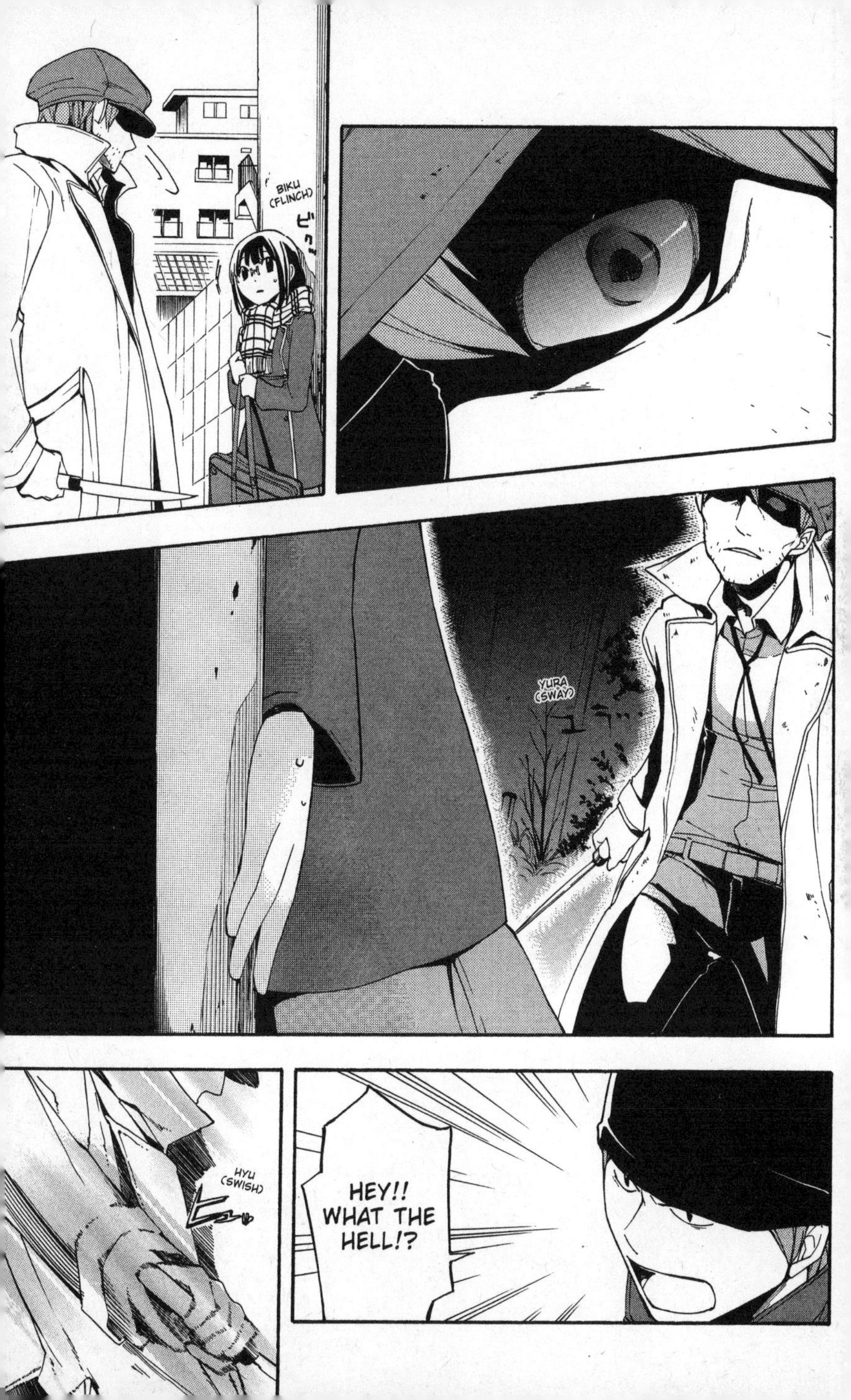
BIKU (FLINCH)
YURA (SWAY)
HEY!! WHAT THE HELL!?
HYU (SWISH)

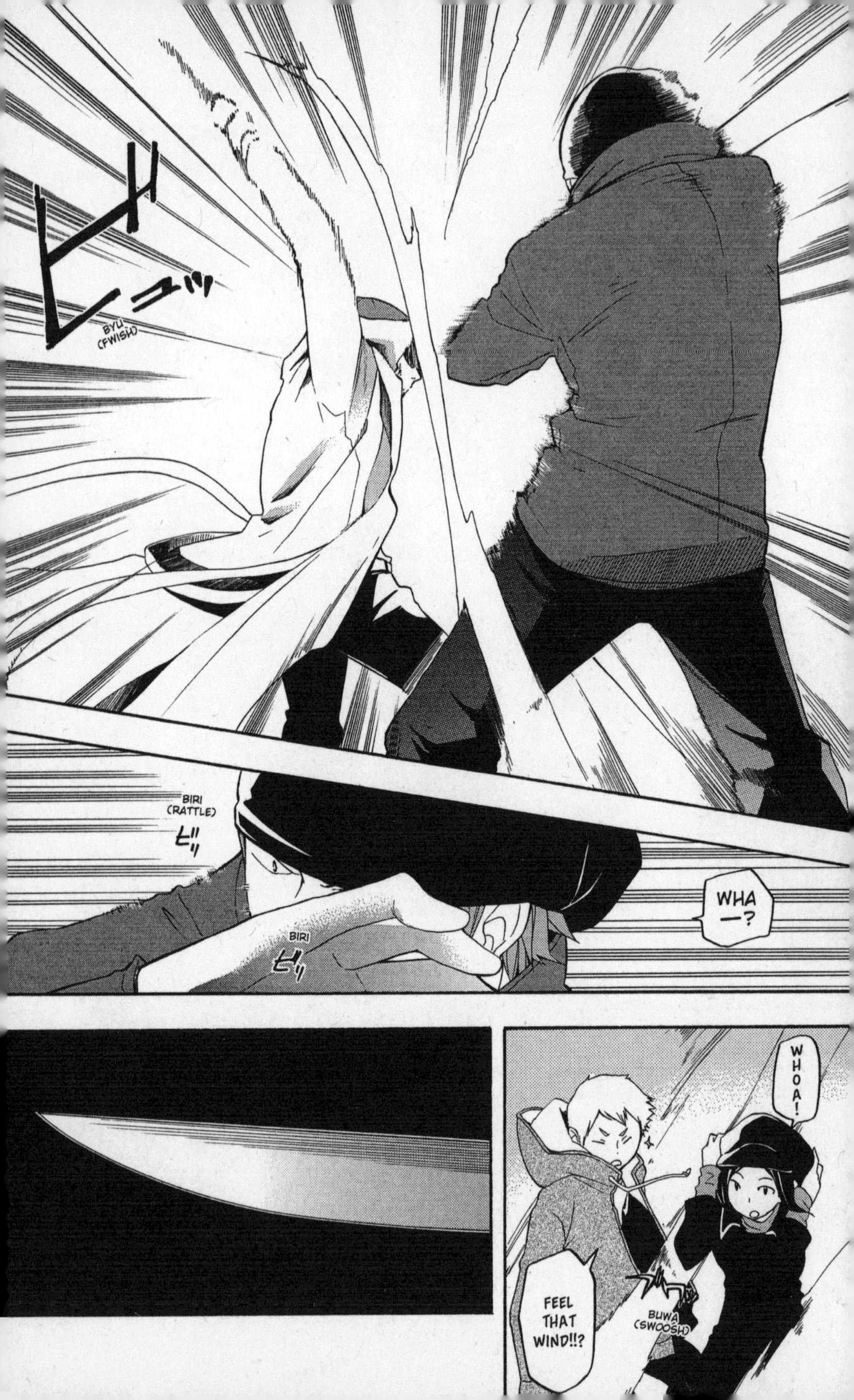
BYU (FWISH)
BIRI (RATTLE)
WHA—?
BIRI
WHOA!
FEEL THAT WIND!!?
BUWA (SWOOSH)

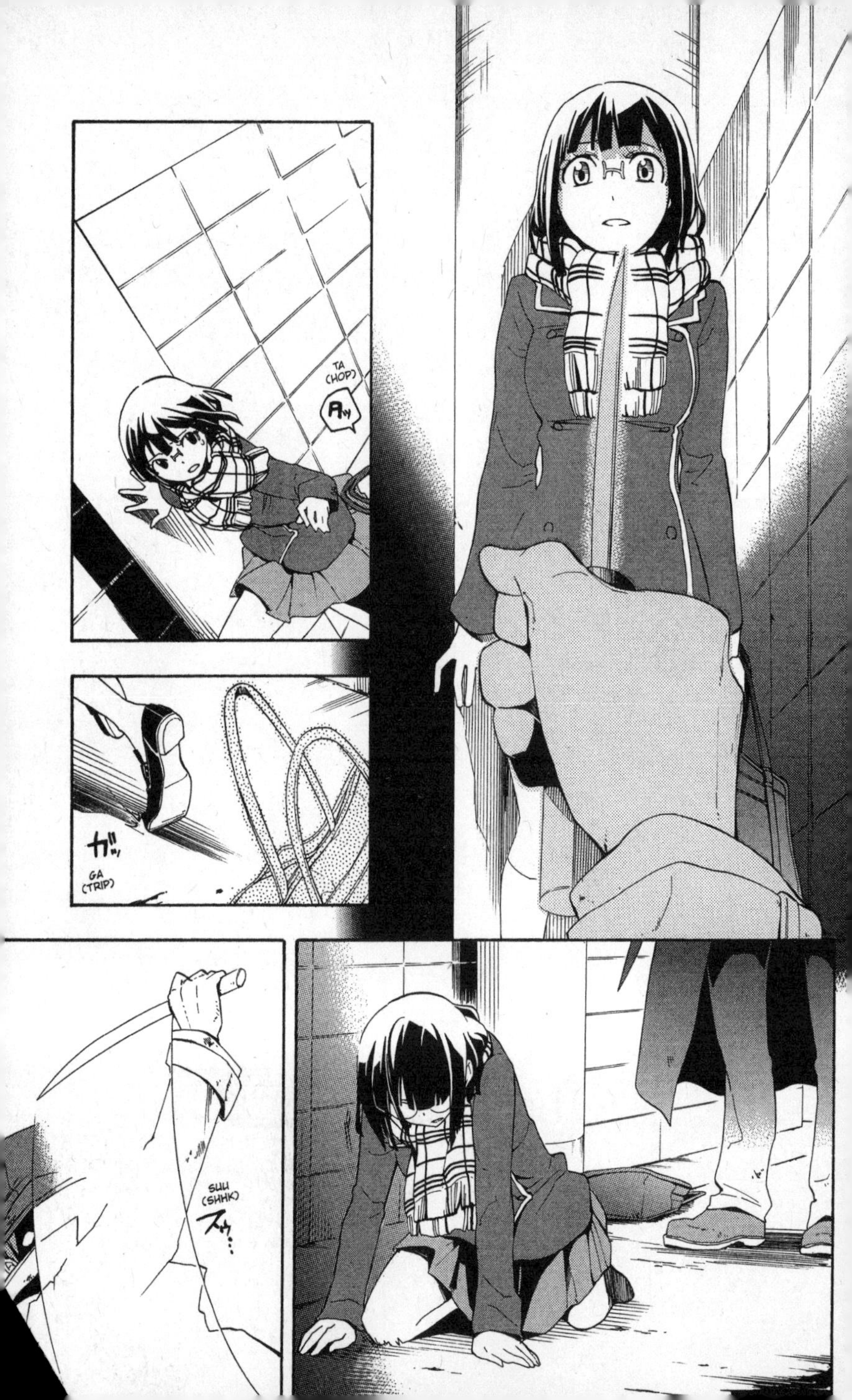

TA
(HOP)
タッ
ガッ
GA
(TRIP)
SUU
(SHHK)
スッ…

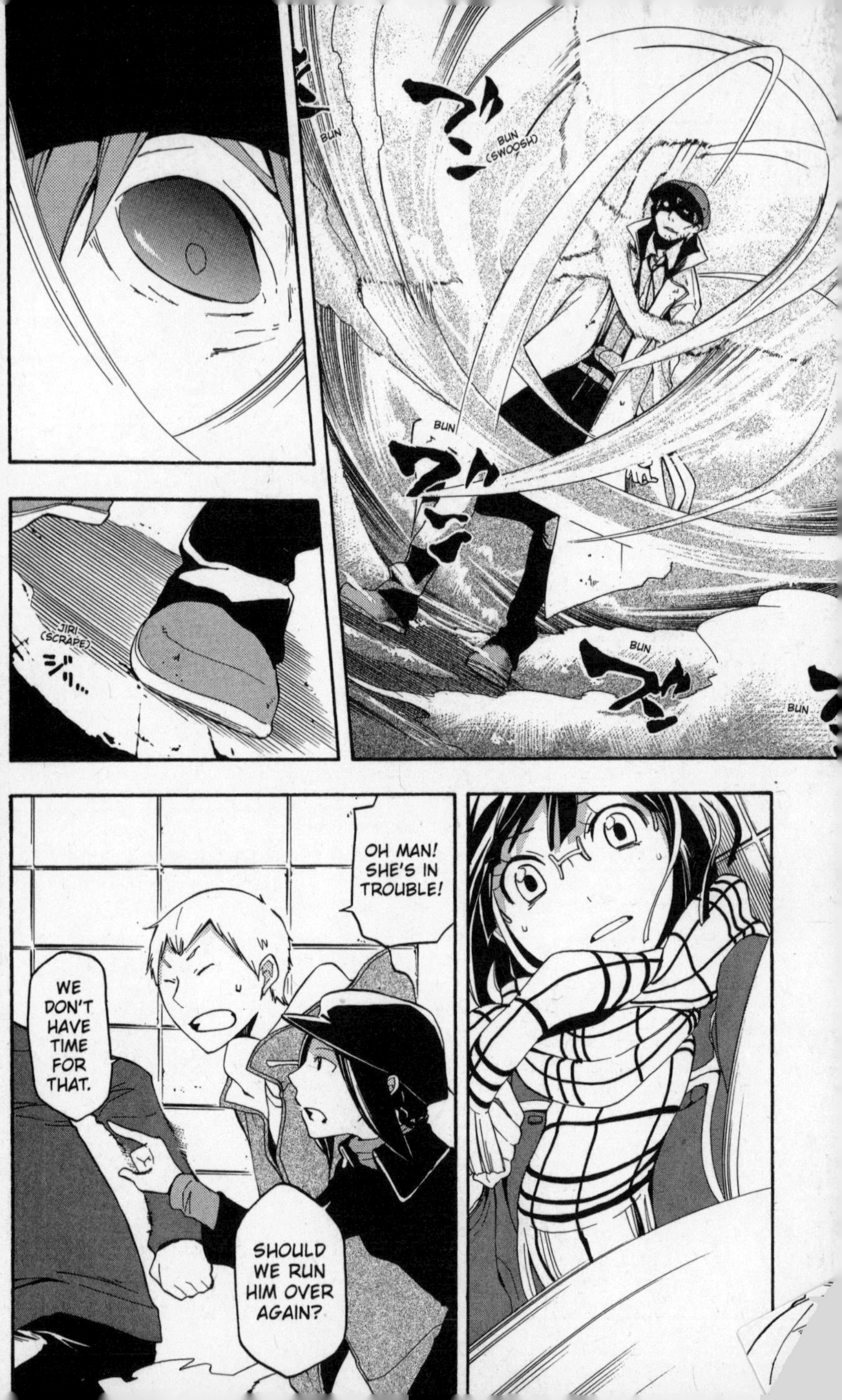
BUN (SWOOSH)
BUN
BUN
BUN
BUN
JIRI (SCRAPE)
OH MAN! SHE'S IN TROUBLE!
WE DON'T HAVE TIME FOR THAT.
SHOULD WE RUN HIM OVER AGAIN?

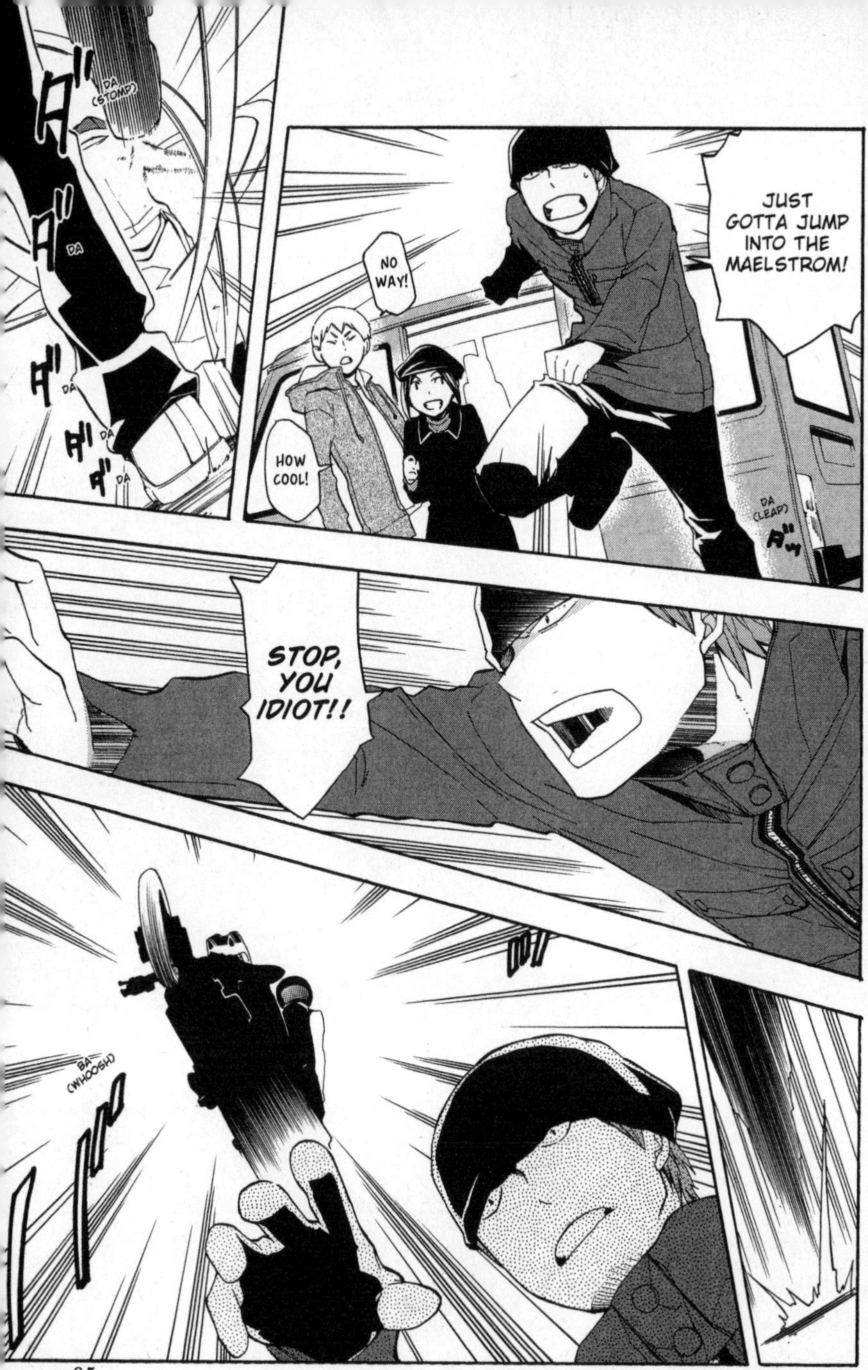
JUST GOTTA JUMP INTO THE MAELSTROM!
NO WAY!
HOW COOL!
DA (LEAP)
DA (STOMP)
DA
DA
DA
DA
STOP, YOU IDIOT!!
BA (WHOOSH)

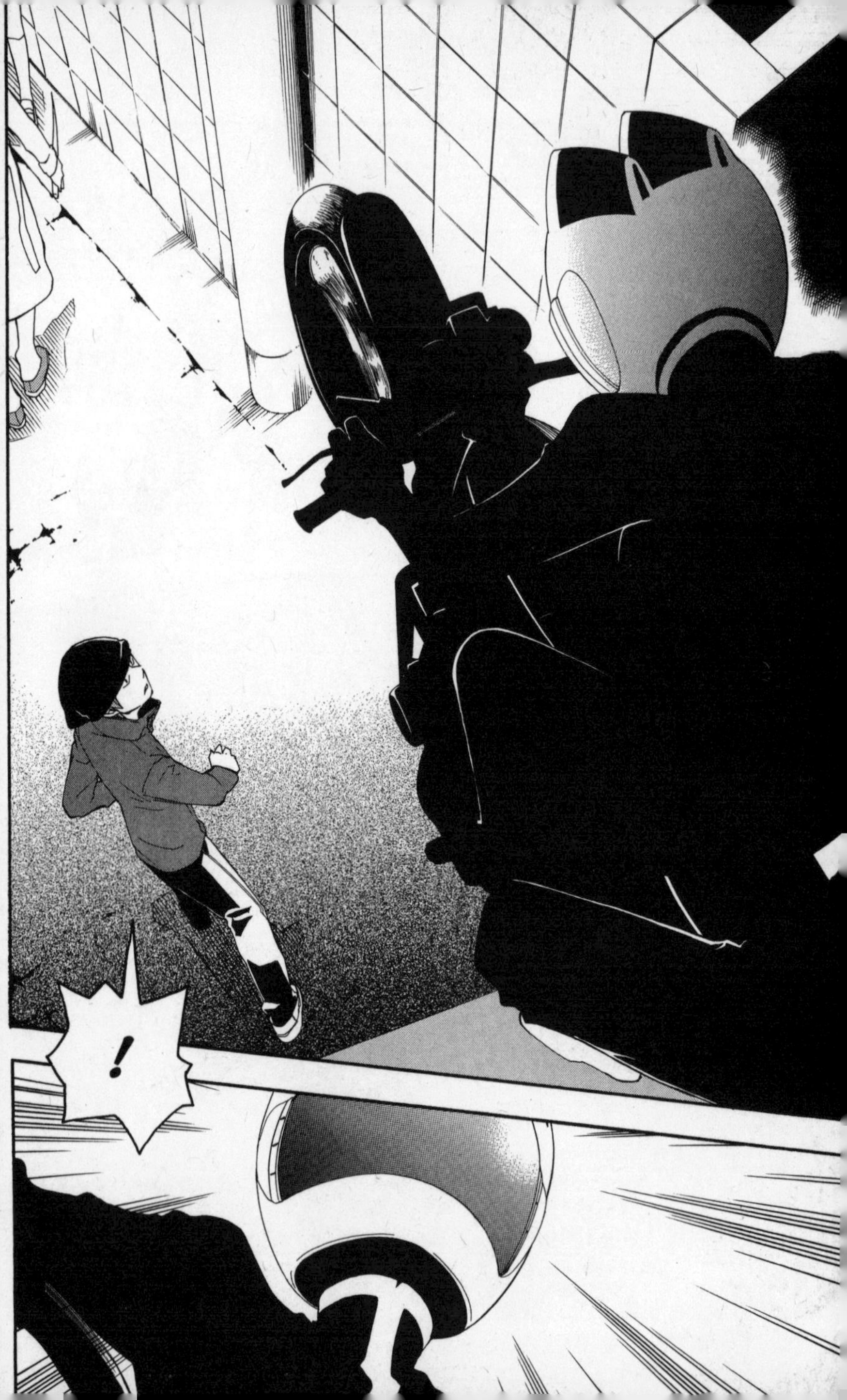
!

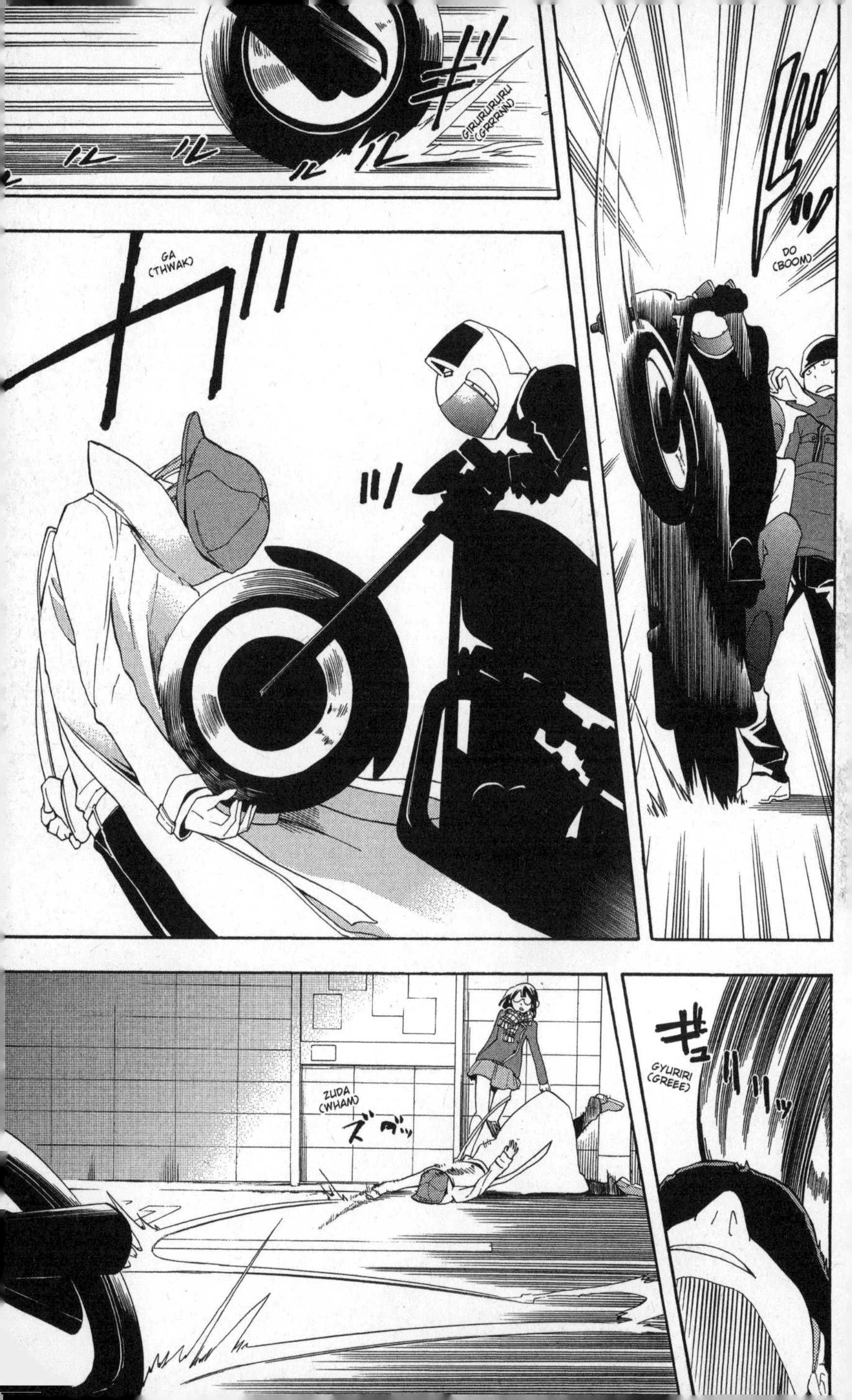
DO (BOOM)
GIRURURURU (GRRRNN)
GA (THWAK)
GYURIRI (GREEE)
ZUDA (WHAM)

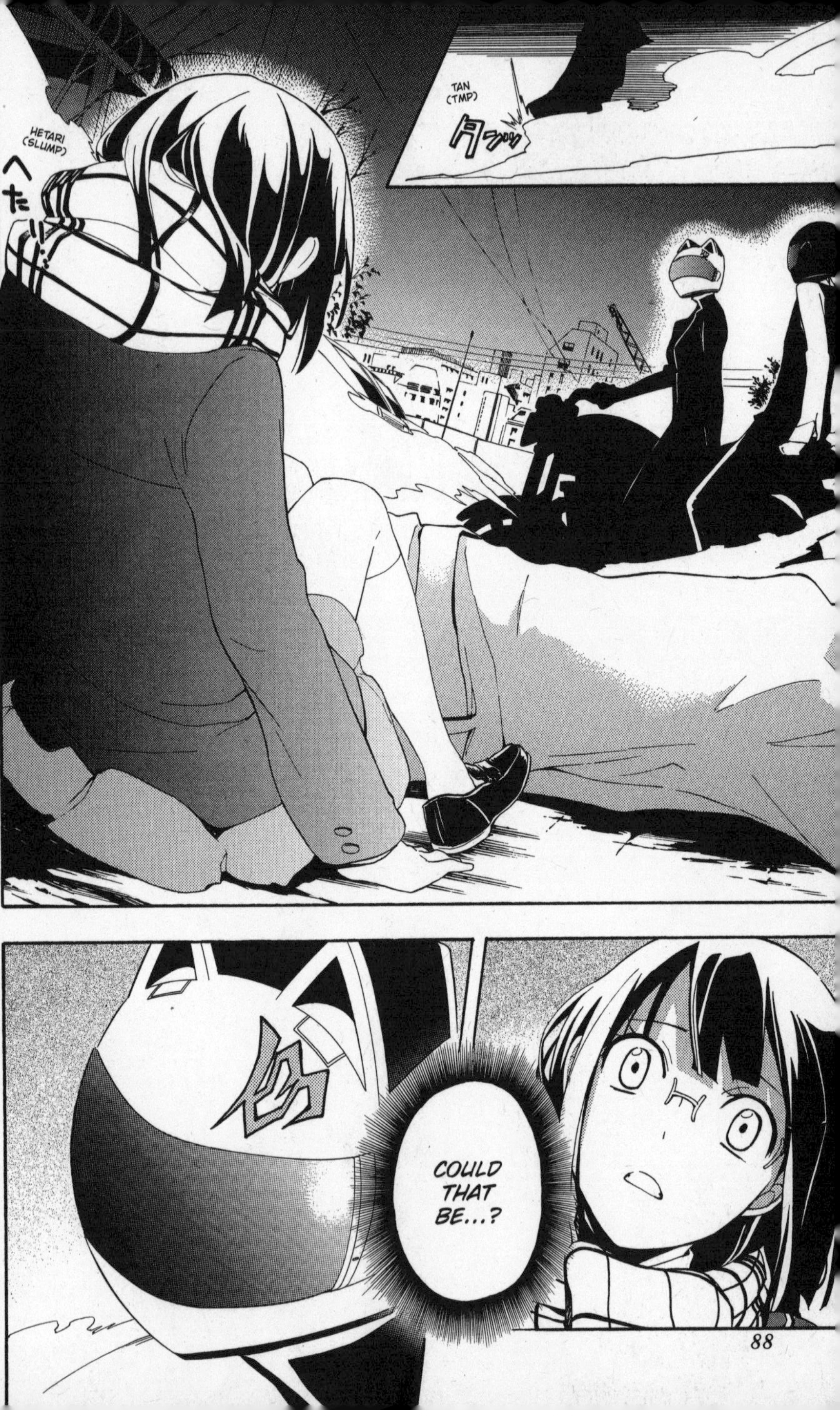
TAN (TMP)
HETARI (SLUMP)
へたり
COULD THAT BE...?

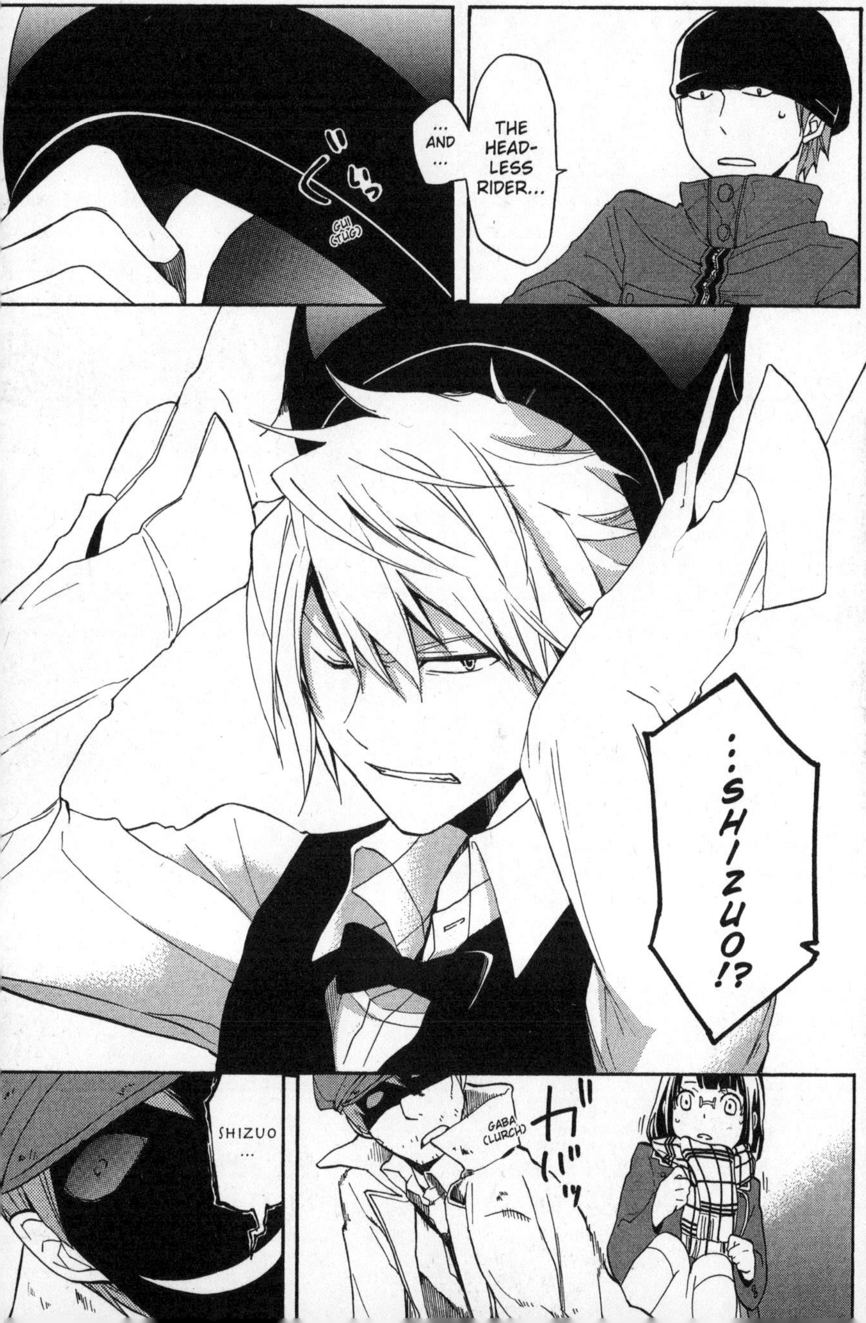
THE HEAD-LESS RIDER...
...AND...
GUI (TUG)
..SHIZUO!?
GABA (LURCH)
SHIZUO ...

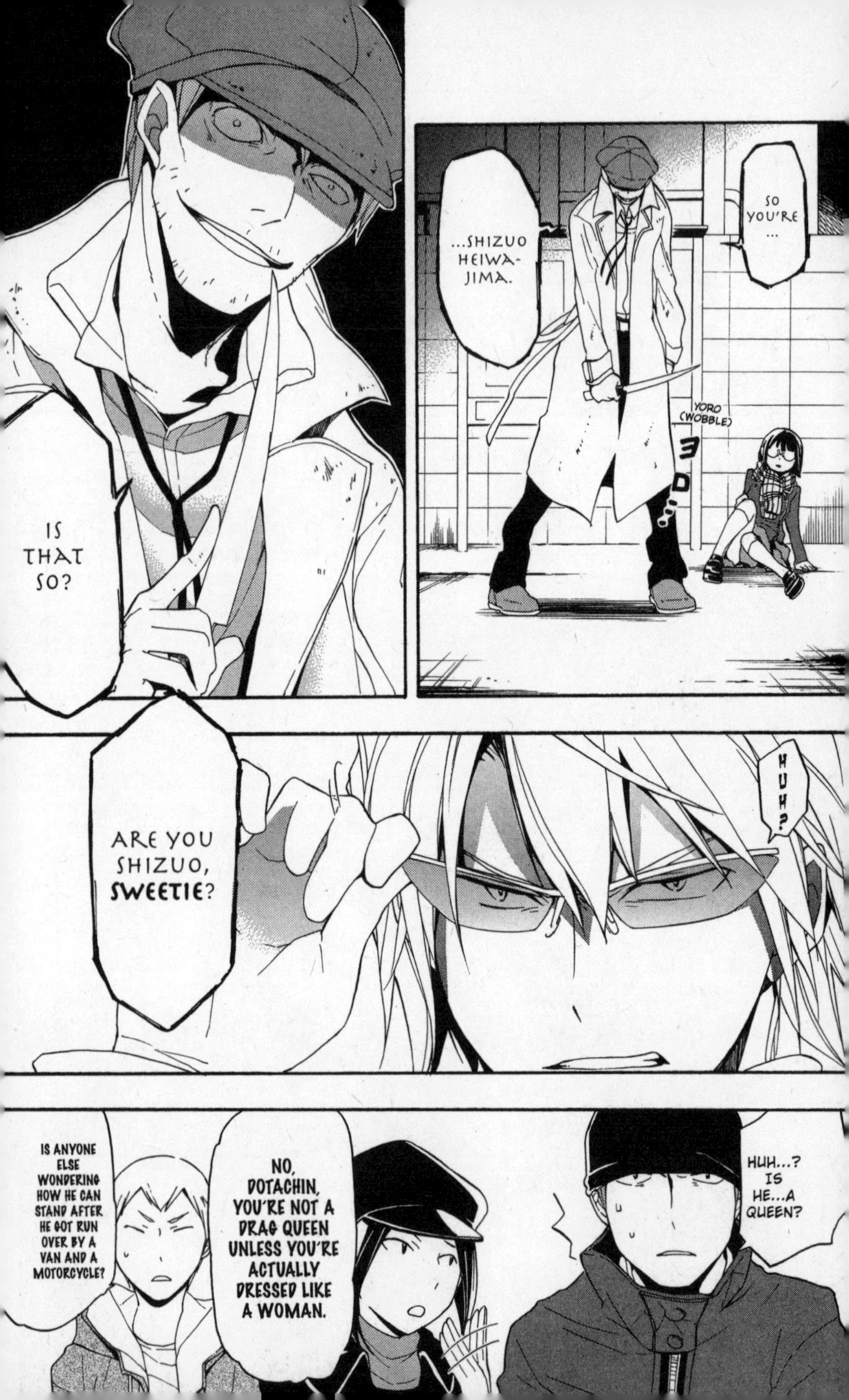
SO YOU'RE ...
...SHIZUO HEIWA-JIMA.
YORO (WOBBLE)
IS THAT SO?
HUH?
ARE YOU SHIZUO, **SWEETIE**?
HUH...? IS HE...A QUEEN?
NO, DOTACHIN, YOU'RE NOT A DRAG QUEEN UNLESS YOU'RE ACTUALLY DRESSED LIKE A WOMAN.
IS ANYONE ELSE WONDERING HOW HE CAN STAND AFTER HE GOT RUN OVER BY A VAN AND A MOTORCYCLE?

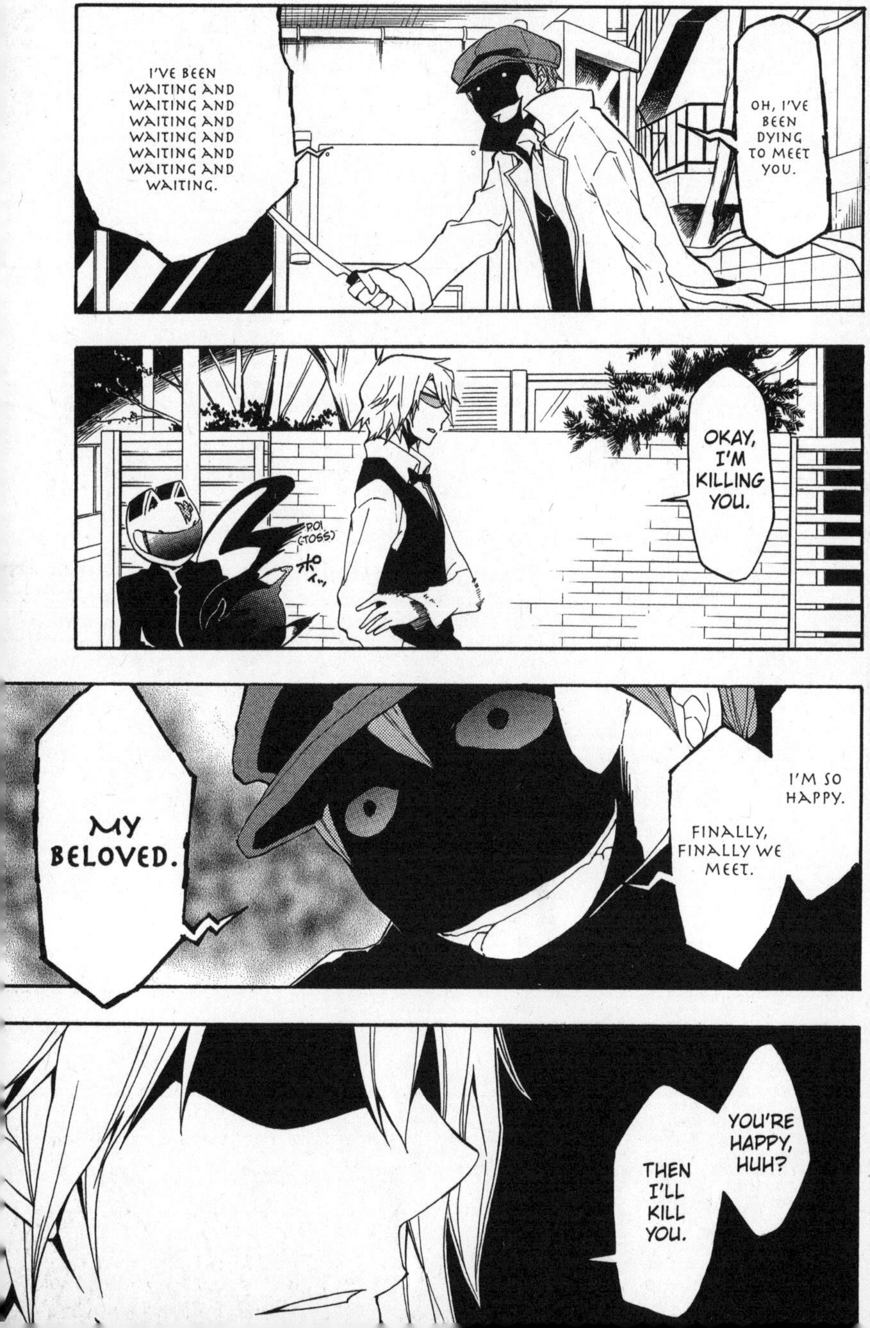

OH, I'VE BEEN DYING TO MEET YOU.
I'VE BEEN WAITING AND WAITING AND WAITING AND WAITING AND WAITING AND WAITING AND WAITING.
OKAY, I'M KILLING YOU.
POI (TOSS)
I'M SO HAPPY.
FINALLY, FINALLY WE MEET.
MY BELOVED.
YOU'RE HAPPY, HUH?
THEN I'LL KILL YOU.

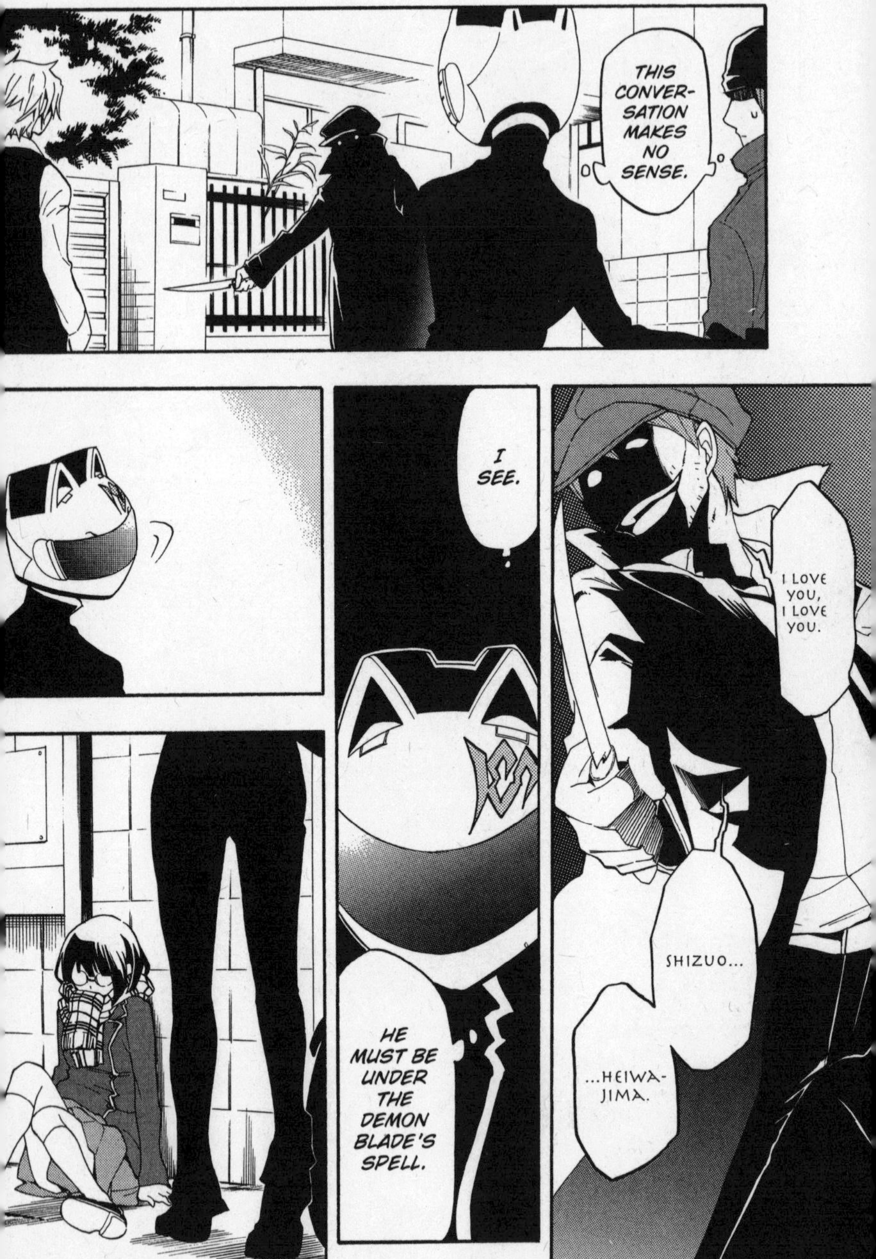
THIS CONVER-SATION MAKES NO SENSE.
I LOVE YOU, I LOVE YOU.
SHIZUO...
...HEIWA-JIMA.
I SEE.
HE MUST BE UNDER THE DEMON BLADE'S SPELL.

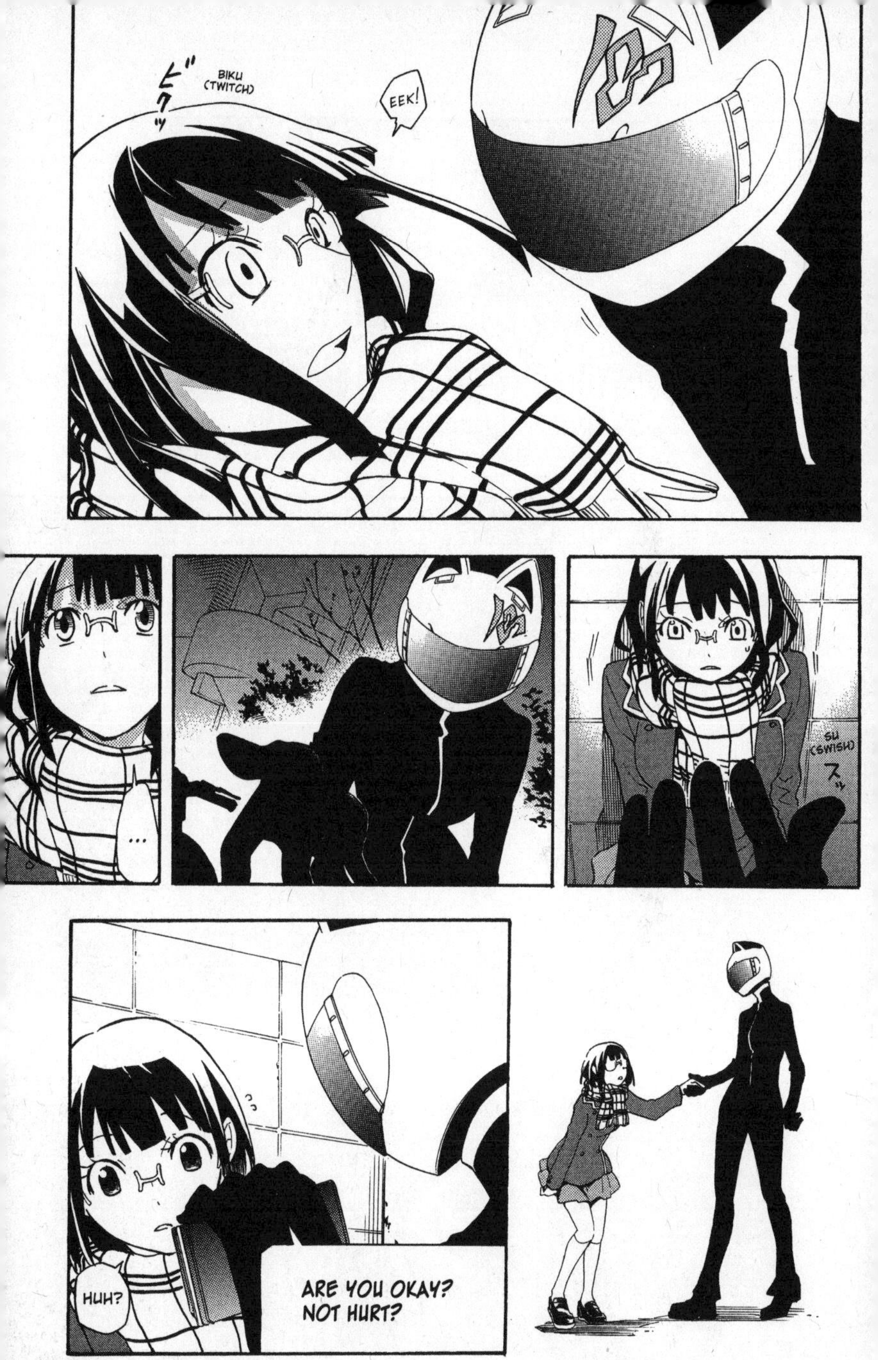

EEK!
ビクッ
BIKU (TWITCH)
スッ
SU (SWISH)
...
ARE YOU OKAY? NOT HURT?
HUH?

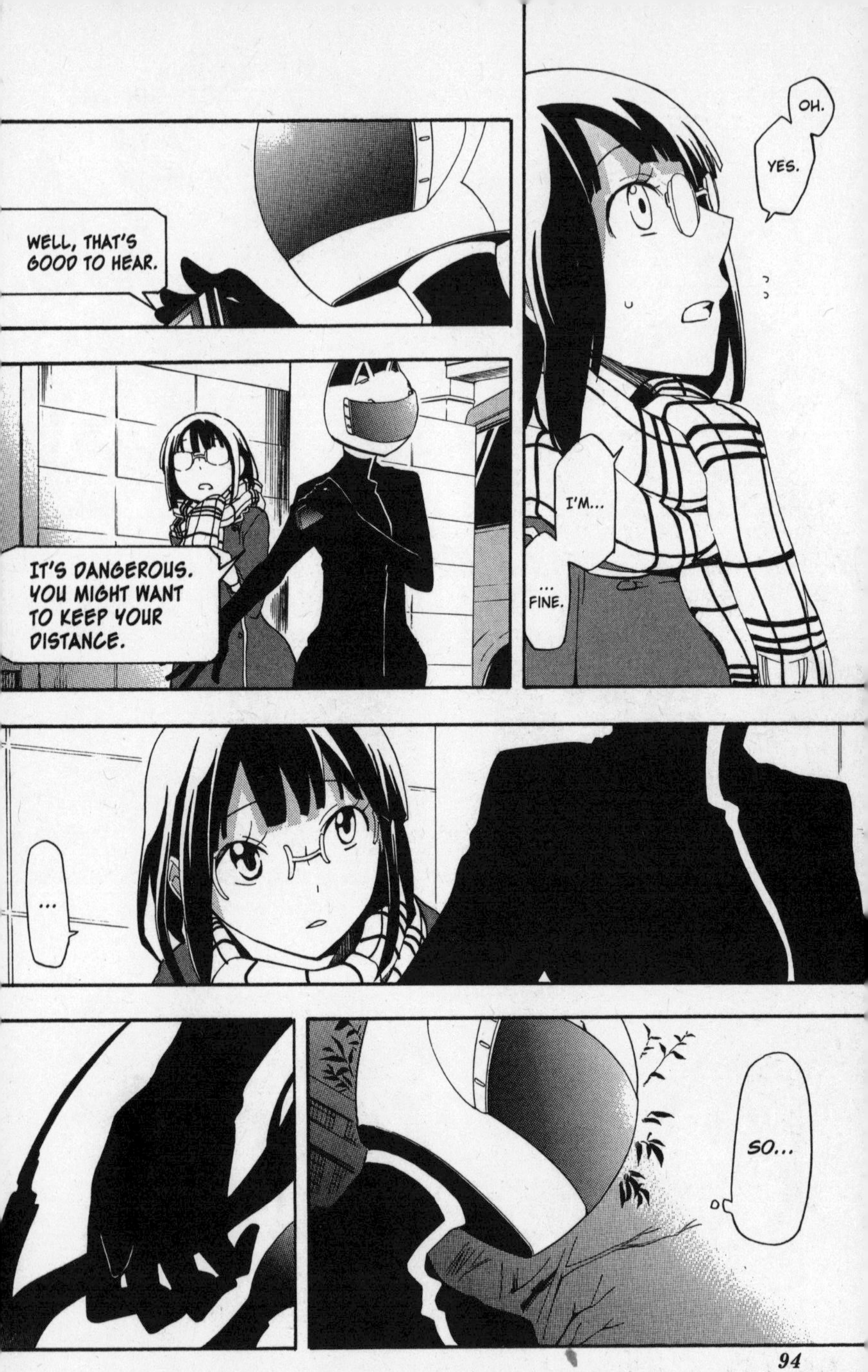
OH.
YES.
I'M...
...FINE.
WELL, THAT'S GOOD TO HEAR.
IT'S DANGEROUS. YOU MIGHT WANT TO KEEP YOUR DISTANCE.
...
SO...

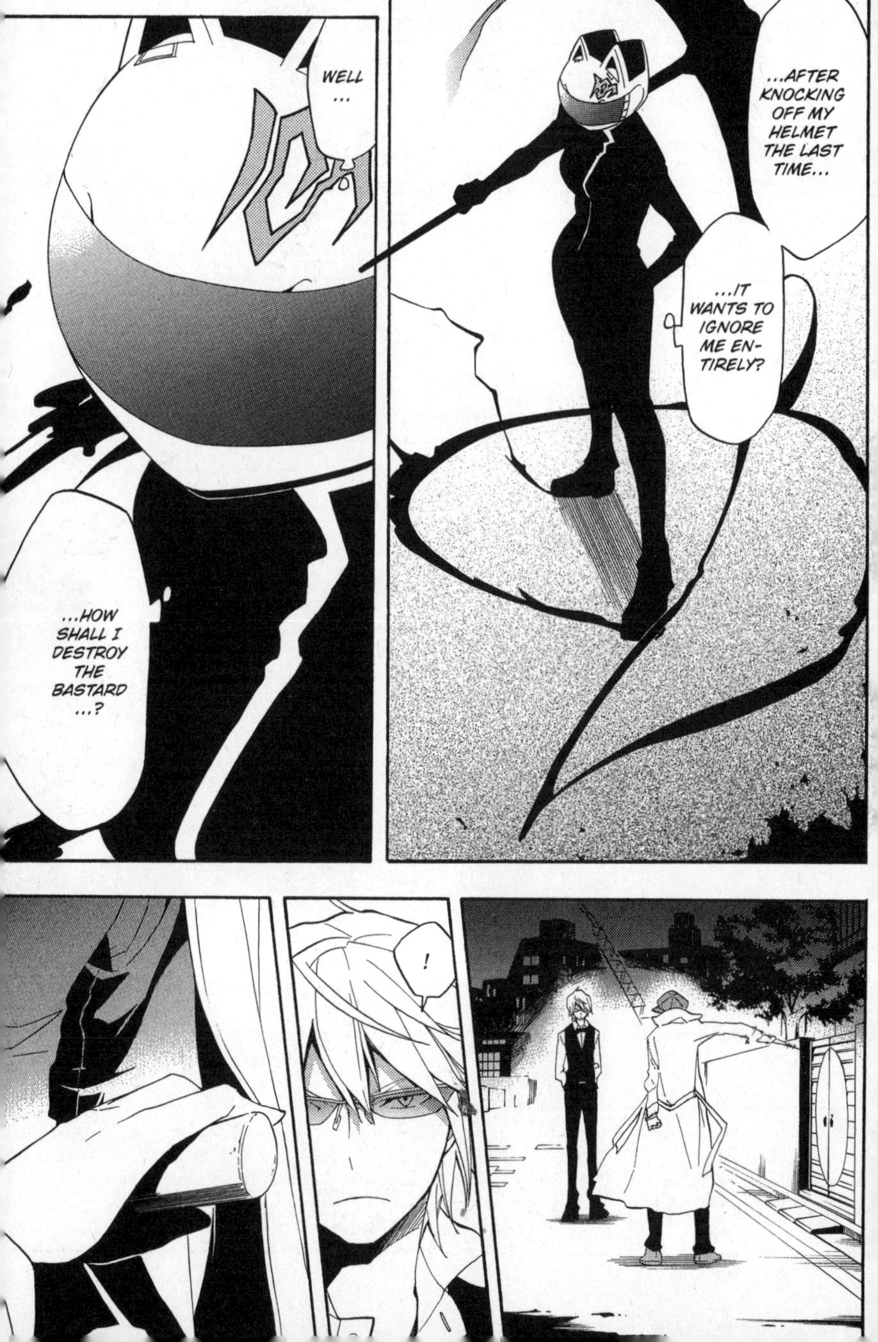
...AFTER KNOCKING OFF MY HELMET THE LAST TIME...
...IT WANTS TO IGNORE ME EN-TIRELY?
WELL...
...HOW SHALL I DESTROY THE BASTARD...?
!

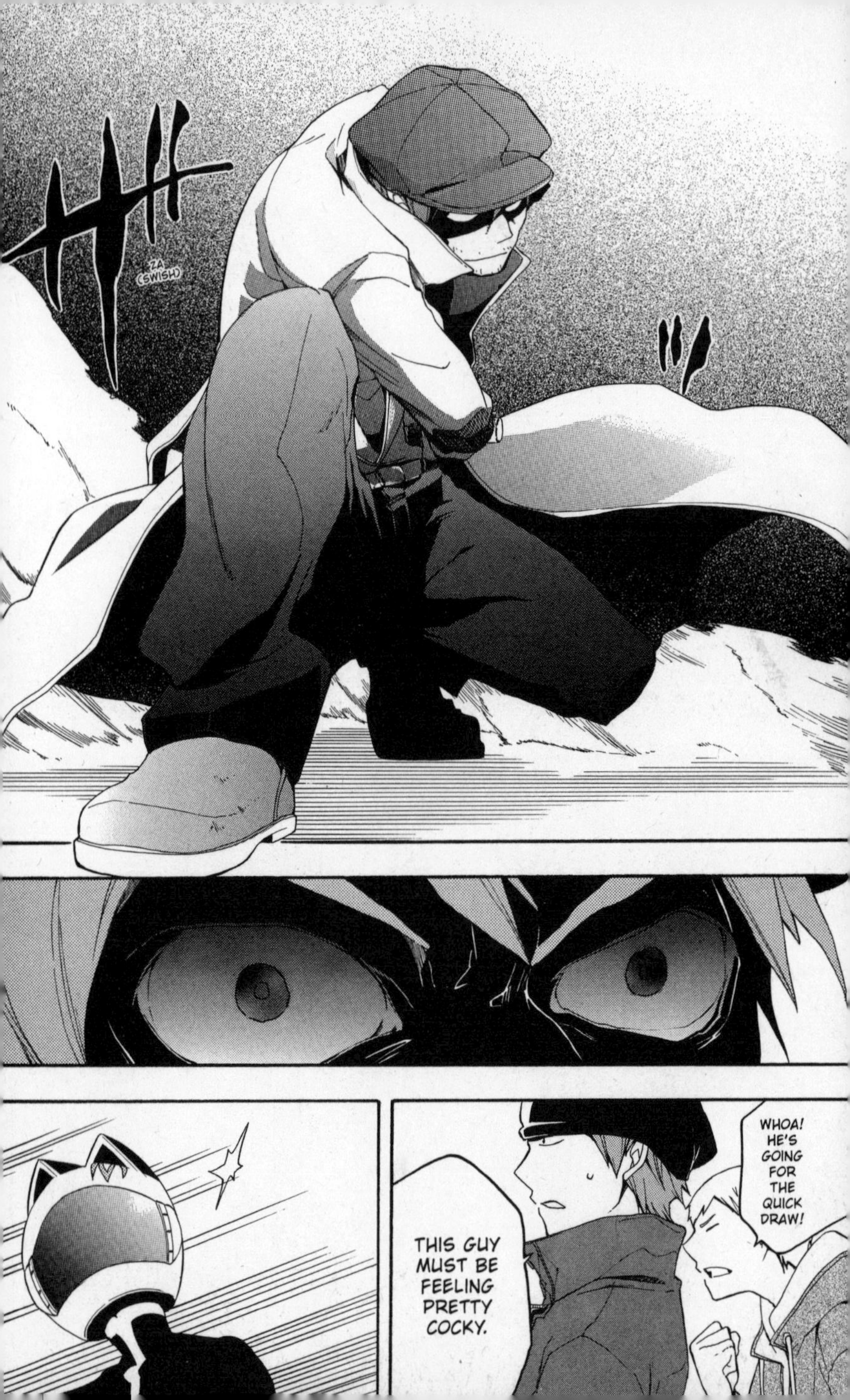
ZA (SWISH)
WHOA! HE'S GOING FOR THE QUICK DRAW!
THIS GUY MUST BE FEELING PRETTY COCKY.

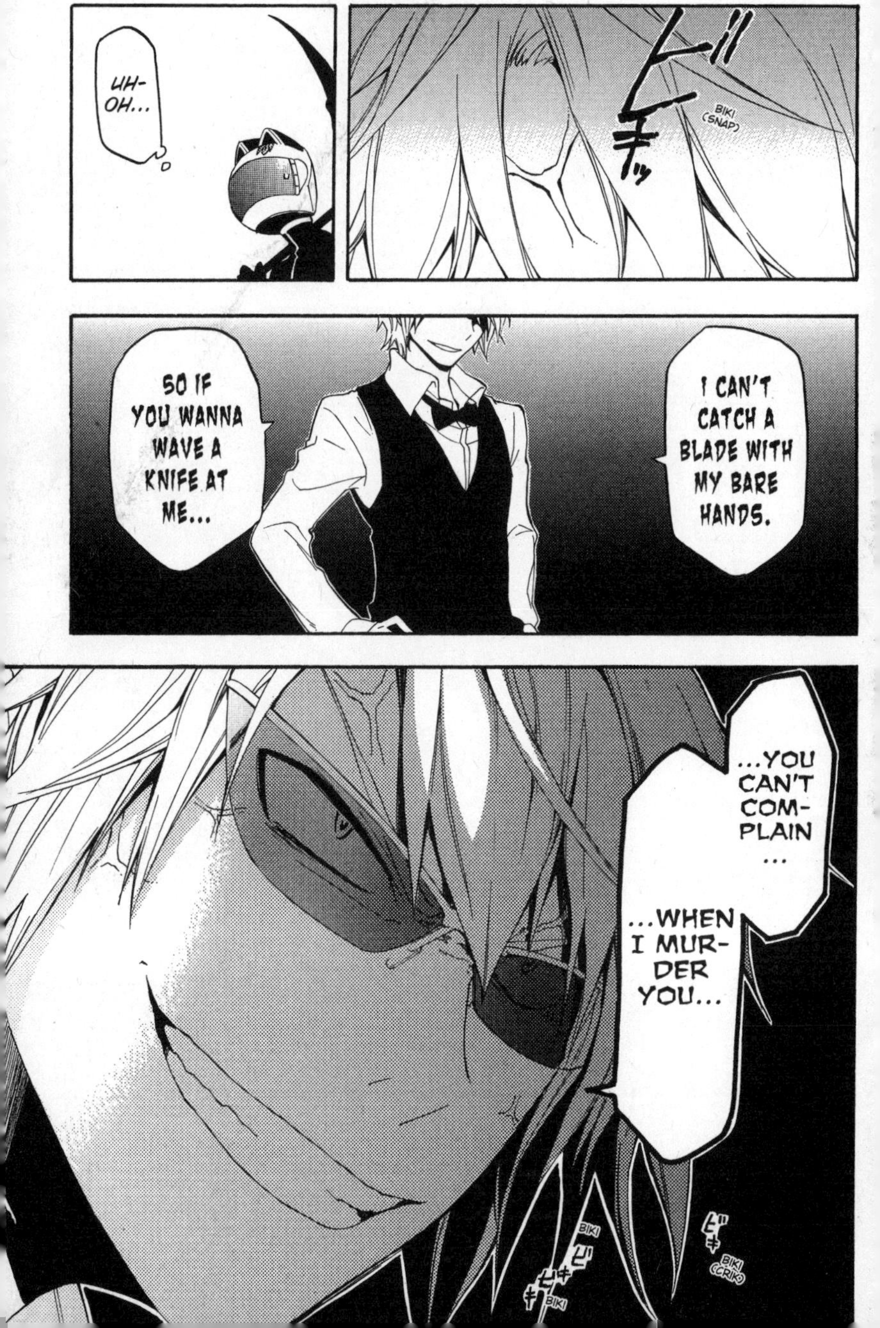
BIKI (SNAP)
UH-OH...
I CAN'T CATCH A BLADE WITH MY BARE HANDS.
SO IF YOU WANNA WAVE A KNIFE AT ME...
...YOU CAN'T COMPLAIN...
...WHEN I MURDER YOU...
BIKI (CRIK)
BIKI
BIKI

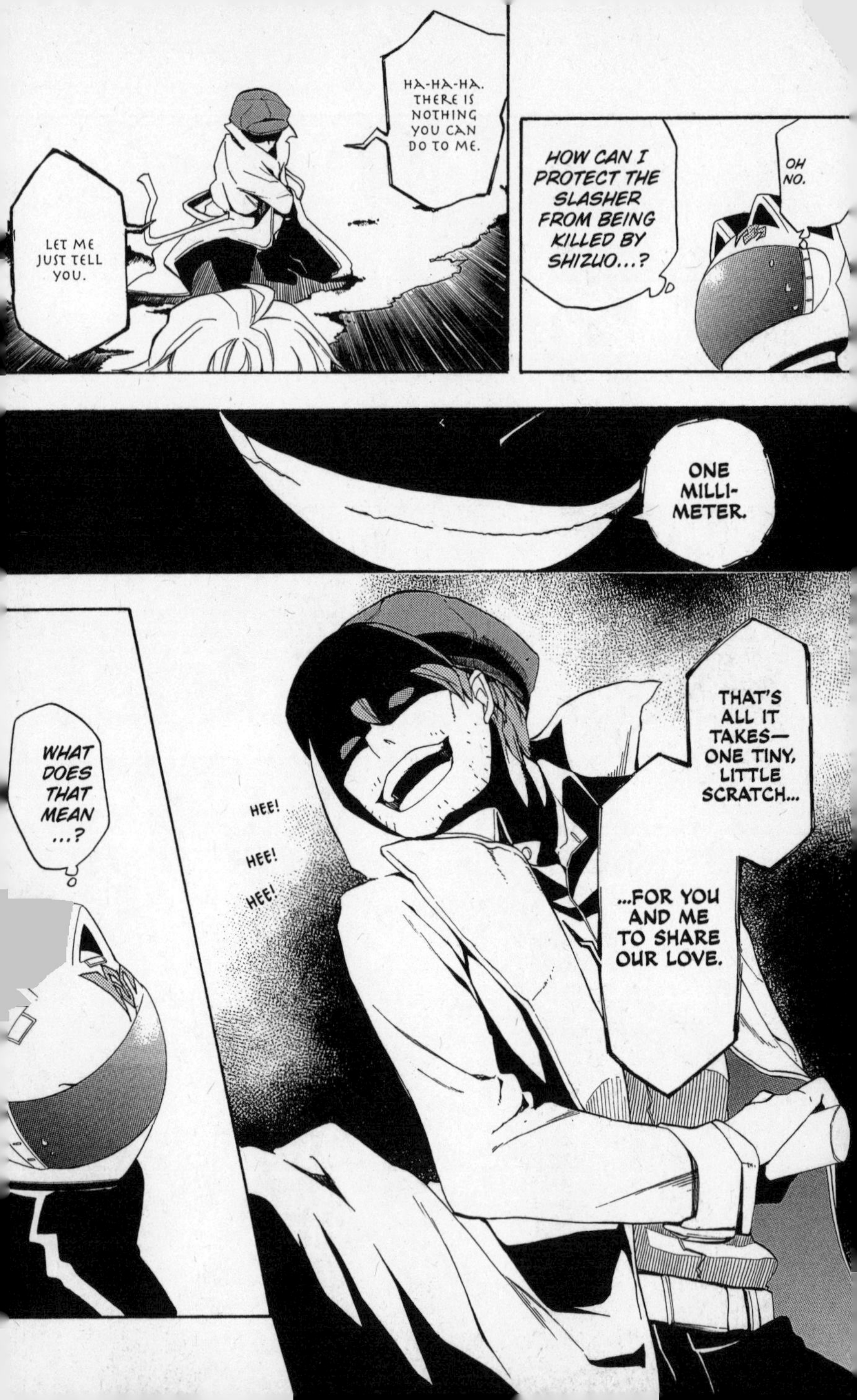
OH NO.
HOW CAN I PROTECT THE SLASHER FROM BEING KILLED BY SHIZUO...?
HA-HA-HA. THERE IS NOTHING YOU CAN DO TO ME.
LET ME JUST TELL YOU.
ONE MILLI-METER.
THAT'S ALL IT TAKES—ONE TINY, LITTLE SCRATCH...
...FOR YOU AND ME TO SHARE OUR LOVE.
HEE! HEE! HEE!
WHAT DOES THAT MEAN...?

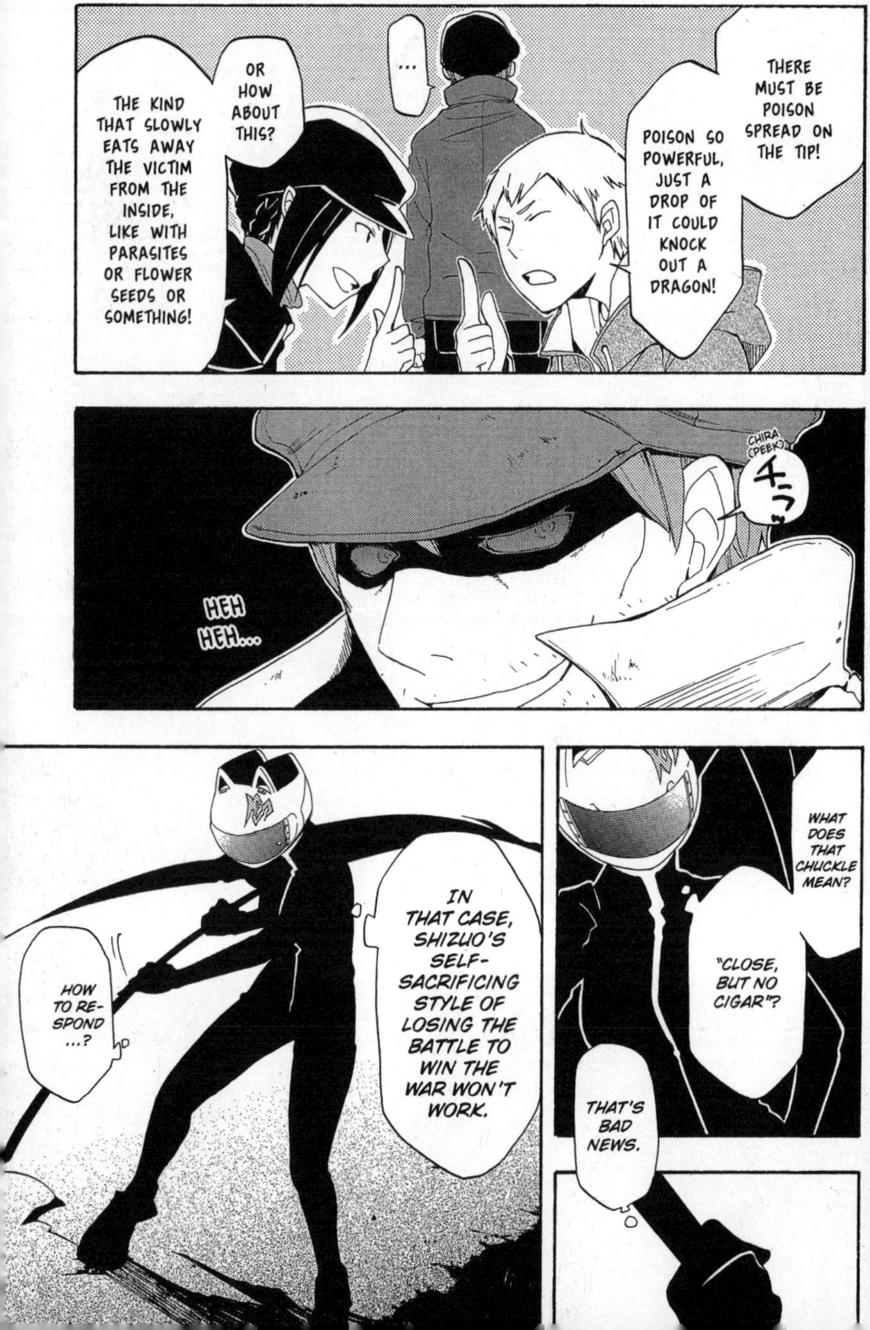
THERE MUST BE POISON SPREAD ON THE TIP!
POISON SO POWERFUL, JUST A DROP OF IT COULD KNOCK OUT A DRAGON!
...
OR HOW ABOUT THIS?
THE KIND THAT SLOWLY EATS AWAY THE VICTIM FROM THE INSIDE, LIKE WITH PARASITES OR FLOWER SEEDS OR SOMETHING!
CHIRA (PEEK)
チラッ
HEH HEH...
WHAT DOES THAT CHUCKLE MEAN?
"CLOSE, BUT NO CIGAR"?
THAT'S BAD NEWS.
IN THAT CASE, SHIZUO'S SELF-SACRIFICING STYLE OF LOSING THE BATTLE TO WIN THE WAR WON'T WORK.
HOW TO RE-SPOND ...?

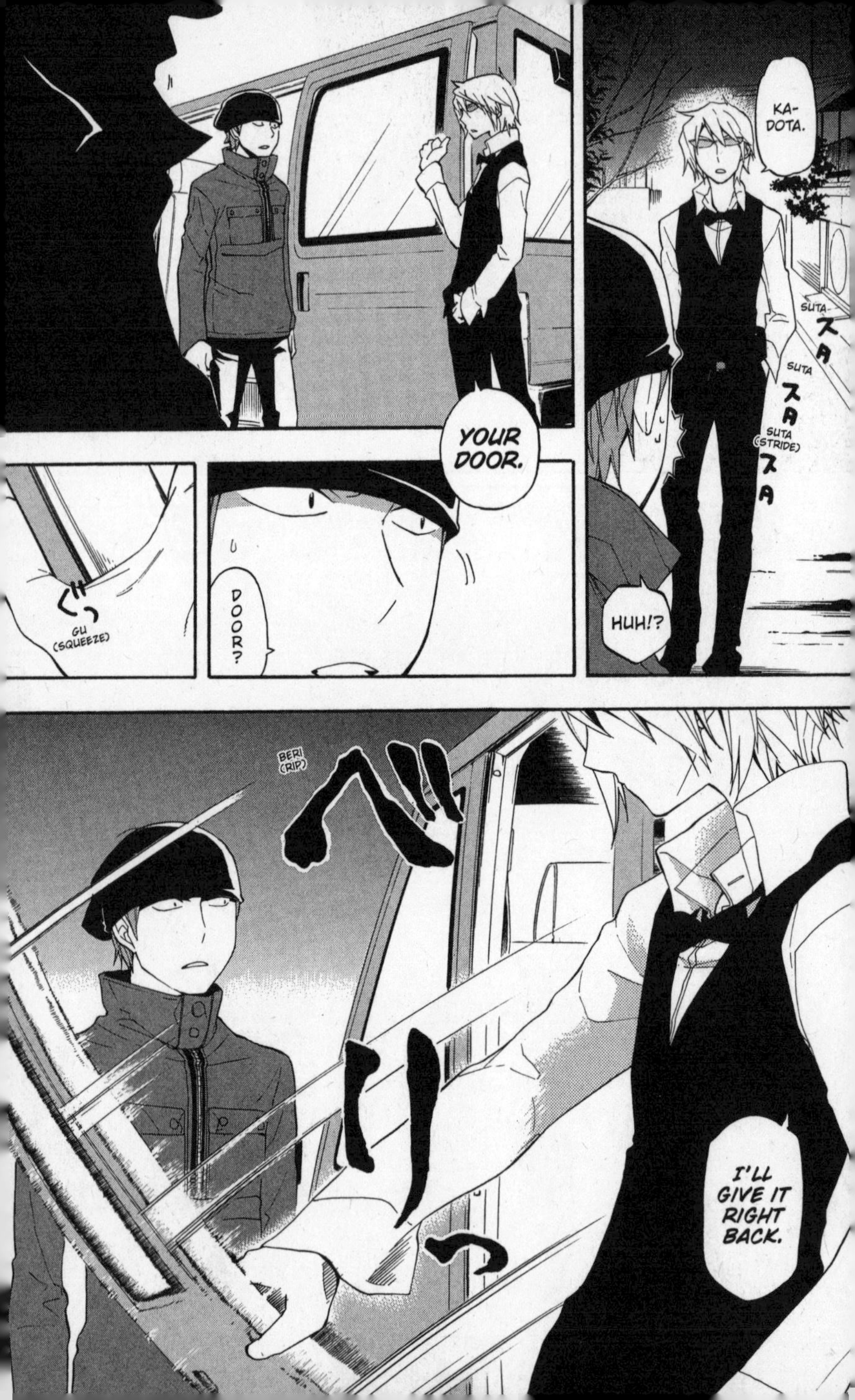
KA-DOTA.
SUTA
SUTA
SUTA (STRIDE)
HUH!?
YOUR DOOR.
DOOR?
GU (SQUEEZE)
BERI (RIP)
I'LL GIVE IT RIGHT BACK.

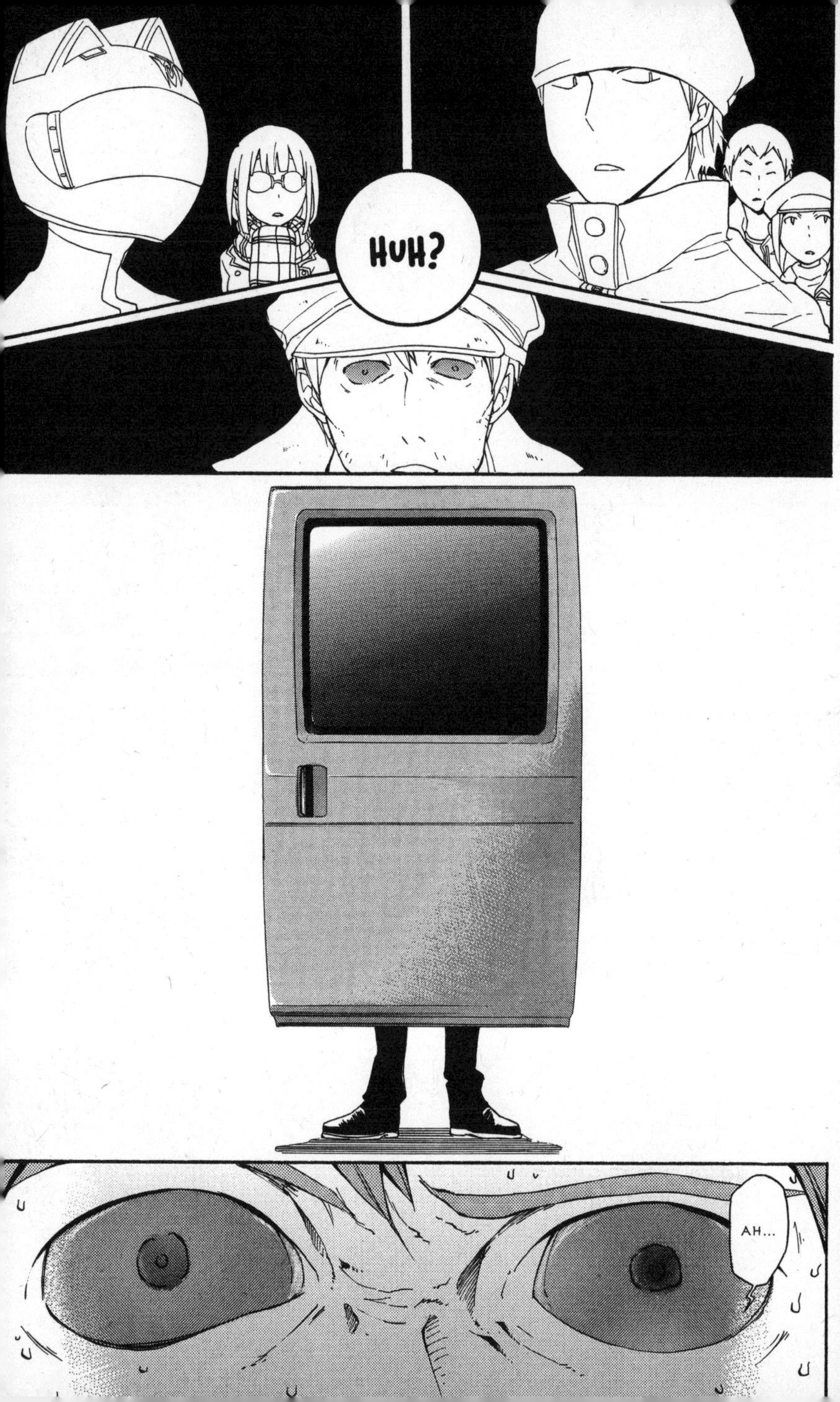
HUH?
AH...

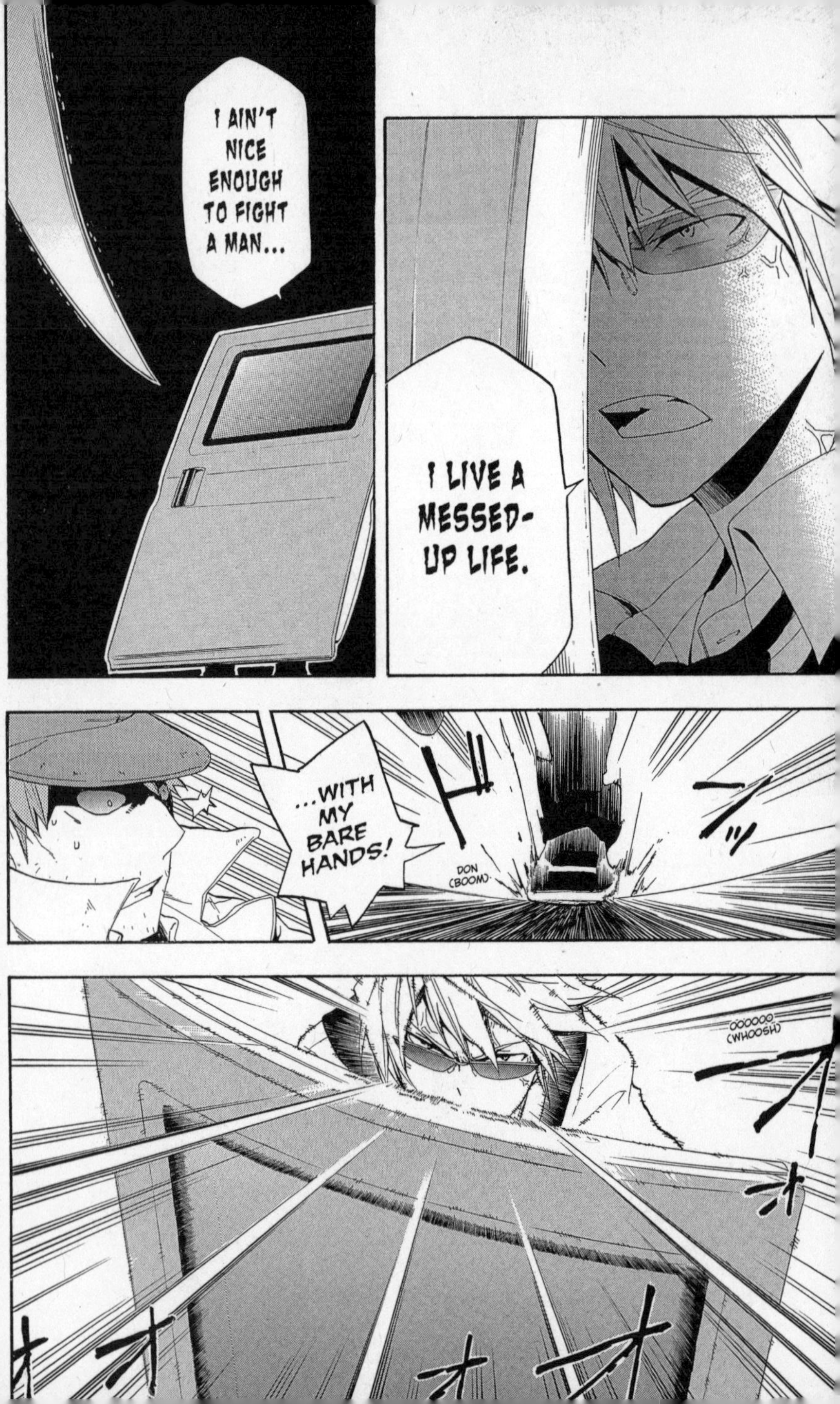
I LIVE A MESSED-UP LIFE.
I AIN'T NICE ENOUGH TO FIGHT A MAN...
DON (BOOM)
...WITH MY BARE HANDS!
OOOOOO (WHOOSH)

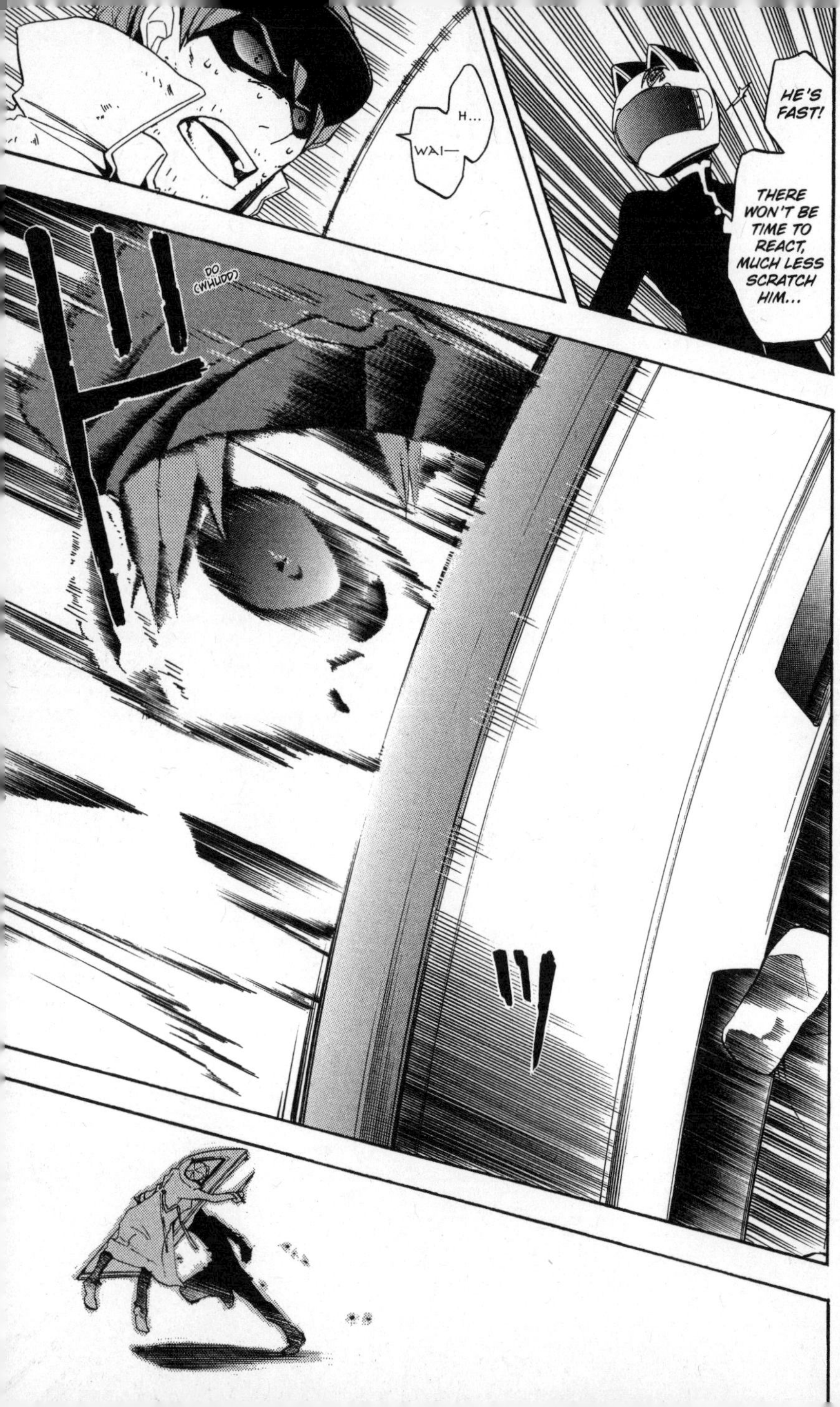
HE'S FAST!
THERE WON'T BE TIME TO REACT, MUCH LESS SCRATCH HIM...
H... WAI—
DO (WHUDD)

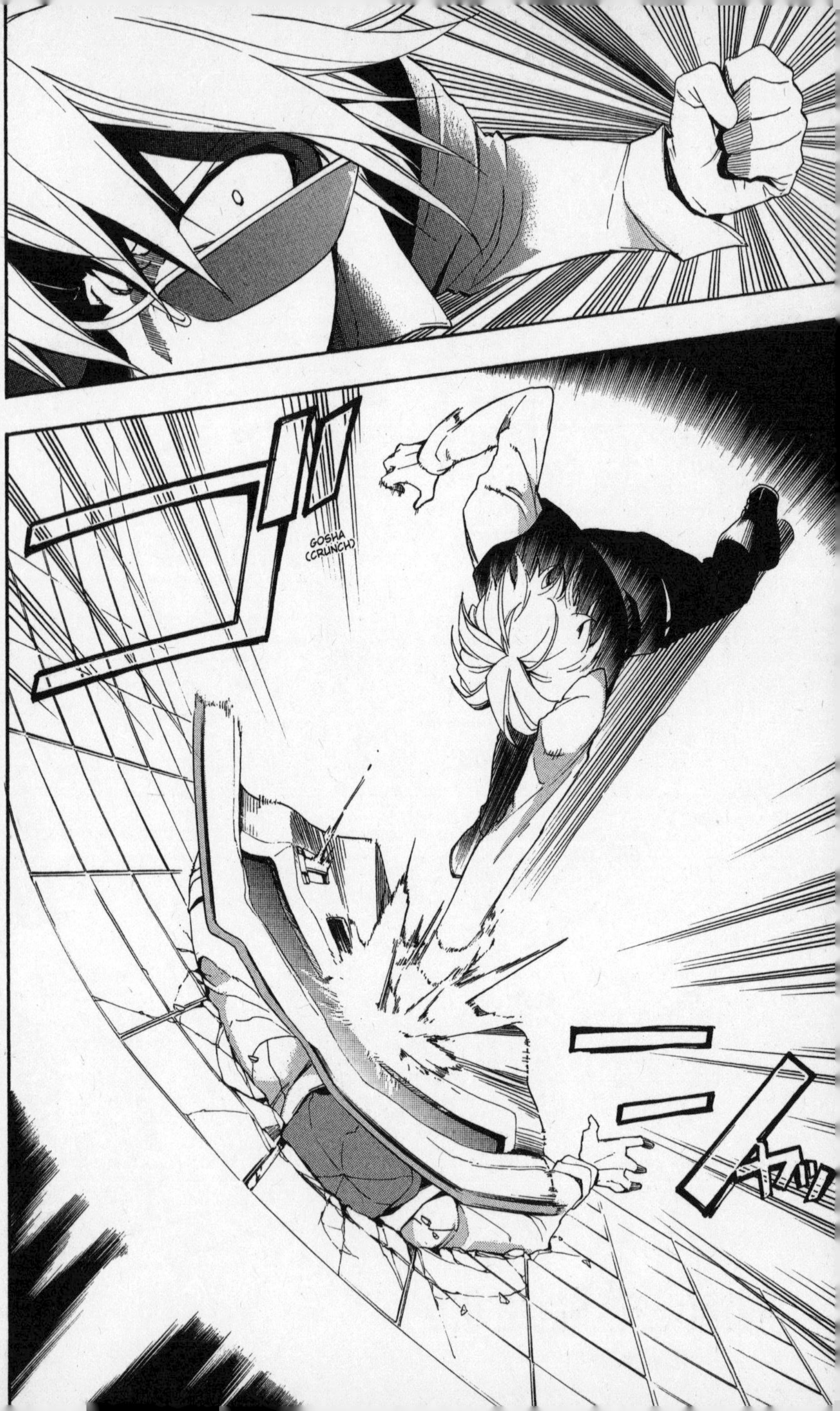
GOSHA (CRUNCH)

Durarara!! Saika Arc

DRRR!!

CHAPTER 9: BLADE FLASH, RED SHADOW

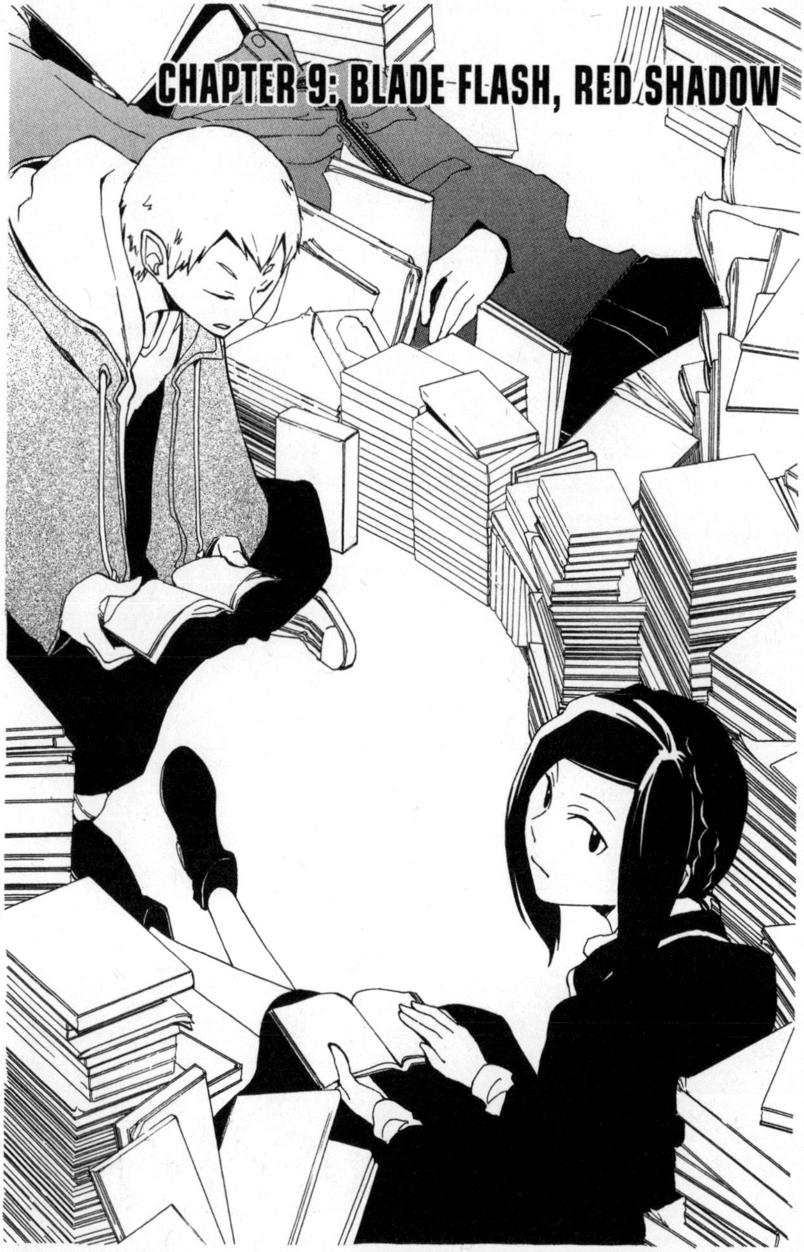

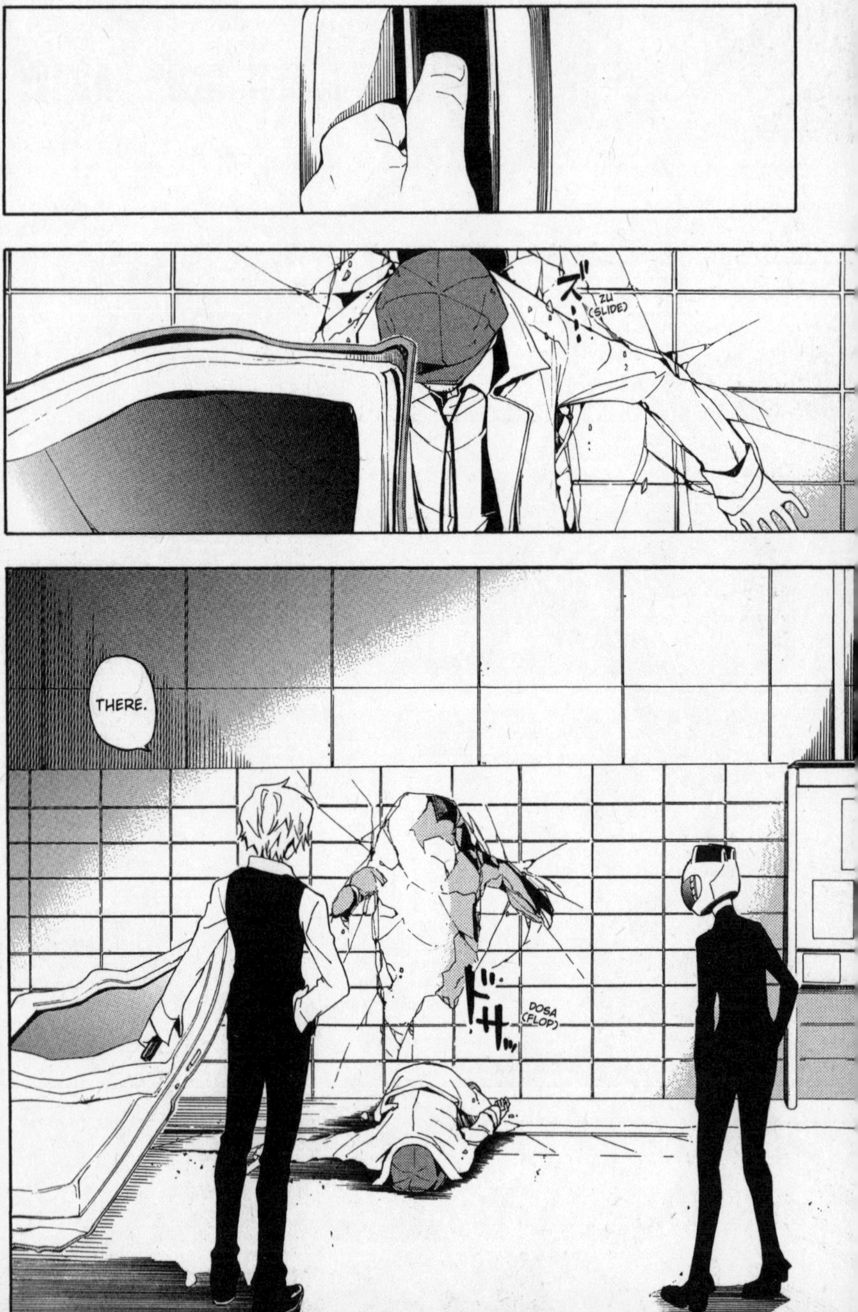
ズ…
ZU (SLIDE)
THERE.
ドサッ
DOSA (FLOP)

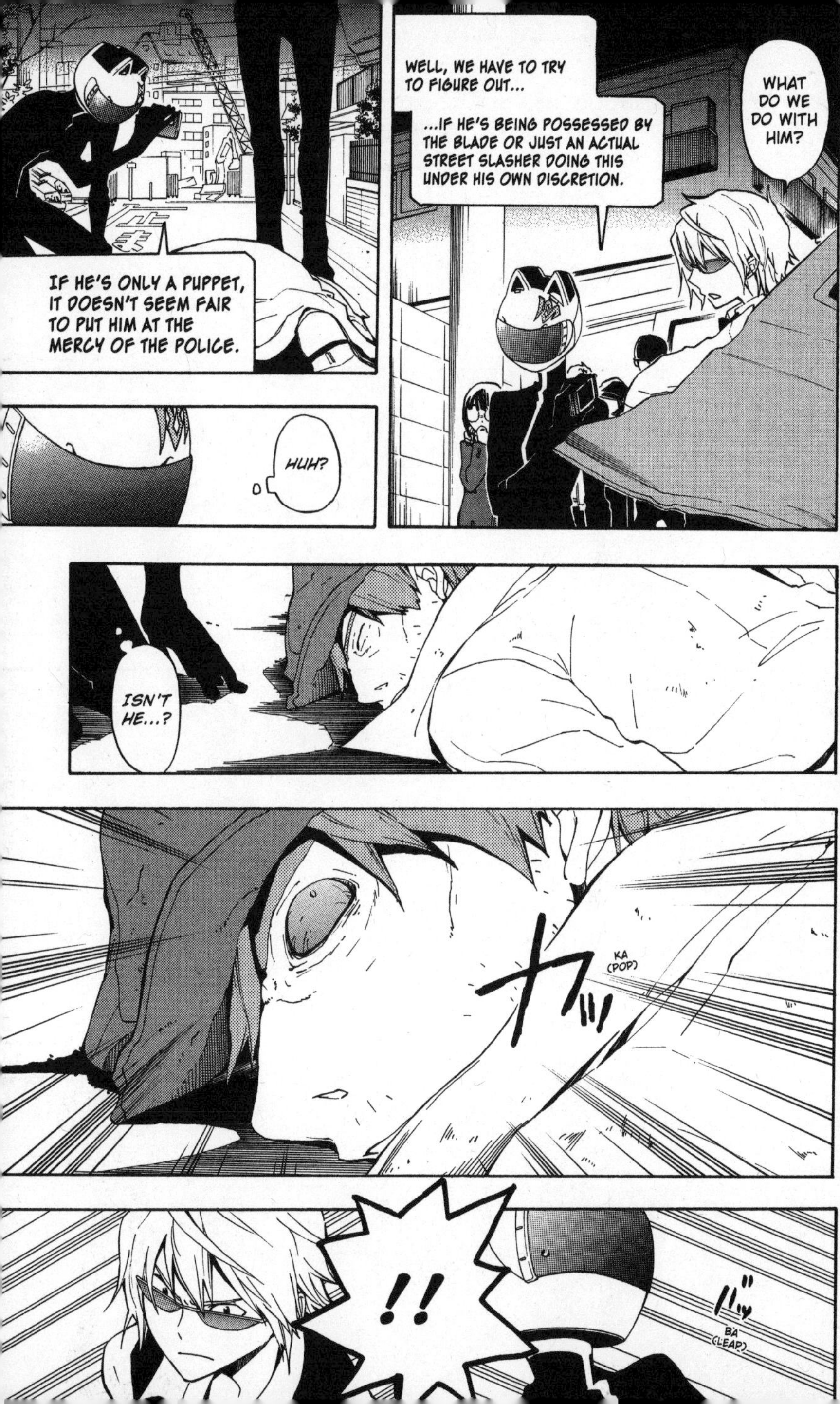
WHAT DO WE DO WITH HIM?
WELL, WE HAVE TO TRY TO FIGURE OUT...
...IF HE'S BEING POSSESSED BY THE BLADE OR JUST AN ACTUAL STREET SLASHER DOING THIS UNDER HIS OWN DISCRETION.
IF HE'S ONLY A PUPPET, IT DOESN'T SEEM FAIR TO PUT HIM AT THE MERCY OF THE POLICE.
HUH?
ISN'T HE...?
KA (POP)
!!
BA (LEAP)

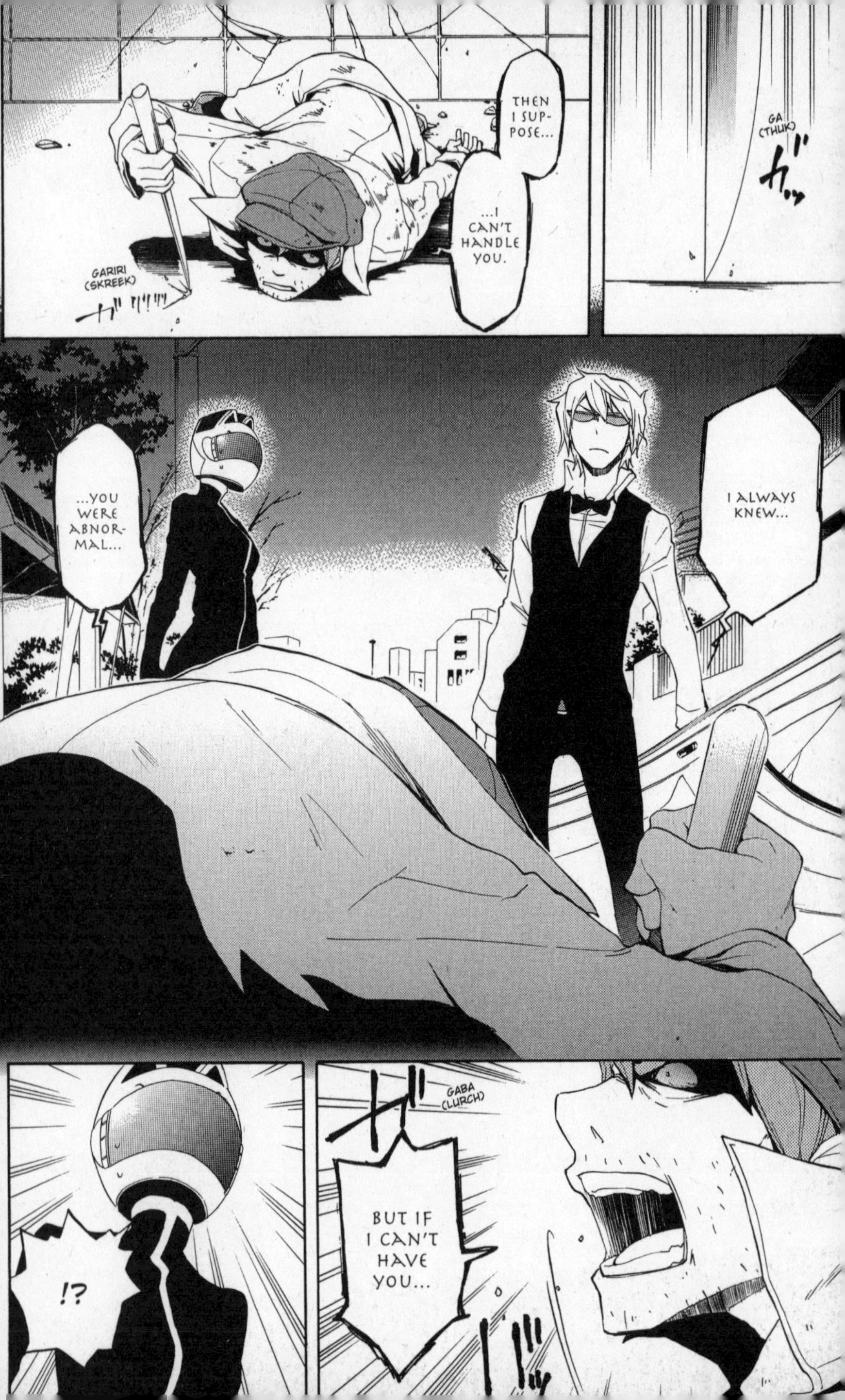
GA (THUK)
THEN I SUPPOSE...
...I CAN'T HANDLE YOU.
GARIRI (SKREEK)
I ALWAYS KNEW...
...YOU WERE ABNORMAL...
GABA (LURCH)
BUT IF I CAN'T HAVE YOU...
!?

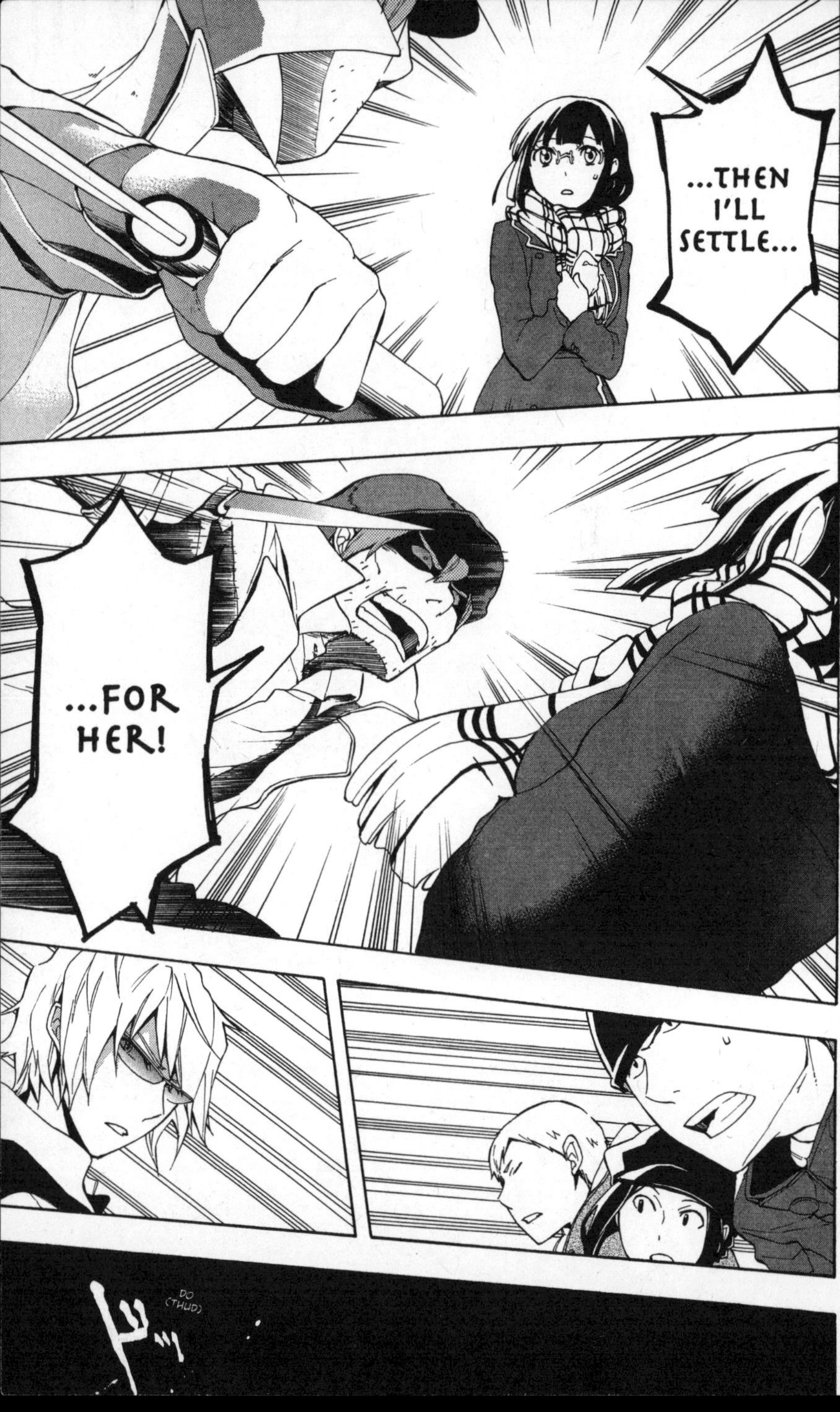
...THEN I'LL SETTLE...
...FOR HER!
DO (THUD)

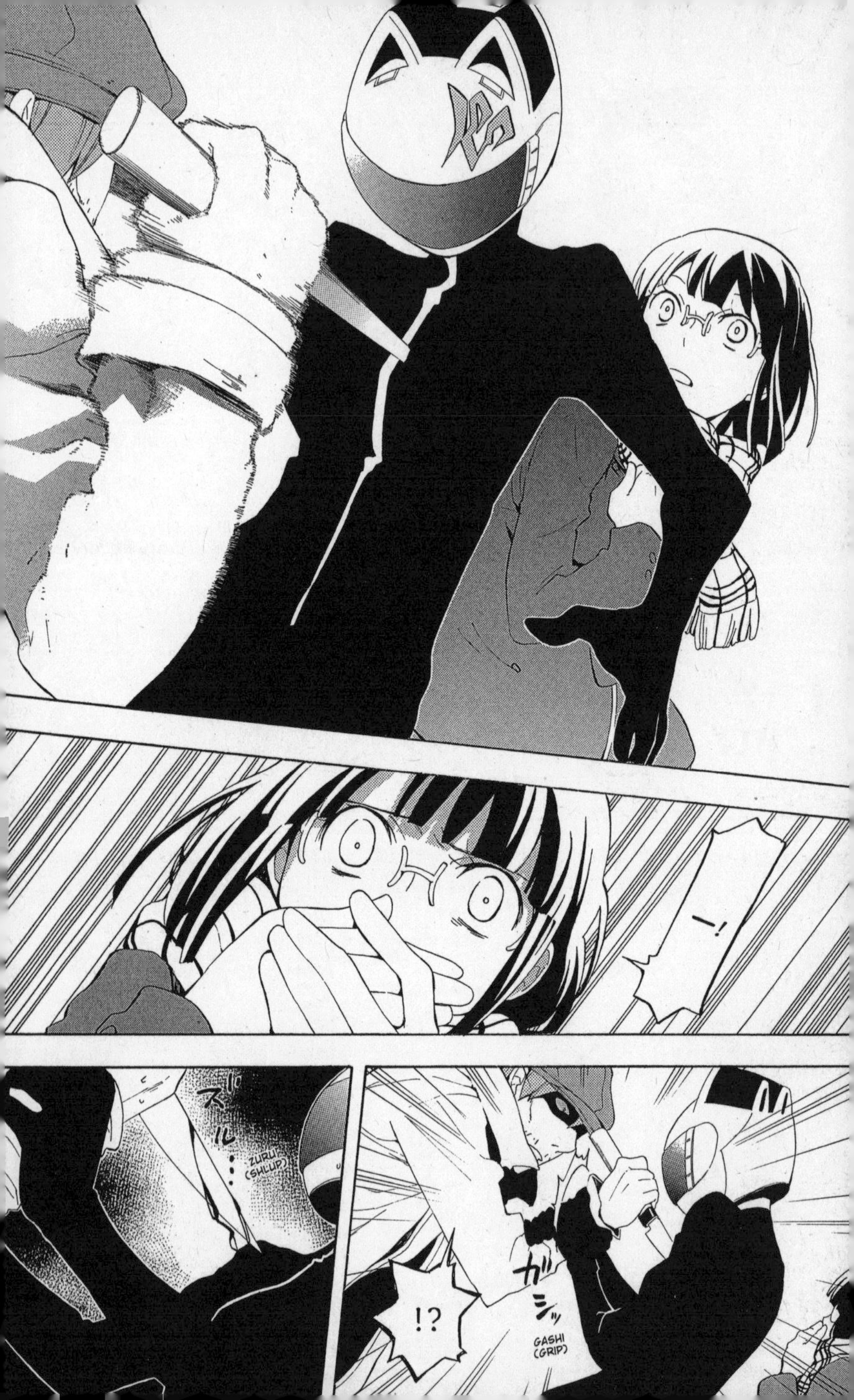
—!
ガシッ
GASHI (GRIP)
!?
ズル…
ZURU (SHLUP)

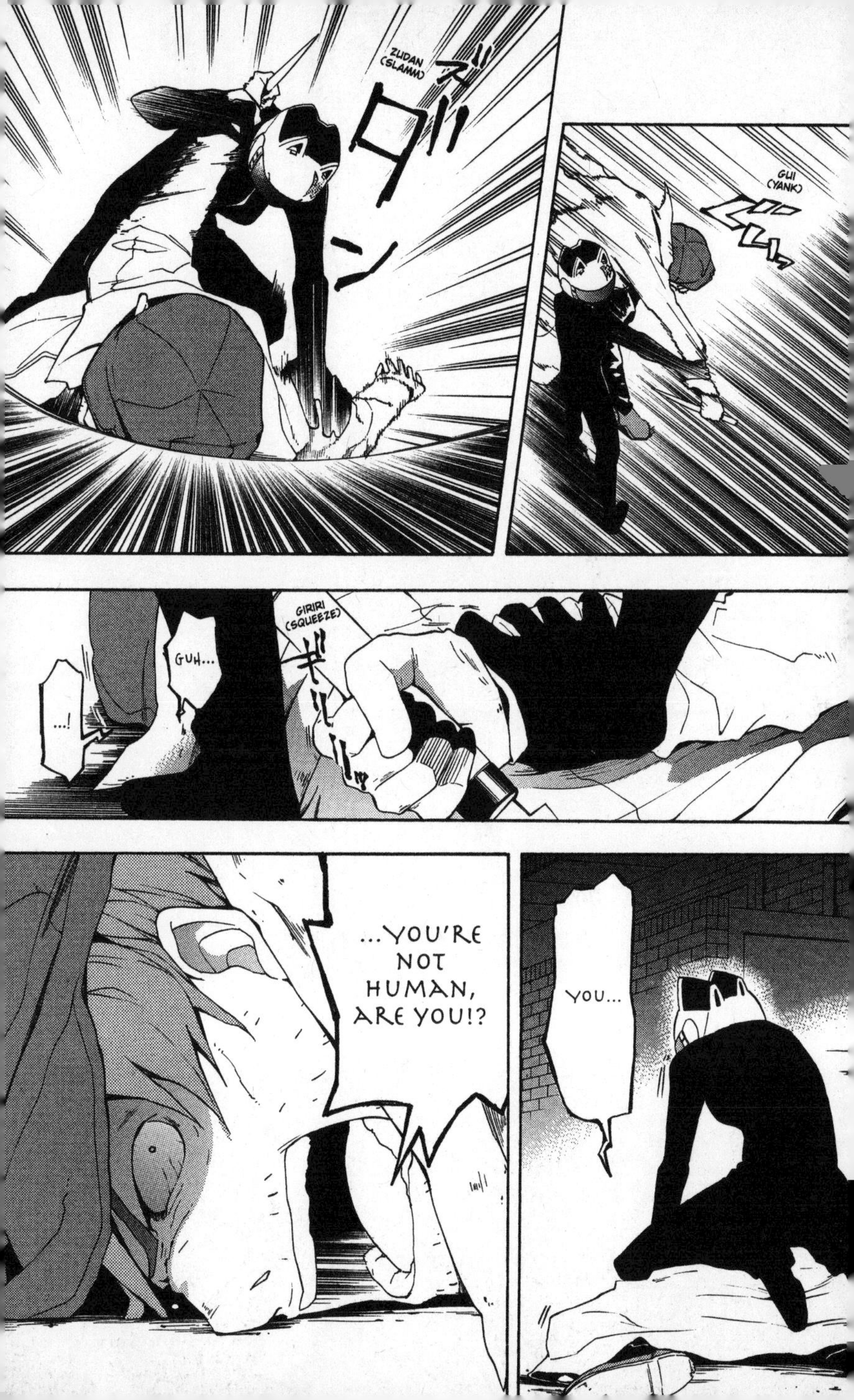
GUI (YANK)
ZUDAN (SLAMM)
GIRIRI (SQUEEZE)
GUH...
...!
YOU...
...YOU'RE NOT HUMAN, ARE YOU!?

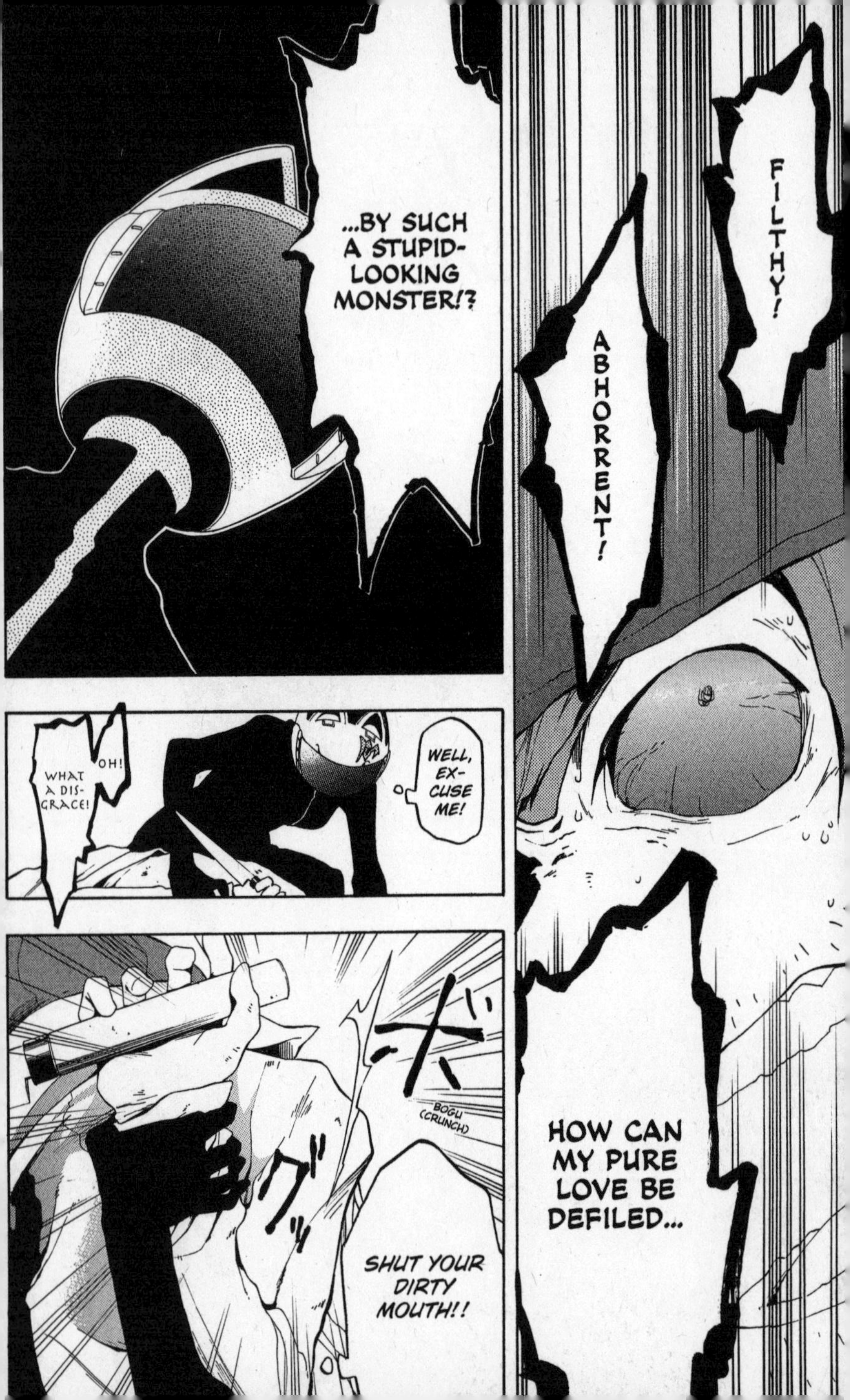
FILTHY!
ABHORRENT!
HOW CAN MY PURE LOVE BE DEFILED...
...BY SUCH A STUPID-LOOKING MONSTER!?
WELL, EX-CUSE ME!
OH!
WHAT A DIS-GRACE!
BOGU (CRUNCH)
SHUT YOUR DIRTY MOUTH!!

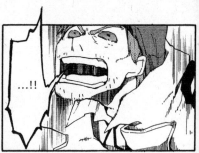

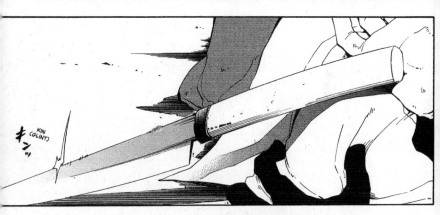

...!!
キンッ
KIN (GLINT)
NOW I JUST NEED TO KEEP THE WEAPON AWAY, TIE HIM UP, AND WAIT FOR HIM TO REGAIN CONSCIOUS-NESS.
IF HE WAS JUST BEING POS-SESSED BY THE BLADE...
...THEN HE'S ONLY A VICTIM.
THE MOST SUR-PRISING THING...
...SAIKA IS ACTUALLY A KITCHEN KNIFE?

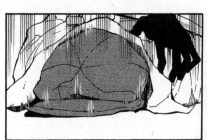

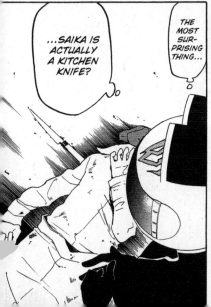

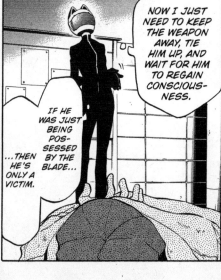

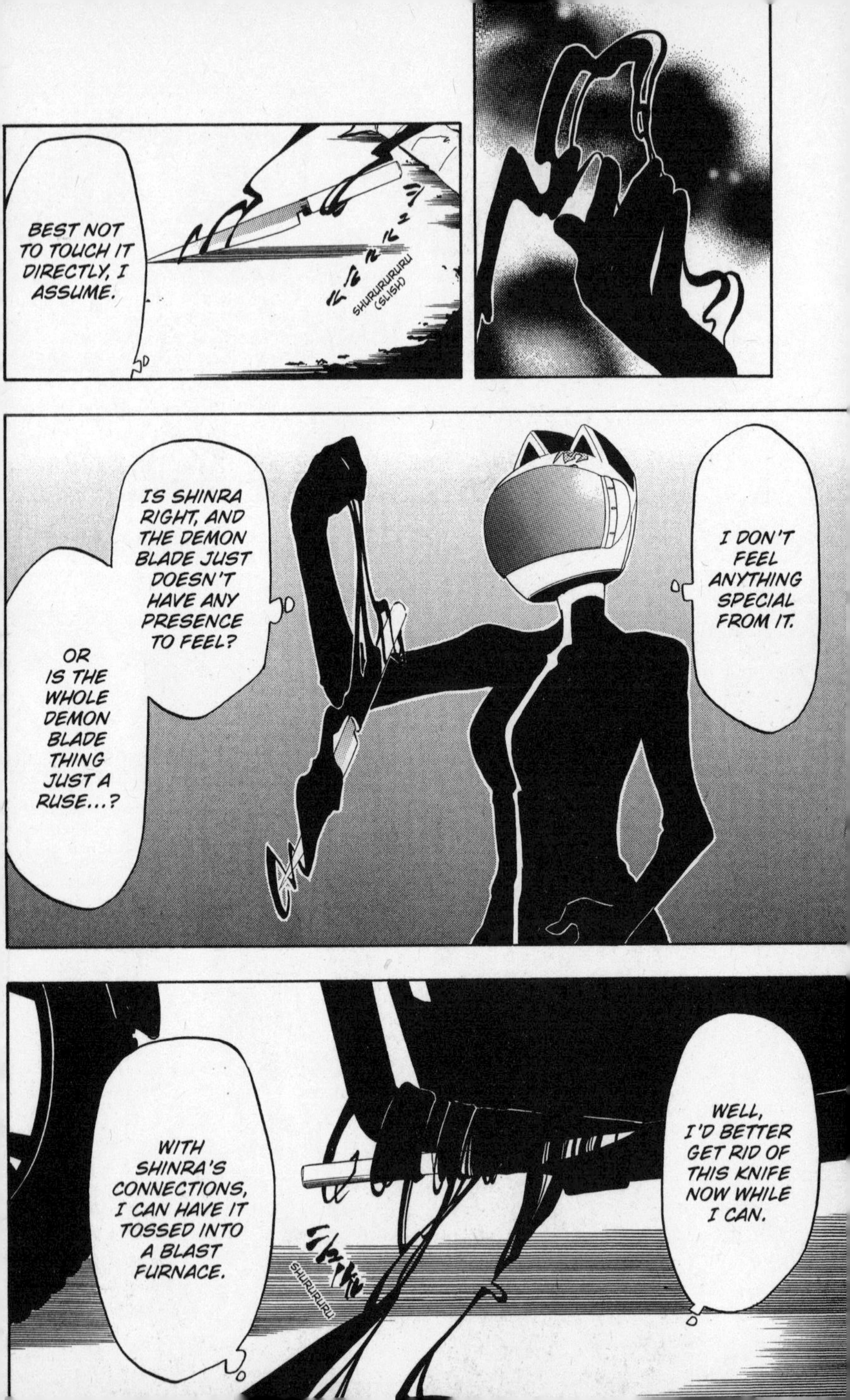
BEST NOT TO TOUCH IT DIRECTLY, I ASSUME.
SHURURURU (SLISH)
I DON'T FEEL ANYTHING SPECIAL FROM IT.
IS SHINRA RIGHT, AND THE DEMON BLADE JUST DOESN'T HAVE ANY PRESENCE TO FEEL?
OR IS THE WHOLE DEMON BLADE THING JUST A RUSE...?
WELL, I'D BETTER GET RID OF THIS KNIFE NOW WHILE I CAN.
SHURURURU
WITH SHINRA'S CONNECTIONS, I CAN HAVE IT TOSSED INTO A BLAST FURNACE.

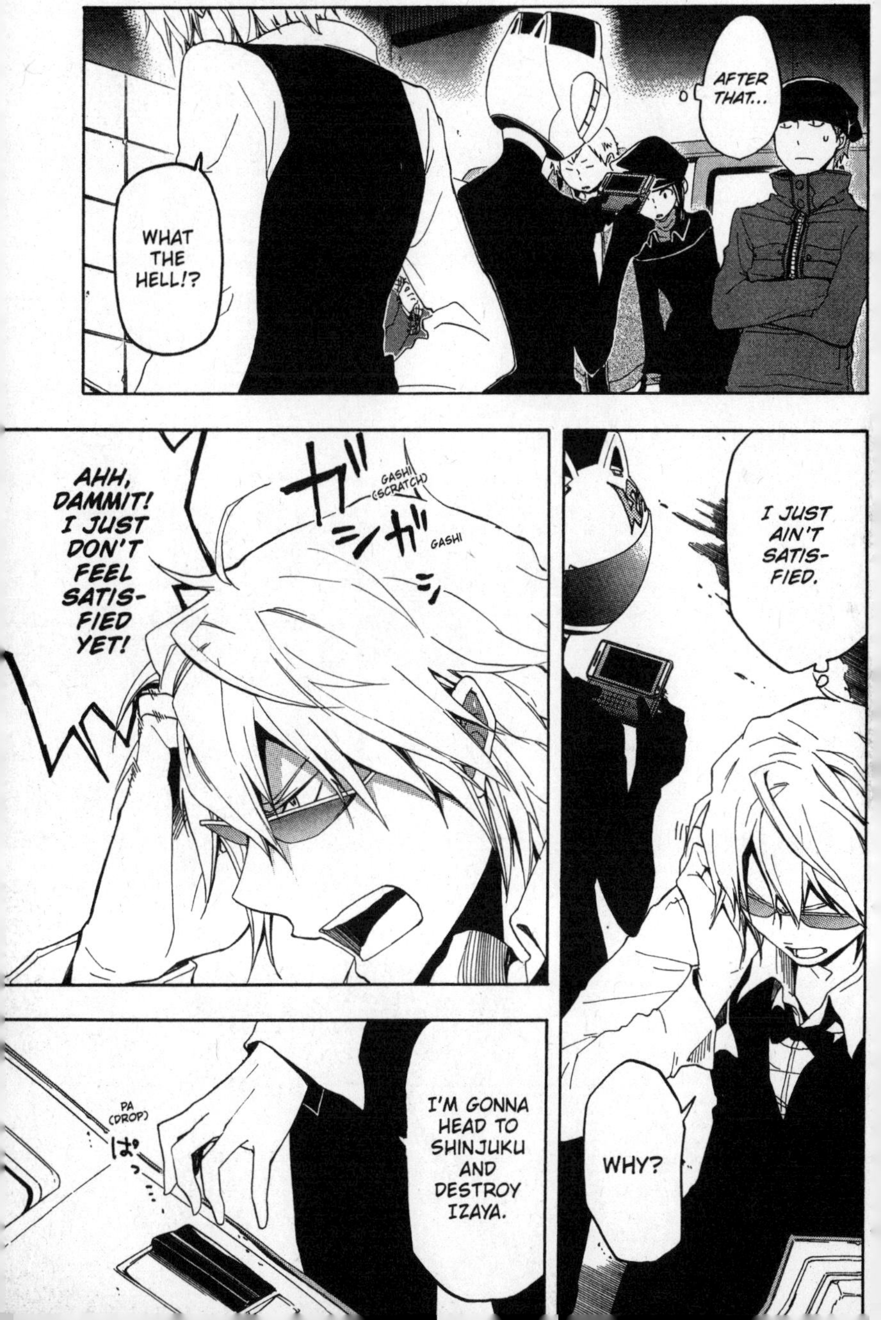
AFTER THAT...
WHAT THE HELL!?
I JUST AIN'T SATIS-FIED.
WHY?
AHH, DAMMIT! I JUST DON'T FEEL SATIS-FIED YET!
GASHI (SCRATCH)
GASHI
PA (DROP)
I'M GONNA HEAD TO SHINJUKU AND DESTROY IZAYA.

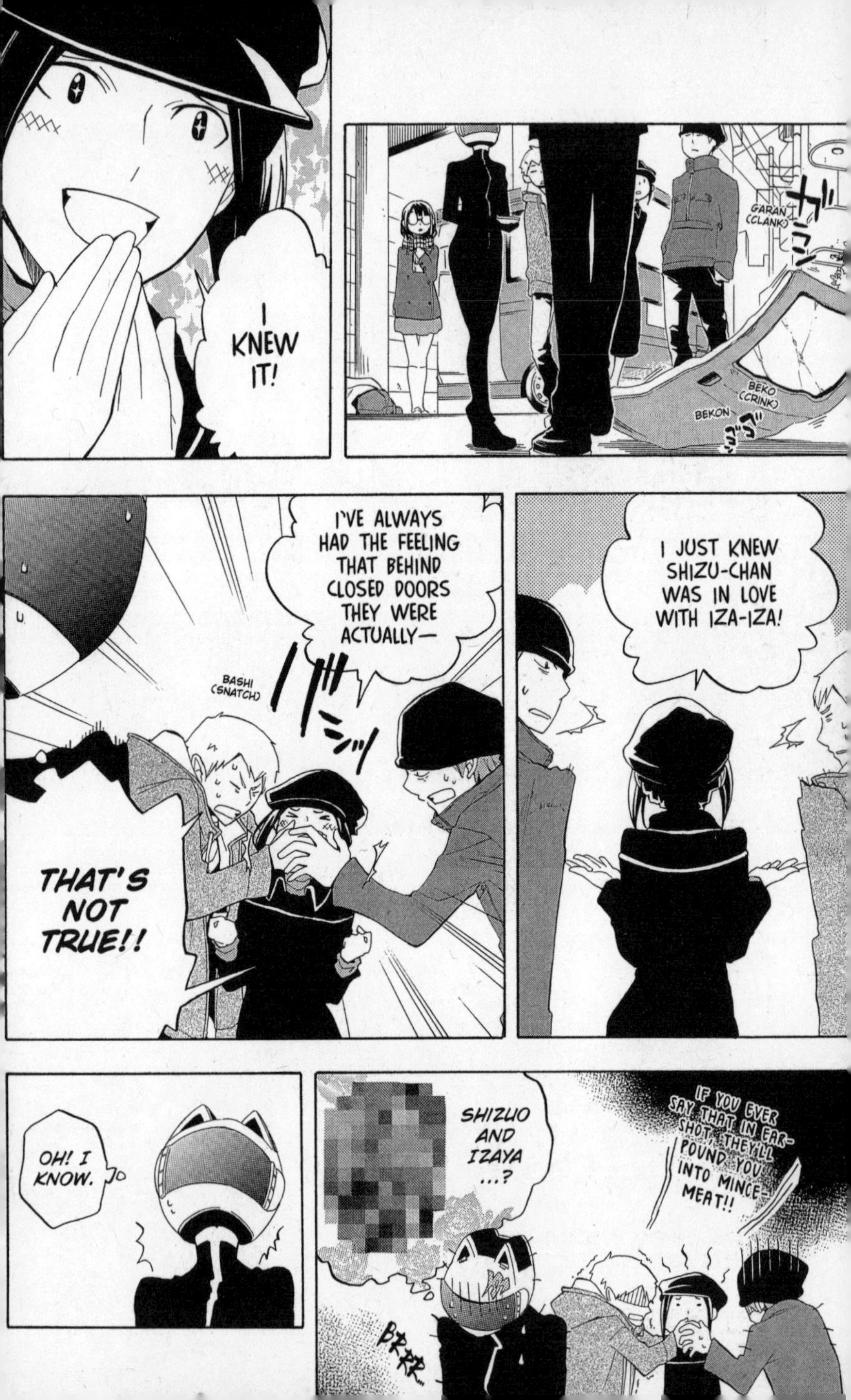
GARAN (CLANK)
BEKO (CRINK)
BEKON
I KNEW IT!
I JUST KNEW SHIZU-CHAN WAS IN LOVE WITH IZA-IZA!
I'VE ALWAYS HAD THE FEELING THAT BEHIND CLOSED DOORS THEY WERE ACTUALLY—
BASHI (SNATCH)
THAT'S NOT TRUE!!
SHIZUO AND IZAYA ...?
IF YOU EVER SAY THAT IN EAR-SHOT, THEY'LL POUND YOU INTO MINCE-MEAT!!
BRRR...
OH! I KNOW.

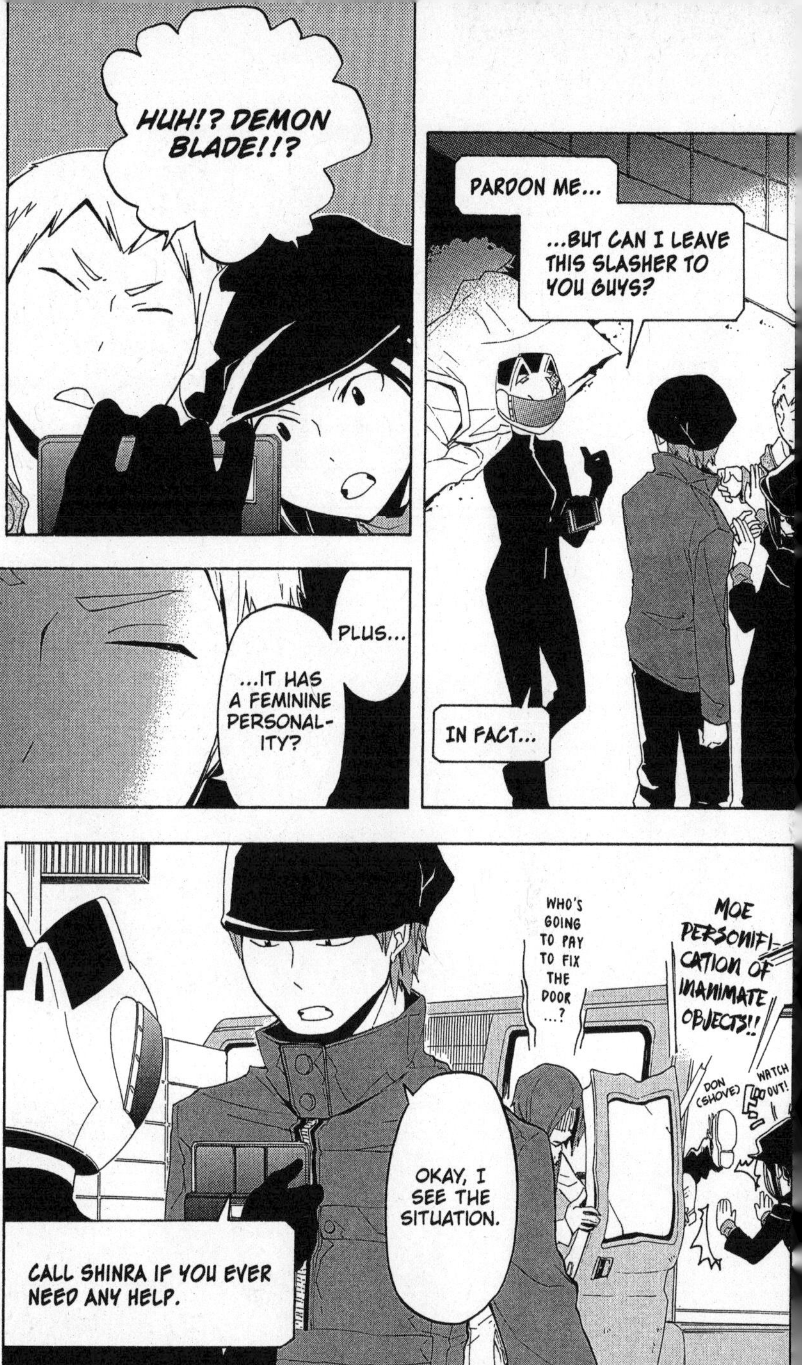
PARDON ME...
...BUT CAN I LEAVE THIS SLASHER TO YOU GUYS?
IN FACT...
HUH!? DEMON BLADE!!?
PLUS...
...IT HAS A FEMININE PERSONAL-ITY?
MOE PERSONIFI-CATION OF INANIMATE OBJECTS!!
WATCH OUT!
DON (SHOVE)
WHO'S GOING TO PAY TO FIX THE DOOR ...?
OKAY, I SEE THE SITUATION.
CALL SHINRA IF YOU EVER NEED ANY HELP.

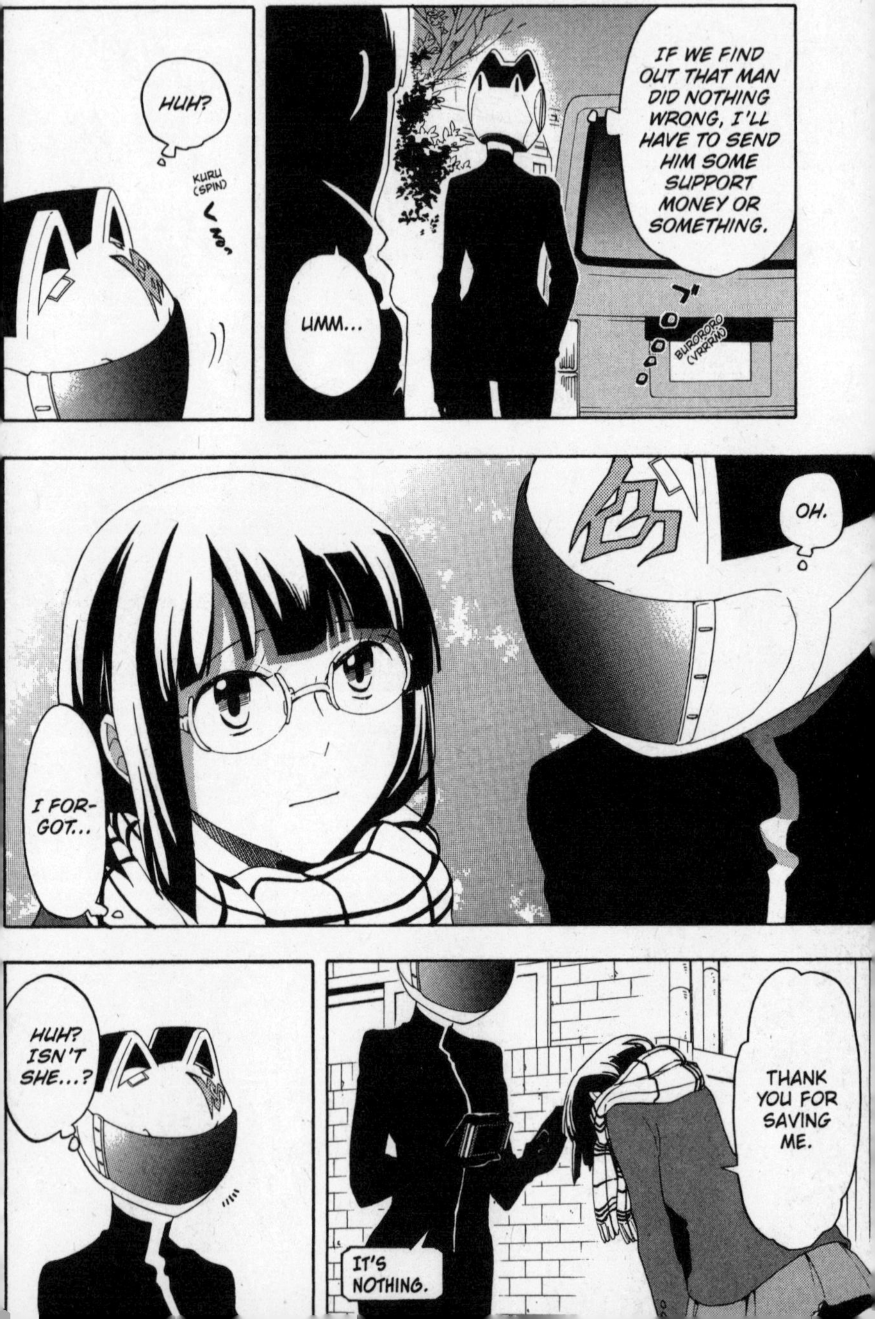
IF WE FIND OUT THAT MAN DID NOTHING WRONG, I'LL HAVE TO SEND HIM SOME SUPPORT MONEY OR SOMETHING.
BURORORO (VRRRN)
UMM...
HUH?
KURU (SPIN)
OH.
I FOR-GOT...
THANK YOU FOR SAVING ME.
IT'S NOTHING.
HUH? ISN'T SHE...?

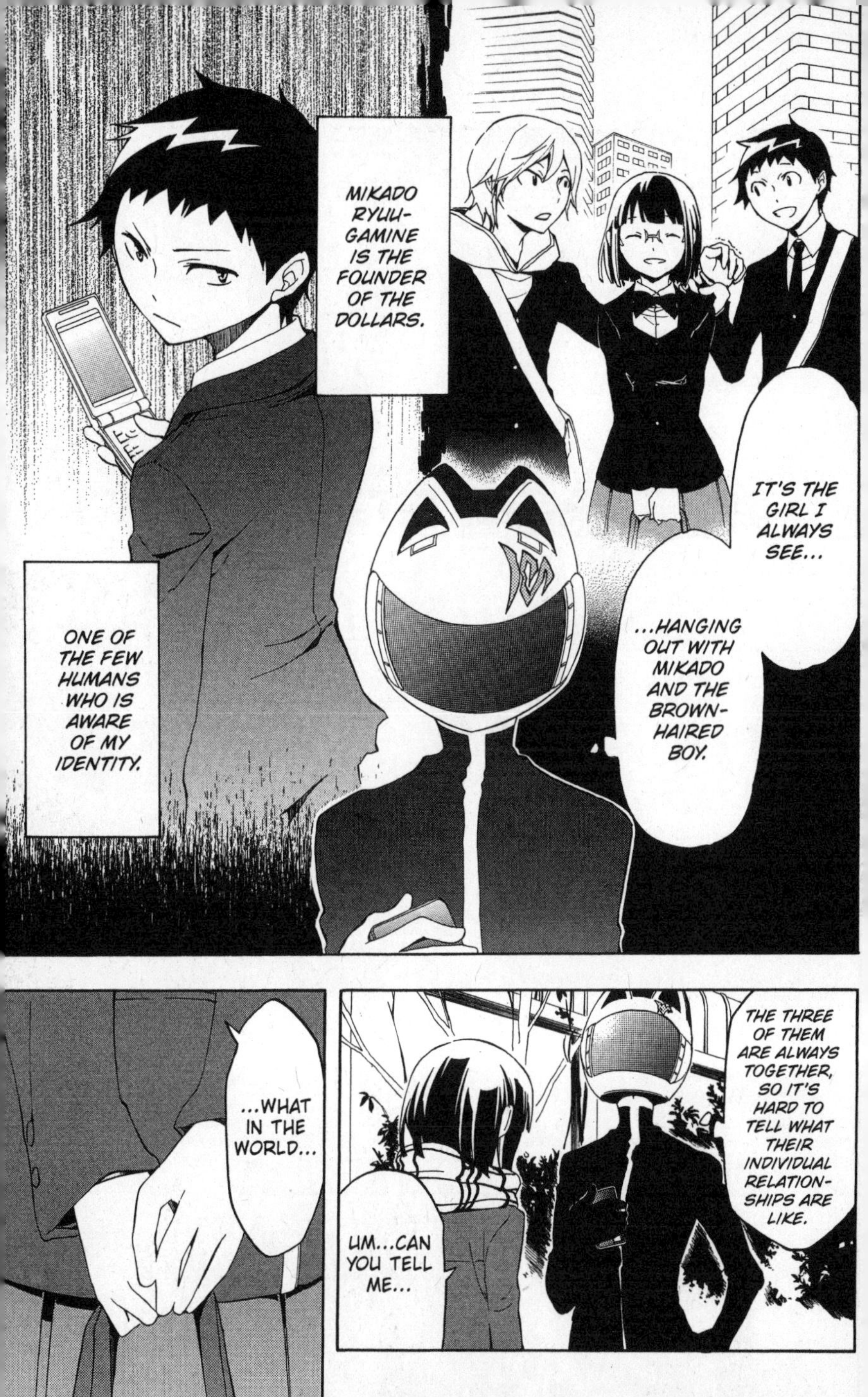
IT'S THE GIRL I ALWAYS SEE...
...HANGING OUT WITH MIKADO AND THE BROWN-HAIRED BOY.
MIKADO RYUU-GAMINE IS THE FOUNDER OF THE DOLLARS.
ONE OF THE FEW HUMANS WHO IS AWARE OF MY IDENTITY.
THE THREE OF THEM ARE ALWAYS TOGETHER, SO IT'S HARD TO TELL WHAT THEIR INDIVIDUAL RELATION-SHIPS ARE LIKE.
UM...CAN YOU TELL ME...
...WHAT IN THE WORLD...

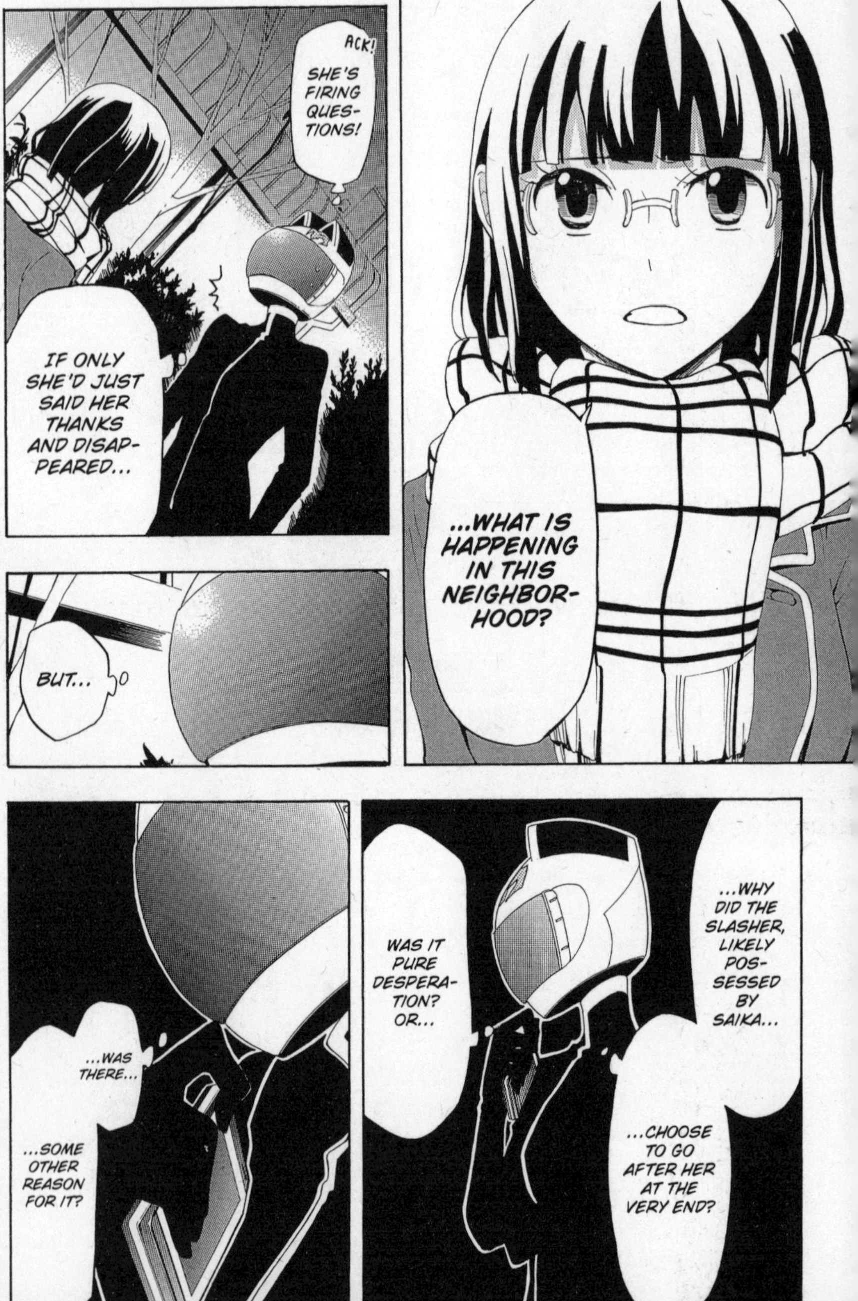
...WHAT IS HAPPENING IN THIS NEIGHBOR-HOOD?
ACK!
SHE'S FIRING QUES-TIONS!
IF ONLY SHE'D JUST SAID HER THANKS AND DISAP-PEARED...
BUT...
...WHY DID THE SLASHER, LIKELY POS-SESSED BY SAIKA...
...CHOOSE TO GO AFTER HER AT THE VERY END?
WAS IT PURE DESPERA-TION? OR...
...WAS THERE...
...SOME OTHER REASON FOR IT?

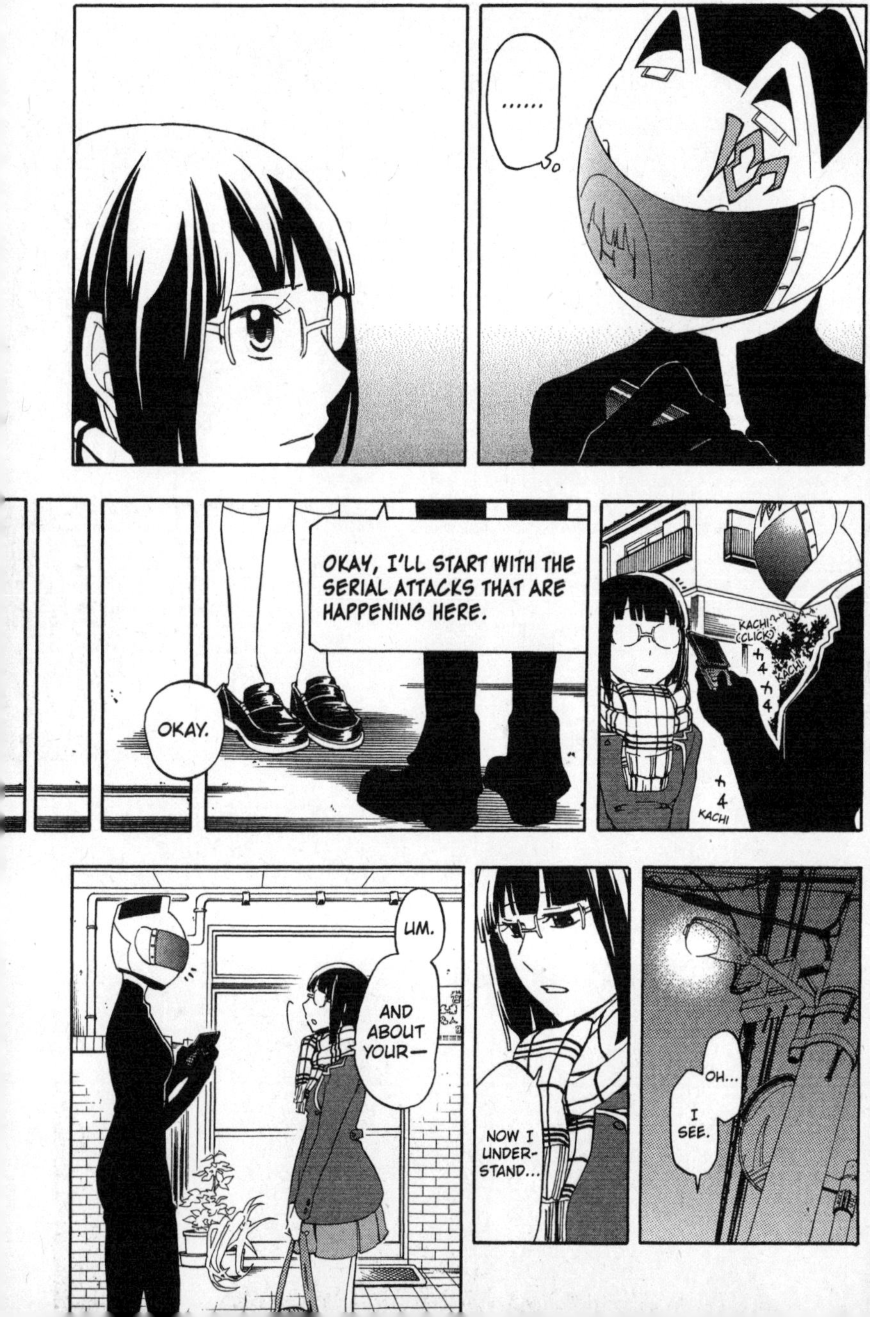
......
KACHI (CLICK)
KACHI
KACHI
OKAY, I'LL START WITH THE SERIAL ATTACKS THAT ARE HAPPENING HERE.
OKAY.
OH... I SEE.
NOW I UNDER-STAND...
UM.
AND ABOUT YOUR—

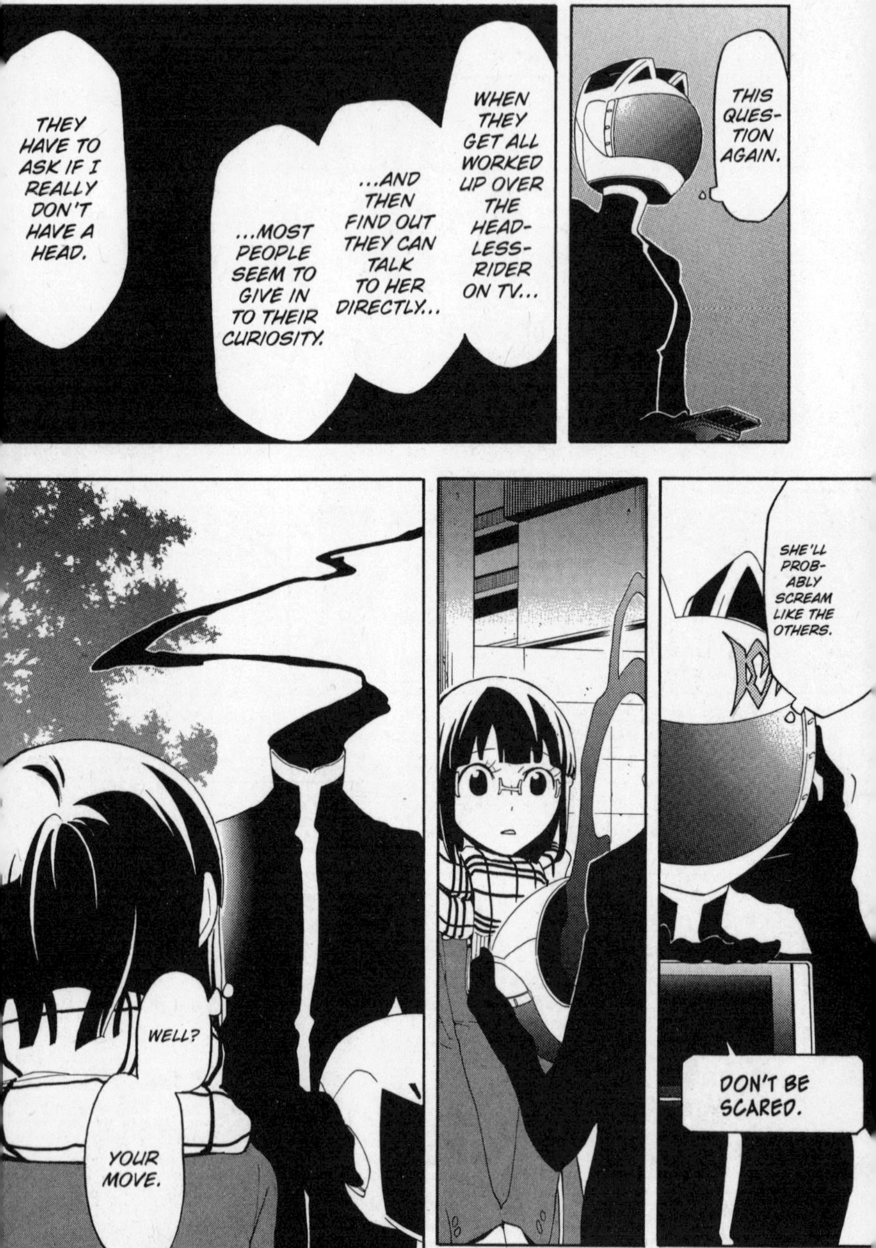
THIS QUESTION AGAIN.
WHEN THEY GET ALL WORKED UP OVER THE HEADLESS-RIDER ON TV...
...AND THEN FIND OUT THEY CAN TALK TO HER DIRECTLY...
...MOST PEOPLE SEEM TO GIVE IN TO THEIR CURIOSITY.
THEY HAVE TO ASK IF I REALLY DON'T HAVE A HEAD.
SHE'LL PROBABLY SCREAM LIKE THE OTHERS.
DON'T BE SCARED.
WELL?
YOUR MOVE.

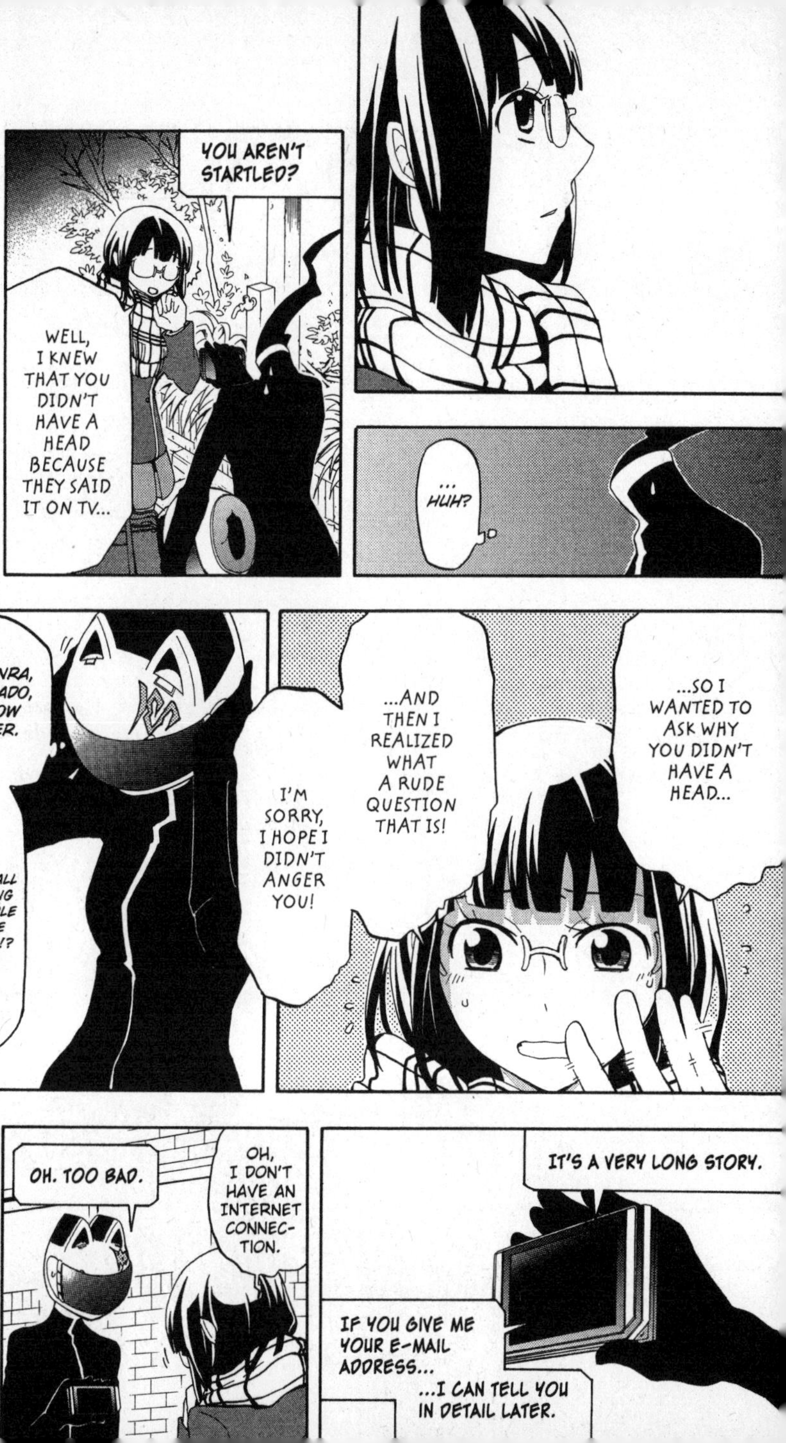
YOU AREN'T STARTLED?
WELL, I KNEW THAT YOU DIDN'T HAVE A HEAD BECAUSE THEY SAID IT ON TV...
...HUH?
...SO I WANTED TO ASK WHY YOU DIDN'T HAVE A HEAD...
...AND THEN I REALIZED WHAT A RUDE QUESTION THAT IS!
I'M SORRY, I HOPE I DIDN'T ANGER YOU!
SHINRA, MIKADO, NOW HER.
ARE ALL YOUNG PEOPLE LIKE THIS!?
IT'S A VERY LONG STORY.
IF YOU GIVE ME YOUR E-MAIL ADDRESS...
...I CAN TELL YOU IN DETAIL LATER.
OH, I DON'T HAVE AN INTERNET CONNECTION.
OH. TOO BAD.

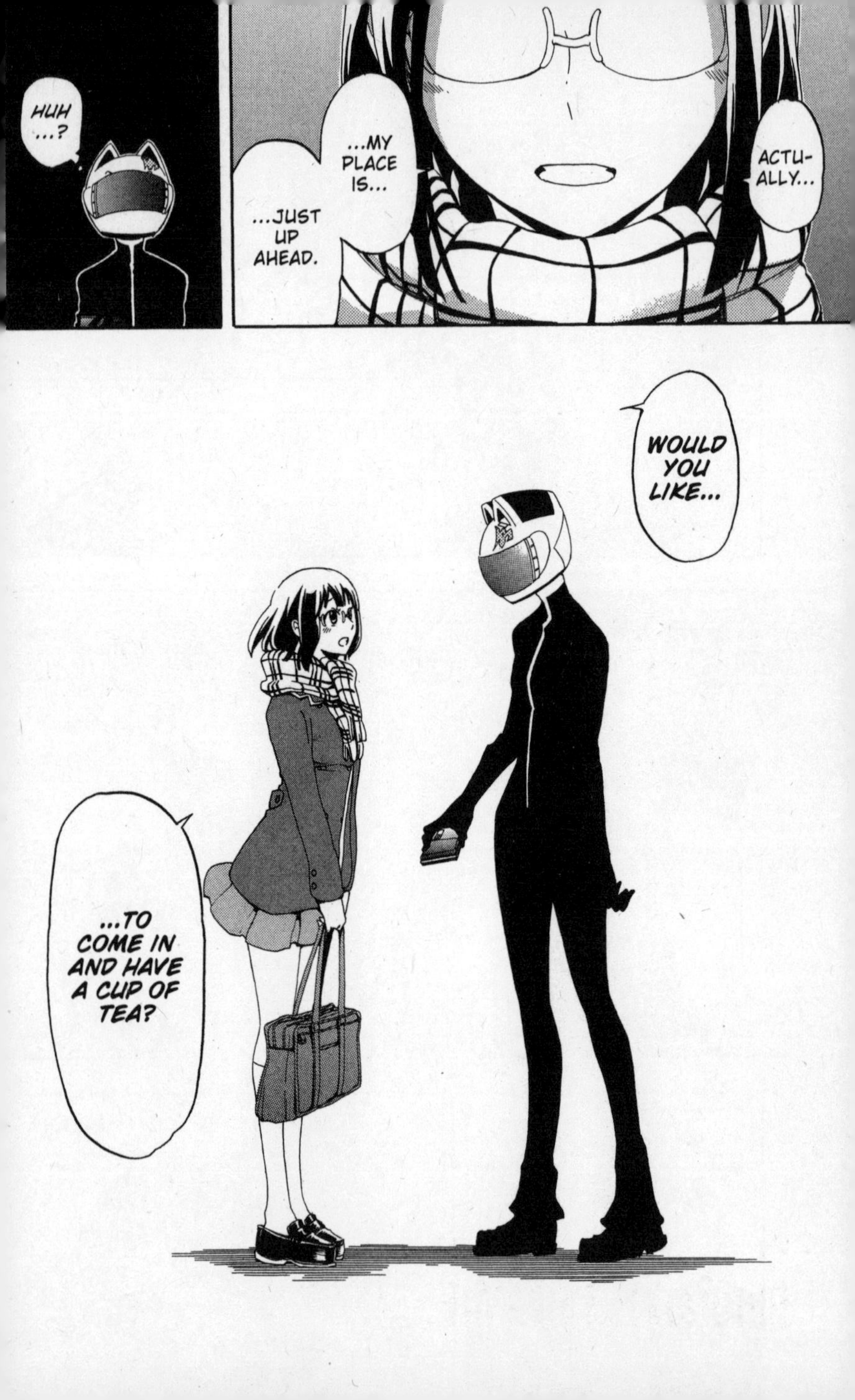
ACTU-ALLY...
...MY PLACE IS...
...JUST UP AHEAD.
HUH ...?
WOULD YOU LIKE...
...TO COME IN AND HAVE A CUP OF TEA?

Durarara!! Saika Arc

DRRR!!

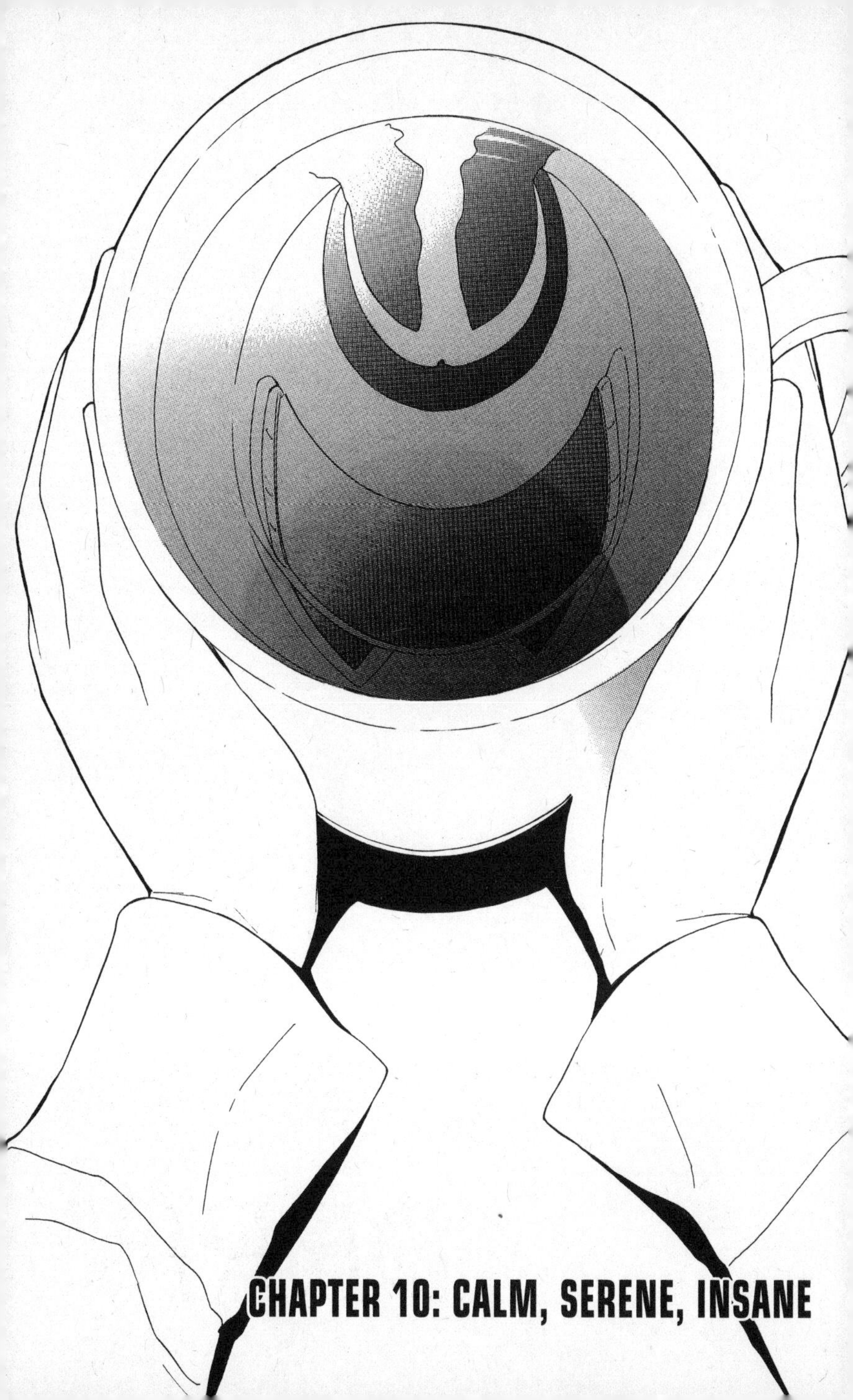

CHAPTER 10: CALM, SERENE, INSANE

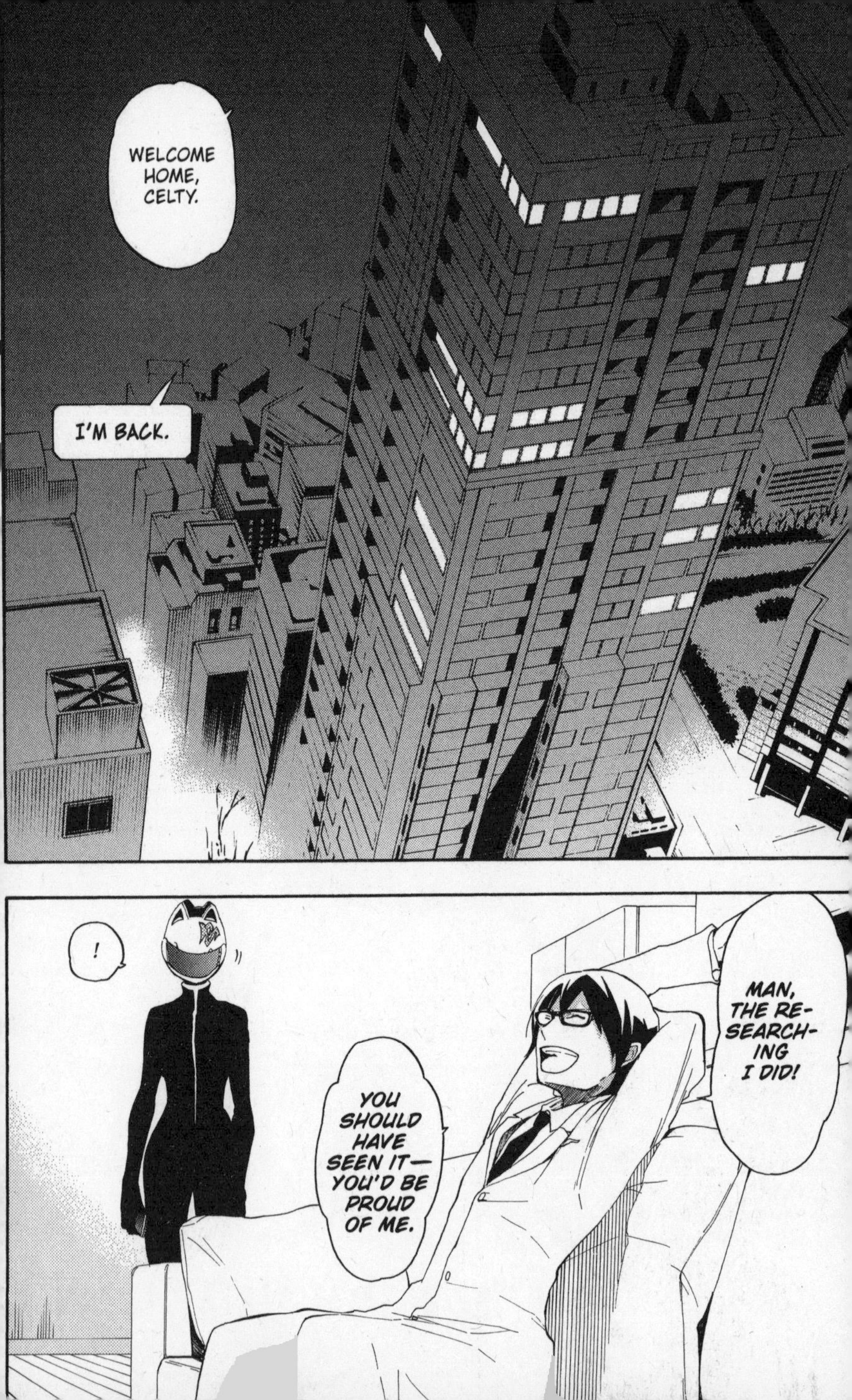
WELCOME HOME, CELTY.
I'M BACK.
MAN, THE RE-SEARCHING I DID!
YOU SHOULD HAVE SEEN IT—YOU'D BE PROUD OF ME.
!

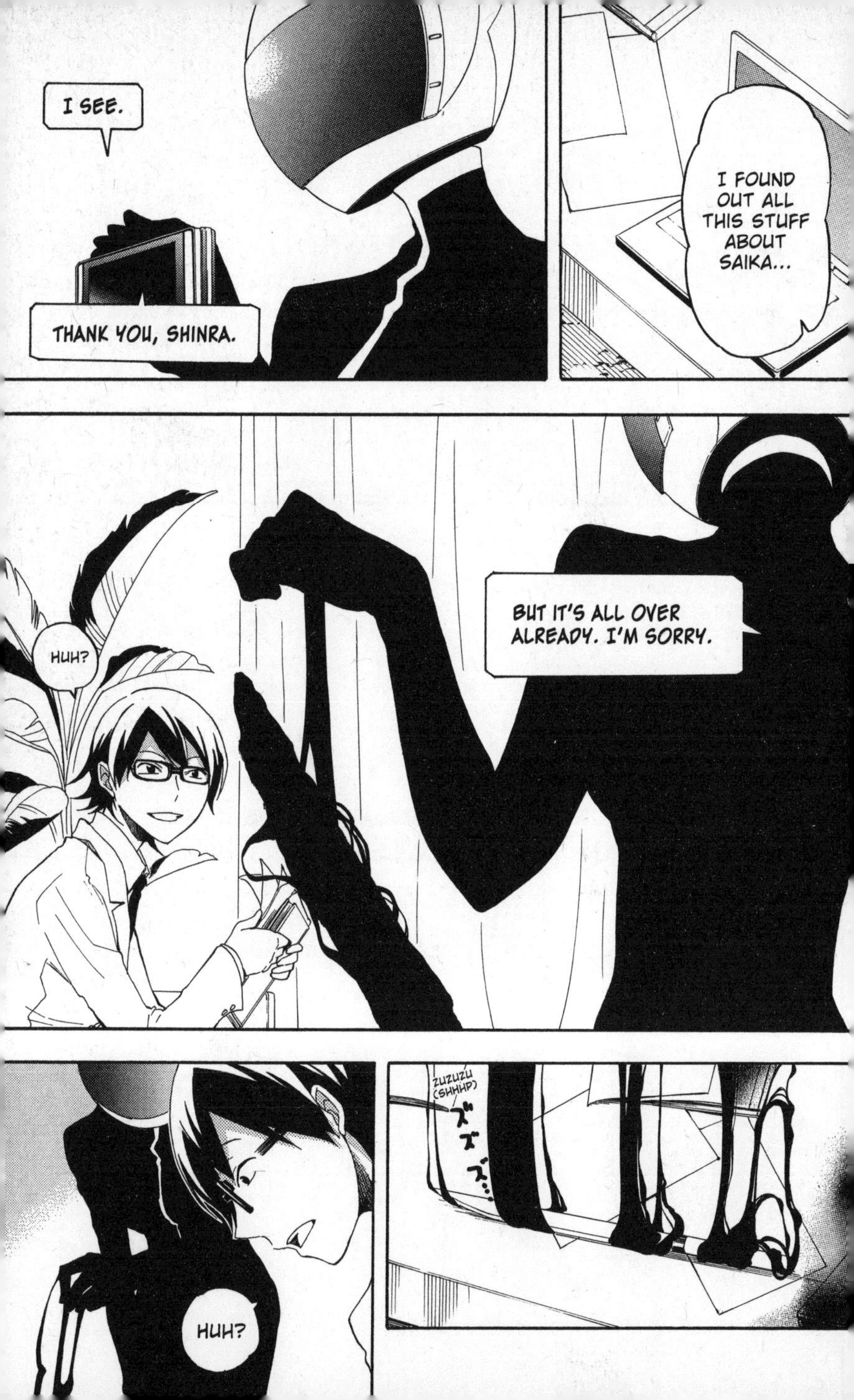
I FOUND OUT ALL THIS STUFF ABOUT SAIKA...
I SEE.
THANK YOU, SHINRA.
BUT IT'S ALL OVER ALREADY. I'M SORRY.
HUH?
ZUZUZU (SHHHP)
ズズズ…
HUH?

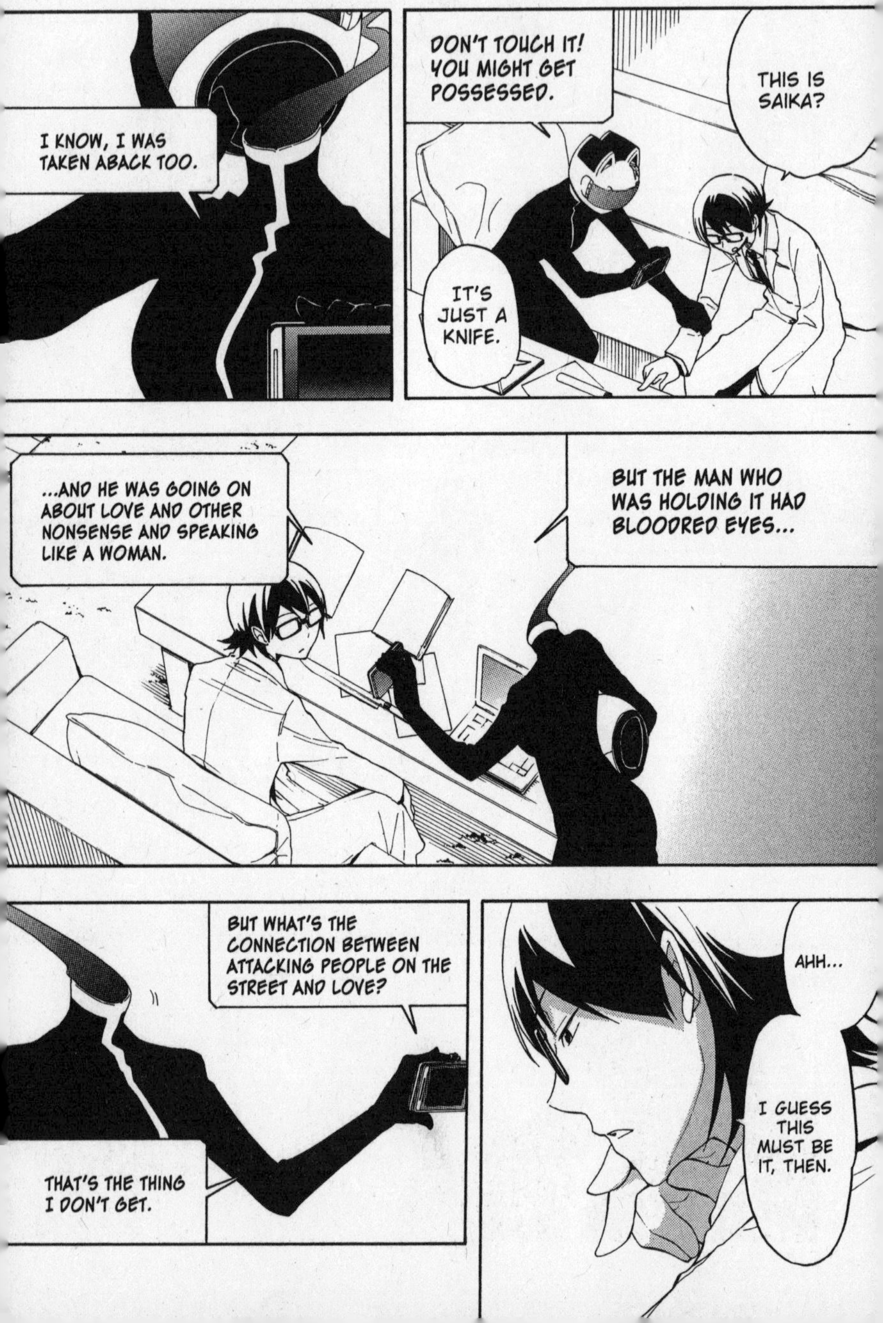
THIS IS SAIKA?
DON'T TOUCH IT! YOU MIGHT GET POSSESSED.
IT'S JUST A KNIFE.
I KNOW, I WAS TAKEN ABACK TOO.
BUT THE MAN WHO WAS HOLDING IT HAD BLOODRED EYES...
...AND HE WAS GOING ON ABOUT LOVE AND OTHER NONSENSE AND SPEAKING LIKE A WOMAN.
AHH...
I GUESS THIS MUST BE IT, THEN.
BUT WHAT'S THE CONNECTION BETWEEN ATTACKING PEOPLE ON THE STREET AND LOVE?
THAT'S THE THING I DON'T GET.

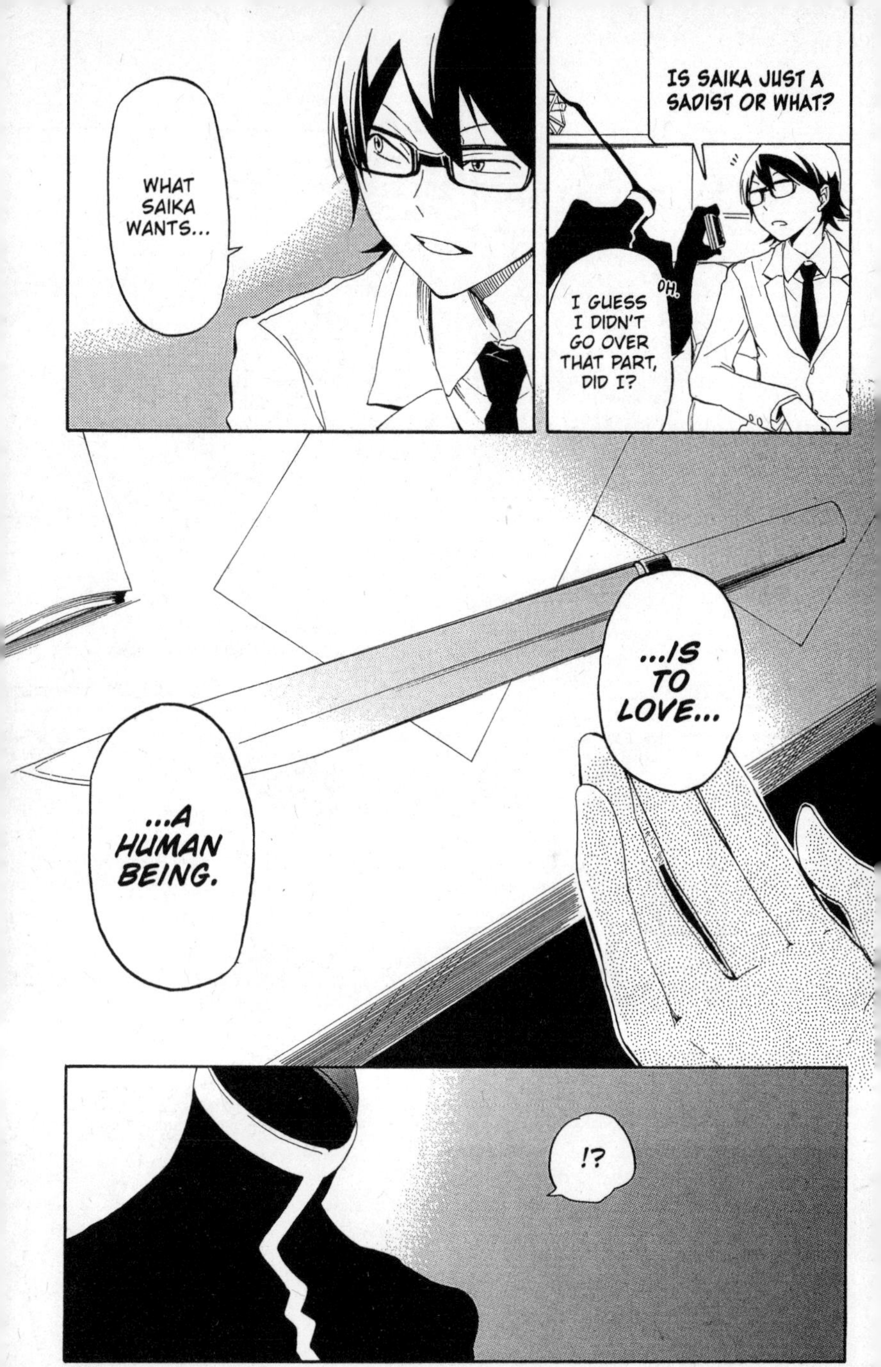
IS SAIKA JUST A SADIST OR WHAT?
OH.
I GUESS I DIDN'T GO OVER THAT PART, DID I?
WHAT SAIKA WANTS...
...IS TO LOVE...
...A HUMAN BEING.
!?

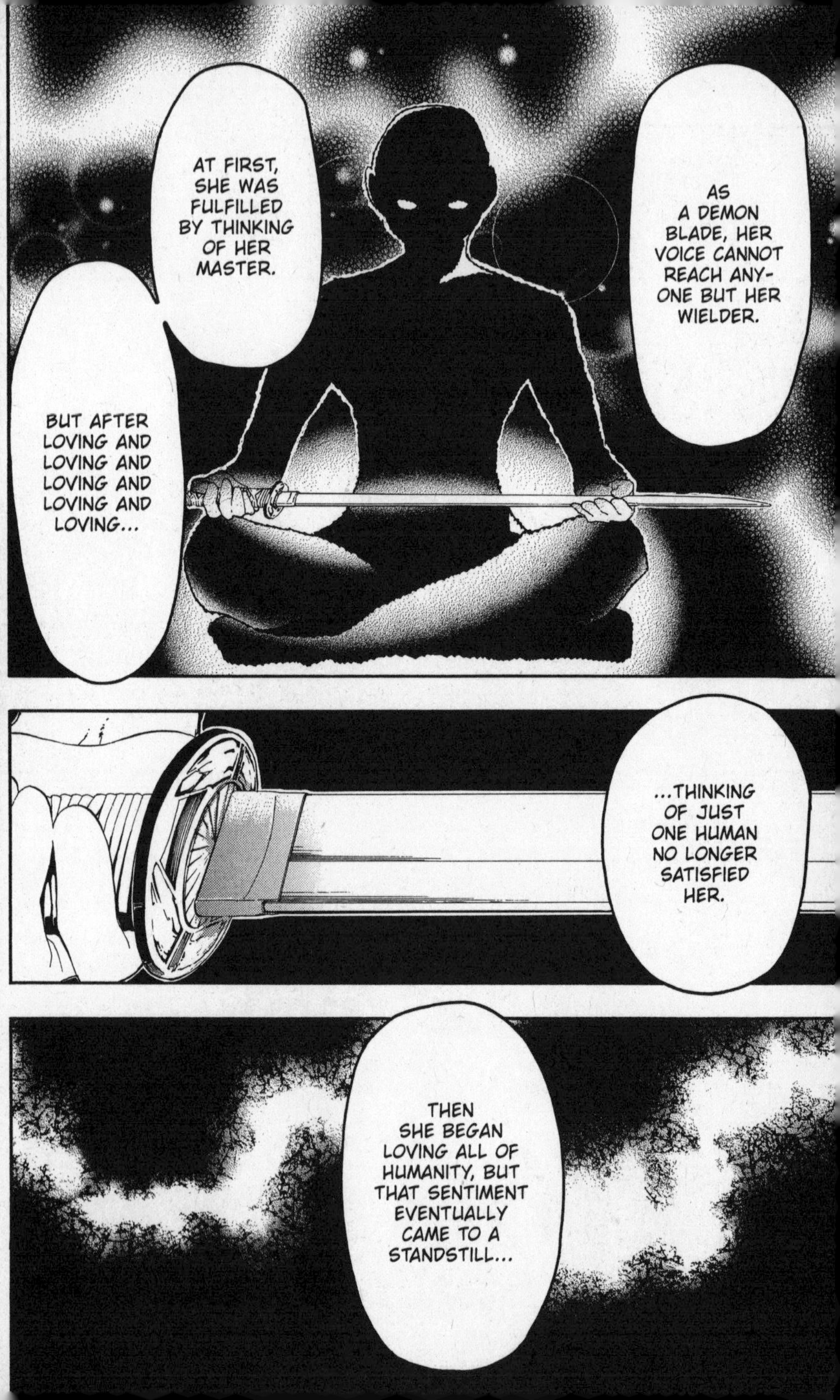
AS A DEMON BLADE, HER VOICE CANNOT REACH ANY-ONE BUT HER WIELDER.
AT FIRST, SHE WAS FULFILLED BY THINKING OF HER MASTER.
BUT AFTER LOVING AND LOVING AND LOVING AND LOVING AND LOVING...
...THINKING OF JUST ONE HUMAN NO LONGER SATISFIED HER.
THEN SHE BEGAN LOVING ALL OF HUMANITY, BUT THAT SENTIMENT EVENTUALLY CAME TO A STANDSTILL...

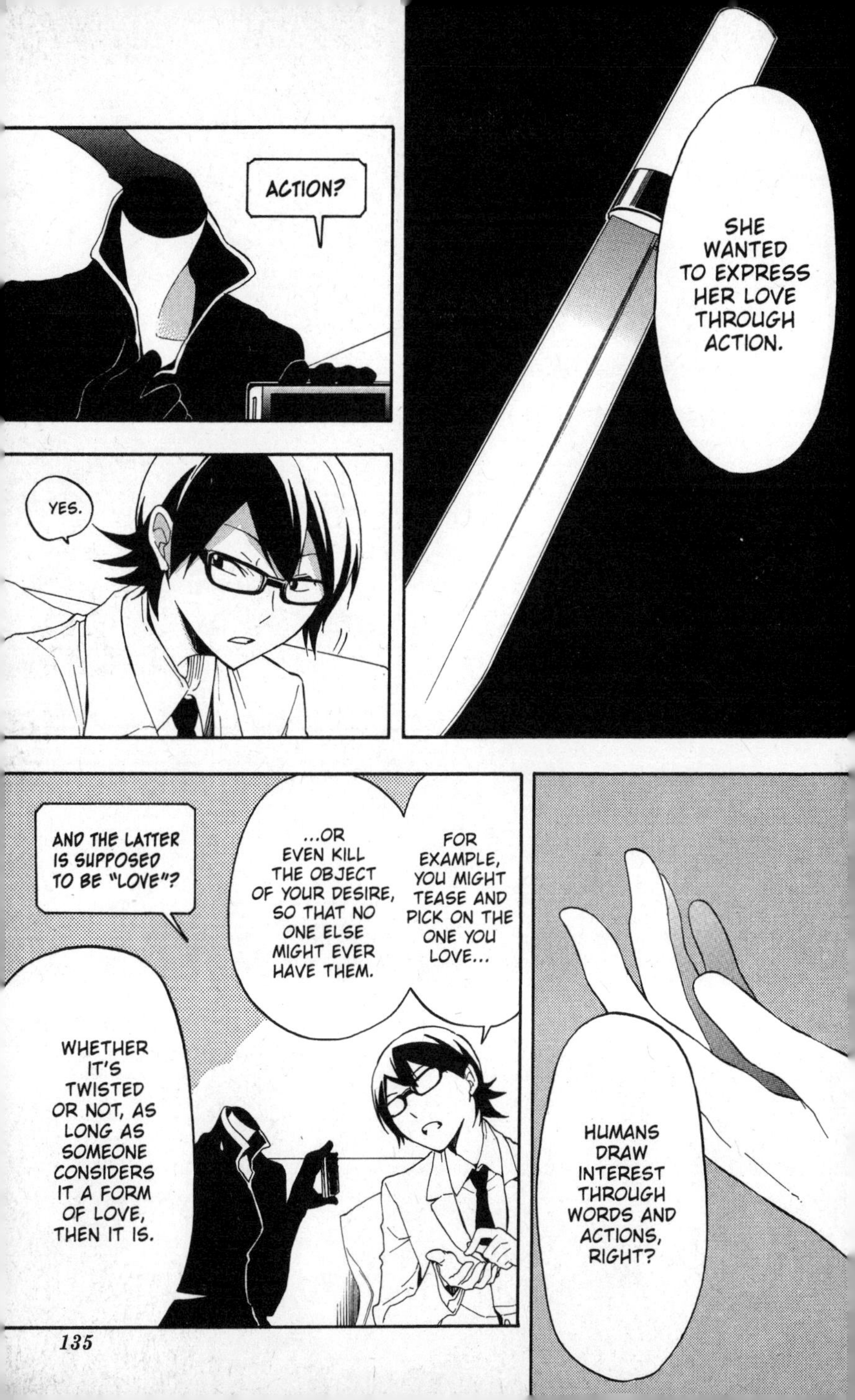
SHE WANTED TO EXPRESS HER LOVE THROUGH ACTION.
ACTION?
YES.
HUMANS DRAW INTEREST THROUGH WORDS AND ACTIONS, RIGHT?
FOR EXAMPLE, YOU MIGHT TEASE AND PICK ON THE ONE YOU LOVE...
...OR EVEN KILL THE OBJECT OF YOUR DESIRE, SO THAT NO ONE ELSE MIGHT EVER HAVE THEM.
AND THE LATTER IS SUPPOSED TO BE "LOVE"?
WHETHER IT'S TWISTED OR NOT, AS LONG AS SOMEONE CONSIDERS IT A FORM OF LOVE, THEN IT IS.

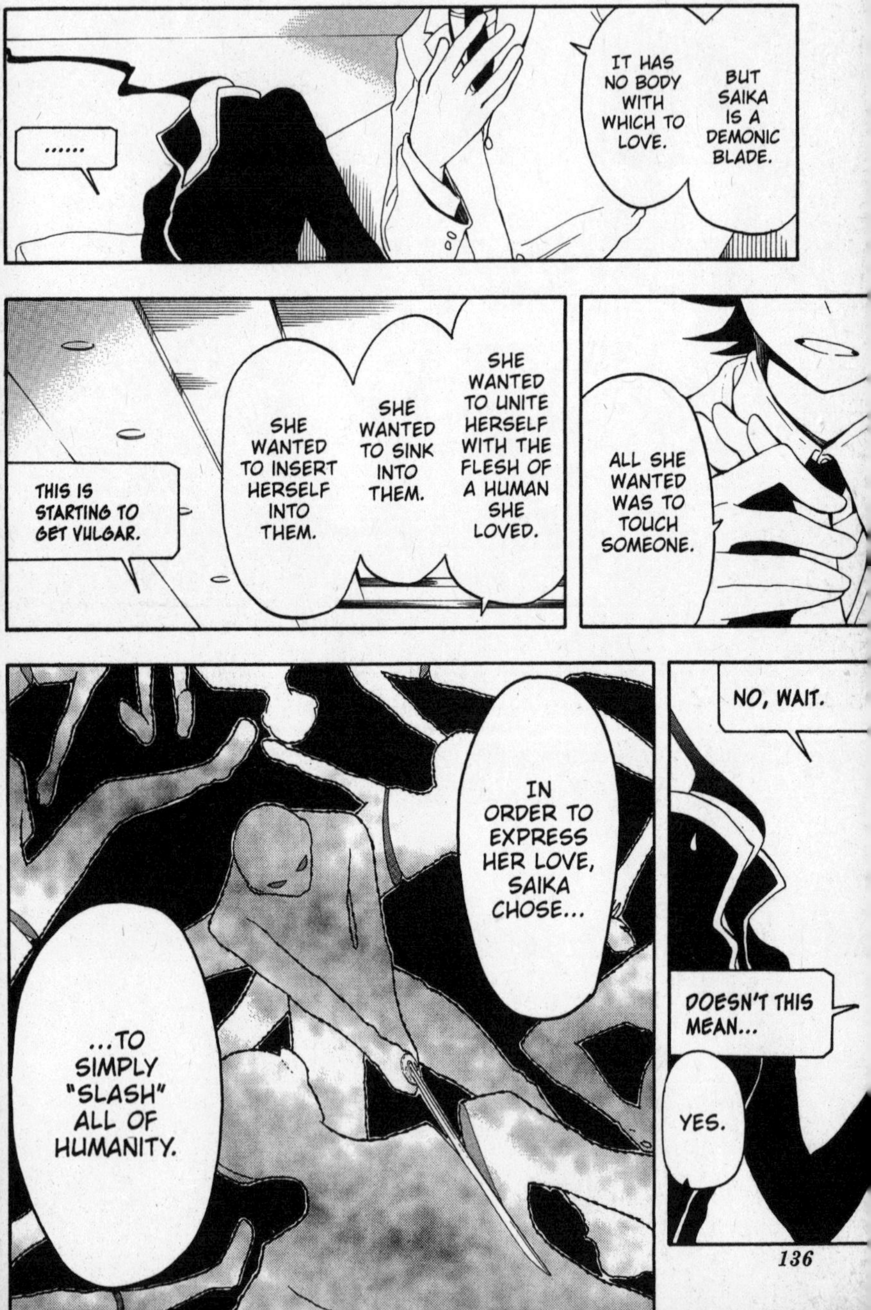
BUT SAIKA IS A DEMONIC BLADE.
IT HAS NO BODY WITH WHICH TO LOVE.
......
ALL SHE WANTED WAS TO TOUCH SOMEONE.
SHE WANTED TO UNITE HERSELF WITH THE FLESH OF A HUMAN SHE LOVED.
SHE WANTED TO SINK INTO THEM.
SHE WANTED TO INSERT HERSELF INTO THEM.
THIS IS STARTING TO GET VULGAR.
NO, WAIT.
DOESN'T THIS MEAN...
YES.
IN ORDER TO EXPRESS HER LOVE, SAIKA CHOSE...
...TO SIMPLY "SLASH" ALL OF HUMANITY.

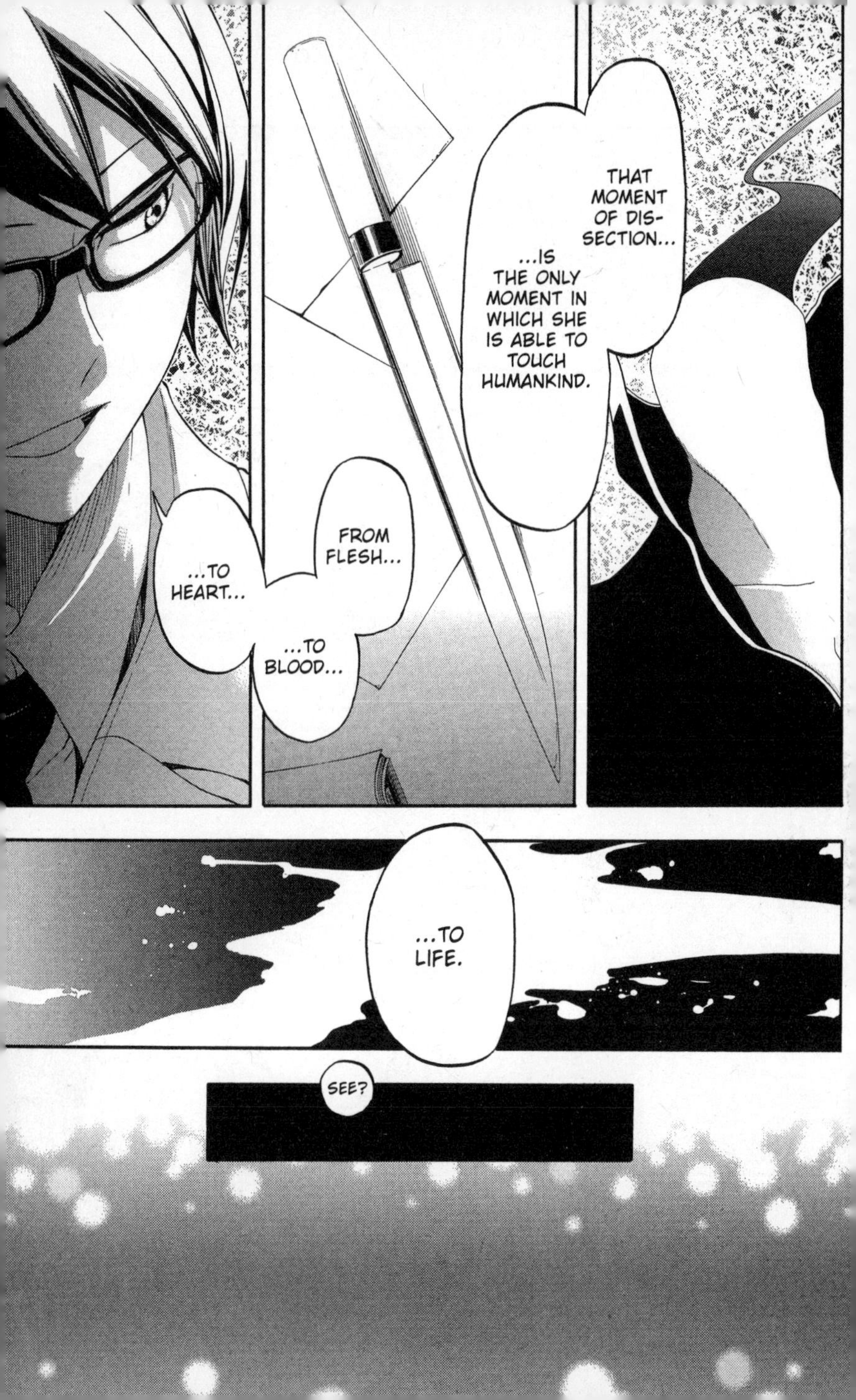
THAT MOMENT OF DIS-SECTION...
...IS THE ONLY MOMENT IN WHICH SHE IS ABLE TO TOUCH HUMANKIND.
FROM FLESH...
...TO HEART...
...TO BLOOD...
...TO LIFE.
SEE?

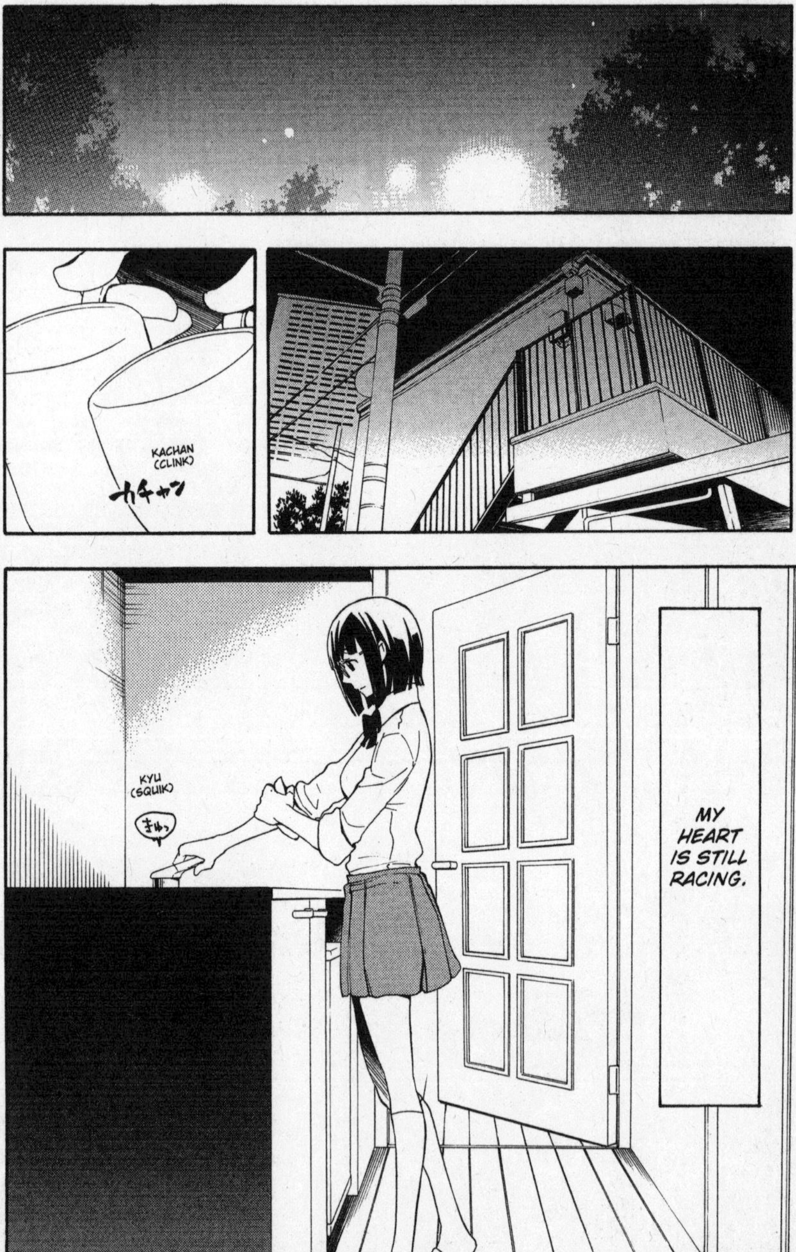
KACHAN (CLINK)
カチャン
MY HEART IS STILL RACING.
KYU (SQUIK)
きゅっ

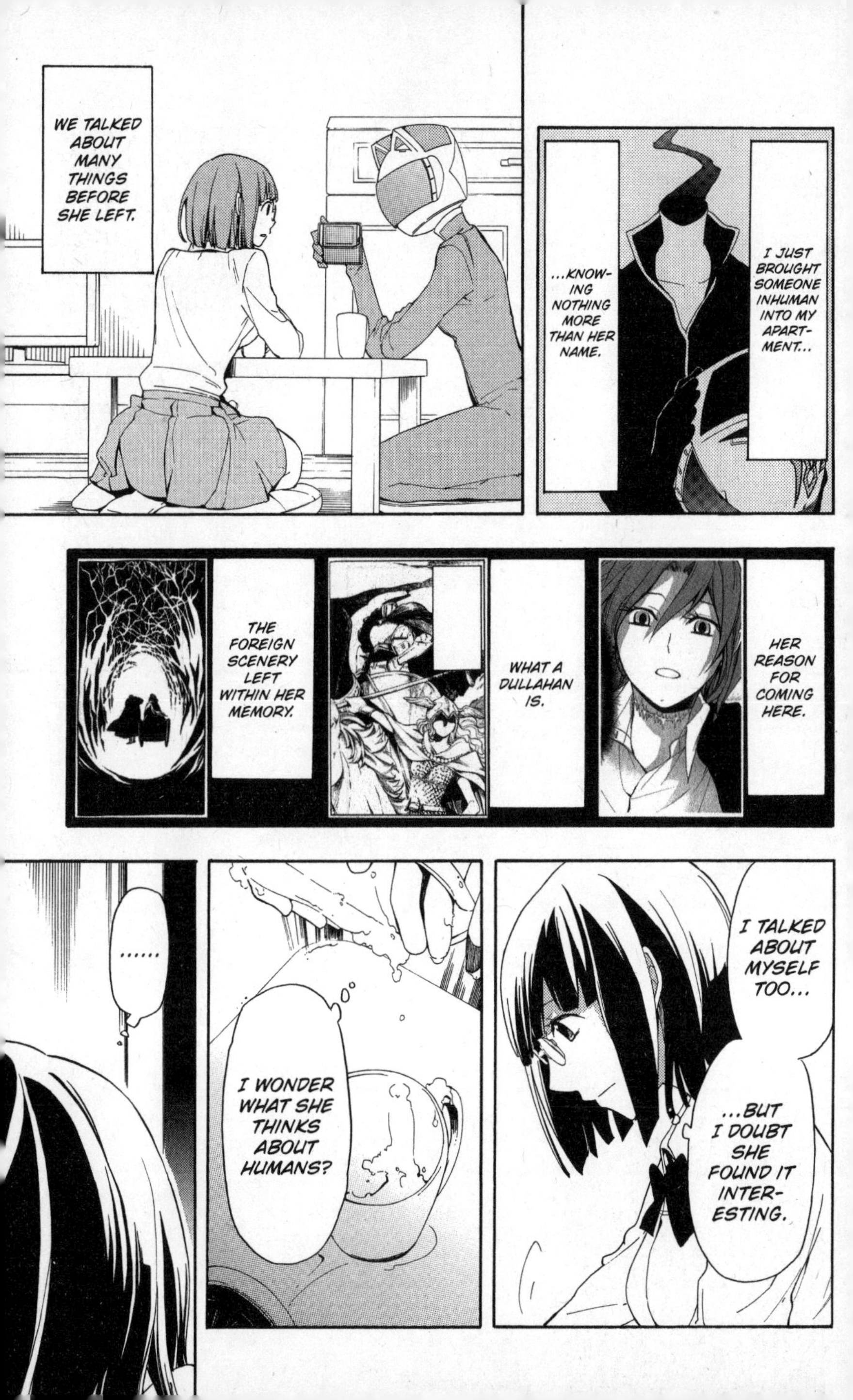
I JUST BROUGHT SOMEONE INHUMAN INTO MY APARTMENT...
...KNOWING NOTHING MORE THAN HER NAME.
WE TALKED ABOUT MANY THINGS BEFORE SHE LEFT.
HER REASON FOR COMING HERE.
WHAT A DULLAHAN IS.
THE FOREIGN SCENERY LEFT WITHIN HER MEMORY.
I TALKED ABOUT MYSELF TOO...
...BUT I DOUBT SHE FOUND IT INTERESTING.
I WONDER WHAT SHE THINKS ABOUT HUMANS?
......

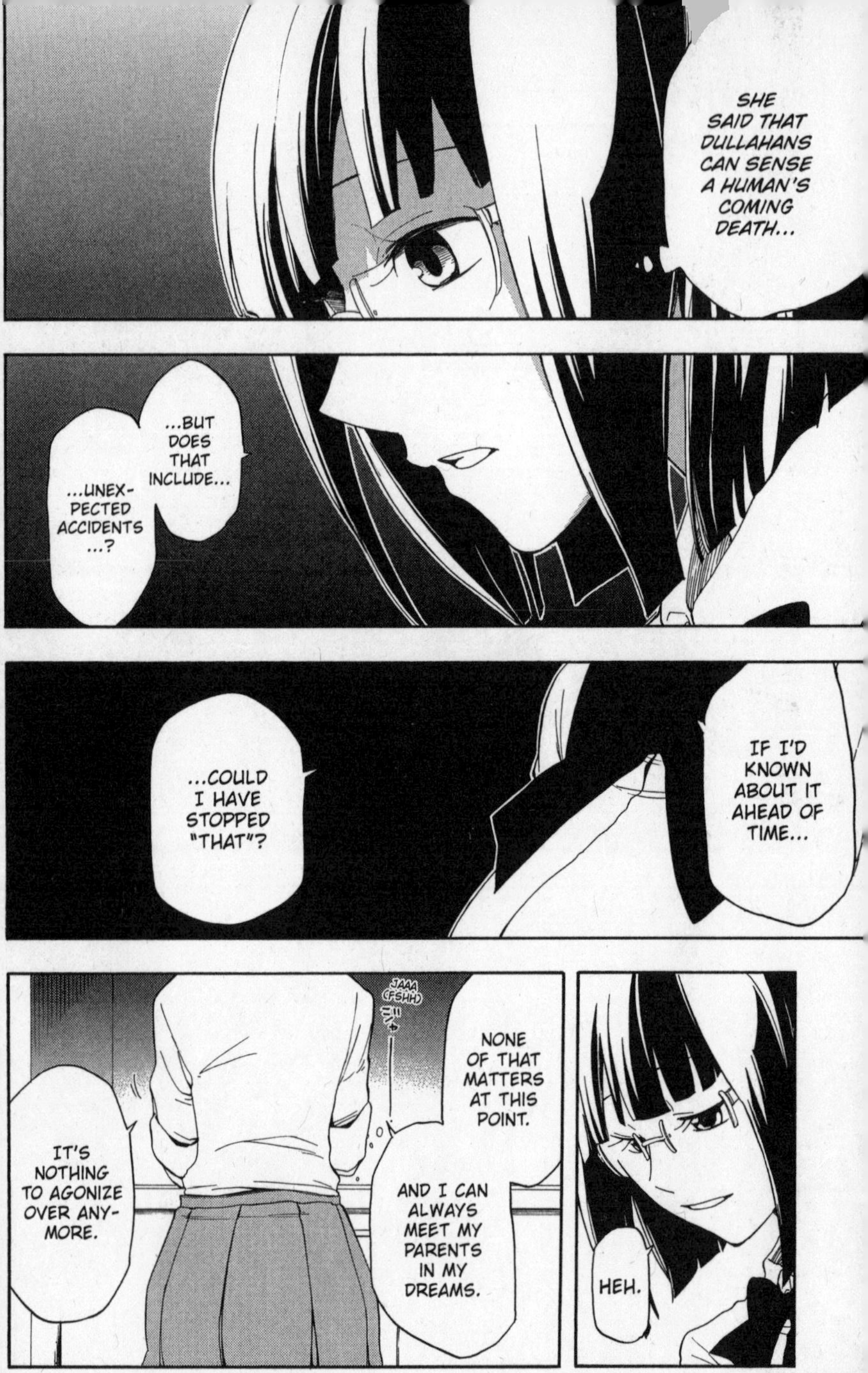
SHE SAID THAT DULLAHANS CAN SENSE A HUMAN'S COMING DEATH...
...BUT DOES THAT INCLUDE...
...UNEXPECTED ACCIDENTS...?
IF I'D KNOWN ABOUT IT AHEAD OF TIME...
...COULD I HAVE STOPPED "THAT"?
HEH.
NONE OF THAT MATTERS AT THIS POINT.
JAAA (FSHH)
AND I CAN ALWAYS MEET MY PARENTS IN MY DREAMS.
IT'S NOTHING TO AGONIZE OVER ANYMORE.

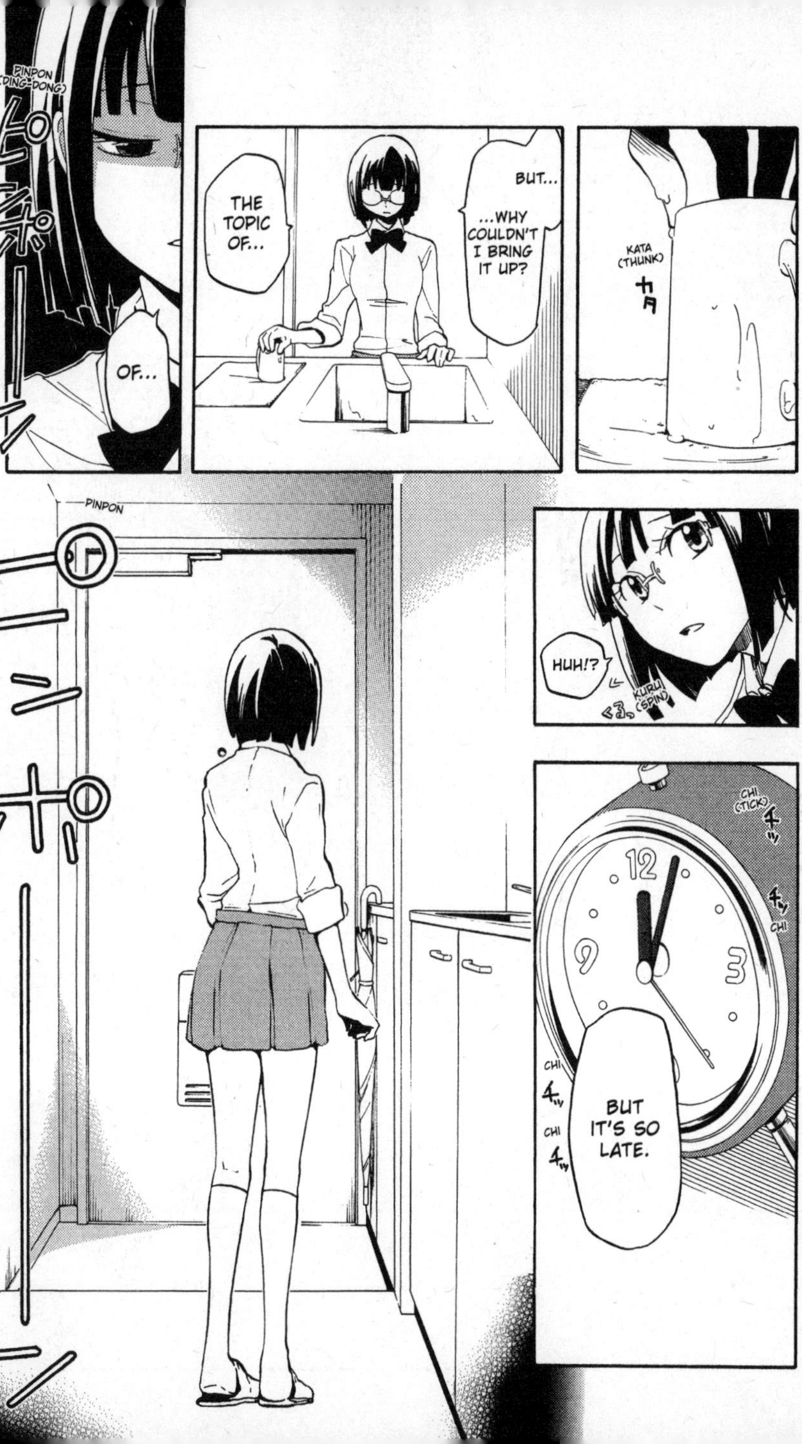
KATA (THUNK)
カタ
BUT...
...WHY COULDN'T I BRING IT UP?
THE TOPIC OF...
PINPON (DING-DONG)
ピンポーン
OF...
HUH!?
KURU (SPIN)
くるっ
CHI (TICK)
チッ
CHI
チッ
BUT IT'S SO LATE.
CHI
チッ
CHI
チッ
PINPON
ピンポーン

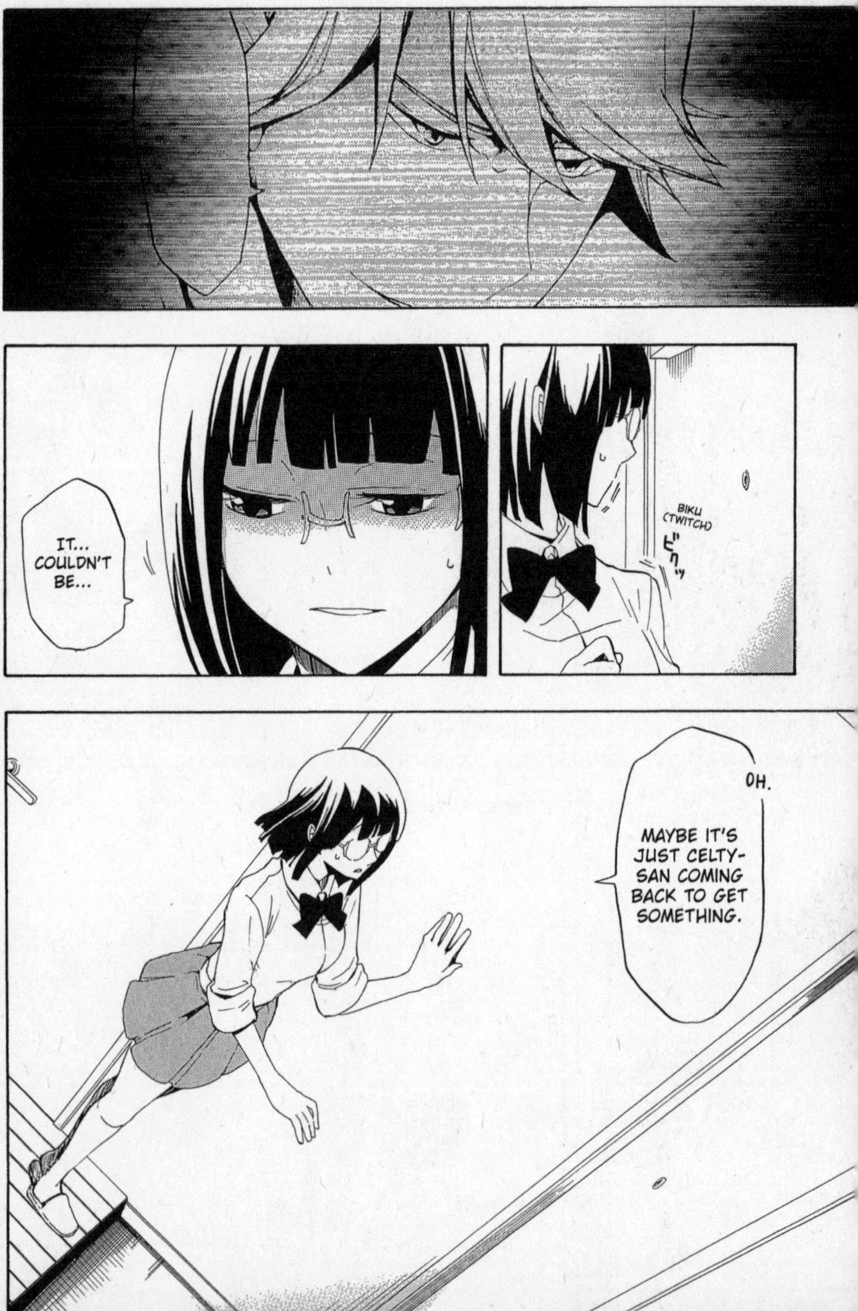
BIKU (TWITCH)
ビクッ
IT... COULDN'T BE...
OH.
MAYBE IT'S JUST CELTY-SAN COMING BACK TO GET SOMETHING.

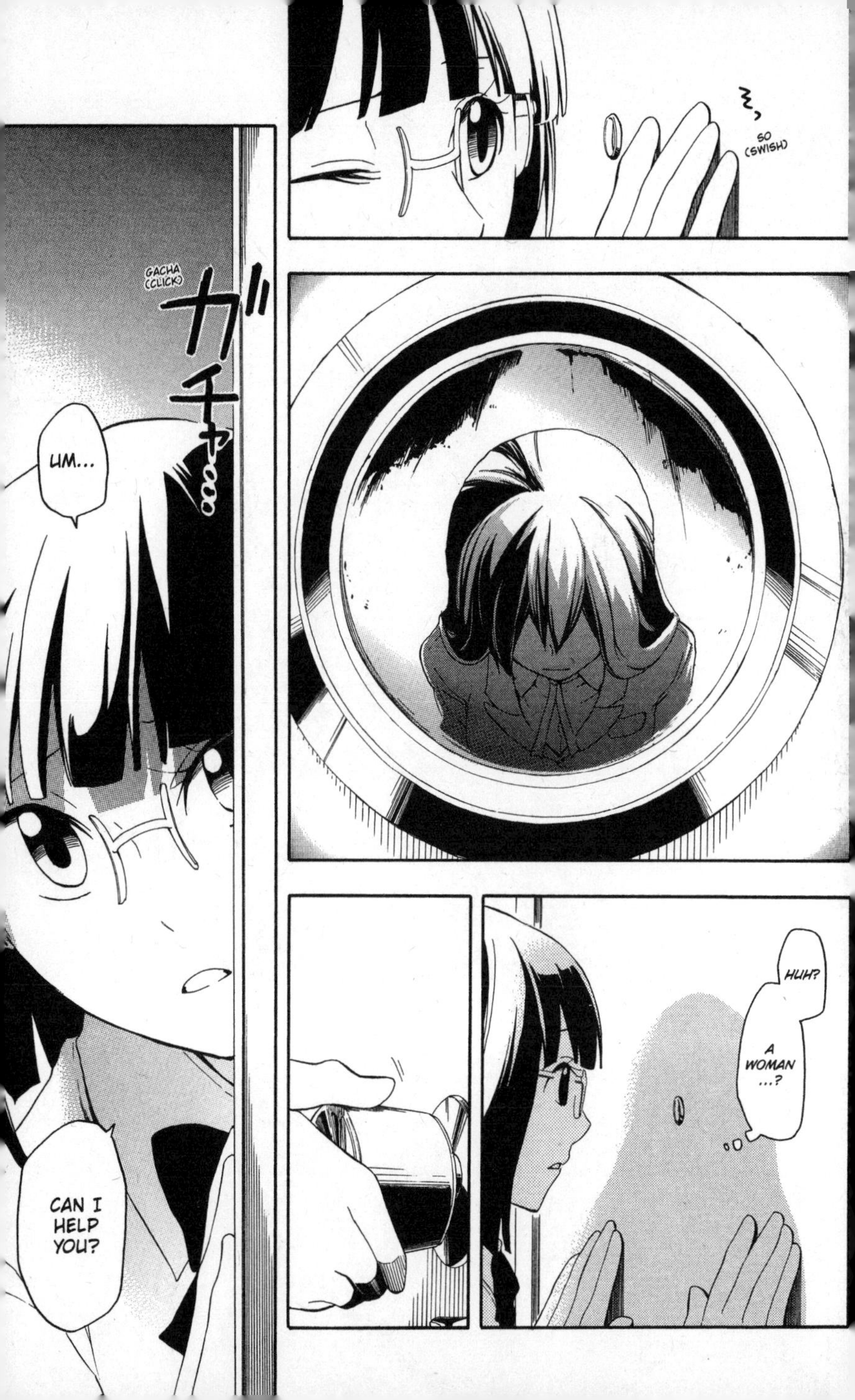
SO (SWISH)
HUH?
A WOMAN ...?
GACHA (CLICK)
ガチャ
UM...
CAN I HELP YOU?

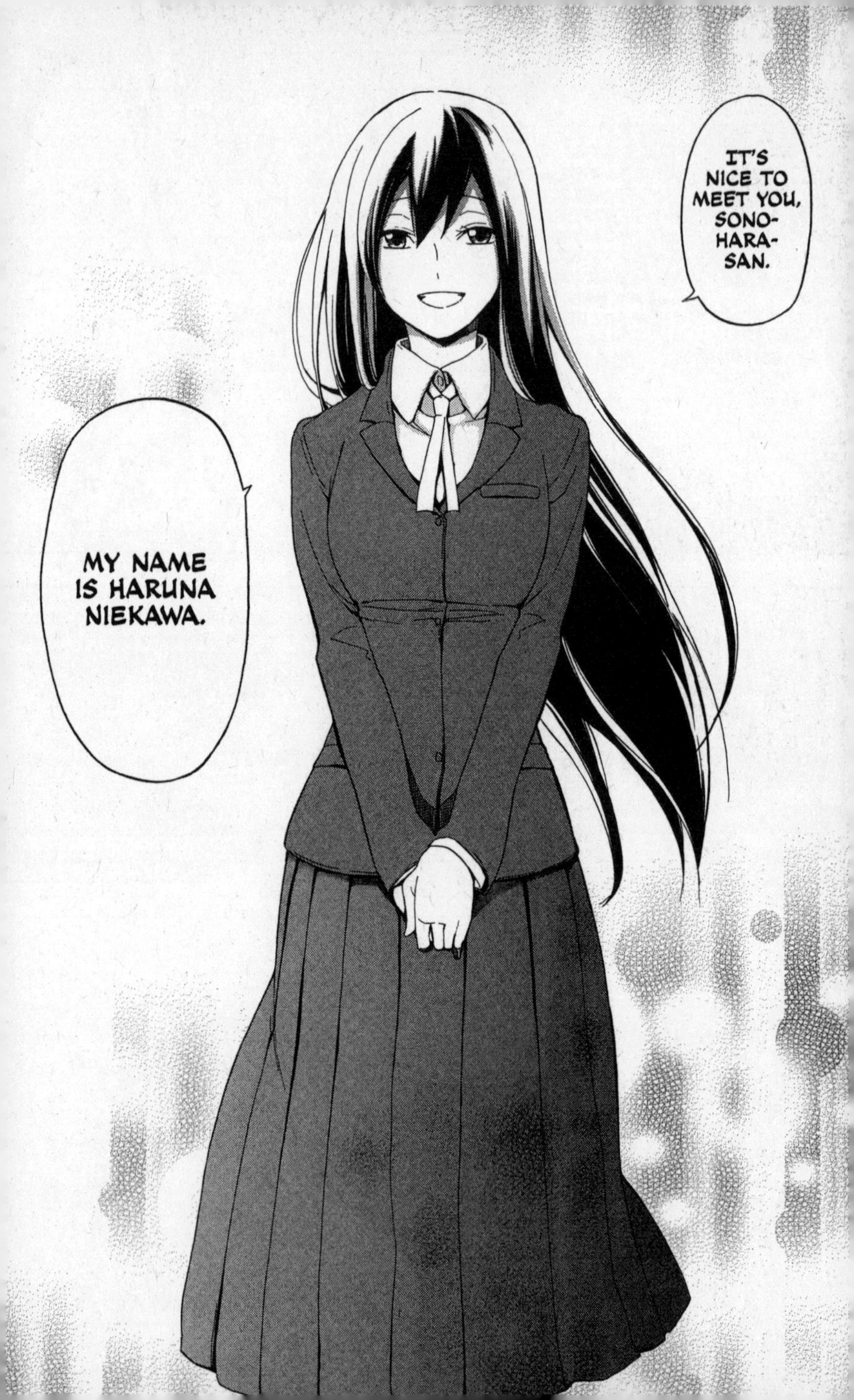
IT'S NICE TO MEET YOU, SONO-HARA-SAN.
MY NAME IS HARUNA NIEKAWA.

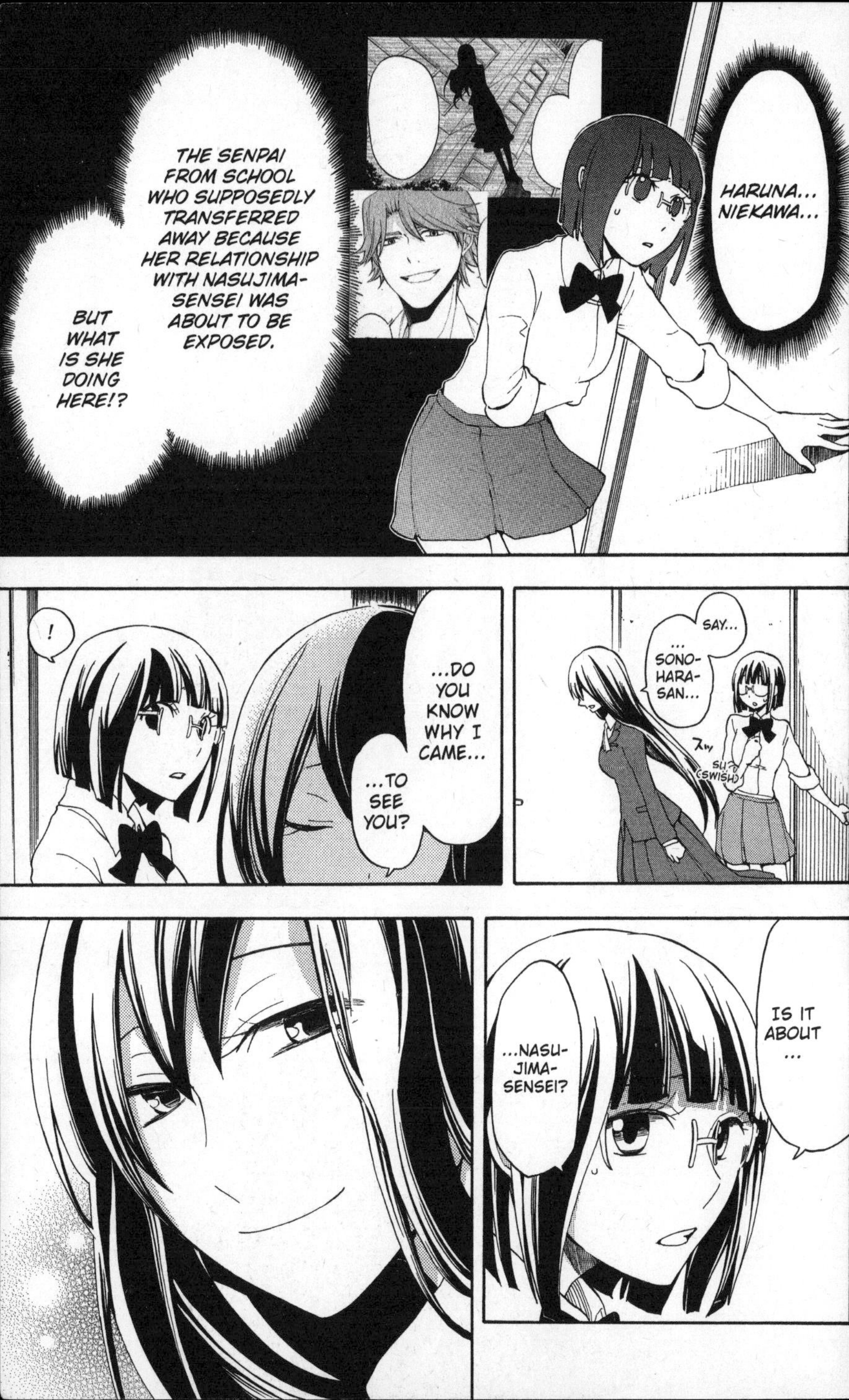
HARUNA... NIEKAWA...
THE SENPAI FROM SCHOOL WHO SUPPOSEDLY TRANSFERRED AWAY BECAUSE HER RELATIONSHIP WITH NASUJIMA-SENSEI WAS ABOUT TO BE EXPOSED.
BUT WHAT IS SHE DOING HERE!?
SAY...
...SONOHARA-SAN...
スッ
SU (SWISH)
...DO YOU KNOW WHY I CAME...
...TO SEE YOU?
!
IS IT ABOUT ...
...NASUJIMA-SENSEI?

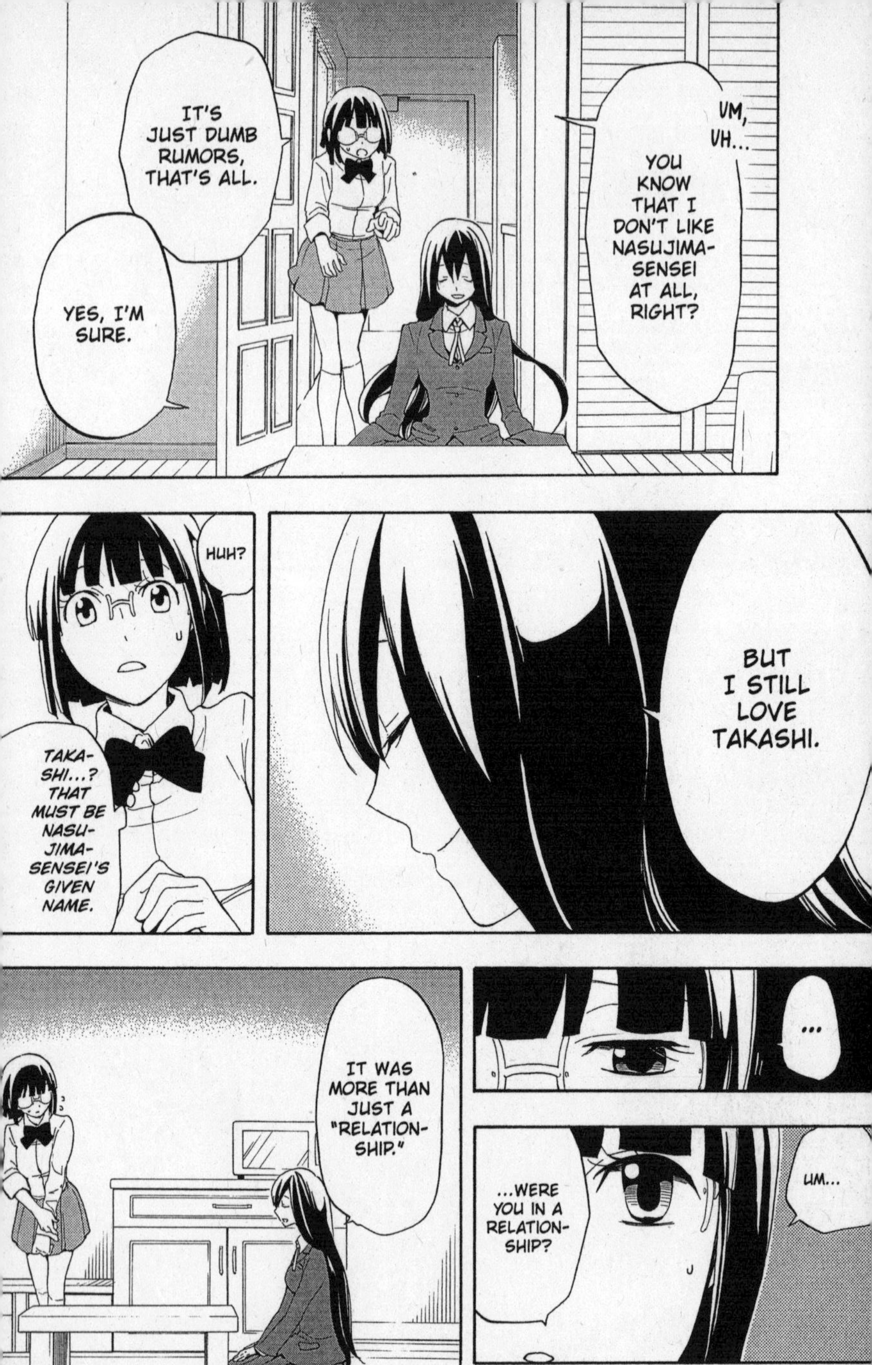
UM, UH...
YOU KNOW THAT I DON'T LIKE NASUJIMA-SENSEI AT ALL, RIGHT?
IT'S JUST DUMB RUMORS, THAT'S ALL.
YES, I'M SURE.
BUT I STILL LOVE TAKASHI.
HUH?
TAKASHI...? THAT MUST BE NASUJIMA-SENSEI'S GIVEN NAME.
...
UM...
...WERE YOU IN A RELATIONSHIP?
IT WAS MORE THAN JUST A "RELATIONSHIP."

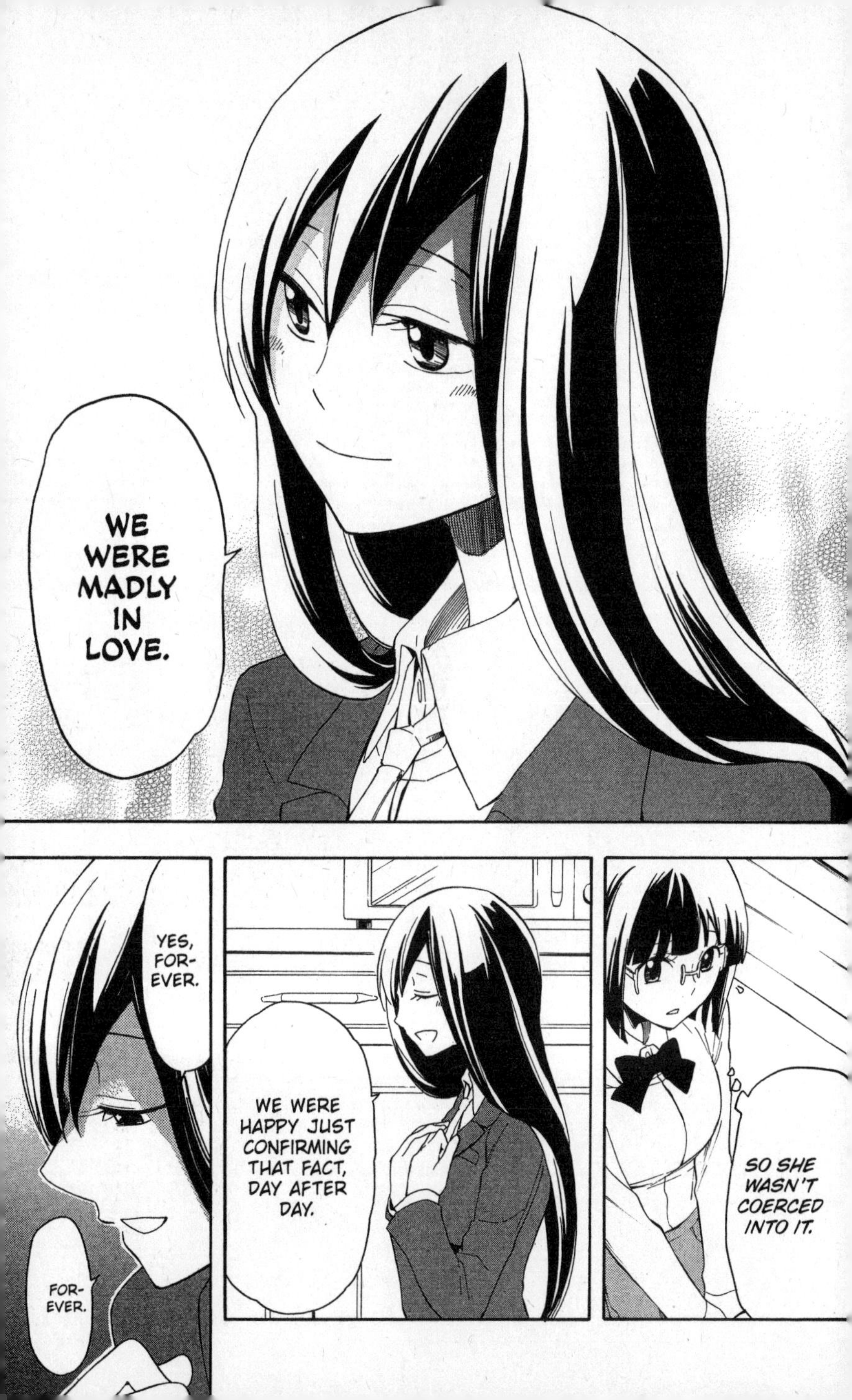
WE WERE MADLY IN LOVE.
SO SHE WASN'T COERCED INTO IT.
WE WERE HAPPY JUST CONFIRMING THAT FACT, DAY AFTER DAY.
YES, FOR-EVER.
FOR-EVER.

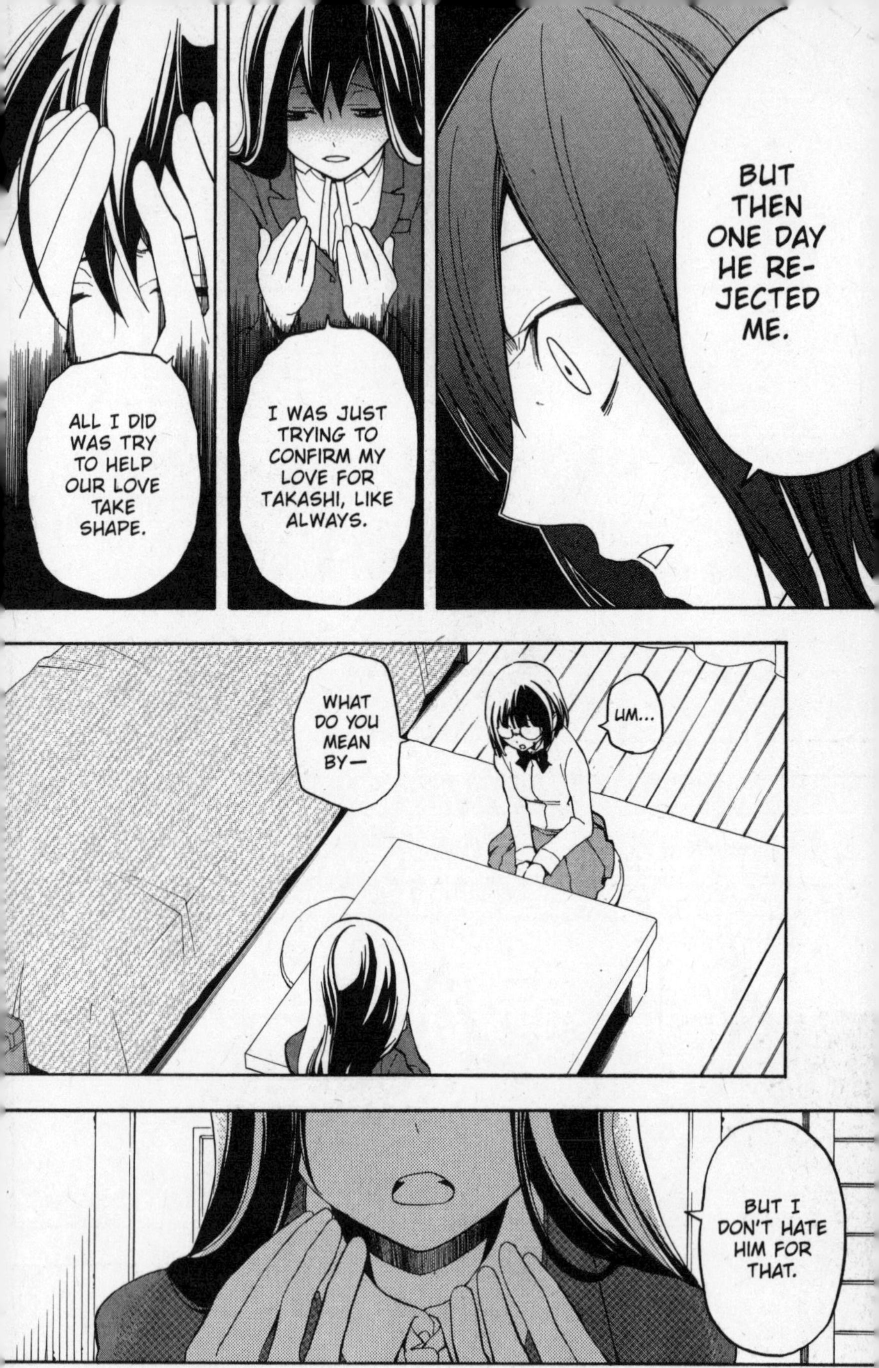
BUT THEN ONE DAY HE RE- JECTED ME.
I WAS JUST TRYING TO CONFIRM MY LOVE FOR TAKASHI, LIKE ALWAYS.
ALL I DID WAS TRY TO HELP OUR LOVE TAKE SHAPE.
UM...
WHAT DO YOU MEAN BY—
BUT I DON'T HATE HIM FOR THAT.

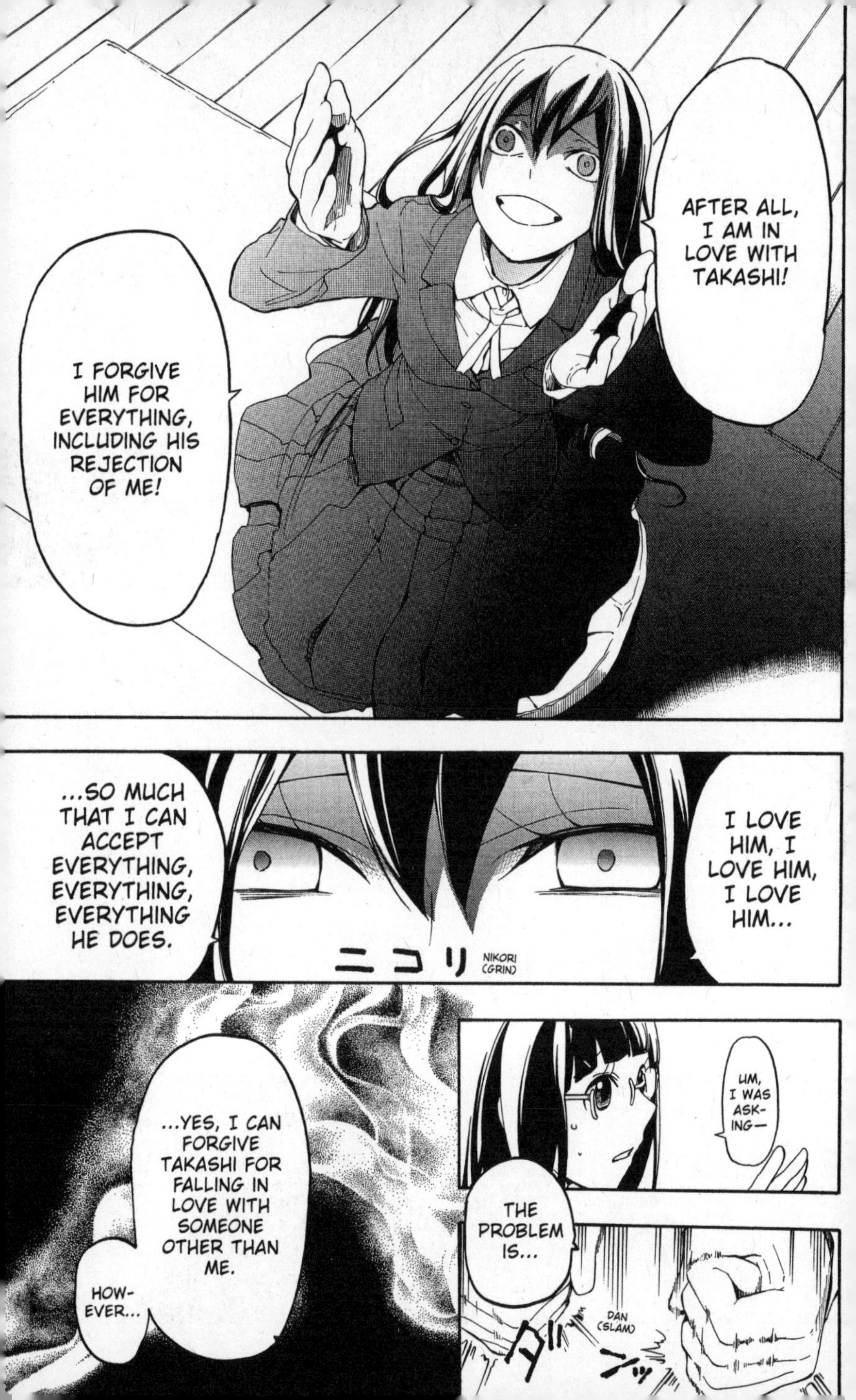
AFTER ALL, I AM IN LOVE WITH TAKASHI!
I FORGIVE HIM FOR EVERYTHING, INCLUDING HIS REJECTION OF ME!
I LOVE HIM, I LOVE HIM, I LOVE HIM...
...SO MUCH THAT I CAN ACCEPT EVERYTHING, EVERYTHING, EVERYTHING HE DOES.
ニコリ
NIKORI (GRIN)
UM, I WAS ASK-ING—
THE PROBLEM IS...
DAN (SLAM)
...YES, I CAN FORGIVE TAKASHI FOR FALLING IN LOVE WITH SOMEONE OTHER THAN ME.
HOW-EVER...

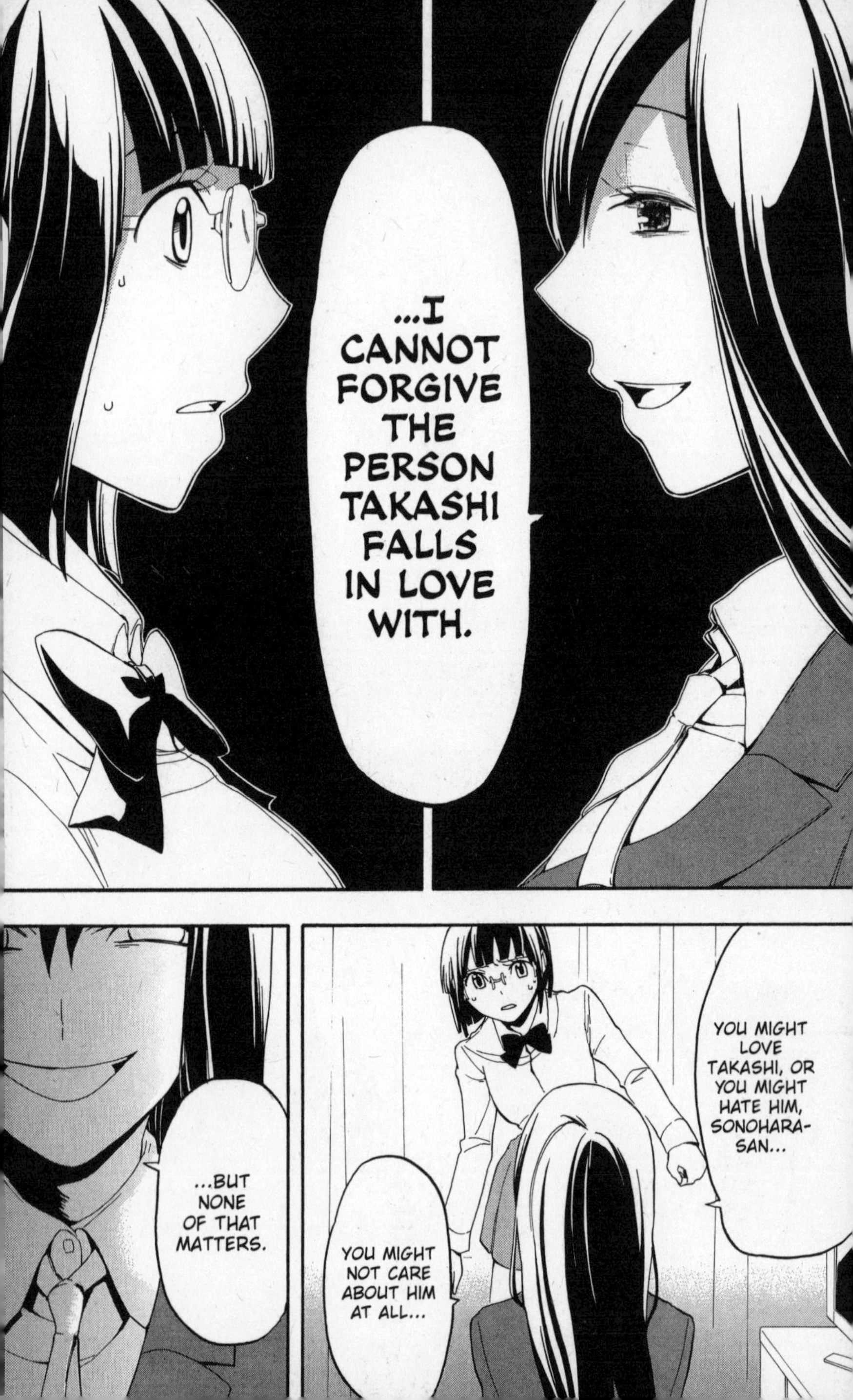
...I CANNOT FORGIVE THE PERSON TAKASHI FALLS IN LOVE WITH.
YOU MIGHT LOVE TAKASHI, OR YOU MIGHT HATE HIM, SONOHARA-SAN...
YOU MIGHT NOT CARE ABOUT HIM AT ALL...
...BUT NONE OF THAT MATTERS.

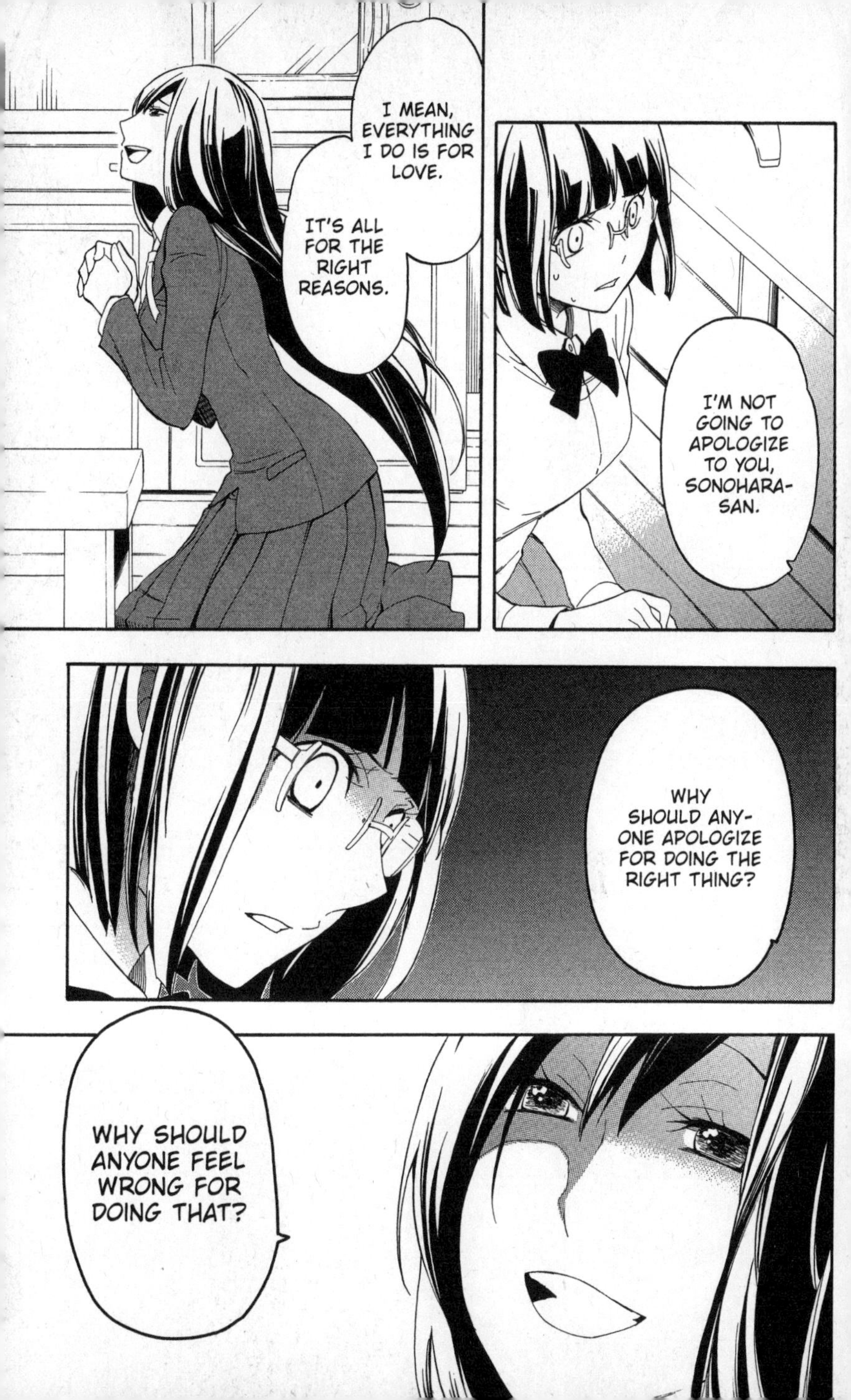

I'M NOT GOING TO APOLOGIZE TO YOU, SONOHARA-SAN.
I MEAN, EVERYTHING I DO IS FOR LOVE.
IT'S ALL FOR THE RIGHT REASONS.
WHY SHOULD ANYONE APOLOGIZE FOR DOING THE RIGHT THING?
WHY SHOULD ANYONE FEEL WRONG FOR DOING THAT?

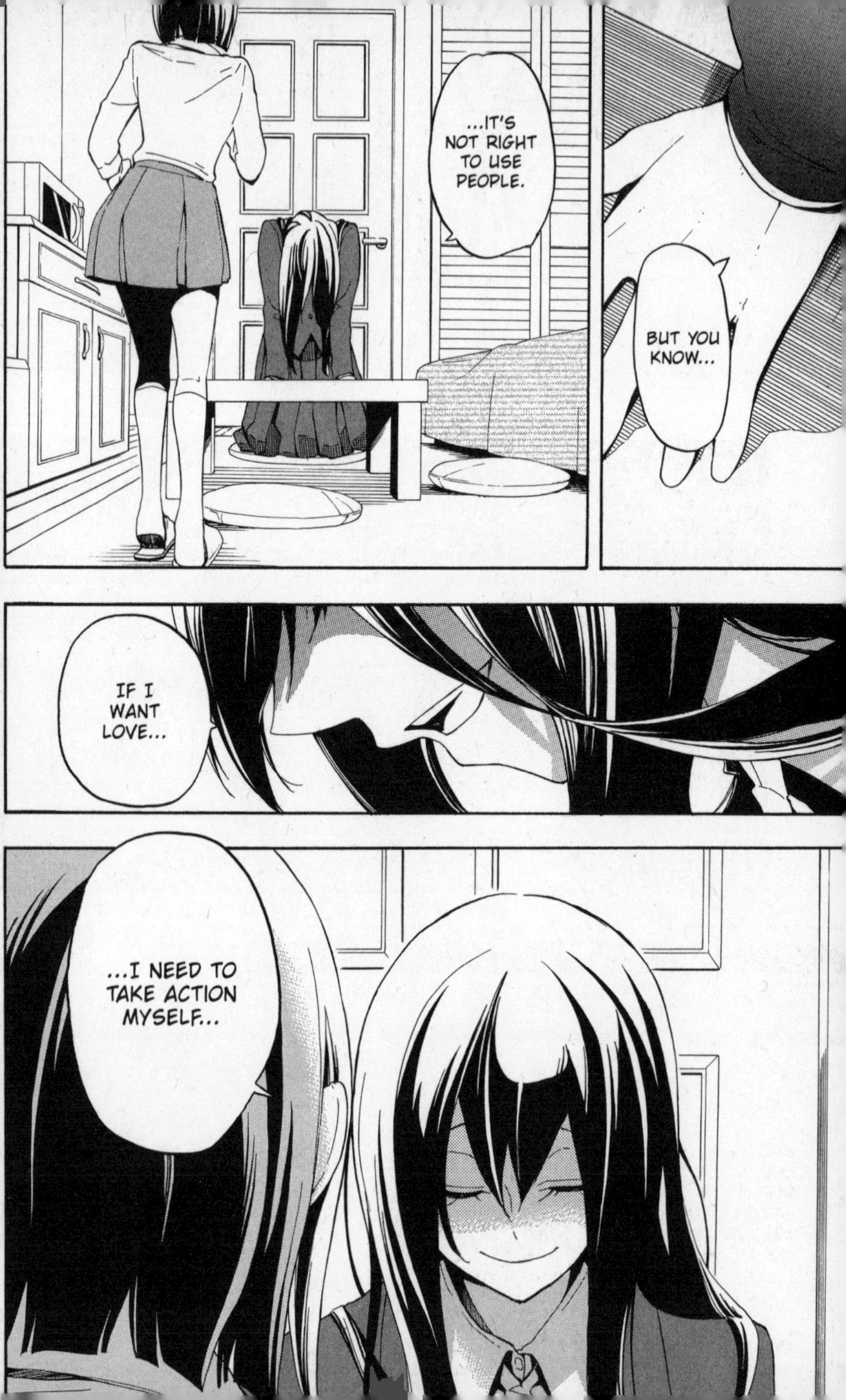
...IT'S NOT RIGHT TO USE PEOPLE.
BUT YOU KNOW...
IF I WANT LOVE...
...I NEED TO TAKE ACTION MYSELF...

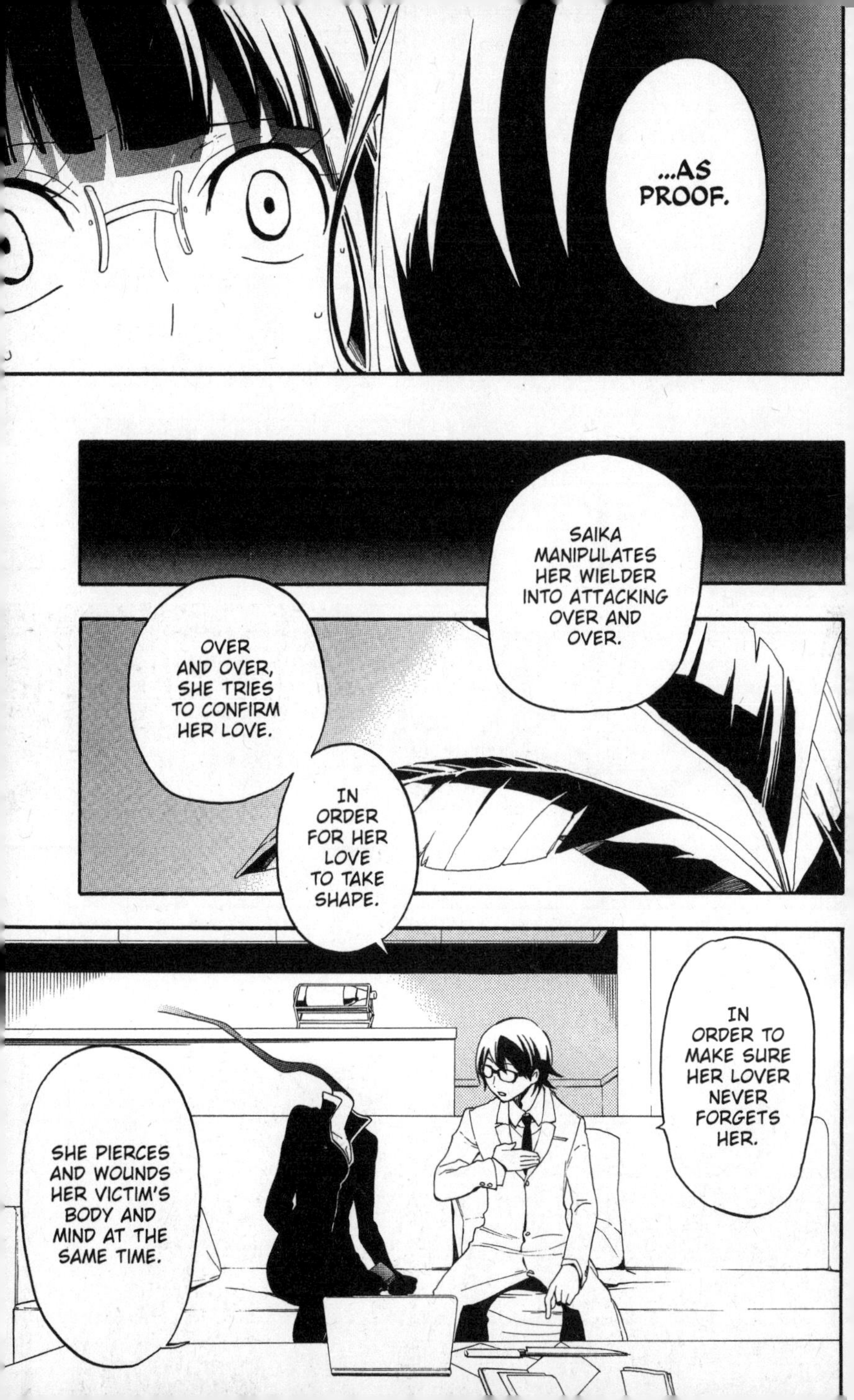
...AS PROOF.
SAIKA MANIPULATES HER WIELDER INTO ATTACKING OVER AND OVER.
OVER AND OVER, SHE TRIES TO CONFIRM HER LOVE.
IN ORDER FOR HER LOVE TO TAKE SHAPE.
IN ORDER TO MAKE SURE HER LOVER NEVER FORGETS HER.
SHE PIERCES AND WOUNDS HER VICTIM'S BODY AND MIND AT THE SAME TIME.

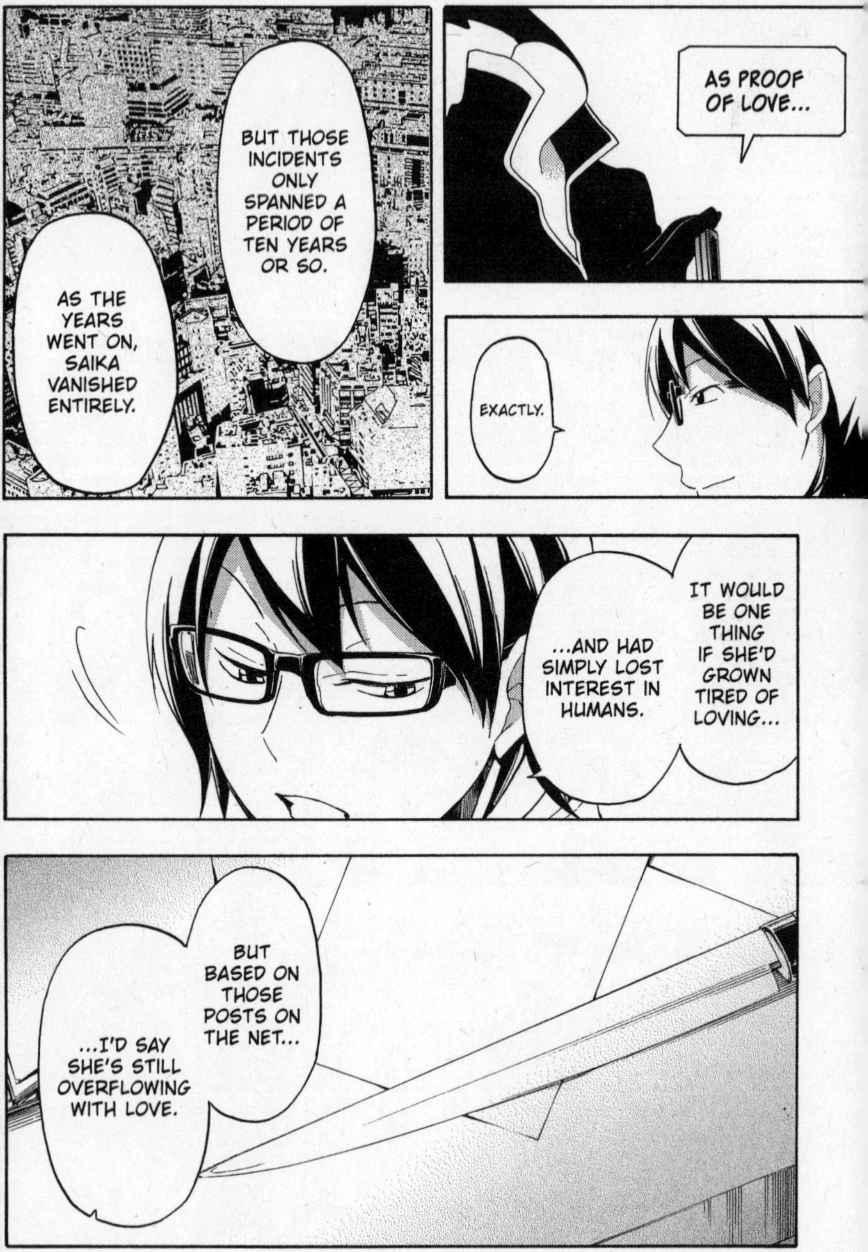
AS PROOF OF LOVE...
EXACTLY.
BUT THOSE INCIDENTS ONLY SPANNED A PERIOD OF TEN YEARS OR SO.
AS THE YEARS WENT ON, SAIKA VANISHED ENTIRELY.
IT WOULD BE ONE THING IF SHE'D GROWN TIRED OF LOVING...
...AND HAD SIMPLY LOST INTEREST IN HUMANS.
BUT BASED ON THOSE POSTS ON THE NET...
...I'D SAY SHE'S STILL OVERFLOWING WITH LOVE.

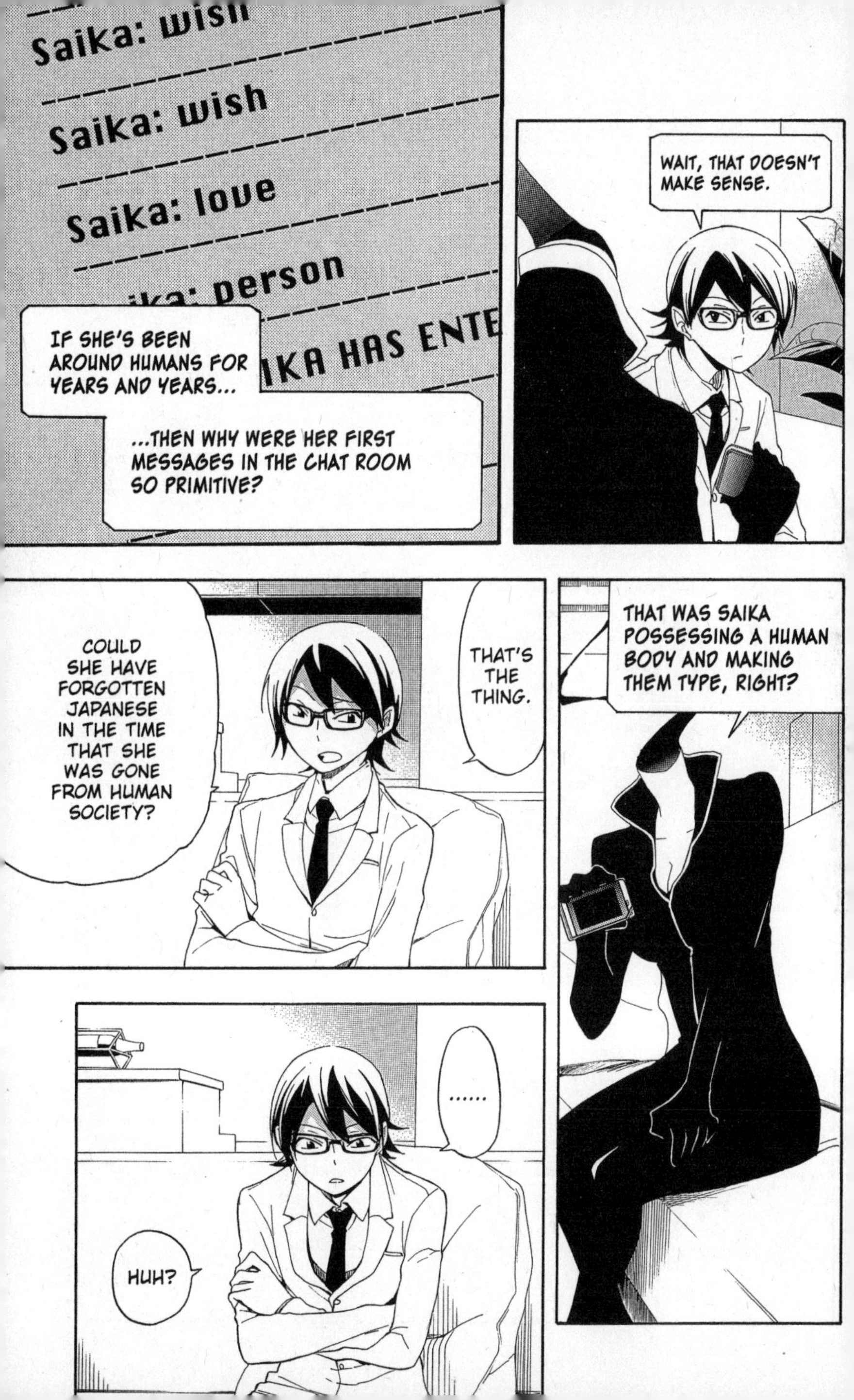
WAIT, THAT DOESN'T MAKE SENSE.
Saika: wish
Saika: wish
Saika: love
ika: person
IKA HAS ENTE
IF SHE'S BEEN AROUND HUMANS FOR YEARS AND YEARS...
...THEN WHY WERE HER FIRST MESSAGES IN THE CHAT ROOM SO PRIMITIVE?
THAT WAS SAIKA POSSESSING A HUMAN BODY AND MAKING THEM TYPE, RIGHT?
THAT'S THE THING.
COULD SHE HAVE FORGOTTEN JAPANESE IN THE TIME THAT SHE WAS GONE FROM HUMAN SOCIETY?
......
HUH?

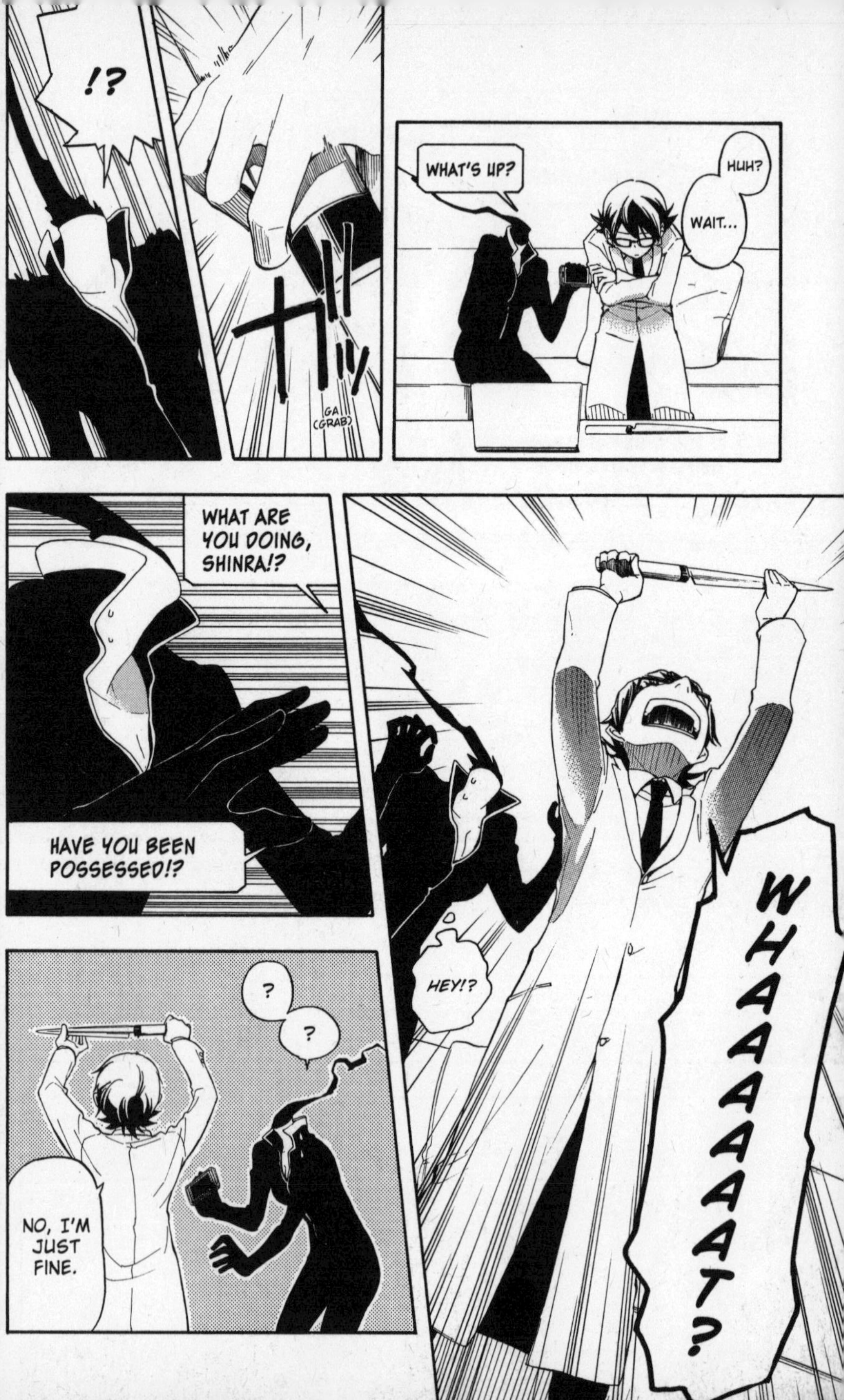
HUH?
WAIT...
WHAT'S UP?
GA (GRAB)
!?
WHAAAAAAAT!?
HEY!?
WHAT ARE YOU DOING, SHINRA!?
HAVE YOU BEEN POSSESSED!?
?
?
NO, I'M JUST FINE.

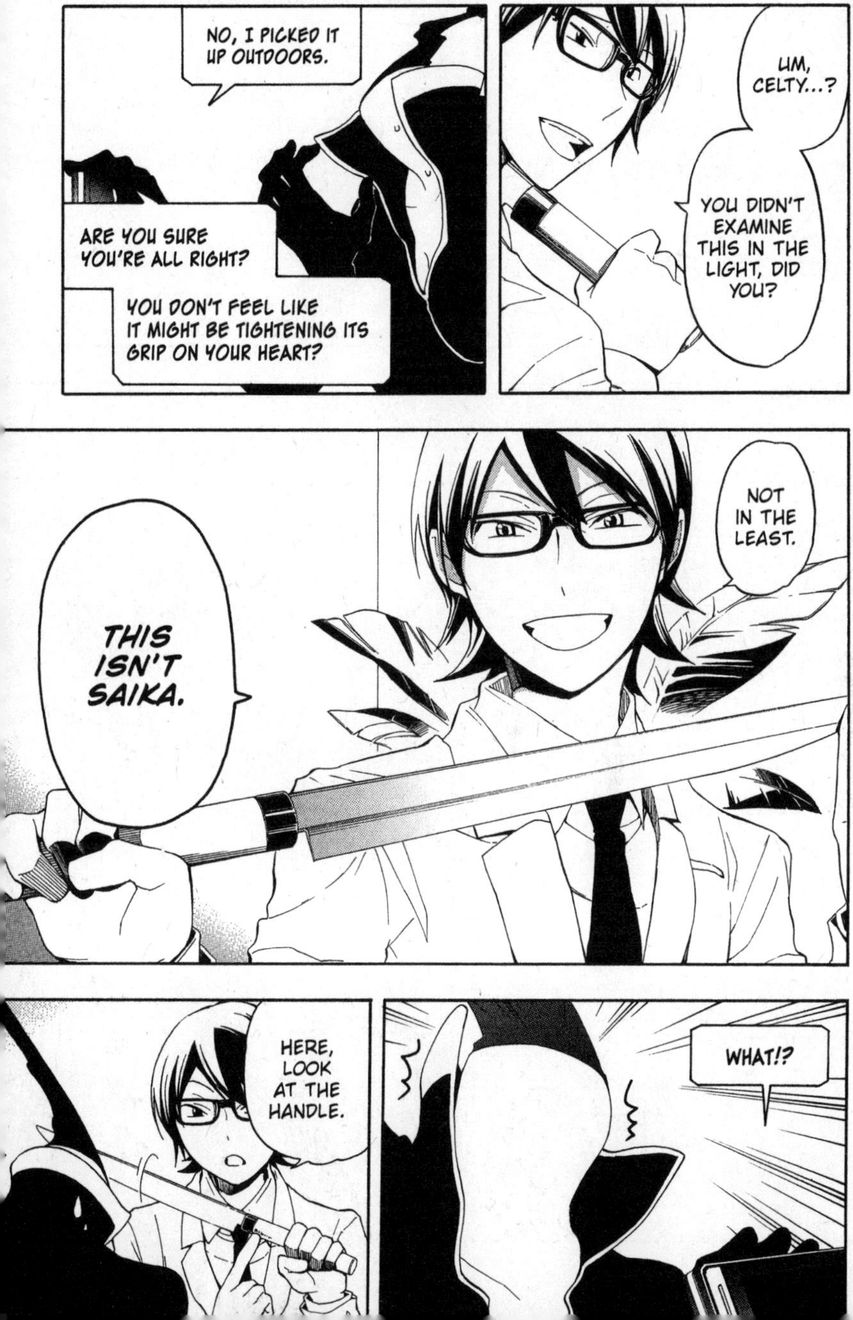
UM, CELTY...?
YOU DIDN'T EXAMINE THIS IN THE LIGHT, DID YOU?
NO, I PICKED IT UP OUTDOORS.
ARE YOU SURE YOU'RE ALL RIGHT?
YOU DON'T FEEL LIKE IT MIGHT BE TIGHTENING ITS GRIP ON YOUR HEART?
NOT IN THE LEAST.
THIS ISN'T SAIKA.
WHAT!?
HERE, LOOK AT THE HANDLE.

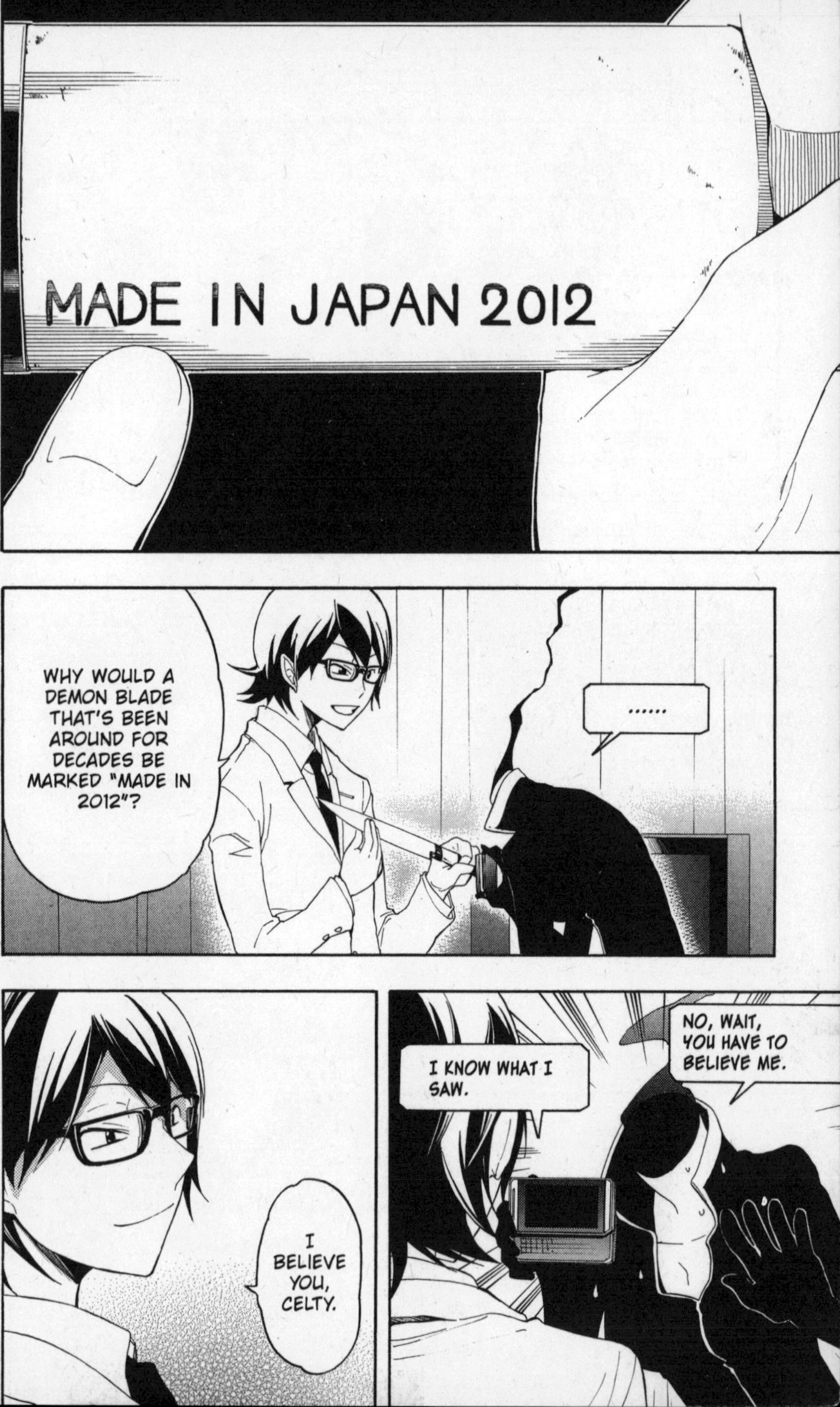
MADE IN JAPAN 2012
......
WHY WOULD A DEMON BLADE THAT'S BEEN AROUND FOR DECADES BE MARKED "MADE IN 2012"?
NO, WAIT, YOU HAVE TO BELIEVE ME.
I KNOW WHAT I SAW.
I BELIEVE YOU, CELTY.

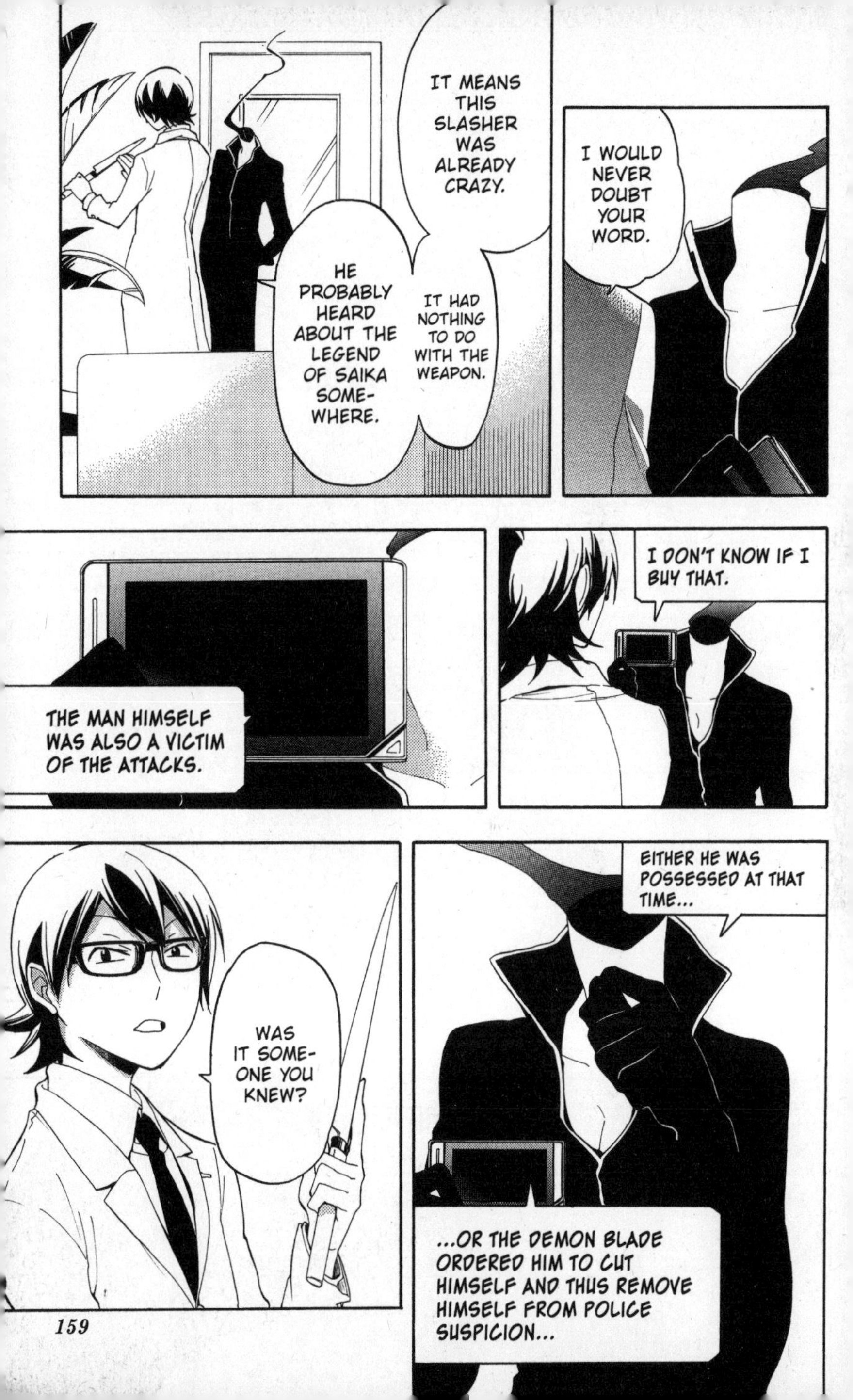
I WOULD NEVER DOUBT YOUR WORD.
IT MEANS THIS SLASHER WAS ALREADY CRAZY.
IT HAD NOTHING TO DO WITH THE WEAPON.
HE PROBABLY HEARD ABOUT THE LEGEND OF SAIKA SOME-WHERE.
I DON'T KNOW IF I BUY THAT.
THE MAN HIMSELF WAS ALSO A VICTIM OF THE ATTACKS.
EITHER HE WAS POSSESSED AT THAT TIME...
...OR THE DEMON BLADE ORDERED HIM TO CUT HIMSELF AND THUS REMOVE HIMSELF FROM POLICE SUSPICION...
WAS IT SOME-ONE YOU KNEW?

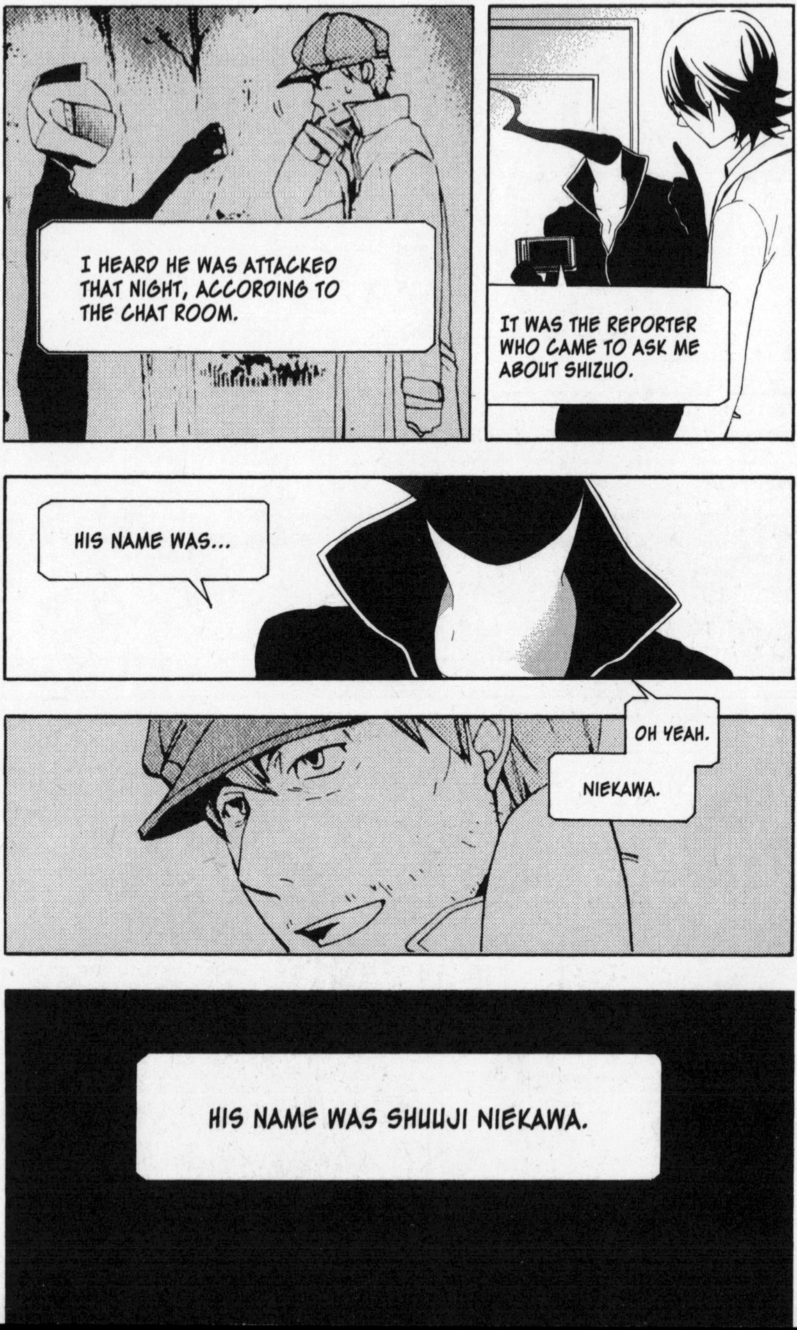
IT WAS THE REPORTER WHO CAME TO ASK ME ABOUT SHIZUO.
I HEARD HE WAS ATTACKED THAT NIGHT, ACCORDING TO THE CHAT ROOM.
HIS NAME WAS...
OH YEAH.
NIEKAWA.
HIS NAME WAS SHUUJI NIEKAWA.

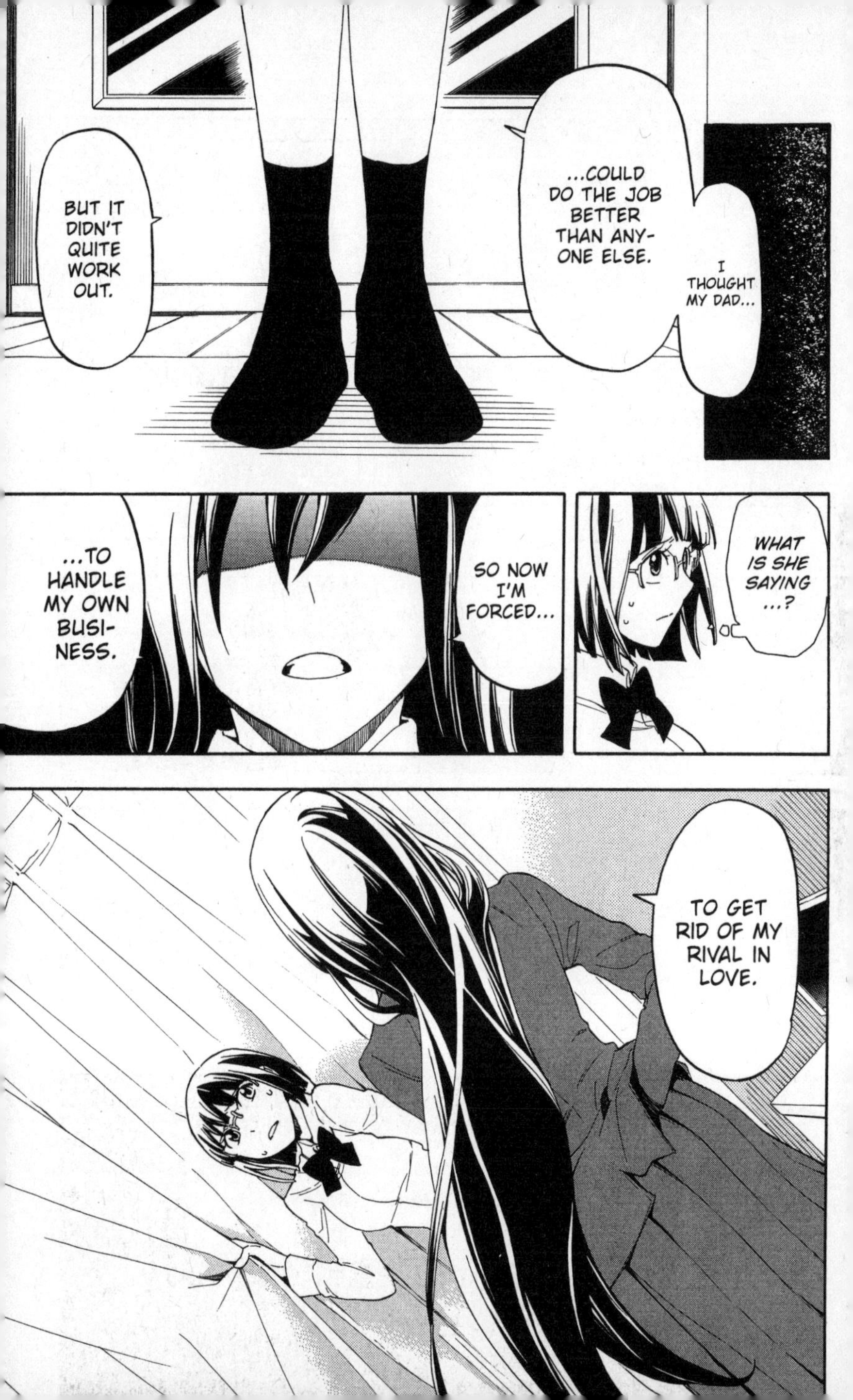
I THOUGHT MY DAD...
...COULD DO THE JOB BETTER THAN ANYONE ELSE.
BUT IT DIDN'T QUITE WORK OUT.
WHAT IS SHE SAYING ...?
SO NOW I'M FORCED...
...TO HANDLE MY OWN BUSINESS.
TO GET RID OF MY RIVAL IN LOVE.

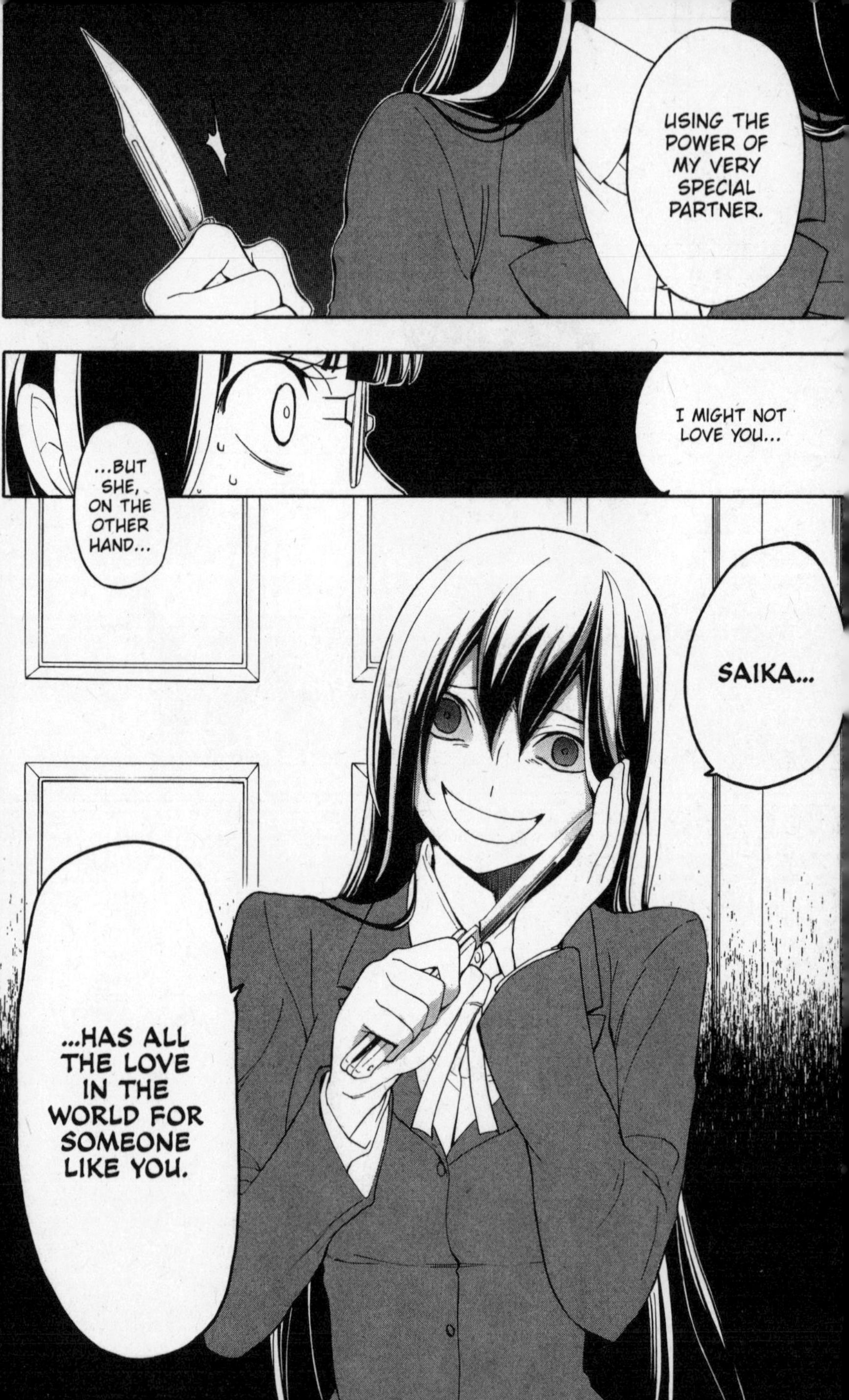
USING THE POWER OF MY VERY SPECIAL PARTNER.
I MIGHT NOT LOVE YOU...
...BUT SHE, ON THE OTHER HAND...
SAIKA...
...HAS ALL THE LOVE IN THE WORLD FOR SOMEONE LIKE YOU.

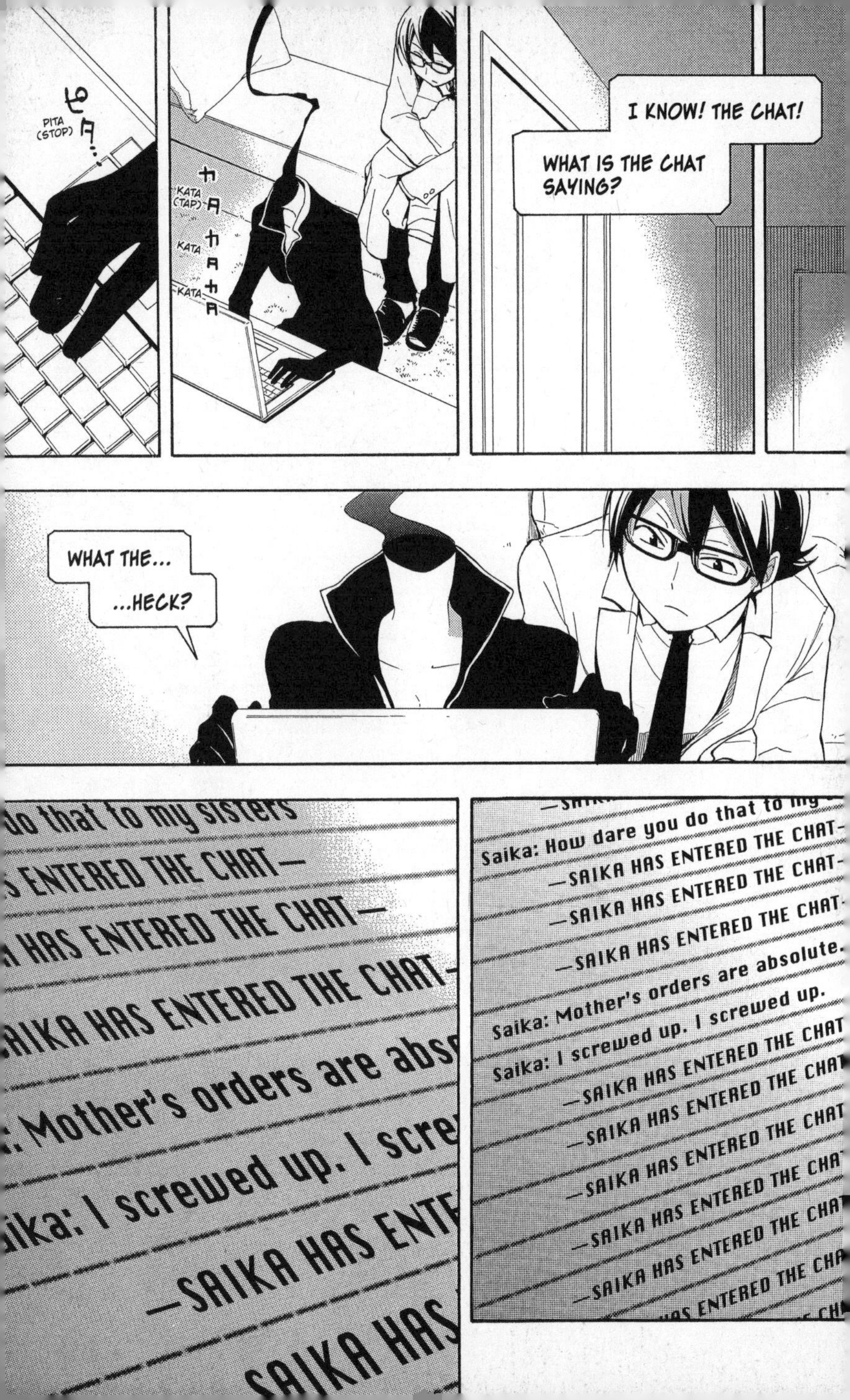
I KNOW! THE CHAT!
WHAT IS THE CHAT SAYING?
KATA (TAP)
KATA
KATA
PITA (STOP)
WHAT THE...
...HECK?
Saika: How dare you do that to my
—SAIKA HAS ENTERED THE CHAT—
—SAIKA HAS ENTERED THE CHAT—
—SAIKA HAS ENTERED THE CHAT—
Saika: Mother's orders are absolute.
Saika: I screwed up. I screwed up.
—SAIKA HAS ENTERED THE CHAT
—SAIKA HAS ENTERED THE CHAT
—SAIKA HAS ENTERED THE CHAT
—SAIKA HAS ENTERED THE CHAT
—SAIKA HAS ENTERED THE CHAT
—SAIKA HAS ENTERED THE CHA
do that to my sisters
ENTERED THE CHAT—
HAS ENTERED THE CHAT—
HAS ENTERED THE CHAT—
Mother's orders are abs
I screwed up. I scre
SAIKA HAS ENT
—SAIKA HAS
SAIKA HAS

Saika: I will give my love to Shizuo Heiwajima

Saika: If I can love Shizuo, then I'm sure I can love everything of this town, this town humans created, this place called Ikebukuro

—SAIKA HAS ENTERED THE CHAT—

Saika: Come to me, come to me again

—SAIKA HAS ENTERED THE CHAT—

Saika: This time we will love you all at once

Saika: Shizuo

Saika: I'm waiting, Shizuo

Saika: If you don't show, I'll love someone else

Saika: I'll love and love and love and love the people of Ikebukuro

Saika: I'm waiting

Saika: I'll wait all night tonight at South Ikebukuro Park

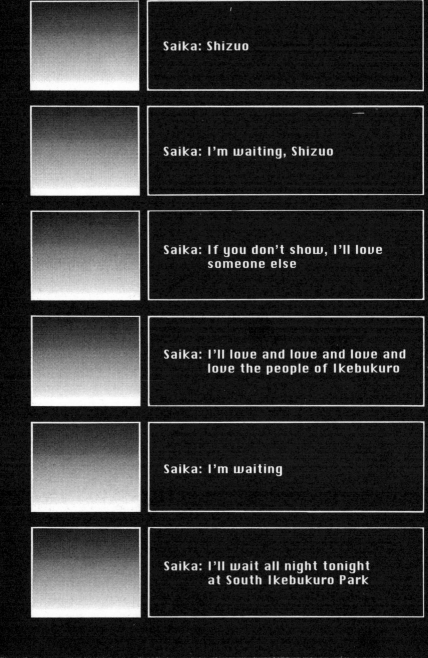

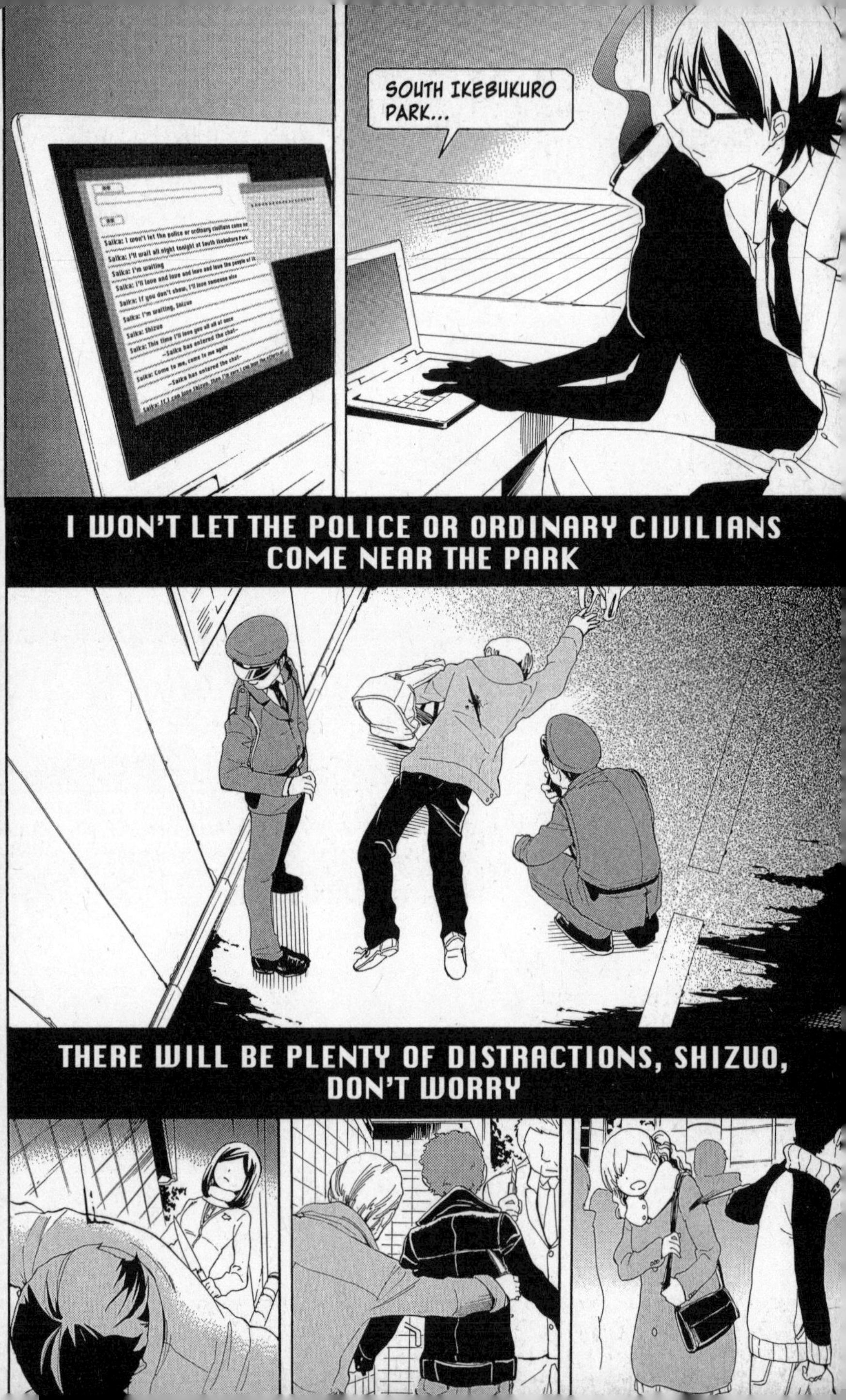
SOUTH IKEBUKURO PARK...
Saika: I won't let the police or ordinary civilians come
Saika: I'll wait all night tonight at South Ikebukuro Park
Saika: I'm waiting
Saika: I'll love and love and love and love the people of
Saika: If you don't show, I'll love someone else
Saika: I'm waiting, Shizuo
Saika: Shizuo
Saika: This time I'll love you all all at once
—Saika has entered the chat—
Saika: Come to me, come to me again
—Saika has entered the chat—
I WON'T LET THE POLICE OR ORDINARY CIVILIANS COME NEAR THE PARK
THERE WILL BE PLENTY OF DISTRACTIONS, SHIZUO, DON'T WORRY

IKEBUKURO WILL BE ROILING WITH CHAOS TONIGHT

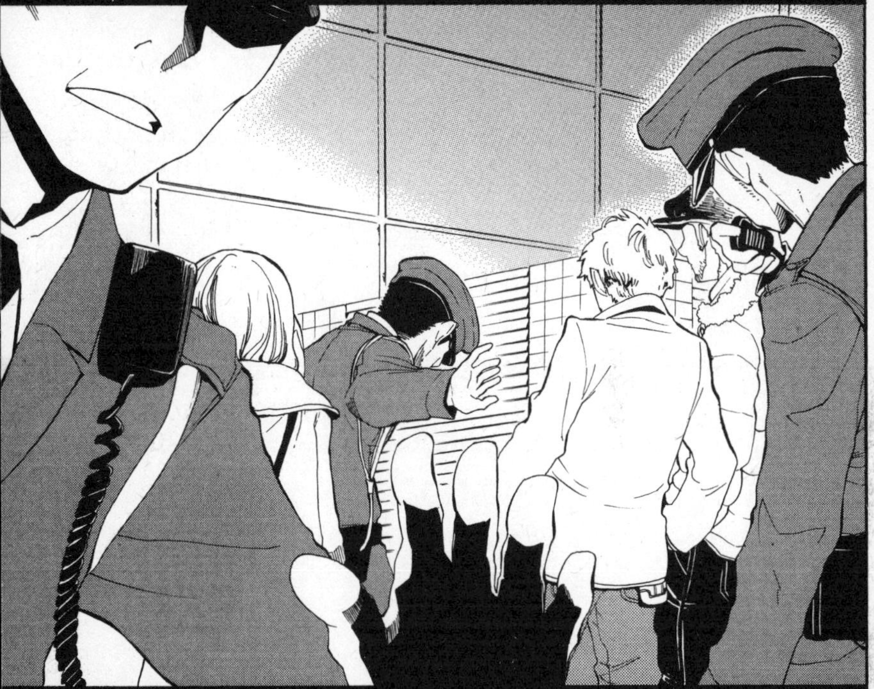

BUT DON'T WORRY, SHIZUO, I WILL LOVE YOU

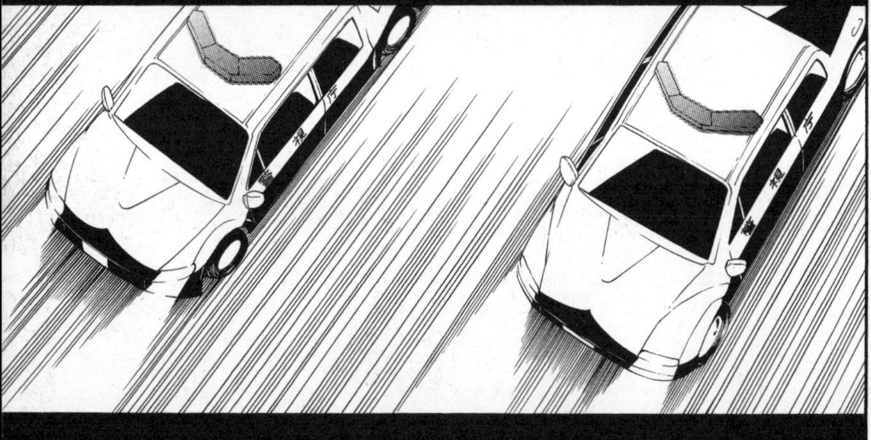

I'LL BE THERE TO LOVE YOU TOO

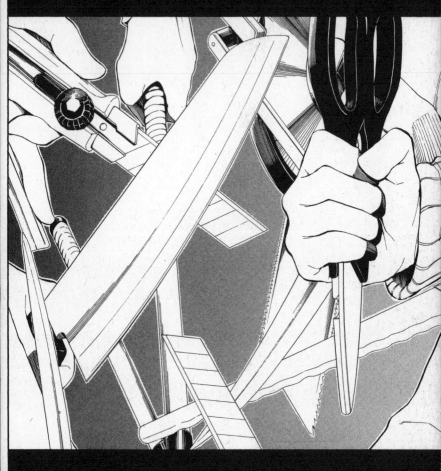

I TOO...

I TOO WILL LOVE YOU.

TRANSLATION NOTES

COMMON HONORIFICS

No honorific: Indicates familiarity or closeness; if used without permission or reason, addressing someone this way would constitute an insult.

-san: The Japanese equivalent of Mr./Mrs./Miss. If a situation calls for politeness, this is the fail-safe honorific.

-kun: Used most often when referring to boys, this indicates affection or familiarity. Occasionally used by older men among their peers, but it may also be used by anyone referring to a person of lower standing.

-chan: An affectionate honorific indicating familiarity used mostly in reference to girls; also used in reference to cute persons or animals of either gender.

PAGE 6
ABC's of Love: A variant on the American baseball sexual metaphor (first base, second base), in which "A" represents kissing, "B" represents touching, and "C" represents sex.

PAGE 26
Raikou: The "coming of the light"—the first rays of sunlight in the early morning, particularly when coming over a mountain peak.

PAGE 61
Fourth Primogenitor, Summon Beasts: Terms from the light novel series *Strike the Blood* by Gakuto Mikumo. In vampiric terms, the primogenitor is the original vampire who has infected all others down the line, and within the story of the novels, the Fourth Primogenitor is a legendary being thought not to exist. He is said to control summon beasts, otherworldly creatures that manifest themselves using the life force of their master.

PAGE 172
Cuticle Detective Inaba: A comedy manga series about a detective whose DNA is human spliced with wolf. He solves crimes by examining human hair. An anime adaptation was announced in August 2012.

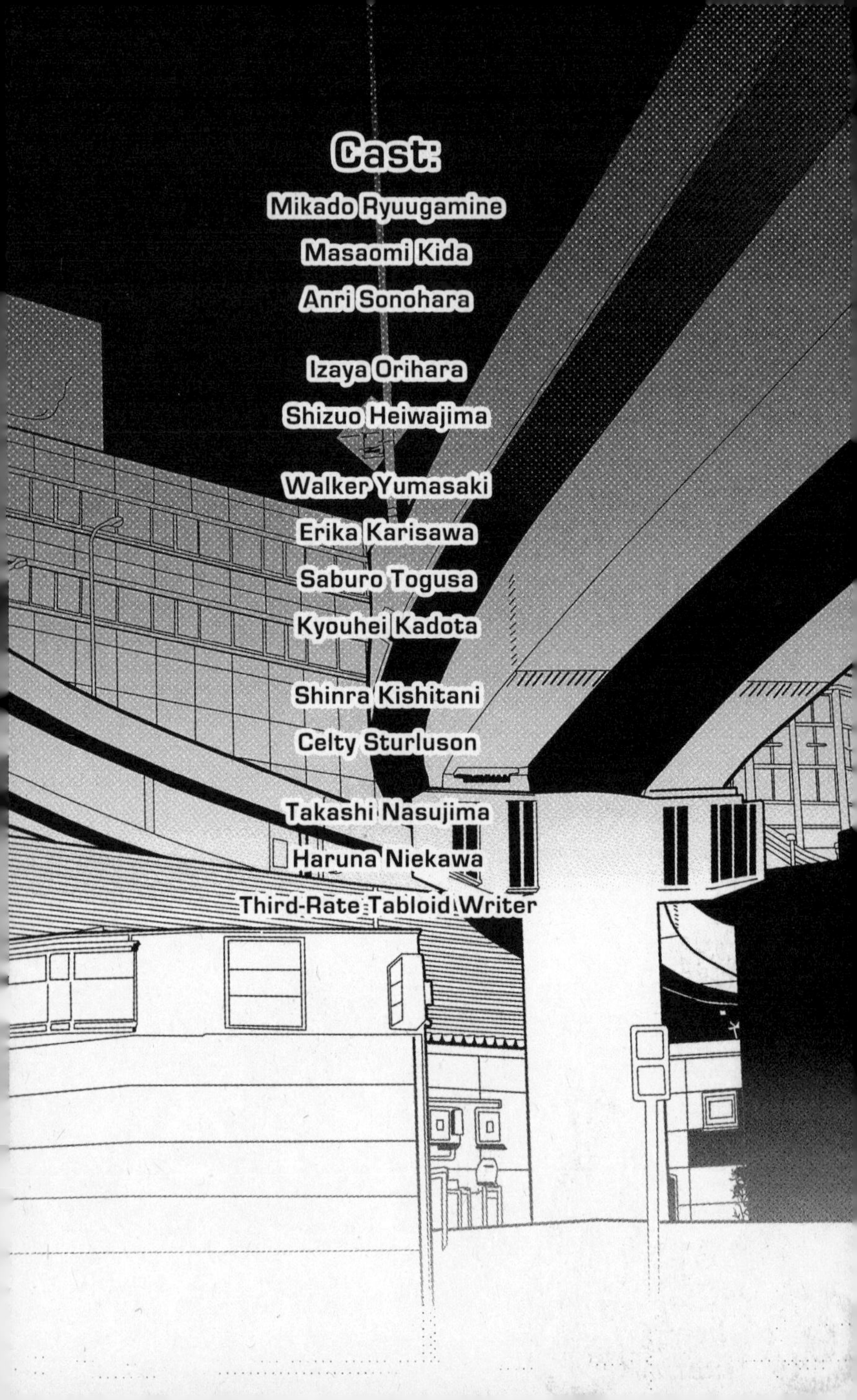

Cast:

Mikado Ryuugamine
Masaomi Kida
Anri Sonohara

Izaya Orihara
Shizuo Heiwajima

Walker Yumasaki
Erika Karisawa
Saburo Togusa
Kyouhei Kadota

Shinra Kishitani
Celty Sturluson

Takashi Nasujima
Haruna Niekawa
Third-Rate Tabloid Writer

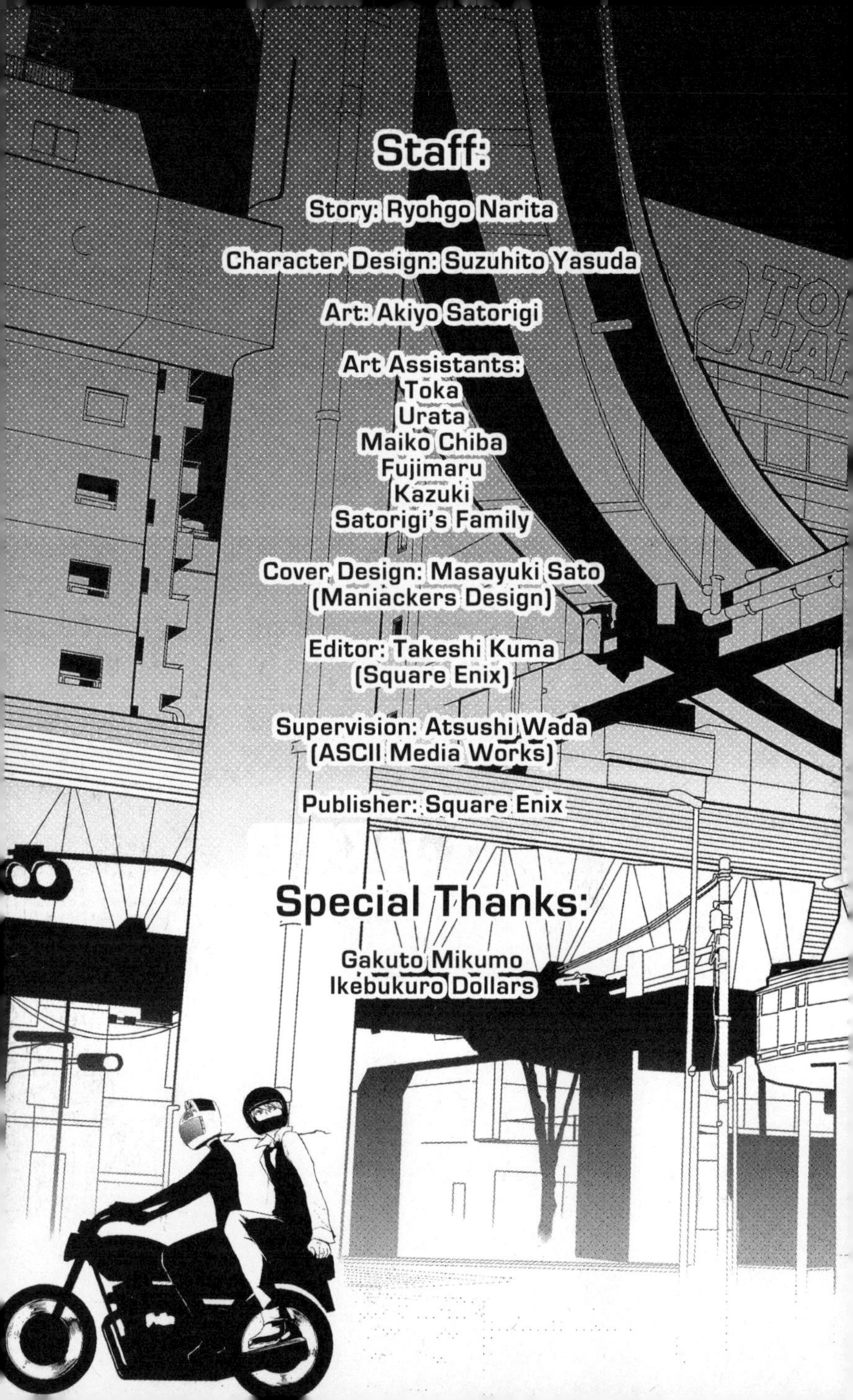

Staff:

Story: Ryohgo Narita

Character Design: Suzuhito Yasuda

Art: Akiyo Satorigi

Art Assistants:
Toka
Urata
Maiko Chiba
Fujimaru
Kazuki
Satorigi's Family

Cover Design: Masayuki Sato
(Maniackers Design)

Editor: Takeshi Kuma
(Square Enix)

Supervision: Atsushi Wada
(ASCII Media Works)

Publisher: Square Enix

Special Thanks:

Gakuto Mikumo
Ikebukuro Dollars

Congratulations to *Cuticle Detective Inaba* for receiving an anime adaptation!

And thus begins my afterword—with a celebratory message for someone else's story. But there's a good reason for this.

As a matter of fact, when *Durarara!!* was made into an anime, I had Yumasaki and Karisawa make a reference to *Inaba* in a conversation, so now I'm paying that dividend down the line! I just can't wait to see the upcoming *Cuticle Detective Inaba* anime!

So, let's try this again—it's nice to see you! I am Ryohgo Narita, the "author" of this mixed-media project known as *Durarara!!* This is the second volume of the Saika Arc.

Illustration: Suzuhito Yasuda

Sometimes I forget these things, since the novels are still ongoing, but the basis for the Saika Arc manga—*Durarara!!* Volume 2—was written over eight years ago...Since my own recollection of the events of the story is growing hazy, reading Satorigi-san's take on it not only jogs my memory, but also gives me that creative shock of seeing it in comic form for the first time. Each and every chapter is deeply stimulating and rewarding.

The climax of the Saika Arc begins in the next volume, and I can remember thinking, "Man, this will be hard to depict visually," at several points while writing it. So I eagerly await these scenes with equal parts excited anticipation and embarrassed regret!

And if any of you Japanese readers happened to think, "Huh? Wait, why didn't this book come out on the usual day of the month that *GFantasy* series get released?" Well, it was actually delayed a bit so that it could be released on the same day as the newest volume of my other humble series, *Baccano!*, coming out from ASCII Media Works!

It's a big hassle to everyone to have the release date of your book delayed, which is why I must give big thanks to my editor Kuma-san for pulling it off! I hope it gets everyone excited for both *Baccano!* and *Durarara!!*

Before I go, I just wanted to say that I got a chance to peek at the cover design for this volume before this afterword goes to print, and I think the reflective foil paper combined with Satorigi-san's tense illustration is just too cool for words!

To everyone who picked up this book and maybe checked out my others, or those who have read my novels and wanted to see the manga edition as well, I hope you enjoy it!

And to Satorigi-san, my editor Kuma-san, the *GFantasy* editorial department, and all of the dedicated readers out there, my deepest appreciation! Thank you so much!

Ryohgo Narita

Creator Ryohgo Narita
Character Design Suzuhito Yasuda
Art Akiyo Satorigi

DURARARA!!
DRRR!!
SAIKA ARC ×2

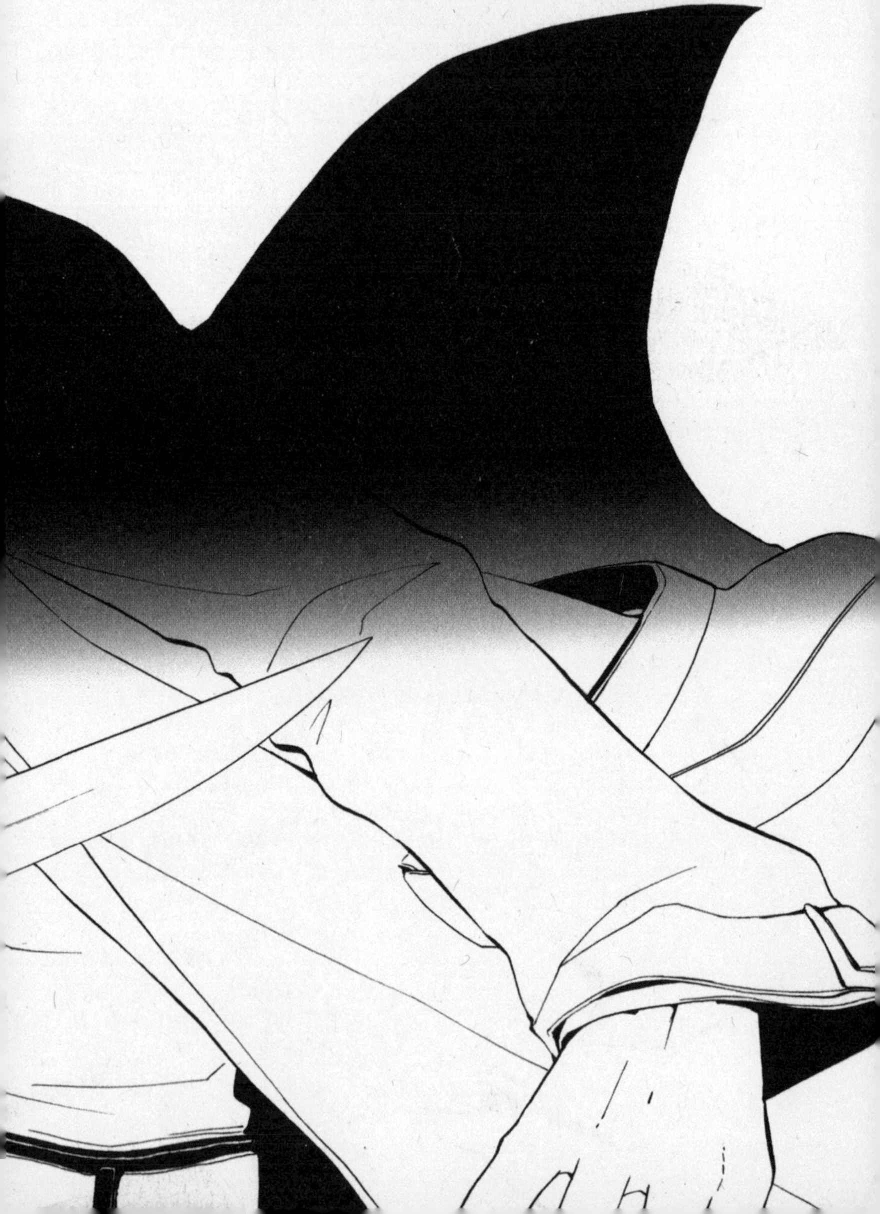

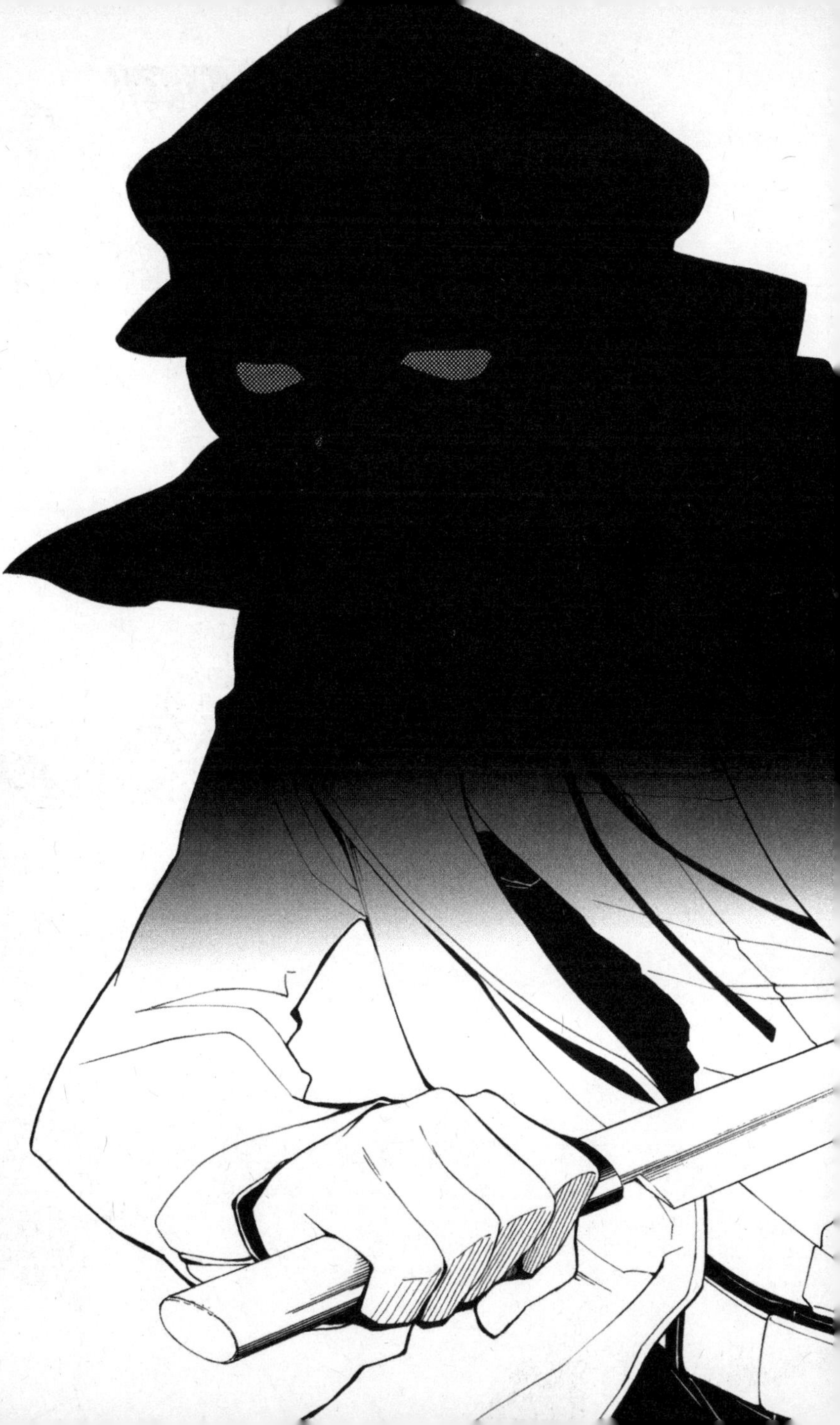

Can't wait for the next volume? You don't have to!

Keep up with the latest chapters of some of your favorite manga every month online in the pages of YEN PLUS!

READ IT THE SAME DAY AS JAPAN!

SOUL EATER NOT!

MAXIMUM RIDE

SOULLESS

WITCH & WIZARD

THE INFERNAL DEVICES
CLOCKWORK ANGEL

Visit us at
www.yenplus.com
for details!

DURARARA!! SAIKA ARC ❷

RYOHGO NARITA
SUZUHITO YASUDA
AKIYO SATORIGI

Translation: Stephen Paul

Lettering: Lys Blakeslee

DURARARA!! SAIKA-HEN Vol. 2
© 2012 Ryohgo Narita
© 2012 Akiyo Satorigi / SQUARE ENIX
Licensed by KADOKAWA CORPORATION ASCII MEDIA WORKS
First published in Japan in 2012 by SQUARE ENIX CO., LTD. English translation rights arranged with SQUARE ENIX CO., LTD. and Hachette Book Group through Tuttle-Mori Agency, Inc.

Translation © 2013 by SQUARE ENIX CO., LTD.

Yen Press
Hachette Book Group
237 Park Avenue, New York, NY 10017

www.HachetteBookGroup.com
www.YenPress.com

Yen Press is an imprint of Hachette Book Group, Inc. The Yen Press name and logo are trademarks of Hachette Book Group, Inc.

First Yen Press Edition: May 2013

ISBN: 978-0-316-25094-8

10 9 8 7 6 5 4 3 2

BVG

Printed in the United States of America